U.S. ARMY COUNTERINSURGENCY AND CONTINGENCY OPERATIONS DOCTRINE 1860-1941

by

Andrew J. Birtle

CENTER OF MILITARY HISTORY
UNITED STATES ARMY
WASHINGTON, D.C., 2004

FOREWORD

Throughout its history, the U.S. Army has conducted a wide variety of military operations in service to the nation. Over the past two centuries, America's soldiers have served the Republic as governors, constables, judges, diplomats, explorers, colonizers, educators, administrators, and engineers. These myriad missions have often been overlooked as soldiers and scholars alike focused their studies on major wars and on the strategic and tactical doctrines that governed them. Comparatively little attention has been paid to the underlying theories, concepts, and methods that American soldiers have employed in the conduct of their many less "conventional," yet exceedingly traditional, missions.

Over the years the Center of Military History has attempted to rectify this omission in military historiography. Center publications such as *Soldier-Statesmen of the Constitution*; *Military Government in the Ryukyu Islands, 1945–1950*; *The U.S. Army in the Occupation of Germany, 1944–1946*; *United States Army Unilateral and Coalition Operations in the 1965 Dominican Republic Intervention*; the multivolume *Role of Federal Military Forces in Domestic Disorders*; and *The Demands of Humanity: Army Medical Disaster Relief* have examined some of the many roles the U.S. Army has played off the conventional battlefield. *U.S. Army Counterinsurgency and Contingency Operations Doctrine, 1860–1941*, adds to this body of literature on the Army's experience in operations other than war. It is the first of a two-volume work examining how the Army has performed two of its most important unconventional missions: the suppression of insurgent or other irregular forces and the conduct of overseas constabulary and contingency operations. The second volume will carry the story of the evolution of Army doctrine for counterinsurgency and contingency operations up through the end of the Vietnam War.

Although the events discussed in this volume occurred long ago, many of the issues raised in it have enduring relevance for today's Army. People, places, and events may change, but the fundamental questions involved in suppressing insurrections, fighting irregulars, administering civilian populations, and conducting foreign interventions remain surprisingly constant. By studying how American soldiers dealt with these complex issues in the past, this book offers valuable insights to guide current and future soldiers when called upon to conduct similar operations.

Washington, D.C.
10 October 1997

JOHN W. MOUNTCASTLE
Brigadier General, USA
Chief of Military History

THE AUTHOR

Andrew J. Birtle received a B.A. degree in history from Saint Lawrence University in 1979 and M.A. and Ph.D. degrees in military history from Ohio State University in 1981 and 1985, respectively. He worked for the U.S. Air Force as a historian for approximately three years before joining the U.S. Army Center of Military History in 1987. He is the author of a number of articles and monographs as well as a book on American military assistance to the Federal Republic of Germany. He is currently writing the second volume in his study of the development of U.S. Army counterinsurgency and contingency operations doctrine.

Preface

It has long been accepted that the U.S. Army did not have an official, codified, written doctrine for the conduct of counterguerrilla, pacification, and nation-building activities prior to World War II. The absence of a formal, written doctrine, however, does not mean that American soldiers did not develop concepts and theories about such activities, some of which became enduring principles that guided Army operations for decades despite their meager mention in the manuals of the day. It is the contention of this book that there was a strong continuity in the manner in which the U.S. Army performed counterinsurgency and overseas constabulary missions in the century that preceded the outbreak of World War II and that some of the central principles governing the conduct of such operations were indeed incorporated into official Army doctrinal literature prior to America's entry into that conflict.

Intellectual history—the tracing of the evolution of thought and ideas over time—is a tricky business. Showing continuity and change in thought and action is difficult, but explaining how it came about is even tougher. Writers studying the evolution of military doctrine are usually aided in their endeavors by the existence of official manuals that codify the state of military thinking at a particular point in time. Unfortunately, such manuals are often silent on the less conventional aspects of the military art. Moreover, one must remember that a system of comprehensive doctrinal manuals in the modern sense did not exist in the nineteenth century and was still in its infancy during the early decades of the twentieth. Consequently, the student of military theory is forced to cast a wider net, studying not only manuals, but curricular materials, textbooks, war plans, and the less official publications of individual soldiers. Murkier still, but no less real, is the realm of personal experience, folkways, and institutional norms that can be acquired and passed down over time. Anthropologists maintain that oral tradition can be a powerful force governing the conduct of human cultures and institutions. The fact that such traditions are not written down denies neither their existence nor their significance. Students of military thought, therefore, must look at deeds as well as words, because by studying the actions of past soldiers, we may gain insight into the principles and beliefs underlying their behavior. I examined all such sources then, official and unofficial, words as well as deeds, to gain insights into the Army's approach to counterinsurgency and contingency operations.

This volume covers a lot of ground—nearly a century of time and occurrences that span the globe. Although many different events are mentioned, this book is not intended to be an operational history. Similarly, while the volume touches upon subjects as diverse as military government, military law, and tactics, it does not present a comprehensive review of each of these distinct doctrinal areas. Rather, it examines these and other subjects selectively to gain insight into what the pre–World War II Army came to call "small wars"—the interrelated fields of counterguerrilla warfare, pacification, and overseas constabulary and contingency operations. Though never credited with a manual of its own, during the century that preceded the outbreak of World War II a loose body of theory, doctrine, thought, and precedent gradually evolved within the U.S. Army into what one might call, to paraphrase Russell Weigley, an American way of small wars.

Many people, far too many to name, assisted in the production of this volume. I would like to extend a general word of appreciation to the staffs of the National Archives and Records Administration, the Library of Congress, the U.S. Army Center of Military History (CMH), the U.S. Army Military History Institute (MHI), and the Pentagon, Infantry School, and Command and General Staff College libraries. Individuals worthy of special mention are Wilbert Mahoney of the National Archives; Richard J. Sommers, David Keough, and Pamela Cheney at MHI; and at CMH, Albert Cowdrey, James Knight, Hannah Zeidlik, Geraldine Harcarik, Catherine Heerin, W. Scott Janes, Arthur Hardyman, S. L. Dowdy, Beth MacKenzie, and indexer Florence Brodkey. I am especially grateful to Diane Arms, who edited the book. Thanks also go to the panel of scholars who reviewed the manuscript and made many helpful suggestions: Edward Coffman, Timothy Nenninger, Lawrence Yates, Allan Millett, Brian Linn, Jeffrey Clarke, and Mary Gillett. Finally, I would like to thank my parents and my wife, without whose support this work would not have been possible.

Though many people contributed to this volume, the author alone is responsible for all interpretations and conclusions, as well as for any errors that may appear.

Washington, D.C.   ANDREW J. BIRTLE
10 October 1997

CONTENTS

Chapter	Page
1. Introduction	3
Concepts and Doctrine	3
Antebellum Antecedents	7
2. The War of the Rebellion, 1861–1865	23
Pacification, 1861–1863	24
Francis Lieber and General Orders 100	32
Pacification, 1863–1865	36
Tactics and Techniques of the Counterguerrilla War	40
The Legacy of the War of the Rebellion	47
3. The Constabulary Years, 1865–1898	55
Reconstruction, 1865–1877	55
Constabulary Duty on the Western Frontier	58
Indian Warfare and Military Thought	60
U.S. Army Counterguerrilla Operations on the Western Frontier	67
The Army and Indian Pacification	76
The New Professionalism and the Legacy of the Constabulary Army	86
4. Cuba and the Philippines, 1898–1902	99
The Army's Approach to Overseas Nation Building	100
The Military Government of Cuba, 1898–1902	104
The Philippine War, 1899–1902	108
5. The Imperial Constabulary Years, 1900–1913	147
The Peking Relief Expedition, 1900–1901	147
Policing the Philippines, 1902–1907	153
Governing the Moros, 1900–1913	159
The Second Cuban Intervention, 1906–1909	168
The Imperial Constabulary Mission and Army Doctrine	174

Chapter	Page
6. Military Interventions During the Wilson Administration, 1914–1920	191
Vera Cruz, 1914	192
The Mexican Punitive Expedition, 1916–1917	199
Wilson and Russia	208
Panama, 1918–1920	226
Army Doctrine and the Wilson Interventions	230
7. The Interwar Years, 1920–1941	239
Overseas Duty in Panama, Germany, and China	240
The Sources of U.S. Army Small Wars Doctrine	244
U.S. Army Small Wars Doctrine in the Interwar Period	247
Theory Into Practice—Small War Exercises and Plans	256
Army Doctrine on the Eve of World War II	260
8. Conclusion: The Development of Small Wars Doctrine in Retrospect	271
Select Bibliography	285
Index	311

MAPS

No.		
1.	U.S. Army Small War Activities, 1861–1938	8
2.	The Philippines, 1899	109
3.	China, 1900–1938	149
4.	Mexico, 1914–1916	194
5.	U.S. Army Expeditions in the Union of Soviet Socialist Republics, 1918–1920	212
6.	Panama, 1918	228

ILLUSTRATIONS

Confederate Cavalry, Partisan Rangers, and Guerrillas Attack a Supply Train	24
Lt. Gen. Henry W. Halleck	29
Maj. Gen. William T. Sherman	32
Maj. Gen. Philip H. Sheridan	37
Lt. Gen. Ulysses S. Grant	38

	Page
A Blockhouse and Encampment Protect a Railroad Bridge	42
Dismounted Skirmish Drill Given to Cadets at West Point	62
The Army Protecting the Overland Mail	64
A Unit of Apache Indian Scouts Camps Near the Mexican Border	68
The Army Used Soldiers, Civilians, and Indians as Scouts	70
Maj. Gen. George Crook	71
The Cavalry Was the Army's Primary Offensive Weapon During the Pacification of America's Inland Empire	73
Capt. Henry W. Lawton's Mixed Column of Cavalry, Scouts, and Pack Mules on Geronimo's Trail	75
Geronimo and His Apache Warriors Shortly After Surrender	76
Indian Company Practices Saber Exercises	81
Indian Irrigation Project	84
Operations During the Philippine Rainy Season	110
Soldiers of the Philippine Insurgent Army on a Firing Line	111
Infantry Unit on a Hike	115
American Infantrymen on Patrol Riding Native Ponies	115
A Detachment of Macabebe Scouts in American Service	117
American Infantrymen Advance in Single-File Formation Down a Filipino Road	118
American Soldiers Feed Filipino Children	120
American Soldiers Detailed as Teachers With Their Filipino Students	121
U.S. Army Band Serenades Filipino Civilians	124
Infantry Unit Forms Up After Destroying a Barrio	127
U.S. Infantrymen Demonstrate the Water Cure	133
A Surrender Ceremony	134
Soldiers and Civilians Intermingle in the Philippines	137
U.S. Troops Guard Boxer Prisoners at Tientsin	151
American Soldiers on Police Detail During the Occupation of Peking	151
Chinese Village Lies in Ruins After a Visitation by Allied Forces	152
The Philippine Constabulary	155
Moro Soldiers of the U.S. Army's Philippine Scouts	157
Moro Warrior in Full Armor	160
Maj. Gen. Leonard Wood	161
Maj. Hugh L. Scott and the Sultan of Jolo	163
American Soldiers Storm the Moro *Cotta* of Fort Bacolod	165
An Elite Provo Company Crosses the Rio Grande River on Mindinao	166

	Page
U.S. Artillery Bombards *Dato* Ali's Fort	167
One-Room Schoolhouse Built by the Army of Cuban Pacification	172
Road-Building Project	173
Street Improvements Instituted by the U.S. Army in Vera Cruz	197
Maj. Frank Tompkins' Cavalry Column Searches for Pancho Villa	204
U.S. Army Indian Scouts Who Participated in the Punitive Expedition	206
The Wagons of the Old Army Seem To Have an Edge Over Newer Forms of Transportation	207
An Infantry Regiment Disembarks at Archangel	211
Small American Outpost in North Russia	214
American Convoy Winds Its Way Along a Forest Road in North Russia	215
American Soldiers Guard Bolshevik Prisoners at Archangel	215
American Soldiers Share Their Rations With the Children of Archangel	216
American Soldiers in Winter Camouflage Clothing in North Russia	217
This American Blockhouse Withstood Several Communist Attacks	218
Camouflaged Train of the Czech Legion	219
Cossack Commander Ataman Semenoff and Maj. Gen. William S. Graves	221
Suchan Mining District in Eastern Siberia	224
American, French, British, and Italian Soldiers of the International Military Guard	241
Spit and Polish Was the Credo of the 15th Infantry in Tientsin	242
Soldiers of the 31st Infantry Defend Shanghai's Foreign Quarter	243

Illustrations courtesy of the following sources: cover, *The Long Column*, by Frank C. McCarthy © 1974 The Greenwich Workshop, Inc.; pp. 24, 29, 32, 37, 38, 42, 64, 68, 71, 75, 76, 81, 84, 111, 115 (top/bottom), 117, 118, 121, 124, 133, 134, 157, 160, 163, 165, 166, 197, 206, 207, 214, 215 (top/bottom), 217, 218, 219, 221, 224, 241, 242, 243, National Archives; 62, Special Collections Division, United States Military Academy Library, West Point, New York; 70, 73, 110, 120, 137, 151 (top/bottom), 152, 155, 161, 167, 172, 173, 204, Library of Congress; and 127, 211, 216, U.S. Army Military History Institute.

U.S. Army Counterinsurgency and Contingency Operations Doctrine 1860-1941

1

INTRODUCTION

Throughout its history, the U.S. Army has focused most of its organizational and doctrinal energies preparing for conventional warfare against a similarly armed opponent. Nevertheless, the Army has spent the majority of its time not on the conventional battlefield, but in the performance of myriad operations other than war. In the century and a half between the founding of the Republic and America's entry into World War II, the Army conducted explorations, governed territories, guarded national parks, engaged in public works, provided disaster relief, quelled domestic disturbances, and supported American foreign policy short of engaging in open warfare. Similarly, much of the Army's combat experience prior to World War II was gained not in conventional battles against regular opponents, but in unconventional conflicts against a bewildering array of irregulars, from American Indians to Bolshevik partisans.

Despite the Army's continuous engagement in operations other than war, relatively little has been written about the Army's conceptual and doctrinal approach to "unconventional" situations prior to World War II.[1] This study partially addresses that gap by examining how the Army performed two of its many traditional, yet unconventional, functions—counterinsurgency and contingency operations.

Concepts and Doctrine

For the purposes of this book, the term *counterinsurgency* embraces all of the political, economic, social, and military actions taken by a government for the suppression of insurgent, resistance, and revolutionary movements. *Contingency operations*, on the other hand, are limited operations undertaken in areas where the Army initially lacks, or has a very limited, base of operations. Although contingency operations can be undertaken for any number of political, humanitarian, or punitive purposes, this monograph confines itself to two circumstances: operations of interposition, in which Army forces are inserted into a foreign country for the purpose of protecting American lives and property during a period of instability, and operations of intervention, in which the Army seeks to alter the political behavior of another country, either by restoring order, quelling an insurrection, imposing punitive measures, recasting institutions, or enforcing a change in government.

Although counterinsurgency and contingency operations can be quite diverse, they often share several underlying factors that permit them to be considered as an entity. First, such missions frequently occur in relatively underdeveloped areas where transportation systems are rudimentary, and topographical and climatic conditions pose significant obstacles to the conduct of operations. Second, combat in such situations usually pits the Army against irregular or semi-irregular forces that employ guerrilla warfare. Finally, and most importantly, political considerations play a central role in these activities at both the operational and tactical levels. Not only is the close coordination of political, diplomatic, and military measures crucial during counterinsurgency and contingency operations, but the ultimate success of these operations often depends on the interaction of soldiers with indigenous civilian populations. Consequently, soldiers engaged in these areas have to exercise political and diplomatic skills above and beyond the martial arts normally required on the conventional battlefield.[2]

In the decades prior to the outbreak of World War II, the Army borrowed the term *small wars* from British soldier-author Sir Charles E. Callwell to describe the type of actions encompassed by the more contemporary terms *counterinsurgency* and *contingency operations*. Small wars, as the pre–World War II Army defined them, were operations undertaken for the purpose of suppressing an insurrection, establishing order, or dispensing punishment in which the Army usually faced a poorly trained or irregular foe. However, since small wars were often peacetime affairs of a quasi-police nature, the term *constabulary operations* is perhaps equally appropriate.

The U.S. Army's constabulary and small wars operations were inherently civil-military in scope and frequently required that the military undertake what officers in the early twentieth century called pacification. In the broadest sense, *pacification* encompassed all actions taken to establish or maintain peace, order, and government authority in an area that was either openly or potentially hostile. It had two main features: military operations against irregulars and civil operations. The

INTRODUCTION

relative balance between these two components fluctuated from situation to situation. Similarly, the exact nature of the Army's civil involvement varied widely depending on the purpose of the operation. At a minimum, it entailed developing working relationships with local civil authorities. In more extreme cases, it encompassed the establishment of military government, the imposition of controls of varying severity over the population, and the introduction of measures designed to ameliorate the conditions that precipitated the unrest. Finally, the military's civil actions sometimes became programs of social engineering designed to reshape the subject society.

Although civil and military activities were inexorably linked in most counterinsurgency and constabulary operations, for the sake of analysis the monograph separates the purely military aspects of counterguerrilla tactics from measures directed at the civilian population, which the study treats under the heading of "pacification." By examining the evolution of the Army's doctrinal approach to the interrelated areas of counterirregular warfare and pacification, the book focuses on a genre of military activity that constituted much of the Army's operational employment not only before World War II, but thereafter as well. Indeed, the Army's experience in constabulary and small war operations during the late nineteenth and early twentieth centuries is particularly relevant in the post–Cold War world, where every crisis is no longer colored by the brush of Marxist-Leninist doctrine and Maoist revolutionary theory.

One last term, *doctrine*, must be defined to understand the focus of this history. There are probably as many definitions of the word as there are soldiers and military theorists. For the purpose of this study, doctrine is that body of knowledge disseminated through officially approved publications, school curriculums, and textbooks that represents an army's approach to war and the conduct of military operations. Doctrine offers a distillation of experience, furnishing a guide to methods that have generally worked in the past and which are thought to be of some enduring utility. By providing a common orientation, language, and conceptual framework, doctrine helps soldiers navigate through the fog of war.[3]

For most of the century and a half prior to America's entry into World War II, the U.S. Army lacked an extensive, formal, written doctrine for the conduct of small wars. Nevertheless, during this period the Army evolved what might be termed an "informal" doctrine comprised of custom, tradition, and accumulated experience that was transmitted from one generation of soldiers to the next through a combination of official and unofficial writings, curricular materials, con-

5

versations, and individual memories. This process, while somewhat haphazard, was not unusual, especially since the Army lacked any formal system for generating doctrine for much of the period covered by this study. Moreover, while some doctrinal developments may be revolutionary, the process of creating and changing doctrine is for the most part an evolutionary one, in which field experience is gradually distilled and codified, only to be eventually modified and replaced after new experiences have demonstrated the inadequacy of existing thought. This study, therefore, approaches the development of Army small wars doctrine by examining both the formal and informal evolution of Army thought and practice with regards to the conduct of counterguerrilla and pacification campaigns.

After taking a cursory look at the antebellum period, the book focuses on the largest insurrection that has ever faced the United States government, the War of the Rebellion. During this conflict the Army developed policies governing the treatment of guerrillas and hostile populations that would serve as guides into the twentieth century. The monograph then takes a look at the Army's extensive experience in irregular warfare and constabulary operations during the post–Civil War Indian campaigns. Less than a decade after the conclusion of these campaigns, the Army found itself performing politico-military constabulary functions once again, this time overseas in Cuba, Puerto Rico, the Philippines, and China. During the first decade of the twentieth century, the U.S. Army gained a wealth of experience in counterinsurgency and population management from operations in these areas. Next, the history examines the Army's growing role as an instrument of foreign policy during President Woodrow Wilson's Mexican and Russian interventions, before concluding with a discussion of the state of Army thinking about small wars on the eve of World War II. (*Map 1*)

Although the book reviews "internal" conflicts such as the Indian and Civil Wars and Reconstruction, it generally does not address riot duty or the utilization of military force in domestic disturbances. Similarly, while the broad outline of civil affairs and military government doctrine is of great importance to the study of pacification, the monograph makes no attempt to examine in detail the technical and administrative aspects of military government doctrine. Finally, this work is not meant to be a narrative history of the Army's many small wars and constabulary operations. Rather, it conveys only those facts necessary to provide the reader with a sufficient background with which to understand the evolution of theory and practice. Readers who are interested in obtaining a more detailed understanding of the events touched upon in this volume can find many sources in the footnotes and bibliography to help them do so.

Antebellum Antecedents

The U.S. Army's approach to pacification and counterguerrilla operations during the nineteenth century stemmed from three sources—frontier experience, antebellum instruction given at the U.S. Military Academy at West Point concerning the art and conduct of war, and the application of those principles by Maj. Gen. Winfield Scott during the Mexican War.

The U.S. Army was in many ways the child of the frontier. With the exception of a few brief interludes of conventional warfare against the British and Mexicans, the antebellum Army spent the bulk of its time policing the nation's ever-changing western boundary. Overworked, underfunded, and dispersed among many small posts, the nation's tiny Army struggled to enforce laws and treaties, explore and govern new territories, punish hostile aggression, and regulate Indian-white contact. Prior to 1822, the Army operated government trading houses, or "factories," in an effort to smooth Indian-white relations through equitable commercial dealings between the two societies. Even after the full privatization of Indian commerce, the War Department retained control over Indian policy until 1849, when the government transferred that responsibility to the Department of the Interior. The frontier was thus an integral part of the antebellum Army's existence, and consequently it inherited a rich heritage of Indian warfare experience that dated back to the colonial era.

In their campaigns against the Eastern woodland Indians during the eighteenth and early nineteenth centuries, British colonists and their American descendants had learned that the best way to bring their elusive opponents to a decisive engagement was to attack their villages. Sometimes this was done using a single force, as Maj. Gen. Anthony Wayne employed in 1794, while at others multiple, converging columns were employed, as during the Sullivan-Clinton campaign of 1779. In either case, expeditions of this nature, if well conceived and carefully organized, compelled the Indians either to abandon their villages, with the loss of crops, property, and prestige, or to stand and fight on European terms. Moreover, as adept as the Indians were in ambushing their enemies, they were notoriously lax when it came to guarding their own camps and settlements, thereby giving their adversaries a chance to turn the tables on them. Such expeditions were not easy, as they usually involved marching long distances over difficult and unfamiliar terrain.

COUNTERINSURGENCY DOCTRINE, 1860–1941

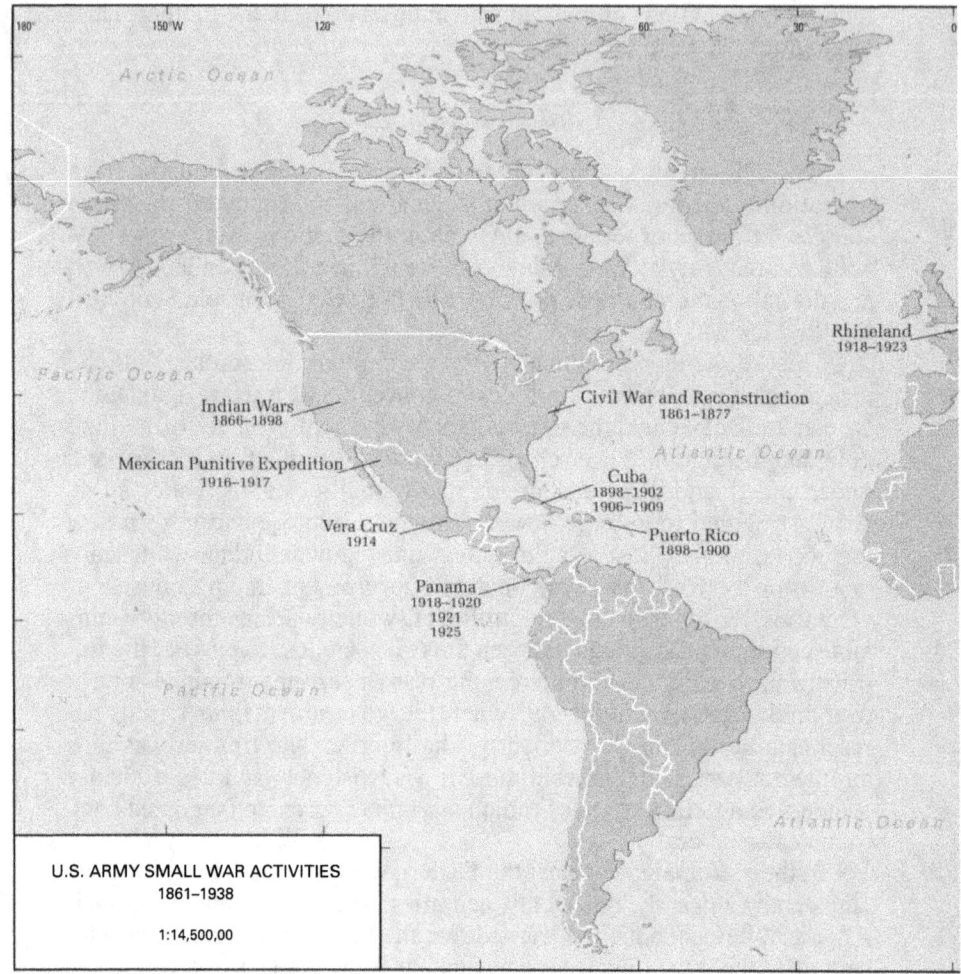

MAP 1

Logistical problems were numerous, as were the difficulties presented by the low caliber of soldiers and militiamen upon whom commanders had to rely. To make up for these deficiencies, Anglo-American commanders of the eighteenth and early nineteenth centuries adopted several expedients. They lightened their columns as much as possible, improved training, developed march and camp procedures to minimize the danger of ambush, organized special corps of light infantry and riflemen skilled in open order combat, and augmented their forces with small bodies of irregulars—frontiersmen, rangers, and Indians—for use

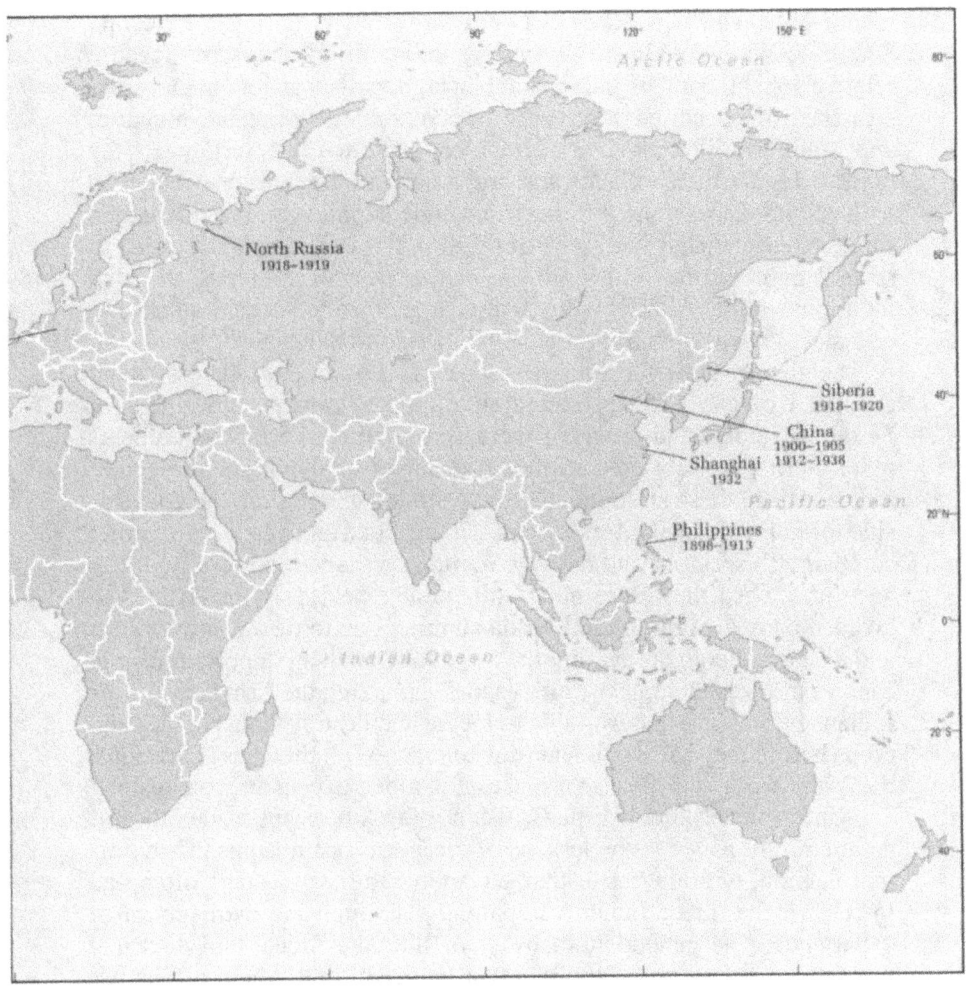

as guides and auxiliaries. Rather than abandoning traditional European methods of warfare for Indian ways, they blended the strong points of each, combining European-style discipline, organization, and firepower with Indian-style raiding. It was through the use of such columns, conventionally based but modified to meet the circumstances of the North American wilderness, that the British and Americans had broken the back of Indian resistance east of the Mississippi.[4]

One reason behind Anglo-American success was the fact that most Eastern tribes were fairly sedentary, and their villages were readily identifiable. The U.S. Army was not so fortunate during the Second Seminole War of 1835–1842. During this conflict, the Army faced a relatively small band of Indian and black guerrilla warriors in an extensive tract of uncharted and nearly impenetrable swampland in central and southern Florida. The Seminoles exploited the terrain to the utmost, hiding their villages and crops deep in the interior. Weakened by heat and disease, the government's undersupplied and overextended forces spent the first few years of the war stumbling around Florida in several cumbersome, converging columns in a vain attempt to catch their elusive foe. Although the Army came close to success on several occasions, it was not until it modified its traditional tactics that it finally was able to draw the war to a close. The Army's ultimate strategy consisted of two elements. First, it impeded the free movement of Seminole raiders and provided increased security to white settlements in northern Florida by establishing a cordon of small posts. Patrols radiated out from these strongpoints every other day, scouring the countryside for guerrilla infiltrators. Second, it launched an aggressive summer campaign to seek out and destroy Seminole villages and food supplies at a time when they were most vulnerable. Previously the Army had avoided campaigning in the Florida summer due to the ravages of heat and disease, thereby providing the Seminoles with an important respite each year. By launching an "off-season" campaign the Army caught the Indians by surprise and was able to locate and destroy their villages and crops before they had sufficient time to react. With these modifications, the Army brought the war to a successful, albeit expensive, conclusion.[5]

Unfortunately, neither the British nor the Americans made much of an attempt to preserve the lessons of these early campaigns in any formal fashion, with the result that successive military leaders often had to relearn the art of Indian campaigning through the hard school of experience. The general immaturity of the educational and doctrinal development systems of the day, the tendency of soldiers to dismiss "savage" warfare as a form of conflict less worthy of study than "civilized" wars, and the universal reluctance of legislatures, be they located in London, Philadelphia, New York, or Washington, to allocate sufficient funds for the establishment of stable, professional military forces, contributed to this shortcoming. So too did the fact that all Indian conflicts were not alike, amply illustrated by the Seminole War, and that methods that worked in one would not necessarily work in another. Indeed, the essential irregularity of irregular warfare and the multiplicity of political, military, and geographical contexts in which it occurred has always been a factor that has retarded the development of any formal, detailed doctrine for operations of this type. Nevertheless,

INTRODUCTION

some of the lessons of these early campaigns were institutionalized. One needs only to compare the organizational, march, and security procedures employed by Anglo-American armies in the wilderness between 1755 and 1795, for example, to see that certain fundamentals about Indian campaigning were preserved and transmitted. Similarly, the organization of the United States Army between 1792 and 1796 into the Legion of the United States, the only time the entire U.S. Army was structured specifically for counter-Indian warfare, marked a deliberate application of previous lessons learned, as did the somewhat unsuccessful employment of the old converging column technique during the Seminole War.[6]

Several factors contributed to the transmission of frontier experience within American military forces from the colonial and early national periods. Many soldiers served in more than one campaign and were able to apply lessons from one to another. Thus Brig. Gen. William Henry Harrison employed many of the methods he had learned as an aide to General Wayne during the 1790s to his own operations after 1810. Knowledge was also passed by word and example from one generation of soldiers to the next. When, during an 1858 war with the Indians of Washington Territory, Col. George Wright applied techniques of devastation and retribution that he had first observed in the Second Seminole War, his actions were not lost upon young 2d Lt. Philip H. Sheridan, who would himself employ devastation as a weapon against Southern and Native American irregulars over the next thirty years.[7]

Finally, literature also played a role. The orderly books and official correspondence of Anglo-American frontier veterans, such as John Forbes, Henry Bouquet, James Wolf, Robert Rogers, George Washington, John Sullivan, and Anthony Wayne helped preserve irregular warfare experience. So too did unofficial treatises, like Bouquet's "Reflections on War With the Savages," which was contained as an appendix to William Smith's frequently reprinted *An Historical Account of the Expedition Against the Ohio Indians, in the Year 1764*. Another unofficial work, James Smith's *A Treatise on the Mode and Manner of Indian War*, published in 1812, perpetuated many of Bouquet's teachings into the early national period. Nor were more conventional European and American manuals necessarily irrelevant, as they sometimes contained sections on partisan warfare and the movement of troops through difficult terrain that were applicable to frontier conditions. Thus, through a combination of personal experience, word of mouth, and the written word, enough frontier lessons were preserved to produce a basic continuity in the Anglo-American approach to Indian warfare during the eighteenth and early nineteenth centuries.[8]

The movement of the frontier out of the Eastern woodlands and into the vast, open expanses of the trans–Mississippi West, where the indigenous population was often less sedentary and infinitely more mobile than the Eastern tribes, somewhat negated the value of this inheritance. Still, certain underlying principles would remain relevant, while early experiences gained among the Western tribes during the 1840s and 1850s established precedents that post–Civil War soldiers—some of whom had served in the trans–Mississippi West either before or during the Civil War—were destined to follow.[9]

While informal methods were the predominant agents in the preservation and transmission of frontier experience, the U.S. Military Academy also played a role, albeit a limited one. Prior to the Second Seminole War, the academy did not address Indian warfare at all, partly because the subject did not fit the school's conventional focus, and partly because the academy during its early years taught virtually nothing at all about the military art, its curriculum being devoted almost exclusively to engineering. Dennis Hart Mahan first introduced Indian warfare into West Point's curriculum in 1835, when he printed a lithographic note on the subject. Between 1836 and 1840, Indian warfare was a standard part of his lecture series on the science of war, and there is some evidence that he continued to address the subject sporadically throughout his forty years as an instructor at the school (1830–1870).

Mahan's teachings encapsulated the major lessons of a century's worth of American frontier experience. He instructed cadets on march, convoy, and signaling procedures suitable for irregular warfare, described how to construct a blockhouse, and gave tips on ways a beleaguered patrol could convert a farmhouse into a fortress. For the most part, however, he confined his lectures to the principles of Indian warfare rather than the specifics. The single most important principle Mahan taught the nation's young officers was that good soldiers adapted their methods to the characteristics of their enemies.

In the case of Indian warfare, he advised cadets to employ frontiersmen and friendly Indians as auxiliaries and scouts, to take extra precautions with regard to camp and march security, and to gather intelligence for the purpose of exploiting intertribal tensions. Adapting to frontier conditions did not mean, however, that the United States should blindly adopt Indian methods of warfare. Doing so would clearly be disadvantageous to the Army, whose soldiers were man-for-man inferior to the tribesmen in the realms of marksmanship and fieldcraft. Nor would engaging in the Indians' brand of desultory guerrilla warfare achieve the decisive results that the United States desired. Rather than trying to beat the Indian at his own game, Mahan believed the Army should employ science and strategy to force the Indian to fight on the white man's terms. The best way to achieve this end was to send a column deep into enemy territory to destroy the Indians' villages and food supplies. Only by striking at the foundations of Indian society could the Army compel its elusive opponents either to capitulate or to stand and fight on terms favorable to the Army. This was how the nation had defeated the Eastern woodland Indians in its earlier frontier conflicts, and this was the recipe Mahan recommended be employed in the Second Seminole War—a war that the Army eventually won along Mahanian lines.[10]

Despite West Point's rather meager treatment of Indian warfare, there were other elements of the curriculum that illuminated the nature of irregular warfare and pacification activities. Prior to the outbreak of the Civil War, the U.S. Military Academy provided formal training on the conduct of war through a series of classes in ethics commonly referred to as the chaplain's course. Included in the curriculum were the study of international law and the laws of war, both of which were less formal codes than loose bodies of precedents and principles that had evolved over the centuries. One of the more important theorists in this field was the eighteenth-century Swiss diplomat and jurist Emmerich Vattel, whose thoughts on the laws of war were employed in the chaplain's course either directly or through the works of others.[11]

In *The Law of Nations*, Vattel argued that wars should be conducted with as much justice and humanity as possible. He urged soldiers to treat civilians with every consideration, so as to shield them from the lawlessness and disruption that normally accompanies war. Looting and wanton destruction were strictly forbidden, as were any acts that unnecessarily harmed the inhabitants of a disputed region or disrupted normal life. Vattel and other writers on international law believed that prudent conduct on the part of an occupying army both protected civilization and facilitated the restoration of peace. Moreover, moderation redounded to an army's benefit, for by maintaining discipline over its soldiers, an army reduced the chances that the inhabitants would take up arms against it.[12]

Although he conceded that international law did not apply to internal conflicts, such as civil wars and insurrections, Vattel counseled moderation in these circumstances as well. He urged that both sides in a civil war avoid becoming trapped in an escalation of reprisal, execution, and destruction, recommending instead that the government speed reconciliation by granting rebels amnesty.

There was, however, a caveat to Vattel's prescription for humane wars. Relations between the army and the people were not one-sided.

Rather, the laws of war treated the relationship between occupier and occupied as a contract, in which the army offered fair treatment in return for obedience on the part of the people. Should the people fail to live up to their part of the bargain, and instead of submitting, actively resist the occupier, then the contract was broken and the military was free to crush resistance by extraordinary means. Although Vattel hoped commanders would use prudence in exercising the right of retaliation, he conceded that it remained an essential ingredient in the arsenal of war.[13]

The evolution of disciplined armies during the eighteenth century had made Vattel's humane policies a practical possibility in that era. Regular armies were not only more manageable than the armed rabble of centuries past, but the logistical organization that supported them also reduced the necessity for soldiers to forage—one of the activities most likely to arouse hostility among civilians. Uniformed armies were readily distinguishable from the population at large, and the entire philosophy of the humane conduct of war was based upon the possibility of differentiating clearly between combatant and noncombatant. For that reason the laws of war reserved the harshest punishments for actions that blurred the line between soldiers and noncombatants. Little mercy was accorded to armed civilian irregulars who fought in mufti as guerrillas. They were to be treated not as soldiers but as bandits and punished by imprisonment or death.[14]

Just as Vattel's precepts on the laws of war formed the basis of the Army's approach to pacification, the theory of war as taught at West Point rested in large part upon the work of another Swiss writer, Baron Antoine Henri Jomini, a veteran of Napoleon's perilous guerrilla war in Spain. Jomini shared Vattel's distaste for guerrilla warfare on the grounds that it tore the fabric of society and exposed soldier and civilian alike to an endless cycle of lawlessness and retaliation. Like most professional soldiers of his day, Jomini did not believe that undisciplined guerrillas could, by themselves, achieve victory. However, he conceded that partisans represented a serious threat to conventional military forces, especially when used in combination with regular troops. In *The Art of War*, Jomini warned his readers of the difficulties regular armies faced when combating guerrillas:

Each armed inhabitant knows the smallest paths and their connections; he finds everywhere a relative or friend who aids him; the commanders also know the country, and, learning immediately the slightest movement on the part of the invader, can adopt the best measures to defeat his projects; while the latter, without information of their movements . . . is like a blind man: his combinations are failures; and when, after the most carefully concentrated movements and the most rapid and fatiguing marches, he thinks he is about to accomplish his aim and deal a terrible blow, he finds no signs of the enemy but his campfires.[15]

Jomini offered no easy solution to the problem, other than inundating the country with troops and carrying on an aggressive hunt for the guerrillas. However, like Vattel, he also recognized the political side of pacification, and he counseled his readers to "calm popular passions in every possible way, exhaust them by time and patience, display courtesy, gentleness, and severity united, and, particularly, deal justly."[16]

While *The Art of War* provided insights into the nature of guerrilla warfare, it would be to West Point's don of military science, Dennis Hart Mahan, that mid-nineteenth–century officers would turn for an introduction into the tactics and techniques most frequently employed in irregular conflicts. A disciple of Jomini, Mahan shared the conventional view that partisans were a valuable adjunct to regular forces, and consequently he included partisan warfare as one of the ten major subjects covered in the academy's science of war course.[17]

Mahan focused his discussion of partisan warfare not on how to counter guerrillas but rather on how to use partisans and small bodies of regular troops to conduct what eighteenth- and nineteenth-century military theorists commonly referred to as *petite guerre* ("small war"). *Petite guerre* essentially referred to small-unit actions involving outposts, patrols, raids, and reconnaissances conducted for the purpose of gaining information and keeping an enemy off balance. Guerrilla-style tactics of ambush, surprise, and stratagem formed an integral part of such missions. Mahan deemed the study of this kind of action so important that he dedicated his most significant work, *An Elementary Treatise on Advanced-Guard, Out-Post, and Detachment Service of Troops*, to the exposition of its basic principles. As the basic military textbook employed at the U.S. Military Academy during the mid-nineteenth century, *Out-Post* (as the book was commonly known) dispensed advice on the conduct of pickets and patrols, established march security procedures, and laid out the basic principles to be followed in conducting and defending against ambushes and surprise attacks. The book particularly warned its readers of the danger partisans posed to supply convoys. By explaining the tactics and techniques of *petite guerre*, *Out-Post* helped prepare the nation's young officers for the conduct of the type of small-unit operations typically employed in both conventional and unconventional warfare.[18]

The antebellum Army shared Mahan's interest in partisan operations. Washington had employed a number of rifle, legionary, and partisan corps during the Revolution, and the 1857 regulations recommended that field commanders create similar bodies of partisan troops during hostilities. The partisans would harass the enemy and maintain control over the countryside by fostering the goodwill of friendly inhabitants and by intimidating those who were not. Deception, secrecy, speed, espionage, and ambuscade were all prescribed as tools of the partisan's trade. The regulations described partisan warfare in terms that accurately portrayed its later conduct during the Civil War.[19]

Besides classroom instruction and regulations, the antebellum officer corps received "real life" experience in the problems of pacification and irregular warfare not only on the frontier, but also during the Mexican War of 1846–1848. Although he had not attended West Point, the commanding general of the Army at the time of the Mexican War, Maj. Gen. Winfield Scott, had had some legal training before entering the Army and was a devoted student of European military thought and practice. During his campaign against Mexico City, Scott formulated specific policies for the conduct of counterguerrilla and pacification operations that gave tangible expression to the precepts of Vattel and Jomini.

Toward the people of Mexico, Scott held out the hand of reconciliation. No sooner did he begin his campaign than he issued proclamations pledging to protect the lives and property of Mexican citizens. He courted the favor of the Mexican Catholic Church, attending mass himself and ordering his soldiers to salute priests. He encouraged municipal officials to remain in office and did everything in his power to restore to normal the economic and social life of the country. Under Scott's guidance, American military governors distributed free rations to the poor, employed natives to clean the streets, and maintained schools, hospitals, and other public institutions. In addition, Scott demanded impeccable conduct from his soldiers in an effort to minimize friction with the Mexican population. He ignored the War Department's instructions to requisition supplies from the population, preferring to pay for supplies rather than risk alienating the people through harsh extractions. So beneficent was Scott that Ulysses S. Grant stated afterwards that "I question whether the great majority of the Mexican people did not regret our departure as much as they had regretted our coming."[20]

Unfortunately, Scott's benevolent policies did not prevent significant outbreaks of guerrilla warfare. Mixed bands of Mexican patriots, soldiers, and outlaws descended upon his supply lines, ambushing convoys and harassing patrols. Scott took a dim view of these raiders, as did Secretary of War William L. Marcy, who advised the commanding general that guerrilla warfare was "hardly recognized as a legitimate mode of warfare, and should be met with the utmost allowable severity." Scott did just that, announcing a war of extermination against the Mexican irregulars. He denied guerrillas quarter and directed that those who were "accidentally" taken prisoner be held only as long as necessary for a summary court to order their execution. Nor was he much kinder to civilians whom he suspected of aiding the irregulars. Scott held local officials personally responsible for guerrilla acts committed in their districts and confiscated their property whenever they failed to help apprehend the guilty parties. When this did not work, he cast a wider net, fining and burning villages suspected of harboring guerrillas. Scott used the torch with such liberality that the road between Vera Cruz and Mexico City was marked by a black swath of devastation several miles wide. Although the U.S. Army never completely subdued the guerrillas, Scott kept them sufficiently in check to accomplish his mission, in part because he was able to demonstrate to the Mexican people that they had more to lose than to gain by resisting U.S. authority.[21]

Reconciliation and retribution formed the twin policies that governed Army conduct during the Mexican War. The overall success of these policies impressed many younger officers, including several who would later rise to high rank during the War of the Rebellion. One veteran who remembered what Scott had done was Henry W. Halleck. An avid student of military and legal theory, Halleck in 1861 published the book *International Law*, which drew upon Scott's actions in Mexico as well as the writings of a large number of European and American scholars. Halleck reiterated the dual principles of moderation and retaliation that had been taught at West Point and implemented by Scott. On the one hand, he urged armies to treat the inhabitants of an occupied country well, warning that the "inevitable consequences" of indiscipline and unbridled foraging were the "massacre of straggling parties" and the conversion of "the ordinary peaceful and non-combatant inhabitants . . . into bitter and implacable foes." On the other, he maintained that self-appointed bands of guerrillas were not legitimate belligerents and should be treated as criminals. Communities that harbored such individuals were, in Halleck's opinion, collectively responsible for their actions, and generals were free to punish them as Scott had in Mexico. However, while the Army had the right to deal harshly with insurgents and their supporters, Halleck, like Vattel, believed that morality demanded that it resort to such extreme measures only when they were absolutely necessary.[22]

International Law represented views that were widely held, and Halleck's promotion to the post of commanding general of the U.S. Army in mid-1862 ensured that they would strongly influence Army policy. By the time of the Civil War, the legacies of the Indian and

Mexican Wars, combined with the works of Vattel, Jomini, Mahan, Scott, and Halleck, provided the U.S. Army with the conceptual foundation upon which it would build its pacification and counterguerrilla policies. The Civil War would add a significant amount of practical experience to these precepts, experience which would in turn influence the Army's conduct of operations for the next hundred years.

Notes

[1] Some works that do address the subject in various ways are Sam Sarkesian, *America's Forgotten Wars* (Westport, Conn.: Greenwood Press, 1984); John Waghelstein, "Preparing for the Wrong War: The United States Army and Low Intensity Conflict, 1755–1890" (Ph.D. diss., Temple University, 1990); John Gates, "Indians and Insurrectos: The U.S. Army's Experience With Insurgency," *Parameters* 13 (March 1983): 59–68; Robert Asprey, *War in the Shadows: The Guerrilla in History*, 2 vols. (Garden City, N.Y.: Doubleday, 1975); Ian Beckett, ed., *The Roots of Counter-Insurgency: Armies and Guerrilla Warfare, 1900–45* (New York: Blandford Press, 1988).

[2] Todd Greentree, *The United States and the Politics of Conflict in the Developing World* (Langley Air Force Base, Va.: Army-Air Force Center for Low Intensity Conflict, 1990); William Olson, "The Concept of Small Wars," *Small Wars and Insurgencies* 1 (April 1990): 39–46; Michael Klare, "The Interventionist Impulse: U.S. Military Doctrine for Low-Intensity Warfare," in *Low-Intensity Warfare*, ed. Michael Klare and Peter Kornbluh (New York: Pantheon, 1988), pp. 49–79.

[3] Joint Chiefs of Staff, *Dictionary of Military and Associated Terms*, JCS Publication 1 (1987), p. 118; U.S. Army, Field Manual (FM) 100–5, *Operations*, 1986, p. 6; E. S. Johnston, "A Science of War," in *Art of War Colloquium* (Carlisle Barracks, Pa.: Army War College, November 1983), pp. 63–64, 50; Robert Doughty, *The Evolution of U.S. Army Tactical Doctrine, 1946–76* (Fort Leavenworth, Kans.: U.S. Army Command and General Staff College, 1979), p. 1; Jay Shafritz et al., *Dictionary of Military Science* (New York: Facts on File, 1989), pp. 148–49; Vardell Nesmith, "The Quiet Paradigm Change: The Evolution of the Field Artillery Doctrine of the United States Army, 1861–1905" (Ph.D. diss., Duke University, 1977), pp. 1–3; Wayne Hall, "A Critique of the Doctrine-Training Fit," *Military Review* (June 1985): 34.

[4] Examples of such campaigns include those of Maj. Gen. John Sullivan in 1779, Maj. Gen. Anthony Wayne in 1794, Brig. Gen. William Henry Harrison in 1811, and Maj. Gen. Andrew Jackson in 1813–1814 and 1817. Of course, not all expeditions succeeded, as Maj. Gen. Arthur St. Clair and Bvt. Brig. Gen. Josiah Harmar demonstrated. For a discussion of how Anglo-American armies adapted (or sometimes failed to adapt) to frontier conditions, see Peter Russell, "Redcoats in the Wilderness: British Officers and Irregular Warfare in Europe and America, 1740–1760," *William and Mary Quarterly* 35 (October 1978): 629–52; Mott Hooton, "Certain Historical Data Regarding Extended Order," *Journal of the Military Service Institution of the United States* 16 (1895): 550 (hereafter cited as *JMSIUS*); John Mahon, "Anglo-American Methods of Indian Warfare, 1676–1794," *Mississippi Valley Historical Review* 45 (September 1958): 254–75; King L. Parker, "Anglo-American Wilderness Campaigning, 1754–64: Logistical and Tactical Developments" (Ph.D. diss., Columbia University, 1970); Asprey, *War in the Shadows*, pp. 101–04; John Dederer, "The Origins and Development of American Conceptions of War to 1775" (Ph.D. diss., University of Alabama, 1988), pp. 27, 160, 170; Russell Weigley, *History of the United States Army* (Bloomington: Indiana University Press, 1984), pp. 24–27; William Guthman, *March to Massacre* (New York: McGraw-Hill, 1975), pp. 11, 94–96, 127; Russell Weigley, *The American Way of War* (Bloomington: Indiana University Press, 1973), pp. 67–68.

⁵ John Trussell, "Seminoles in the Everglades," *Army* 12 (December 1961): 41–45; Eben Swift, "Services of Graduates of West Point in Indian Wars," in *The Centennial of the United States Military Academy at West Point, New York*, 2 vols. (Washington, D.C.: Government Printing Office, 1904), 1:526. For a comprehensive account of the Seminole War, see John Mahon, *History of the Second Seminole War* (Gainesville: University of Florida Press, 1967).

⁶ Mahon, *Seminole War*, p. 320; Weigley, *History of the U.S. Army*, pp. 92–93; Francis Prucha, *The Sword of the Republic* (Bloomington: Indiana University Press, 1969), pp. 30–38; Fletcher Pratt, *Eleven Generals: Studies in American Command* (New York: Sloane, 1949), pp. 37–58.

⁷ Dennis Vetock, *Lessons Learned: A History of United States Army Lesson Learning* (Carlisle Barracks, Pa.: U.S. Army Military History Institute, 1988), pp. 13–14, 16.

⁸ Henry Bouquet, "Reflections on War With the Savages of North America," app. to William Smith, *An Historical Account of the Expedition Against the Ohio Indians, in the Year 1764* (Philadelphia: W. Bradford, 1765); James Smith, *A Treatise on the Mode and Manner of Indian War* (Paris, Ky.: Joel R. Lyle, 1812); Parker, "Anglo-American Campaigning," pp. 301–30; O. L. Spaulding, "The Military Studies of George Washington," *American Historical Review* 29 (July 1929): 678–79; Edward Williams, ed., *The Orderly Book of Colonel Henry Bouquet's Expedition Against the Ohio Indians, 1764* (Pittsburgh, 1960); Anthony Wayne, "General Wayne's Orderly Book," *Michigan Pioneer Historical Society Collection* 34 (1904): 341–733. For examples of early military texts that contained discussions of partisan warfare that could be applied to the frontier, see De Jeney, *The Partisan* (London, 1760); William Young, *Manoeuvers, or Practical Observations on the Art of War* (1771); Roger Stevenson, *Military Instructions for Officers Detached in the Field; Containing a Scheme for Forming a Corps of a Partisan, Illustrated With Plans of the Manoeuvers Necessary in Carrying on Petite Guerre* (Philadelphia: Aitken, 1775); Epaphras Hoyt, *Practical Instructions for Military Officers* (Westport, Conn.: Greenwood Press, 1971).

⁹ Robert Utley, *Frontiersmen in Blue: The United States Army and the Indian, 1848–65* (New York: Macmillan, 1967), pp. 342–46.

¹⁰ Vetock, *Lessons Learned*, p. 24; Thomas Griess, "Dennis Hart Mahan: West Point Professor and Advocate of Military Professionalism, 1830–1871" (Ph.D. diss., Duke University, 1968), pp. 306–07; John Brinsfield, "The Military Ethics of General William T. Sherman: A Reassessment," *Parameters* 12 (June 1982): 37; Robert Wooster, *The Military and United States Indian Policy* (New Haven, Conn.: Yale University Press, 1988), pp. 56–57; Stephen Ambrose, "Dennis Hart Mahan," *Civil War Times* 2 (November 1963): 35; Trussell, "Seminoles in the Everglades," pp. 41–45; Swift, "Services of Graduates," p. 526; Thomas Smith, "West Point and the Indian Wars," presentation at the U.S. Military Academy, Sep 93, pp. 18–22, copy in Historians files, CMH; Dennis Hart Mahan, "Composition of Armies," lithographic text, 1836, pp. 33–36, George L. Welker Papers, U.S. Military Academy, West Point, N.Y.

¹¹ Brinsfield, "Military Ethics," p. 38; Ralph Gabriel, "American Experience With Military Government," *American Historical Review* 49 (July 1944): 631–32; Robert Futrell, "Federal Military Government in the South, 1861–65," *Military Affairs* 15 (Winter 1951): 181.

INTRODUCTION

[12] Emmerich Vattel, *The Law of Nations* (Philadelphia: T. & J. W. Johnson, 1863), pp. 348–66; James Kent, *Commentaries on American Law*, 2 vols. (New York: O. Halsted, 1826), 1:85–87.

[13] Vattel, *Law of Nations*, pp. 352, 366, 422–25.

[14] Kent, *Commentaries on American Law*, 1:89; Brinsfield, "Military Ethics," p. 38. For the continuity in the laws of war as they were taught at West Point, see *The Centennial of the U.S. Military Academy at West Point, New York*, 1:440–41; Vattel, *Law of Nations*; Henry Wheaton, *Elements of International Law* (Philadelphia: Lea & Blanchard, 1846); Theodore Woolsey, *Introduction to the Study of International Law* (Boston: James Monroe, 1864); Henry W. Halleck, *International Law; or, Rules Regulating the Intercourse of States in Peace and War* (New York: Van Nostrand, 1861); George B. Davis, *Outlines of International Law* (London: Sampson, Low, Marston, Searle & Rivington, 1888).

[15] Antoine Henri Jomini, *The Art of War* (Philadelphia: J. B. Lippincott, 1862), pp. 29–34.

[16] Ibid., p. 33. *The Art of War* was first published in French in 1838 and republished in English in the United States in 1854 and 1862. Only a handful of antebellum officers formally studied *The Art of War* at West Point, since the class of 1859–1860 was the only one which used this work as a textbook. Nevertheless, many officers were exposed to Jomini's ideas, either through lectures on partisan warfare presented by Dennis Hart Mahan or through individual study. George Winton, "Ante-Bellum Military Instruction of West Point Officers and Its Influence Upon Confederate Military Organization and Operations" (Ph.D. diss., University of South Carolina, 1972), p. 50; *Centennial of the U.S. Military Academy*, 1:464; Richard Beringer et al., *Why the South Lost the Civil War* (Athens: University of Georgia Press, 1986), pp. 17–18; Herman Hattaway and Archer Jones, *How the North Won* (Chicago: University of Illinois Press, 1983), pp. 12–13; T. Harry Williams, *The History of American Wars From Colonial Times to World War I* (New York: Alfred Knopf, 1981), pp. 195–96; Griess, "Mahan," p. 366.

[17] Griess, "Mahan," pp. 222, 366.

[18] Dennis Hart Mahan, *An Elementary Treatise on Advanced-Guard, Out-Post, and Detachment Service of Troops With the Essential Principles of Strategy and Grand Tactics* (New York, 1847 edition), preface, and (New York: John Wiley, 1863 edition), pp. 42, 155, 166–68. For background on partisan and guerrilla warfare in Western military thought prior to the Civil War, see Beringer et al., *Why the South Lost*, pp. 171, 340–41, 437; Henry W. Halleck, *Elements of the Military Art* (New York, 1846), p. 43; Peter Paret, "Colonial Experience and European Military Reform at the End of the Eighteenth Century," *Bulletin of the Institute of Historical Research* 37 (May 1964): 53–58; Russell, "Redcoats in the Wilderness," pp. 630–41; Stevenson, *Military Instructions for Officers*; Hoyt, *Practical Instructions for Military Officers*, pp. vi, 78, 221.

[19] War Department, *Regulations for the Army of the United States, 1857* (New York: Harper & Brothers, 1857), pp. 86–87; War Department, *Revised United States Army Regulations of 1861* (Washington, D.C.: Government Printing Office, 1863), pp. 95–96.

[20] Justin Smith, *The War With Mexico*, 2 vols. (New York: Macmillan, 1919), 2:210, 220–21, 229; Gabriel, "Military Government," pp. 633–36. Grant quote from Justin Smith, "American Rule in Mexico," *American Historical Review* 23 (January 1918):

301, and see also 287–88, 291–98. Provost Marshal General's School, Military Government Under Winfield Scott, Training Packet 58, n.d., pp. 15–17, 26–27, 72–73, copy in Historians files, CMH.

[21] Quote from Smith, *War With Mexico*, 2:423, and see also 2:170–73, 421. Headquarters of the Army, Mexico, GO 372, 12 Dec 1847; Headquarters of the Army, Jalapa, GO 127, 29 Apr 1847; Smith, "American Rule in Mexico," pp. 289–90. Other American commanders in Mexico, including Maj. Gen. Zachary Taylor, adopted policies similar to Scott's. See Waghelstein, "Wrong War," pp. 171–77; K. Jack Bauer, *The Mexican War, 1846–48* (New York: Macmillan, 1974), pp. 220–23, 269, 333–34.

[22] Gabriel, "Military Government," p. 637; Provost Marshal General's School, Military Government, An Historical Approach, Training Packet 9, n.d., p. 112. Quotes from Halleck, *International Law*, pp. 458–61, and see also pp. 386–88, 796–97.

2

THE WAR OF THE REBELLION 1861-1865

In 1861 Southern nationalists launched an insurrection to liberate themselves from United States authority. As in many modern insurrections, the rebels pursued independence on a multiplicity of fronts. They organized governments, launched political campaigns to undermine the Northern war effort and win foreign recognition, and employed a mix of regular and irregular forces to combat government troops and maintain control over those Southerners who did not share their goals.

Though the rebels focused their military energies on the creation and employment of conventional forces, Southern irregulars made significant contributions to the secessionist war effort. As federal troops advanced into the South, rebel guerrillas sniped at pickets, ambushed patrols, harried detachments, and disrupted lines of communications and supply. Employing classic techniques of stealth, surprise, speed, and deception, mounted irregulars avoided federal concentrations and sought out weak points, striking their targets quickly before melting back into forest, mountain, and swamp.

Initially, such actions were performed by individuals ("bushwhackers") and small, self-constituted bands of secessionist sympathizers. As the war progressed, rebel authorities reinforced these bands with regularly constituted units of Partisan Rangers and cavalry detached for "partisan service." These irregulars were so effective that they tied down as much as one-third of the U.S. Army at certain stages of the war, rendering Union forces too weak to defeat decisively rebel main force units like the Army of Northern Virginia. Moreover, rebel irregulars, supported by sympathetic elements of the population, effectively undermined federal authority throughout the southern and border states by terrorizing loyal citizens and disrupting efforts to restore the legitimate govern-

Confederate cavalry, partisan rangers, and guerrillas posed a constant threat to federal rear areas and supply columns.

ment. "In no other way," wrote President Abraham Lincoln, "does the enemy give us so much trouble, at so little expense to himself."[1]

The Army responded to the challenges posed by rebel irregulars and disloyal citizens in a variety of ways. As the Army occupied disaffected territory, federal officers acted as constables, governors, jurists, and lawmakers. They chased guerrillas, restored government authority, and implemented a host of other measures designed to pacify disaffected regions. The Army's experience in conducting occupation and counterguerrilla operations during the War of the Rebellion established important precedents that would influence its approach to counterinsurgency situations far into the future.

Pacification, 1861–1863

President Lincoln set the tone of federal pacification endeavors during the Civil War. A humane man, Lincoln favored mild and conciliatory policies on both moral and political grounds. A moderate course, he felt, would help bind the wounds created by the conflict and mollify those in the southern and border states who were not entirely hostile to the Union. The president believed that most Southerners did not really want to leave the Union but rather had been duped into supporting secession by a few fire-eating demagogues. A firm display of the government's martial prowess, coupled with leniency, would, in his estimation, quickly reconvert most Southerners into loyal citizens. Besides, the conquered rebel would soon become a voter, on whom the postwar government of the South would ultimately depend, and the president—a subtle and accomplished politician—was well aware that in a few years his party might need the ballots of those who were currently in rebellion against the Union. The president's mild policies complemented the precepts on the conduct of war as taught at West Point, and together they became the basis of the Army's approach to the pacification of the South.[2]

One of the first Army officers to establish concrete pacification measures was Maj. Gen. George B. McClellan. In May 1861, when the rebellion was but a few weeks old, McClellan sent a small army into western Virginia to reassert federal authority. A West Point graduate and a veteran of the Mexican War, McClellan shared Lincoln's hope that the insurrection could be put down with as little disruption as possible. Recognizing that Virginians were deeply divided over secession, McClellan attempted to win support by adopting a moderate course. In a series of proclamations issued in May and June, he promised to protect the rights and property of the people of western Virginia, including their right to own slaves. He reinforced these promises by exhorting his soldiers to "use every effort to conciliate the people and strengthen Union feeling."[3] "Bear in mind," he continued, "that you are in the country of friends, not of enemies, that you are here to protect, not to destroy. Take nothing, destroy nothing . . . respect the right of private opinion; you will punish no man for opinion's sake. Show to the world that . . . we inaugurate no reign of terror where we go."[4]

Other commanders entering disaffected territory in 1861–1862 followed a similar course. Lincoln reinforced this approach by reprimanding and occasionally replacing commanders whose actions undercut his moderate policies. In addition, the president moved to impose quasi-civilian government in occupied areas. Although the federal government controlled little territory south of the Mason-Dixon line during the first year of the rebellion, Lincoln desired to demonstrate to Southerners his determination to restore quickly some semblance of normalcy wherever federal forces had made some headway. In 1862 he appointed military governors for North Carolina, Louisiana, Arkansas, Texas, and Tennessee. For the most part, Lincoln chose politicians and lawyers who he believed would be better suited for the task than professional soldiers. The following year he took these measures a step further by establishing a generous amnesty program and by promising to restore full civil government in any rebellious state where a mere 10 percent of the electorate had taken oaths of loyalty to the federal government.[5]

The Army's responsibilities in administering occupied regions during the insurrection were complex. The initial task was to reestablish order by creating new police and judicial authorities. In some areas the Army reestablished the civil courts, while in others military commissions and provost courts functioned. Some military courts presided over purely civil and criminal matters, handling everything from fraud to divorce.[6]

With the basic mechanisms of order in place, the military governments turned to civil administration. The Army removed patently disloyal officials and appointed others, relying wherever possible upon civilians to conduct the daily business of local government. When this was not possible, the Army stepped in, providing essential services and issuing ordinances that governed every aspect of public life. Military officials supervised elections; collected taxes; fed, clothed, and sheltered the destitute; and regulated economic and business affairs.

In New Orleans Maj. Gen. Benjamin F. Butler imposed strict sanitary controls in the hope of preventing epidemics. He paid the poor to clean the streets, flushed drainage ditches daily, instituted regular trash collection, and ordered all dwellings and businesses to remain tidy. Army commanders showed similar concerns for health and sanitation in other parts of the South as well. In Virginia, Tennessee, and Mississippi, the Army instituted compulsory inoculations for smallpox, while in North Carolina one stickler for cleanliness issued an ordinance forbidding people to allow their hogs to roam freely in the streets. The officer was overruled by his superior, however, on the grounds that meandering hogs were "an old custom of the place."

Many measures instituted by the Army were done in its own interest. Fire departments created by the military helped protect military property, labor laws ensured military access to civilian labor, and regulations aimed at suppressing disease, vice, and alcohol safeguarded the health of the soldiery. Nonetheless, such measures benefited the community as well and served the Lincoln administration's goal of restoring goodwill in the South.[7]

The linchpin of the Army's administration of civil affairs was the provost marshal. The Army established provosts in every district under martial law, and in many areas they represented the only governmental authority. They maintained order and monitored the activities of the disloyal, administering loyalty oaths, collecting fines, arresting rebels, prosecuting criminals, and distributing food and material to the needy. By and large the provosts operated fairly, although there were cases of corruption and abuse, especially when they were local men who bore grudges against their secessionist neighbors.[8]

Despite much effort and goodwill, however, benevolent pacification proved less than successful. In part, this was because federal commanders were never able to stamp out unauthorized foraging, looting, and other acts of petty criminality on the part of their troops that alienated the Southern population and undermined government efforts to win popular support. More fundamental, however, was the fact that benevolent pacification rested upon a faulty premise. Lincoln's estimation that the mass of Southerners were latently pro-Union proved to be incorrect. Confederate loyalties were deeply held by many, while Lincoln's concessions were often misinterpreted by Southerners as a sign of weakness. Complicating matters, federal defeats in the field steadily forced Lincoln to adopt more stringent measures, including in September 1862 the emancipation of slaves. This measure alone irrevocably alienated the mass of white Southerners and doomed any hope for reconciliation. Consequently, secessionists held fast to the hope of victory and refused to return their allegiance to the Union as long as Southern armies remained in the field. Until federal forces could defeat the main rebel armies, the government could only attempt to control, rather than convert, the disaffected.[9]

But victory remained elusive. The constant ebb and flow of the battle lines meant that federal officials rarely controlled any part of the South long enough to establish solid military or civil governments. The Army occupied so little territory in Texas and North Carolina that the Lincoln military governorships had little real authority, while effective federal rule in Arkansas was delayed until late in the war. Even in southern and border state areas that were generally under federal control, raids and incursions from adjacent rebel-dominated regions seriously disrupted pacification efforts.

Particularly effective were the numerous bands of rebel irregulars that prowled behind federal lines both in the South and in loyal border states that contained significant pro-Southern populations, most notably Missouri, Kentucky, and the newly created states of Kansas and West Virginia. Though it is difficult to determine the number of secessionist sympathizers that served in irregular capacities during the rebellion, there was hardly a theater of the war where federal soldiers and Unionist civilians were not harassed by rebel bushwhackers and partisans. Guerrillas kidnapped and assassinated government officials, attacked economic targets, and attempted to enforce Confederate edicts in federally controlled areas. The favorite targets of the irregulars were the provost marshals. Although most partisans were content to kill provosts, the rebel cavalryman Col. John H. Morgan preferred to subvert them instead, by kidnaping and terrorizing them into agreeing to protect, rather than persecute, secessionist civilians.[10]

Against Unionist civilians, rebel partisans waged similar terror campaigns. Using a mixture of threats and violence, the guerrillas either intimidated the neutral and pro-government population into submission or forced them to flee, often burning their homes and robbing them in the process. Federal officials understood that their inability to protect the population from the guerrillas on account of troop shortages essentially doomed progress in pacification. As General Butler explained in June 1862,

in the present temper of the country here it is cruel to take possession of any point unless we continue to hold it with an armed force, because when we take possession of any place those well disposed will show us kindness and good wishes; the moment we leave, a few ruffians come in and maltreat every person who has not scowled at the Yankees. Therefore it is that I have been very chary of possessing myself of various small points which could easily be taken.[11]

More than any other factor, it was the political and military disruption created by the guerrillas and their civilian sympathizers that led the Army to stiffen its pacification policies in 1861 and 1862. Army officers responded in line with their education and experience, refusing to treat bushwhackers or their civilian allies as legitimate combatants. In western Virginia General McClellan took the first step in this regard in June 1861 by threatening to treat guerrillas and their civilian accomplices "according to the severest rules of military law." Two months later Maj. Gen. John C. Fremont, the Army's senior commander in Missouri, resurrected Scott's military commissions, declaring that he would execute anyone found guilty of bearing arms in the state. Henry W. Halleck, Fremont's successor as commander of the Department of the Missouri, placed the military commissions on a more formal basis later that year, and by 1862 military tribunals were widely employed in all theaters as a standard weapon in the counterguerrilla war.[12]

Halleck, however, did not consider military commissions as his only means of punishing the guerrillas, and in December 1861 he adopted Winfield Scott's policy of authorizing soldiers to shoot down guerrillas who were caught in the act of burning bridges and destroying telegraph lines. In a passage that could have been taken from his recently published book, Halleck explained to his soldiers that "it is a well-established principle that insurgents, not militarily organized under the laws of the State, predatory partisans, and guerrilla bands are . . . not legitimately in arms. . . . They are, in a legal sense, mere freebooters and banditti, and are liable to the same punishment which was imposed upon guerrilla bands by Napoleon in Spain and by Scott in Mexico."[13]

General Halleck

Halleck reiterated his "no-quarter" policy in the spring of 1862 just before President Lincoln elevated him to be commanding general of the Army. From his new post he disseminated his views on guerrilla warfare to the Army as a whole. He found a receptive audience. Already the War Department had announced that guerrillas were "the common enemies of mankind, and should be hunted and shot without challenge wherever found." Halleck encouraged this view, and as the war progressed an increasing number of officers either denied the guerrillas quarter or tried them by military commissions. But in doing so they ran afoul both of the president's soft heart and of his acute political sense.[14]

Lincoln undermined the effectiveness of military commissions when, in the fall of 1861, he insisted upon personally reviewing all death sentences imposed by military courts, in part out of concern that the Confederates would execute federal prisoners in retaliation. Lincoln's action greatly agitated Army officers. General Butler felt that the delay created by having to send cases to Washington for review undermined any deterrent effect that an execution might have, while Halleck estimated that the odds were seven to one in favor of a guilty party escaping punishment. Lincoln worsened the situation in 1862 when, in the interests of reconciliation, he announced a general amnesty for all civilian prisoners.[15]

In practice, the president's leniency backfired. By releasing suspects and overturning convictions, he created a revolving door through which suspects were released with nothing more than a loyalty oath to ensure their future good conduct. In most cases, those set free were no more loyal than when they were arrested, and many resumed their old habits. The natural reaction of the frustrated and harried soldiers in the field was to adopt a no-quarter policy of their own. Col. George Crook, the commander of the 36th Ohio Volunteer Infantry that was stationed in West Virginia on counterguerrilla duty during the fall and winter of 1861–1862, recollected that "when an officer returned from a scout he would report that they had caught so-and-so, but in bringing him in he slipped off a log while crossing a stream and broke his neck, or that he was killed by an accidental discharge of one of the men's guns, and many like reports. But they never brought back any more prisoners."[16]

Unit commanders winked at the practice, which quickly became common regardless of whether department commanders approved or disapproved of denying quarter to guerrillas. Congress came to the aid of frustrated officers in 1864 by passing an act that permitted department commanders to execute guerrillas convicted by military commissions, without referring the cases to Washington. By that time, however, the issue was almost moot, for no-quarter policies were already widely in force.[17]

Federal officers also turned against the civilian population that abetted the irregulars. Recognizing that "the mild and indulgent course heretofore pursued" had failed to deter the secessionists, General Halleck in the winter of 1861–1862 called for the adoption of a more severe policy designed to make secessionist civilians "begin to feel the presence of the war." The most common method of control adopted by the Army was administering loyalty oaths. Initially, the government required only office holders and former Confederate soldiers to take the oath, but over time it extended the practice to nearly everyone living in the southern and border states. The Army usually demanded that people taking the oath put up a bond guaranteeing their good conduct. Violation of the oath resulted in forfeiture plus other unpleasant consequences, ranging from confiscation to exile, imprisonment, and even death.[18]

Life was still less pleasant for those who candidly registered themselves as disloyal. Such individuals lost the right to participate in local politics and bore the brunt of special levies imposed by the government. Even so, many resisted taking the oath, prompting some officers to devise special incentives. In Tennessee, for example, Maj. Gen. William S. Rosecrans threatened to ship anyone who refused to take the oath beyond government lines. When the threat failed to make any converts, he arrested 100 leading secessionist citizens. Soon thereafter, 10,000 Tennesseans rushed to profess their loyalty and to post bonds ranging from $1,000 to $5,000 as proof of their sincerity. Although many individuals took the oath purely out of expediency, the stiff punishments inflicted for violations probably acted as somewhat of a deterrent.[19]

The Army supplemented loyalty oaths by punishing whole communities for the activities of guerrillas. Federal forces first resorted to such measures during the summer of 1861 in western Virginia and Missouri. Brig. Gen. John Pope, a Mexican War veteran, announced a policy of fining Missouri towns within a five-mile radius of any guerrilla attack, unless the inhabitants could prove that they had attempted to prevent the deed. He employed a similar policy a year later in the East, as commander of the Army of Virginia. Brig. Gen. John Wool, commander of the Department of Virginia, reinforced Pope's action. During the Mexican War, Wool had adopted a policy of holding communities responsible for the damages done by guerrillas. Now, fifteen years later, he reinstated those same policies, proclaiming in July 1862 that he would hold civilians accountable not just for guerrilla actions, but also for failing to notify the Army of the presence of guerrillas. Other commanders followed suit, and the imposition of fines and assessments quickly became a common feature of the war.[20]

When assessments proved insufficient or impractical, the Army turned to more drastic measures, confiscating property and arresting thousands of civilians. Individuals suspected of aiding the insurgents were tried by military commissions and, if convicted, sentenced to imprisonment or (with Lincoln's rare approval) death. Many were not charged but were held for various lengths of time and then released. Union officers also arrested individuals for use as hostages, holding them until such time as the community paid a fine or helped apprehend local irregulars. Hostages and other detainees could also expect to be banished, as the Army forced thousands of civilians to leave their homes for a variety of reasons. Sometimes the rationale was to punish especially recalcitrant citizens, like five women who walked out of a Vicksburg church when the minister read a prayer for Lincoln. More often, civilians were banished in retaliation for guerrilla attacks, as was the case in the fall of 1862 when Maj. Gen. William T. Sherman exiled ten secessionist families for every boat on the Mississippi River that came under rebel fire.[21]

The net effect of all these actions—oaths and bonds, fines and assessments, arrests and banishments—was to give officers charged with pacification duties the muscle they felt they needed to motivate the population to abandon the insurrection and partake of the administration's generous terms of reconciliation. Although a few extremists believed that nothing short of the most stringent measures would suc-

Counterinsurgency Doctrine, 1860–1941

General Sherman

ceed in crushing the rebellion, most officers by the end of the war's second year still believed that a judicious mixture of moderation and severity would eventually bring Southerners to see the error of their ways. Maj. Gen. John M. Schofield, who spent a good deal of his Civil War career fighting guerrillas and their pro-secessionist allies in Missouri, was typical. While he took a hard line toward active secessionists by imposing fines, confiscating property, and denying quarter to bushwhackers, he ordered his subordinates to treat the population with respect on the grounds that "many may be reclaimed by justice mingled with kindness." In the winter and spring of 1862–1863, the War Department reaffirmed this dual approach to pacification by distributing two documents that attempted to clarify the issue for commanders in the field.[22]

Francis Lieber and General Orders 100

The first document, *Guerrilla Parties Considered With Reference to the Laws and Usages of War*, originated as a response to the creation of the Partisan Rangers in the spring of 1862. The rangers represented an attempt by rebel authorities to legitimize and gain greater control over their guerrilla warriors by formally making them a part of the Confederate Army. The creation of this new class of irregular forced the federal government to reassess its own policy. What troubled Commanding General Halleck was not the concept of formal partisan troops, which had long been accepted in European and American military circles, but whether the rebels could extend the cloak of legitimacy to the many less formally organized bushwhacker and guerrilla bands that operated in civilian dress. In August 1862 he asked Dr. Francis Lieber, a noted legal scholar, for his views on the subject. Lieber responded by writing *Guerrilla Parties*.

In his pamphlet, Lieber attempted to dispel the confusion over the treatment of rebel irregulars by dividing them into several categories:

the partisan, the guerrilla, the "war-rebel," and the armed prowler (or bushwhacker). He essentially agreed with Confederate authorities that Partisan Rangers were legitimate combatants, as long as they were regularly enrolled, paid, officered, uniformed, and subordinated to proper authority. Such partisans, he maintained, were fully entitled to the protection of the laws of war, as long as they themselves did not violate them.[23]

Lieber took a dimmer view of guerrilla bands. He defined them as self-constituted groups, not formally tied to the organization and administration of an army, which carried on a "petty war . . . by raids, extortion, destruction, and massacre, and who . . . generally give no quarter." He regarded guerrillas of this type to be "particularly dangerous because they easily evade pursuit, and by laying down their arms become insidious enemies." For this reason, Lieber opined that the government had the right to deal with guerrillas harshly. Nevertheless, he recommended in the interest of humanity that the government treat captured guerrillas as regular prisoners of war unless specific crimes could be proved against them.[24]

Lieber was less generous to the other categories of irregulars—the war-rebel and the armed prowler. War-rebel was a label Lieber assigned to civilians in occupied areas who took up arms against an occupying power, while the armed prowler or bushwhacker was merely an individual who took it upon himself to shoot down sentinels. By wearing civilian dress and taking shelter amongst the population, war-rebels and bushwhackers undermined the distinction between combatant and noncombatant that was the foundation upon which the laws of war rested, and consequently, Lieber believed the Army should treat them as brigands. Civilians who provided information and assistance to the irregulars were equally subject to harsh treatment. Essentially, Lieber advocated treating irregulars according to their deeds. Those who abided by the rules of war deserved humane treatment, while those who did not were to be treated severely, regardless of whether they were regular soldiers, partisans, guerrillas, or civilians.[25]

The government took Lieber's advice and in November 1862 declared that it would treat partisans who abided by the laws of war as legitimate combatants. Halleck was so pleased with Lieber's approach that he ordered 5,000 copies of the pamphlet distributed throughout the Army. Encouraged by the response, Lieber suggested that the government publish a more formal code governing the conduct of federal forces in the field. Recognizing the merit of the proposal, Halleck commissioned a panel consisting of Lieber, Maj. Gen. Ethan Allan Hitchcock, and three other officers to draft such a document, which the

War Department published under Lincoln's signature on 24 April 1863 as General Orders (GO) 100, *Instructions for the Government of Armies of the United States in the Field.*[26]

General Orders 100 provided a practical synthesis of the laws of war as they had evolved by the mid-nineteenth century. Like those laws, GO 100 attempted to ameliorate the harshness of war by striking a balance between humanitarian impulses and brutal necessity. Lieber reminded American soldiers that "men who take up arms against one another in public war do not cease on this account to be moral beings, responsible to one another and to God."[27]

Since the object of war was not the death of one's foe but rather the restoration of peace, the code exhorted soldiers not to do anything that would impede the achievement of that end. Moderation was especially needed in occupation duty, and the order admonished soldiers to respect the personal and property rights of unarmed citizens, as well as their religious and social customs. The order strictly forbade all forms of wanton destruction, looting, and pillaging, as well as acts of cruelty, torture, or revenge. Although General Orders 100 recognized that military necessity sometimes required stern measures, including the destruction of property, Lieber reminded officers that "unjust or inconsiderate retaliation removes the belligerents farther and farther from the mitigating rules of regular war, and by rapid steps leads them nearer to the internecine wars of savages."[28]

Although moderation and conciliation were his central themes, Lieber's tolerance had limits. Like his predecessors in the realm of international law, Lieber considered the relationship between soldier and civilian to be reciprocal in nature. Should the civilian population spurn the hand of reconciliation by taking up arms and supporting guerrillas, then military necessity required that the Army adopt stern measures. As in Lieber's earlier pamphlet, General Orders 100 maintained that partisans were legitimate combatants only when they wore uniforms and were an integral part of a larger army. Irregulars who masked their true nature by assuming "the semblance of peaceful pursuits, divesting themselves of the character or appearance of soldiers," were engaging in private, rather than public, war and were to be treated summarily as pirates, rather than as legitimate combatants. Among the punishments the orders prescribed for disloyal civilians during an insurrection were expulsion, relocation, imprisonment, fines, and confiscation.[29]

General Orders 100 was a landmark document because it marked the first time a government had issued official guidelines regulating how its army should conduct itself in relation to an enemy's army and civilian population. Prior works on the laws of war, including those studied at the academy, had been of a theoretical and scholarly nature that lacked the compulsion of state policy. What Lieber had done was to assemble into a concise and practical guide the loose collection of theory and precedent that made up the laws of war.

The code had a profound impact on the development of military policy and legal theory both at home and abroad. GO 100 caused a sensation in Europe, as Prussia, France, and Great Britain all used it as a model to develop similar codes for their own armies. Moreover, the code became one of the pillars upon which the first formal international agreements on the laws of war, the Hague Conventions of 1899 and 1907, were based. General Orders 100 was equally revered at home. In 1875 the U.S. Military Academy made a systematic study of the code mandatory for cadets, and it remained an integral part of the U.S. military doctrine until the Army issued its first field manual on the laws of war in 1914. Even then, the 1863 code lived on, as both the new manual and its successor, Field Manual 27–10, *Rules of Land Warfare*, published in 1940, incorporated many of its ideas. GO 100 thus enshrined in American military policy a practical blend of moderation and stringency that would characterize the Army's approach to military government, counterguerrilla, and pacification operations for the next one hundred years.

Yet for all of its influence upon future generations of Army leaders, General Orders 100 had surprisingly little impact on the conduct of the Civil War itself. One reason was that it was issued only as guidance, since the War Department believed that local commanders were best equipped to decide the proper boundary between leniency and severity. More important was the fact that Lieber's code was based upon the same concepts that federal commanders had used to govern their actions from the beginning of the war. The orders heightened awareness of these principles and provided a useful guide for applying them but did not essentially change them. What GO 100 really did was to sanction virtually everything federal commanders had done prior to its publication. Lieber's guerrilla pamphlet and the general orders codified what Halleck and most of his officers already believed to be the proper policies. The imposition of fines and assessments on the disloyal; the imprisonment and possible execution of civilians who aided the enemy; the denial of quarter to guerrillas who themselves took no prisoners or who disguised themselves as civilians; and the dispensing of summary justice for certain violations of the laws of war—all were sanctioned by GO 100. The degree to which any or all of these measures were imposed was left to the discretion of individual commanders. But all were included in the commander's arsenal and, as the war grew ever harsher, were applied with an unsparing hand.[30]

Pacification, 1863–1865

After the publication of General Orders 100, the War Department reaffirmed its November 1862 decision to treat captured guerrillas as prisoners of war, even to the extent of including them in regular prisoner exchanges. Many guerrillas were exchanged, especially if they were caught wearing uniforms or were not known to have committed any particularly heinous act. However, the War Department attached so many caveats to this policy that it was never consistently carried out.

For one thing, guerrillas taken in border states could only be released with the approval of the governor, a clear recognition of the fact that guerrilla warfare was as much political in its effects as it was military. For another, commanders were allowed to try captured guerrillas whom they believed had committed crimes, and some commanders put virtually all guerrilla prisoners on trial. Even when guerrilla prisoners were not charged with any specific offense, the Army reserved the right to withhold them from routine exchanges. Finally, the War Department continued to permit commanders to refuse quarter to guerrillas who had violated the rules of war. Halleck's successor as commanding general of the Army, Lt. Gen. Ulysses S. Grant, himself ordered Maj. Gen. Philip H. Sheridan to "hang without trial" members of Col. John S. Mosby's battalion of Virginia Partisan Rangers, who routinely donned civilian garb to escape capture.

The effect of all these qualifications was that guerrillas received treatment as prisoners of war only when and where local commanders deemed such a policy advisable. As the war progressed, fewer and fewer commanders chose to grant such favors. No-quarter policies, either official or unofficial, became increasingly common. So too did mass arrests, banishments, and the confiscation and destruction of property, as the Army turned increasingly to heavy-handed tactics in dealing with the recalcitrant population. Indeed, the last two years of the war, from the publication of General Orders 100 in April 1863 to Lee's surrender at Appomattox in April 1865, witnessed growing severity on the part of federal forces.[31]

The greatest spokesman for the "hard war" approach was General Sherman. Sherman realized that the Army was "not only fighting hostile armies, but a hostile people, and must make old and young, rich and poor, feel the hard hand of war." Since Southerners "could not be made to love us," he theorized, then they should be made to "fear us and dread the passage of troops through their country." "Fear," he concluded, "is the beginning of wisdom." Halleck agreed. So too did General Grant, who "understood that he was engaged in a people's war and that the people as well as the armies of the South must be conquered, before the war could end." By striking at the people themselves, the Army hoped to undermine their willingness to support the insurrection in general and the guerrillas in particular.[32]

The harshest measures employed by the government in the counterguerrilla war involved the confiscation or destruction of property and the wholesale removal of civilians from guerrilla-infested areas.

General Sheridan

Although the Army experimented with population removal early in the war, the first major removal scheme surfaced in the fall of 1862, when Halleck authorized Grant to confiscate property and deport all active secessionists living in western Tennessee and northern Mississippi. A year later Brig. Gen. Thomas Ewing, Jr., removed nearly the entire population of three and a half western Missouri counties where guerrilla warfare was particularly rife. Halleck eventually rescinded the order, on the grounds that it harmed the loyal as well as the disloyal.

Nevertheless, over the next two years the Army occasionally used a combination of mass arrests and banishments to attack the informal network of active civilian sympathizers upon which the guerrillas relied for food, shelter, and information. One of the more notable efforts occurred in Virginia in 1864, when General Grant ordered the arrest of the families of known guerrillas as well as "all able-bodied male citizens under the age of fifty . . . suspected of aiding, assisting, or belonging to guerrilla bands" in the area between Harper's Ferry, West Virginia, and Washington, D.C. When this did not succeed in rooting out the guerrillas, Grant contemplated removing the entire population of northern Virginia living east of the Blue Ridge Mountains, due to "the necessity of cleaning out that country so that it will not support Mosby's gang" of partisans.[33]

General Grant

Federal forces supplemented depopulation with devastation. The Army had begun confiscating or destroying private property in retaliation for guerrilla activities in 1861. Initially it destroyed only well-defined targets, such as the houses of known guerrillas or buildings from which sniper fire emanated. However, as the war progressed, some officers began to press for a more liberal use of the torch. Colonel Crook, whose regiment was assigned to counterguerrilla duty in western Virginia in the winter and spring of 1861–1862, was one of the first to do so. Crook found the situation in Webster County to be "so bad that we had to burn out the entire county to prevent the people from harboring" the guerrillas. Other commanders followed suit. Beginning in 1862, the Army and the Navy adopted the policy of destroying towns and farms as retaliation for guerrilla attacks on shipping along the Mississippi River. The Army implemented a similar policy to protect vital railroads. By 1863 a growing consensus existed within the Army that the way to eliminate the guerrillas was, in the words of Col. W. R. Penick, "to destroy all subsistence [in] the country and send off their wives and children." Ewing's depopulation program reflected this trend, as did the actions of commanders in virtually every part of the South in 1863 and 1864.[34]

In North Carolina Brig. Gen. Edward A. Wild, a Harvard-educated physician dubbed the "cousin of Beelzebub" by the inhabitants, destroyed houses, barns, and livestock, took hostages, and hanged captured guerrillas in an effort to pacify the state. In Missouri a combination of banishments and incendiarism left wide areas of the state deserted and desolate, while in Arkansas Maj. Gen. Frederick Steele ordered his troops to make areas infested with guerrillas "uninhabitable." The Army adopted a similar course in West Virginia in 1864, as Maj. Gens. David Hunter and George Crook burned out sections of the Kanawha Valley, destroying crops, livestock, and buildings. Generals Grant and Sheridan took a similar view in neighboring Virginia. Unable to secure the rich and strategically important Shenandoah Valley from the combined threat of rebel main forces, partisans, and bushwhackers, Grant ordered Sheridan to destroy all the crops and seize all the livestock in the valley. Sheridan put the valley to the torch, sparing only houses for humanitarian reasons, although his troopers sometimes burned even these in retaliation for guerrilla attacks.

Having laid waste to the Shenandoah, Sheridan turned his attention to neighboring Loudoun County, the base area of the highly successful rebel partisan, Colonel Mosby. In late November 1864 Sheridan struck at the civilian infrastructure that supported Mosby, destroying or confiscating all forage, livestock, barns, and mills in the county. Though the guerrillas continued to operate, they did so with increasing difficulty and with dwindling support from the war-ravaged inhabitants.[35]

Perhaps the greatest practitioner of devastation was its greatest spokesman, General Sherman. As commander of the Department of the Tennessee in January 1864, he authorized his soldiers to confiscate the livestock of all but proven Unionists to "punish the country well for permitting the guerrillas among them." He took this policy a step further several months later when, as commander of all federal armies in the West, he cut a swath of devastation through the heart of the Confederacy, destroying anything that could conceivably be of use to the rebel military, both to weaken the Confederacy materially and to demoralize the population which formed the underpinning of the insurrection. Although he attempted to respect Southerners' personal and property rights, he did not hesitate to strike even these when guerrillas were afoot. Thus he directed that

in districts and neighborhoods where the army is unmolested, no destruction of [private] property should be permitted; but should guerrillas or bush whackers molest our march, or should the inhabitants burn bridges, obstruct roads, or otherwise manifest local hostility, then army commanders should order and enforce a devastation more or less relentless, according to the measure of such hostility.[36]

The extent to which the policy of destruction was successful in rooting out the guerrillas varied depending upon the circumstances. Nevertheless, commanders had enough success that by 1865 devastation rather than moderation had become the guiding principle of federal armies in suppressing the insurrection. This did not mean that the Army had abandoned moderation entirely. Many officers felt uncomfortable about denying quarter and burning farms and crops, and even those who endorsed the harshest measures endeavored to prevent their soldiers from degenerating into the kind of lawlessness that they so despised in the guerrillas. Indeed, many of the same officers who declared a "war of extermination" against the guerrillas offered generous terms of amnesty to those who voluntarily laid down their arms. Nor did the Army act indiscriminately, for while excesses did occur, for the most part federal actions represented what one historian has described as a "directed severity" that was aimed at specific targets (most notably upper-class secessionists, guerrillas, and military resources) than at Southern society as a whole.[37]

Nevertheless, over the course of four years the balance between moderation and retaliation shifted decisively toward the more radical pole. Even Lincoln, who continuously strove to moderate the actions of his field commanders, accepted the necessity of using "hard" policies in overcoming the insurrection. Although commanders felt uncomfortable with the extreme measures to which they were driven, they assuaged their consciences by holding the Southerners themselves responsible. As Sheridan explained, "The ultimate result of the guerrilla system of warfare is the total destruction of all private rights in the country occupied by such parties."[38]

Tactics and Techniques of the Counterguerrilla War

While the government endeavored to undermine popular support for the insurrection through a combination of moderation and retaliation, the Army struggled with the difficult job of suppressing rebel irregulars in the field. It was a daunting task, for as Crook observed, "it is impossible for any body of troops to march on them without their being apprised of it, and it is impossible to force them to fight unless they want to, for they carry little or no baggage, and can live on little or nothing. When approached they disintegrate and hide in the mountains until all danger is over, when they again reassemble for fresh depredations."[39]

What made the guerrillas particularly difficult to destroy was their ability to blend in with the population at large. Fed, clothed, housed, and informed by civilian sympathizers, the guerrillas assumed a chameleon-like quality, a trait enhanced by their frequent adoption of civilian dress.[40]

If the advantages the irregulars enjoyed in terms of surprise, initiative, mobility, terrain, and intelligence were not enough, the Union Army labored under several additional handicaps. Deficiencies in equipment and shortages of trained cavalry contributed to the difficulties, but a primary problem was an overall dearth of manpower. The Army was whipsawed between Confederate main force units on the one hand and the irregulars on the other. While the guerrillas sapped the Army of the strength it needed to defeat rebel main forces decisively,

Confederate regulars had the same effect on the Army's counterguerrilla campaign. By compelling the Army to concentrate the majority of its resources on the conventional battlefield, the Confederate Army ensured that the U.S. Army would never have enough troops to firmly secure its rear. In addition, many of the troops assigned to rear area security and counterguerrilla work were second-echelon units that were poorly trained, badly equipped, and deficient in morale.[41]

The Army's most common counterguerrilla technique was to establish small posts in the major towns of a disorderly region, with mobile reserves stationed at county seats and other key locations. These posts both protected local populations and resources and served as bases from which patrols radiated out to scour the countryside for guerrillas. The number and size of the posts were contingent upon the available manpower and the nature of the threat. Whether or not such systems worked depended to a great degree on the balance of forces and the initiative demonstrated by local commanders. In Missouri, for example, guerrillas were usually able to infiltrate the strongpoints to strike at less protected targets, keeping federal cavalry in a reactive mode. Moreover, most posts were so small that garrison commanders risked being overrun whenever they split their forces to conduct patrols. Provisioning the many small posts also proved to be a logistical nightmare, since each had to be supplied by convoys that were highly vulnerable to guerrilla attack. Nevertheless, the fortified posts did prove to be of some utility, and throughout 1864 their tiny garrisons repeatedly beat off guerrilla attacks.[42]

The Army particularly favored static defenses for the protection of railroads, the lifelines of Civil War armies, and erected blockhouses to protect bridges and other key points. Some of these defenses evolved into extensive networks of stockades and outposts all carefully connected by systems of patrols. Armored trains and gunboats provided additional firepower. When these failed to work, the Army took more drastic measures. It defoliated the ground on either side of the tracks and at times removed the population as well. It placed civilian hostages on board trains and threatened to hold the local population responsible for any damage done to the line. Although the success of such measures varied, they tied down tens of thousands of government soldiers. Herman Haupt, the U.S. superintendent of railways, ultimately concluded that it was impossible to protect the railroads completely from irregular attack; instead, he perfected rapid repair techniques that enabled the government to reopen damaged facilities quickly.[43]

Federal forces supplemented these passive measures with a variety of patrols, scouts, raids, and sweeps. Most operations were conducted

A blockhouse and encampment typical of many such posts established by the Army to protect important railroad bridges from Confederate raiders.

by small bodies of men that rarely exceeded a regiment in size. At times, however, the Army even conducted division-size sweeps designed to clear areas of guerrilla concentrations. What usually determined the success or failure of these operations was not their size, but the amount of drive and ingenuity exhibited by the commanders. Unfortunately, too many officers demonstrated more complacency than initiative in conducting counterguerrilla operations. That many units employed in rear area work were second-line formations undoubtedly contributed to this problem. So, too, did the desultory nature of guerrilla warfare, which made for many long and uneventful days of monotonous garrison duty and routine patrolling that inevitably took the edge off units. All too often, federal units stuck to the main roads and camped in towns rather than take to the "bush." Nevertheless, there were many resourceful and aggressive officers who rose to the challenge and turned in creditable performances during the counterguerrilla war. Some were veterans of prewar Indian campaigns, while others learned their trade by trial and error.[44]

One of the more successful was George Crook, a West Pointer who arrived in West Virginia in the fall of 1861 after nearly a decade of service fighting Indians in the Pacific Northwest. Crook immediately saw the parallels between Indian and guerrilla warfare and went about applying the techniques that would later become his trademark. His first step was to send some of his most intelligent officers into the countryside to learn as much as they could about the land and its people, paying particular attention to the haunts and habits of the bushwhackers. He supplemented these efforts by recruiting local Unionists to serve as guides. Once this was done, he launched an aggressive campaign in which he used small, flying columns to hunt down the guerrillas and drive them toward other detachments waiting in ambush. He supplemented these activities by burning out disaffected areas and permitting his men to execute captured guerrillas. Crook employed these techniques throughout the war with some success, eventually adding a specially formed scouting unit to his counterguerrilla repertoire.[45]

Many commanders shared Crook's belief that continuous, aggressive small-unit action would eventually wear down the guerrillas. One such person was Maj. Gen. Samuel R. Curtis, a veteran of counterguerrilla operations in Mexico, who urged his subordinates to relentlessly "pursue, strike, and destroy the reptiles." Another was Col. Henry M. Lazelle who, like Crook, had extensive experience in Indian warfare prior to the outbreak of the rebellion. Lazelle argued cogently that the way to defeat the guerrilla was to beat him at his own game. Rather than sending out large bodies of regular cavalry, Lazelle believed that the Army should employ small groups of specially selected men who would travel by night and hide by day, while spies and friendly residents ferreted out information as to the guerrillas' whereabouts. Once this information was obtained, the scout units would ambush the irregulars.[46]

Many officers did just that and adopted the techniques of the guerrillas, moving at night, setting up ambushes, and launching surprise raids on towns and houses to arrest suspected bushwhackers. In some cases they employed spies and "secret service" men to gather information. Others dressed their men as rebels to ferret out the clandestine civilian network that supported the guerrillas. Throughout the South, federal officers learned to increase their effectiveness by traveling light, avoiding the main roads, and employing unobtrusive advance parties of scouts and Unionists to pave the way for counterguerrilla expeditions.[47]

The 13th Indiana Volunteer Infantry provides an example of the flexibility and inventiveness with which federal units approached the guerrilla problem as early as 1861. Like Crook's 36th Ohio, the 13th Indiana spent a portion of the first year of the war on counterguerrilla duty in western Virginia. Not content to patrol the highways, the 13th took to the hills to strike the bushwhackers on their home turf. The unit replaced its conventional wagon train with pack mules to increase its mobility in the back country and developed a patrol system that used small groups of three to six men under the command of a noncommissioned officer. The patrols stayed out in the bush for ten to twelve days at a time, engaging in frequent skirmishes with bushwhackers. The regiment was fairly effective and, on at least one occasion, masqueraded as a rebel unit to penetrate deep into secessionist territory.[48]

Security proved a constant source of worry for federal counterguerrilla units, as the rebels were particularly fond of laying ambushes and picking off sentinels. Federal officers responded by tightening camp and march security and, in some cases, by changing picket procedures so that outpost lines could be more quickly reinforced in case of partisan attack. Local commanders instituted pass systems to control the flow of civilians, and hence information, to the guerrillas. Since rebel irregulars achieved some of their most notable successes by impersonating federal soldiers, some commands adopted recognition signals or wore distinctive pieces of clothing.[49]

Another way in which the Army responded to the challenges of the guerrilla war was through the employment of a variety of special units for counterguerrilla service. One of the most common adaptations was the creation of bodies of mounted infantry to make up for the Army's perennial shortage of cavalry. For the most part mounted infantrymen were handpicked and exempted from normal infantry duty. Instead, they devoted themselves exclusively to reconnaissance, escort, and counterguerrilla work, providing their regimental commanders with an elite, mobile strike force. Most regiments mustered no more than a company's worth of mounted scouts, usually less than a hundred men, although the Army did occasionally convert entire regiments into mounted infantry organizations in an effort to counter the superior mobility enjoyed by mounted rebel raiders.[50]

A second type of unit employed primarily for counterguerrilla and security work were local units recruited in the southern and border states. There were actually several kinds of locally based formations. The first and most common type were militia and home guard organizations. These units often represented the first line of defense against bushwhackers in the border states. Second, the Army occasionally employed independent bands of Unionist guerrillas as guides and saboteurs. More common than Unionist guerrillas were locally raised companies of scouts, which the Army used either as independent counterguerrilla units or as guides for regular troops. Finally, the Army also recruited regular units in the southern and border states. For example, three regiments of Tennessee mounted infantry were raised under the command of Brig. Gen. Alvan Gillem and collectively known as Gillem's Cossacks. Although given line designations, Gillem's Cossacks were regular in name only. They received virtually no conventional training and were employed almost exclusively as raiders and counterguerrillas in eastern Tennessee and North Carolina. They were assisted in these endeavors by two regiments of North Carolina mounted infantry raised by the noted Unionist guerrilla George Kirk. Kirk's regiments were even less "regular" than Gillem's, as many of his men lived at home and only assembled when called. Units like Gillem's and Kirk's were in fact the federal equivalent of the Confederacy's Partisan Rangers, and they proved quite effective in that role.[51]

Relying on local formations for counterguerrilla work had distinct advantages and disadvantages. On the one hand, locally raised units freed the Army's line troops for active service against rebel main forces. Such "native" troops were also familiar with the terrain and people, helping to narrow the advantages the irregulars enjoyed over conventional units. For this reason some commanders preferred them over the regulars for counterguerrilla work. On the other hand, most local units suffered from serious discipline problems, not only because they were poorly trained, but also because of their animosity toward their prosecessionist neighbors, who had persecuted their families and friends. Needless to say, the excesses committed by the Army's "native" troops did not help reestablish peace in the southern and border states.[52]

Finally, during the course of the war the Army raised a few units specifically for counterguerrilla work. Such experiments met with mixed success. One of the first and least successful of the counterguerrilla units was the Jesse Scouts created by General Fremont upon his arrival in West Virginia in April 1862. Commanded by Capt. J. Carpenter, a veteran of both the prewar guerrilla conflict in Kansas and of John Brown's raid on Harper's Ferry, the unit spent most of its time strutting up and down the streets of West Virginia in outlandish costumes and was eventually disbanded in 1863.

A more reputable outfit was the Loudoun County Rangers, which Secretary of War Edwin M. Stanton created in 1862 for the purpose of protecting Unionist citizens and countering guerrillas in northern Virginia. The rangers had a checkered career, suffering several significant defeats at the hands of rebel partisans. Nevertheless, the organization played an active role in many reconnaissance and counterguerrilla operations during the war.[53]

The government had a more promising start when it created the 1st District of Columbia (D.C.) Volunteer Cavalry. This unit, dubbed the "Terror to Evildoers," had its origins as the military arm of the National

Detectives, a police and counterintelligence organization set up by Lafayette Baker to help rid the Washington, D.C., area of traitors and spies. Baker convinced Lincoln and Stanton in the spring of 1863 that he needed a military force to aid his police operations, and the War Department authorized him to raise four companies of cavalry for that purpose. The 1st D.C. Volunteer Cavalry quickly became an elite formation. Not only was it composed of specially selected men and horses, but it was the only cavalry regiment during the war to be outfitted with the magnificent Henry repeating rifle. The unit specialized in making day and night raids to arrest spies and guerrillas in the capital area. Eventually, Stanton's concerns over the partisan threat led him to double the size of Baker's cavalry arm. Like many elite units, however, success had its price. No sooner had the 1st D.C. been increased to a full regiment in 1864 than the Army shipped it south for conventional cavalry duty.[54]

The guerrillas did not go away, and in the summer of 1864 Sheridan began to search for a way to destroy the most effective of northern Virginia's irregulars, Colonel Mosby's battalion of Partisan Rangers. In August Maj. Gen. George Crook, in command of the Army of West Virginia, offered Sheridan the use of one of his elite counterguerrilla units for the purpose of hunting down Mosby. Crook had formed the company-size unit, known as the Legion of Honor, earlier that year by taking select men from a number of regiments in his army and putting them under the command of veteran Indian fighter Capt. Richard Blazer. Sheridan accepted Crook's offer and armed Blazer's Scouts with Spencer repeaters. Blazer's small band arrived in the Shenandoah Valley in mid-August and immediately went to work against Mosby and other guerrilla bands. During his first two months in the valley, Blazer killed, wounded, or captured sixty-eight guerrillas. His success was due not only to his military talents, but also to his public relations skills. One guerrilla complained that Captain Blazer "by his humane and kindly treatment, in striking contrast with the usual conduct of our enemies, had so disarmed our citizens that instead of fleeing on his approach and notifying all soldiers, thus giving them a chance to escape, little notice was taken of him. Consequently, many of our men were 'gobbled up' before they were aware of his presence." Unfortunately, Blazer's success spelled his doom. He became such an annoyance that Mosby targeted him for destruction, and in mid-November Mosby trapped and destroyed the unit, capturing Blazer in the process.[55]

No sooner had Blazer fallen than Sheridan created a new special unit under the command of Maj. Henry Young. Young's men served as scouts and spies for Sheridan's cavalry, often operating in Confederate dress. Sheridan considered Young's Scouts to be quite useful in the counterguerrilla war, and they succeeded in capturing the noted partisan leader Harry Gilmore.[56]

The employment of special counterguerrilla units was not limited to the Virginia theater, as commanders in other areas also dabbled with unconventional measures. Perhaps the most remarkable counterguerrilla unit was the Mississippi Marine Brigade, an amphibious organization created in November 1862 in response to guerrilla attacks on federal shipping along the Mississippi River. Over the course of the next two years the "marines" led an active life, skirmishing with rebel guerrillas, conducting raids, and participating in conventional operations. Although effective, the unit was troubled by morale and discipline problems and soon developed a reputation for robbery and arson as it steamed up and down the Mississippi burning towns, destroying plantations, and carting off loot. Some of this destruction was authorized in line with the Army's tough retaliatory policies, but the brigade exercised little discretion in picking its targets. Moreover, the unit's special boats were costly to maintain, and considerations of economy and reputation eventually led the Army to disband the marine brigade in 1864.[57]

All in all, the Army proved to be fairly adaptable in addressing the tactical aspects of the guerrilla problem. Not every officer was a Crook or a Lazelle, nor did every experiment bear fruit. Nevertheless, the Army demonstrated a willingness to employ a wide variety of methods. It failed, however, to codify the special tactics, with the result that knowledge of these techniques was confined to the memories of veterans. Most practitioners agreed that successful counterguerrilla operations depended on aggressive and innovative officers who knew how to adapt the basic principles of combat and *petite guerre* to the circumstances of guerrilla warfare. That the Army never managed to eliminate the guerrillas completely was due more to larger problems inherent in the nature of the war itself than to any major deficiencies in its methods. In the end, the Army was able to contain the guerrilla threat sufficiently to permit the conventional war to move forward to victory.

The Legacy of the War of the Rebellion

With its armies collapsing, its guerrillas harried, and its population demoralized, the South finally abandoned its quest for independence in April 1865. By adopting measures of "total" warfare, the federal government had raised the price of secession to a level that the South was either unwilling or unable to pay.[58]

In many respects the War of the Rebellion was a defining experience for the U.S. Army—its leaders and campaigns became the object of veneration and study for generations of future American soldiers. In the realm of irregular warfare, the exploits of cavalry raiders on both sides and the measures undertaken by federal authorities to protect railroads from partisan attack were frequently studied, while during the Philippine War (1899–1902) the War Department compiled a thick portfolio on Union counterguerrilla measures to justify similar actions taken against Filipino insurgents.[59] Nevertheless, the post–Civil War Army spent little effort analyzing the counterguerrilla and pacification aspects of the war. Not only had pacification duty proved to be difficult and unrewarding, but the highly political content of the work made the subject unappealing to most soldiers. Moreover, what lessons the Army might have derived from its counterguerrilla experiences were overshadowed by the conventional aspects of the conflict. In the end, it had been the conventional and not the unconventional war that had proved decisive, and it was upon this facet of the rebellion that the postwar Army naturally turned when it came time to derive the tactical and operational lessons of the war.

But perhaps the most fundamental reason why the Army did not reappraise its approach to guerrilla warfare and pacification was that the war had essentially validated the officer corps' preexisting beliefs. This was true not only in tactics, where postwar textbooks used at West Point perpetuated Mahan's contention that conventional, small-unit tactics were essentially applicable to partisan and antipartisan warfare, but more importantly, in policy.[60] Indeed, the greatest contribution of the Civil War to the development of Army doctrine was not in the charting of new ideas but in the validation and sanctification of old ones. Nevertheless, two new and important formulations of old ideas had emerged from the struggle. The first, General Orders 100, codified the dual policies of moderation and retaliation that had served as the basis for the Army's "firm-but-fair" approach to pacification throughout the insurrection and the period of reconstruction that followed. The second was the "hard war" policy advocated by Grant and Sherman. Sherman's march to the sea and Sheridan's devastation of the Shenandoah and Loudoun valleys were particularly emblazoned in the Army's collective consciousness as examples of the extreme measures that the Army could legitimately employ when more temperate policies failed to suppress an insurrection. Together, the words of Francis Lieber and the deeds of General Sherman would become the precepts upon which the U.S. Army would base its pacification policies into the twentieth century.

Notes

[1] Quote from Hattaway and Jones, *How the North Won*, p. 356, and see also pp. 233, 250, 300, 330, 357, 684, 721. Ulysses Grant, *Personal Memoirs of U.S. Grant*, 2 vols. (New York: Charles Webster, 1886), 2:504–05; Archer Jones, *Civil War Command and Strategy* (New York: Free Press, 1992), pp. 151, 234.

[2] Peter Maslowski, *Treason Must Be Made Odious* (Millwood, N.Y.: Kto Press, 1978), pp. 19, 28; Christopher Grimsley, "A Directed Severity: The Evolution of Federal Policy Toward Southern Civilians and Property" (Ph.D. diss., Ohio State University, 1992), pp. 37, 136.

[3] *The War of the Rebellion: A Compilation of the Official Records of the Union and Confederate Armies*, 53 vols. (Washington, D.C.: Government Printing Office, 1880–1901), ser. 1, 2:46. Hereafter cited as *OR*.

[4] Ibid., ser. 1, 2:196–97.

[5] Frank Freidel, "General Orders 100 and Military Government," *Mississippi Valley Historical Review* 32 (March 1946): 546; William Russ, "Administrative Activities of the Union Army During and After the Civil War," *Mississippi Law Journal* 17 (May 1945): 81–82; Gerald Capers, *Occupied City: New Orleans Under the Federals* (Manhattan: University of Kansas Press, 1965), pp. 106–07; Brinsfield, "Military Ethics," p. 41; *OR*, ser. 1, 8:381; Allen Carpenter, "Military Government of Southern Territory, 1861–65," in American Historical Association, *Annual Report for the Year 1900* (Washington, D.C.: Government Printing Office, 1901), pp. 477–78; Futrell, "Federal Military Government," p. 182.

[6] Carpenter, "Military Government of Southern Territory," pp. 483–85.

[7] Hog quote from Futrell, "Federal Military Government," p. 191. Carpenter, "Military Government of Southern Territory," pp. 496–98; Maslowski, *Treason*, pp. 126–36; Howard Nash, *Stormy Petrel: The Life and Times of General Benjamin F. Butler, 1818–93* (Rutherford, N.J.: Fairleigh Dickinson University Press, 1969), pp. 149–59; Capers, *Occupied City*, pp. 72, 88.

[8] Benjamin Thomas and Harold Hyman, *Stanton* (New York: Alfred A. Knopf, 1962), pp. 306, 360–62; Richard Brownlee, *Gray Ghosts of the Confederacy: Guerrilla Warfare in the West, 1861–65* (Baton Rouge: Louisiana University Press, 1958), pp. 151–52; Michael Fellman, *Inside War: The Guerrilla Conflict in Missouri During the American Civil War* (New York: Oxford University Press, 1989), p. 42.

[9] Maslowski, *Treason*, pp. 74, 76, 80, 147–48; Capers, *Occupied City*, pp. 107–11; Brownlee, *Gray Ghosts*, p. 49; James Reston, *Sherman's March and Vietnam* (New York: Macmillan, 1984), p. 59; Grimsley, "Directed Severity," pp. 225, 231; Bruce Catton, *Grant Moves South* (Boston: Little, Brown & Company, 1960), pp. 291–92.

[10] Carpenter, "Military Government of Southern Territory," p. 477; Russ, "Administrative Activities of the Union Army," pp. 82–85; Maslowski, *Treason*, pp. 35–37; James Ramage, *Rebel Raider: The Life of General John Hunt Morgan* (Lexington: University of Kentucky Press, 1986), p. 100; Richard Curry and F. Gerald Ham, "The Bushwhacker's War: Insurgency and Counterinsurgency in West Virginia," *Civil War History* 10 (1964): 431; Jones, *Strategy*, pp. 147–49.

[11] Quote from James Parton, *General Butler in New Orleans* (Boston: Ticknor & Fields, 1866), p. 560. For similar problems elsewhere, see Maslowski, *Treason*, p. 37;

Charles Morse, "The Relief of Chattanooga, October 1863, and Guerrilla Operations in Tennessee," in *Civil War and Miscellaneous Papers, Papers of the Military Historical Society of Massachusetts* (Boston: Military Historical Society of Massachusetts, 1918), 14:74.

[12] McClellan quote from *OR*, ser. 1, 2:196. *OR*, ser. 1, 3:467; *OR*, ser. 1, 8:405–06, 477; Futrell, "Federal Military Government," p. 186.

[13] Quote from *OR*, ser. 1, 8:477–78, and see also 8:439. *OR*, ser. 2, 1:237.

[14] Fellman, *Inside War*, p. 87. Quote from *OR*, ser. 1, vol. 12, pt. 3, p. 169. *OR*, ser. 1, vol. 27, pt. 2, p. 69; *OR*, ser. 1, vol. 16, pt. 2, p. 141.

[15] Carl Beamer, "Gray Ghostbusters: Eastern Theater Union Counterguerrilla Operations in the Civil War, 1861–65" (Ph.D. diss., Ohio State University, 1988), p. 99; Parton, *Butler in New Orleans*, p. 561; Futrell, "Federal Military Government," p. 187; *OR*, ser. 1, 3:466–69.

[16] Quote from George Crook, *General George Crook: His Autobiography* (Norman: University of Oklahoma Press, 1960), p. 87. Curry and Ham, "Bushwhacker's War," p. 418; Beamer, "Gray Ghostbusters," p. 34.

[17] Futrell, "Federal Military Government," p. 187; *OR*, ser. 1, vol. 34, pt. 4, p. 261; War Department GO 231, 18 Jul 1864, p. 4.

[18] First quote from *OR*, ser. 1, 8:405, and see also 8:439. Second quote from Brinsfield, "Military Ethics," p. 42. Beamer, "Gray Ghostbusters," pp. 69, 160; Brownlee, *Gray Ghosts*, pp. 157–58.

[19] Maslowski, *Treason*, p. 61; Carpenter, "Military Government of Southern Territory," p. 495; *OR*, ser. 2, 4:47; *OR*, ser. 1, 8:439.

[20] *OR*, ser. 1, 3:403–04, 421–24; *OR*, ser. 1, vol. 27, pt. 2, p. 69; Wayne Smith, "An Experiment in Counterinsurgency: The Assessment of Confederate Sympathizers in Missouri," *Journal of Southern History* 35 (August 1969): 362; Beamer, "Gray Ghostbusters," pp. 32, 63–65; Smith, *War With Mexico*, pp. 170–71.

[21] Futrell, "Federal Military Government," pp. 187–88; *OR*, ser. 1, vol. 31, pt. 3, p. 58; *OR*, ser. 1, 13:741–43; *OR*, ser. 1, vol. 34, pt. 4, pp. 224–25. The Army refused to sanction the execution of civilian hostages and was even squeamish about executing guerrilla hostages. Nevertheless, the latter was occasionally done. Albert Castel, "The Guerrilla War, 1861–65," *Civil War Times Illustrated* 13 (October 1974): 30; James Prichard, "General Orders No. 59: Kentucky's Reign of Terror," *Civil War Quarterly* 10 (1987): 32–34; *OR*, ser. 1, 4:290–91; *OR*, ser. 1, vol. 34, pt. 2, pp. 136, 174; *OR*, ser. 1, vol. 47, pt. 2, p. 50.

[22] *OR*, ser. 1, 8:607.

[23] Ramage, *Rebel Raider*, p. 67; Carl Grant, "Partisan Warfare, Model 1861–65," *Military Review* (November 1958): 42–43; Richard Hartigan, *Lieber's Code and the Law of War* (Chicago: Precedent, 1983), pp. 35–36, 78; Virgil Jones, *Gray Ghosts and Rebel Raiders* (New York: Henry Holt, 1956), pp. 89–95.

[24] Hartigan, *Lieber's Code*, pp. 33, 41–42.

[25] Brainerd Dyer, "Francis Lieber and the American Civil War," *Huntington Library Quarterly* 2 (July 1939): 453; Hartigan, *Lieber's Code*, pp. 316–44.

[26] Hartigan, *Lieber's Code*, pp. 13, 78, 92; Dyer, "Francis Lieber," pp. 454–56; Freidel, "General Orders 100," pp. 547–48; *OR*, ser. 1, vol. 22, pt. 2, pp. 237–44.

[27] Quote from Hartigan, *Lieber's Code*, p. 48, and see also p. 46.

[28] Quote from ibid., p. 50, and see also pp. 52, 54. *OR*, ser. 3, 3:148–64.

[29] Doris Graber, *The Development of the Law of Belligerent Occupation*,

1863–1914, Columbia Studies in History, Economics, and Public Law 543 (New York: Columbia University Press, 1949), p. 71. Quote from Hartigan, *Lieber's Code*, p. 60, and see also p. 71.

[30] Hartigan, *Lieber's Code*, pp. 1–2, 5, 23; Graber, *Belligerent Occupation*, pp. 14, 20, 38; Freidel, "General Orders 100," pp. 555–56; *Centennial of the U.S. Military Academy*, 1:369; Futrell, "Federal Military Government," p. 181.

[31] *OR*, ser. 2, 5:289, 537–39, 592; *OR*, ser. 2, 8:201, 317, 360; *OR*, ser. 1, vol. 30, pt. 3, p. 34, 106; *OR*, ser. 1, vol. 34, pt. 3, p. 216; *OR*, ser. 1, vol. 34, pt. 4, p. 218; *OR*, ser. 1, vol. 39, pt. 2, pp. 135, 362; *OR*, ser. 1, vol. 41, pt. 2, p. 422; *OR*, ser. 1, vol. 41, pt. 4, p. 631; Prichard, "General Orders No. 59," p. 34; Edward Stackpole, *Sheridan in the Shenandoah* (Harrisburg, Pa.: Stackpole Co., 1961), pp. 377–79; Stephen Starr, *The Union Cavalry in the Civil War*, 3 vols. (Baton Rouge: Louisiana State University Press, 1979), 2:344–47, 362; Jones, *Gray Ghosts*, pp. 181, 308; John Joyce, "Burnside in East Tennessee, Mountain Scenery and Guerrillas," *United Service* (August 1893): 128; Morse, "Relief of Chattanooga," p. 81; Brownlee, *Gray Ghosts*, p. 112; James Williamson, *Mosby's Rangers* (New York: Sturgis & Walton, 1909), p. 421.

[32] First and third quotes from Russell Weigley, *Towards an American Army* (New York: Columbia University Press, 1962), both on p. 86, and see also p. 91. Fourth quote from ibid., p. 93. Stephen Ambrose, *Halleck: Lincoln's Chief of Staff* (Baton Rouge: Louisiana State Press, 1962), pp. 181, 187. Second quote from Hattaway and Jones, *How the North Won*, p. 251.

[33] *OR*, ser. 1, 8:495; Brinsfield, "Military Ethics," p. 42; *OR*, ser. 1, vol. 22, pt. 2, pp. 428–29, 460–61; Fellman, *Inside War*, pp. 96, 127; John Schofield, *Forty-Six Years in the Army* (New York: Century Co., 1897), pp. 78–79, 82–84, 97; Castel, "Guerrilla War," pp. 19–23; Brownlee, *Gray Ghosts*, pp. 115–16, 120, 126; Ann Niepman, "General Orders No. 11 and Border Warfare During the Civil War," *Missouri Historical Review* 66 (January 1972): 185–210. First quote from Jones, *Gray Ghosts*, p. 286. *OR*, ser. 1, vol. 41, pt. 4, p. 276. Second quote from Philip Sheridan, *Personal Memoirs of P.H. Sheridan* (New York: Charles Webster, 1888), p. 487.

[34] First quote from Crook, *Autobiography*, p. 88. *OR*, ser. 1, 13:741–43, 747–49; Castel, "Guerrilla War," p. 33. Second quote from Fellman, *Inside War*, pp. 126–27. Reston, *Sherman's March*, p. 30; Jones, *Gray Ghosts*, pp. 246–48, 281–82, 296–301, 321; *OR*, ser. 1, vol. 43, pt. 2, pp. 345, 348, 565; Starr, *Union Cavalry*, 2:50 and 3:256–57; O. O. Howard, "Is Cruelty Inseparable From War?" *Independent* 54 (15 May 1902): 1162; Beamer, "Gray Ghostbusters," pp. 63–64, 186, 190, 225–29; Parton, *Butler in New Orleans*, pp. 563–64; *OR*, ser. 1, vol. 30, pt. 3, p. 106; *OR*, ser. 1, vol. 29, pt. 1, p. 90.

[35] John Barrett, *The Civil War in North Carolina* (Chapel Hill: University of North Carolina Press, 1963), pp. 152, 178–81; Fellman, *Inside War*, pp. 125–28; *OR*, ser. 1, vol. 34, pt. 2, p. 616; Beamer, "Gray Ghostbusters," p. 230; *OR*, ser. 1, vol. 43, pt. 1, p. 32, and pt. 2, pp. 496–97; *OR*, ser. 1, vol. 37, pt. 1, p. 557; Sheridan, *Memoirs*, p. 484; Stackpole, *Sheridan in the Shenandoah*, pp. 163–64; Jeffrey Wert, *Mosby's Rangers* (New York: Simon & Schuster, 1990), p. 260.

[36] First quote from Grant, "Partisan Warfare," p. 54. Second quote from Brinsfield, "Military Ethics," p. 44.

[37] Wert, *Mosby's Rangers*, pp. 199, 275; Sheridan, *Memoirs*, pp. 99–100; Barrett, *Civil War in North Carolina*, pp. 178–81; Castel, "Guerrilla War," p. 33; Crook, *Autobiography*, p. 88; Beamer, "Gray Ghostbusters," p. 230; Starr, *Union Cavalry*,

2:50; Grimsley, "Directed Severity," pp. 31, 406–24; Waghelstein, "Wrong War," p. 189; Brownlee, *Gray Ghosts*, pp. 47, 49; Reston, *Sherman's March*, pp. 57, 94; William Sherman, *Personal Memoirs of General W.T. Sherman* (New York, 1890), pp. 175–76; *OR*, ser. 2, 5:560, 571; *OR*, ser. 1, 13:402; *OR*, ser. 1, 33:397; *OR*, ser. 1, vol. 34, pt. 2, pp. 616–17; *OR*, ser. 1, vol. 34, pt. 4, pp. 225–26; *OR*, ser. 1, vol. 39, pt. 2, p. 136; *OR*, ser. 1, vol. 41, pt. 4, pp. 262, 918, 928–29; *OR*, ser. 1, vol. 43, pt. 2, pp. 768, 775, 810.

[38] Quote from Beamer, "Gray Ghostbusters," pp. 212–14. Schofield, *Forty-Six Years*, p. 92; James McPherson, *Battle Cry of Freedom* (New York: Ballantine, 1988), p. 809.

[39] *OR*, ser. 1, vol. 12, pt. 3, p. 84.

[40] *OR*, ser. 1, vol. 29, pt. 2, p. 397.

[41] Rick Gutwald, "Low Intensity Conflict as Practiced by John Singleton Mosby in the American Civil War" (Master's thesis, U.S. Army Command and General Staff College, 1986), pp. 32, 122, 145; Beamer, "Gray Ghostbusters," pp. 54, 68, 272; Starr, *Union Cavalry*, 3:423.

[42] Jones, *Gray Ghosts*, p. 79; *OR*, ser. 1, 8:493–94; Brownlee, *Gray Ghosts*, pp. 183, 185, 187.

[43] Morse, "Relief of Chattanooga," p. 73; Beamer, "Gray Ghostbusters," pp. 117, 128, 225–29; William Nichols, "Fighting Guerrillas in West Virginia," *Civil War Times Illustrated* 6 (April 1967): 21; Jones, *Gray Ghosts*, pp. 296–302, 321; *OR*, ser. 1, vol. 43, pt. 2, p. 565; Howard, "Cruelty," p. 1162; Reston, *Sherman's March*, p. 30; Castel, "Guerrilla War," p. 18.

[44] Fellman, *Inside War*, pp. 82, 167; Brownlee, *Gray Ghosts*, p. 192; *OR*, ser. 1, vol. 43, pt. 2, p. 688; Williamson, *Mosby's Rangers*, pp. 427–29; *OR*, ser. 1, vol. 29, pt. 1, p. 90.

[45] Crook, *Autobiography*, pp. 85–88; Beamer, "Gray Ghostbusters," pp. 219, 230.

[46] Quote from *OR*, ser. 1, 13:689. *OR*, ser. 1, vol. 37, pt. 2, pp. 389–90.

[47] *OR*, ser. 1, 8:493–94; *OR*, ser. 1, vol. 34, pt. 4, p. 221; Fellman, *Inside War*, pp. 121–22, 166–69; Jones, *Gray Ghosts*, p. 79; Beamer, "Gray Ghostbusters," p. 55; Frederick Mitchell, "Fighting Guerrillas on the La Forche," in Military Order of the Loyal Legion of the United States, Commandery of the District of Columbia, *War Papers* (1905), 56:3–16; Williamson, *Mosby's Rangers*, pp. 427, 429; Henry Romeyn, "Scouting in Tennessee," in Military Order of the Loyal Legion of the United States, Commandery of the District of Columbia, *War Papers* (1905), 59:3–24; John Forsythe, *Guerrilla Warfare and Life in Libby Prison* (Annandale, Va.: Turnpike Press, 1967), p. 13.

[48] Charles Ross, "Scouting for Bushwhackers in West Virginia in 1861," in *War Papers Read Before the Commandery of Wisconsin, Military Order of the Loyal Legion of the United States* (Milwaukee: Burdick & Allen, 1903), 3:400–412.

[49] Starr, *Union Cavalry*, 3:311; Beamer, "Gray Ghostbusters," p. 140; Ross, "Scouting for Bushwhackers," p. 401; *OR*, ser. 1, vol. 37, pt. 2, pp. 388–89.

[50] Starr, *Union Cavalry*, 3:416; Romeyn, "Scouting in Tennessee," pp. 3–24.

[51] Beamer, "Gray Ghostbusters," p. 30; Curry and Ham, "Bushwhacker's War," pp. 421–22; Castel, "Guerrilla War," pp. 9, 33–36, 38; William Trotter, *Bushwhackers! The Civil War in North Carolina*, vol. 2, *The Mountains* (Greensboro, N.C.: Signal Research, 1988), pp. 113–15, 251, 258, 281–84; Starr, *Union Cavalry*, 3:402–03.

[52] *OR*, ser. 1, vol. 43, pt. 2, pp. 738–39; Maslowski, *Treason*, p. 42; Beamer, "Gray Ghostbusters," p. 272; Ross, "Scouting for Bushwhackers," p. 411; Fellman, *Inside War*, pp. 54, 87, 112, 169–72; *OR*, ser. 1, vol. 34, pt. 2, p. 776.

[53] Beamer, "Gray Ghostbusters," pp. 56, 71; Jones, *Gray Ghosts*, pp. 81, 109–10, 132, 366; Forsythe, *Guerrilla Warfare*, p. 4; Briscoe Goodhart, *History of the Independent Loudoun Virginia Rangers* (Washington, D.C.: McGill & Wallace, 1896), pp. viii, 32, 44, 90, 128–29, 132, 173.

[54] Starr, *Union Cavalry*, 2:399; Robert Mangrum, "Edwin M. Stanton's Special Military Units and the Prosecution of the War, 1862–65" (Ph.D. diss., North Texas State University, 1978), pp. 252, 257–61.

[55] Quote from Beamer, "Gray Ghostbusters," pp. 219–20. Stackpole, *Sheridan in the Shenandoah*, pp. 376–77; Wert, *Mosby's Rangers*, pp. 202–03, 251; John Mosby, "Captain Blazer," *Harper's Weekly* 22 (May 1897): 519.

[56] Sheridan, *Memoirs*, p. 106; Richard Weinert, "The South Had Mosby; The Union, Major Henry Young," *Civil War Times Illustrated* 3 (April 1964): 39–40.

[57] Castel, "Guerrilla War," p. 49; Starr, *Union Cavalry*, 3:200–204; Mangrum, "Special Military Units," pp. 145–50, 152, 155, 185, 187, 200, 206, 210, 213–14; Warren Crandall and Isaac Newell, *History of the Ram Fleet and the Mississippi Marine Brigade in the War for the Union on the Mississippi and Its Tributaries* (St. Louis, 1907), pp. 252, 315.

[58] Beringer et al., *Why the South Lost*, pp. 342–46, 437–39; Hattaway and Jones, *How the North Won*, pp. 686–87.

[59] U.S. Congress, Senate, Philippine Committee, *Hearings Before the Committee on the Philippines*, 57th Cong., 1st sess., 1902, S. Doc. 331, pt. 2, pp. 2789–820.

[60] James Mercur, *Elements of the Art of War* (West Point, N.Y.: U.S. Military Academy Press, 1889), pp. 239–46.

3

THE CONSTABULARY YEARS 1865-1898

"In reality," wrote an officer of the late nineteenth century, "the Army is now a gendarmery—a national police." His observation reflected the reality of postwar America as well as its army. Blessed with weak neighbors and wide ocean buffers and as yet unentangled with significant overseas interests, the nation faced no important military threats during the three decades between the end of the Civil War and the outbreak of the Spanish-American War. As they had before 1861, Americans looked upon their Army as the national jack-of-all-trades, assigning soldiers, in addition to their military duties, the roles of engineer, laborer, policeman, border guard, explorer, administrator, and governor. Of these many responsibilities, two—the Army's occupation of the South following the War of the Rebellion, and its policing of the American West—bear some examination for the insights they provide into the Army's experience with counterguerrilla warfare, pacification, and nation building.[1]

Reconstruction, 1865–1877

The Confederacy's surrender in the spring of 1865 did not end the Army's pacification responsibilities in the South. Between 1865 and 1877 the Army devoted as much as one-third of its strength to supporting the federal government's effort to "reconstruct" Southern society. Reconstruction passed through several phases. Initially, the Army operated military governments throughout the South until such time as state governments were restored under the generous terms offered by President Lincoln and his successor, Andrew Johnson. As during the Mexican and Civil Wars, the Army adopted a firm-but-fair approach to its administration of government, eschewing vengeance in favor of sympathetic policies aimed at restoring tranquility and economic stability. Whenever possible, the Army relied on local civilians to administer civil affairs, both to minimize its own burdens and to speed the restoration of normal civil life. Many commanders also went beyond the basic requirements of maintaining order, suppressing banditry, and administering government and followed wartime precedents by feeding the destitute, enforcing sanitary regulations, and organizing schools. They were assisted in their efforts by the Freedmen's Bureau, which Congress established under the War Department in 1865. Under the leadership of Maj. Gen. Oliver O. Howard, the bureau provided vital medical, educational, legal, social, and political services to tens of thousands of destitute Southerners, black and white.[2]

Reconstruction entered a second phase in 1867, when a Radical Republican Congress replaced the generous Lincoln-Johnson program with more rigorous policies. Motivated by a complex mixture of vindictiveness, idealism, political partisanship, and humanitarian concern, Congress abolished all but one of the South's civilian governments, restored military rule, disenfranchised many former secessionists, and established new requirements for readmission into the Union that included Negro suffrage. The Radicals' goal was to impose a political and social revolution on the South. The task plunged Army officers into a political whirlpool, as they once again administered governments and assisted in the formulation of new state constitutions.

By 1870 all of the formerly rebellious states had been readmitted to the Union under the Radical program. In most cases the new state governments were dominated by white Republicans bolstered by the new black electorate. Still, the Army's work was not done, for over the next seven years it was repeatedly called upon to supervise elections, maintain order, and otherwise protect the Republican governments from the mass of white Southerners who resented the imposition of "alien" Northern policies. Ultimately, however, the Radicals' efforts at revolutionizing Southern society failed. Using a combination of political action and terror, Southern whites succeeded in "redeeming" one state after another, replacing the Republican governments with conservative Democratic ones that erased all vestiges of "black rule." Having lost their bid for independence, white Southerners won their battle to preserve their political and cultural autonomy at the expense of Southern blacks.

The Radicals' attempt to "reconstruct" Southern society failed because it alienated the mass of Southern whites while simultaneously failing to give blacks the political, economic, and social tools they needed to exercise their newly won freedoms. Although some soldiers and Northern politicians had recommended that Southern land be redistributed to give the freedmen a firm socioeconomic base, ultimately schemes of land reform ran afoul of several American shibboleths, such as notions of personal responsibility, the sanctity of private property, and lingering aversions to "big government" activism. Once Congress abolished the Freedmen's Bureau in 1872, Southern blacks had nothing more than the right to vote to assert their interests, a right that was of little use without the presence of federal bayonets to uphold it.

Unfortunately, there was little the Army could do to halt the counterrevolutionary movement waged by Southern conservatives against black rights. By 1872 postwar manpower reductions and the requirements of the frontier had reduced the Army's presence in the old Confederacy (excluding Texas) to about 3,500 men. With most of the Army's cavalry called off to police the West, those troops left in the South lacked the mobility to control effectively the many clandestine societies and paramilitary groups, like the Ku Klux Klan and the Red Shirts, that intimidated and terrorized Republicans, Unionists, and freedmen alike. Frustrated by Southern opposition and anxious to put the bitterness engendered by the war and subsequent occupation behind it, a disenchanted nation abandoned the quest for racial justice in return for national harmony and in 1877 withdrew the last regular troops from the South.[3]

Though he had advocated using "hard war" measures to crush the rebellion, General Sherman had recognized as early as September 1865 that "no matter what change we may desire in the feelings and thoughts of the people [in the] South, we cannot accomplish it by force." Military power might be able to suppress an insurrection, but it could not easily crush its spirit. The course of Reconstruction verified Sherman's view and demonstrated the hazards of using military force to impose fundamental changes in social values and institutions, no matter how virtuous those changes might be. This was a cautionary lesson for any future soldier or politician charged with such a mission, whether it be in the realm of social engineering at home or nation building abroad.

Most officers agreed with Sherman as to the ultimate folly of Reconstruction, yet the Army derived no formal doctrines from its sojourn in the South. Officers regarded their experience as an aberration, so unique that it was unlikely to arise again. Although many officers assembled creditable records in attempting to negotiate the byzantine world of Reconstruction politics, the political nature of their experience defied easy codification into rules and precepts, even if they had been inclined to formulate such doctrines, which they were not. Rather, Reconstruction's primary impact was to reinforce the officer corps' traditional aversion for political involvements of any type. Speaking of his transfer to the Western frontier after several years of service in the Freedmen's Bureau, Lt. Gen. Nelson A. Miles recalled that "it was a pleasure to be relieved of the anxieties and responsibilities of civil affairs, to hear nothing of the controversies incident to race prejudice, and to be once more engaged in strictly military duties." There were few officers who did not share his sentiments and who did not gladly forget about the entire ordeal when it was over.[4]

Constabulary Duty on the Western Frontier

Miles and his fellow officers may have looked forward to their transfer to the frontier, but the job that awaited them was no less challenging. By mid-century the Native American population west of the Mississippi numbered about 270,000 people divided into over 125 distinct tribal, linguistic, and cultural groups. Although the Army tried to shield the Indians from illegal white encroachment, its primary mission was to pursue Indian raiders, punish recalcitrant tribes, and confine the indigenous population to an ever-dwindling area "reserved" for their use. Conflict was the inevitable result of this process. From the signing of a flurry of abortive peace treaties in October 1865 until the suppression of the last Indian uprising at Leech Lake, Minnesota, in October 1898, the Army engaged in over a thousand combats as part of its forcible pacification of the Western Indians.[5]

The nature of the Western Indian tribes, their mode of warfare, and the terrain that they inhabited greatly complicated the Army's task. Unlike the more sedentary Eastern woodland tribes, most Indians on the Great Plains were nomadic hunter-gatherers, inured to the hardships of long treks and uncertain food supplies and possessed with a mobility and knowledge of the terrain that permitted them easily to escape discovery or pursuit. Indian males were trained from childhood in tracking, hunting, horsemanship, and other martial arts, including the use of camouflage. As individual warriors they were superb, man for man superior to the average American soldier. Their method of warfare maximized these advantages. For the most part they avoided set piece battles and waged a guerrilla war of raids, ambushes, and surprise attacks. Traveling light, unincumbered by fixed settlements or supply trains, they struck soldier and settler alike only when they perceived that they had an advantage. After raiding a homestead or ambushing a convoy, they quickly submerged themselves into the security of the endless expanse of arid deserts, roadless mountains, and featureless prairies that constituted the American West. All of this made the task of subduing the Indians, in the words of William T. Sherman, the Army's commanding general for much of the Indian wars period, "the hardest kind of war."[6]

As if the advantages the Indians enjoyed in terms of mobility, skill, and terrain were not enough, the Army labored under a set of equally debilitating burdens. Congressional cuts reduced the size of the Army to 27,442 in 1874, a level that left the Military Division of the Missouri, one of the two major theaters of operations west of the Mississippi, with a ratio of one soldier for every 100 square miles of area. The necessity of providing at least a modicum of protection to all areas of white settlement and travel meant that by 1868 the Army had 116 posts on the frontier, most of which mustered no more than a few skeletonized companies. Commands were so small that post commanders placed themselves at risk every time they divided their paltry garrisons for the purpose of providing an escort or conducting a patrol or pursuit. The only way departmental commanders could undertake effective operations was by pulling together an impromptu force from a variety of posts and units, an arrangement that inevitably lacked cohesiveness. The Army recognized that overdispersion increased logistical costs and impeded sound administration and training, but it was never able to remedy the situation. It simply had too few men to do the job. Moreover, the Army found that it was almost impossible to close a post once it had been established, primarily because forts represented markets and jobs, perks that the local inhabitants and their representatives in Congress were reluctant to give up. Railroads offered some relief, but it was not until the Army had already broken the main Indian powers and forced them onto reservations that it was able to gradually concentrate its forces during the 1880s and 1890s.[7]

Finally, the Army's manpower shortage was complicated by significant problems in the quality of the men available. The Army usually sent recruits to their units with little or no training. Nor did they receive much once they had arrived. Most units were so understrength that all hands had to be employed just to perform the many routine chores of Army life, such as building, maintaining, and guarding posts, chopping firewood, tending gardens, and caring for livestock, not to mention active service escorting wagon trains, mounting patrols, and protecting construction crews. Even if time had not been a problem, financial constraints limited the Army to allocating ten rounds of ammunition per man per month for target practice, hardly enough to turn unskilled shooters into marksmen. More often than not training in marksmanship, horsemanship, and maneuvers could be had only on the job, sometimes with disastrous results. Not surprisingly, the boredom and hardships of frontier duty created a huge turnover in the ranks, and the Army lost between 25 and 40 percent of its enlisted force annually to death, discharge, and desertion. Given these handicaps, it is remarkable that the frontier Army was as successful as it was in Indian warfare.[8]

Indian Warfare and Military Thought

The post–Civil War Army inherited a rich heritage in Indian warfare that dated back to the colonial era. The value of this heritage was mitigated, however, by the absence of a formal system to preserve the lessons of the past, as well as by the difficulty in applying those lessons to the many different environments in which the Army had to operate, from the Pennsylvania woodlands to the Florida swamps, Kansas prairies, New Mexican deserts, and Colorado mountains. Political and cultural differences between tribes further complicated the application of any fixed methods, although sufficient similarities did exist to permit the formulation of some broad principles.

As noted in Chapter 1, while the Army had never developed a formal doctrine for Indian warfare, it had gradually evolved a theory that blended conventional with unconventional techniques to attack the social and economic resources upon which Indian power rested. Essentially, this amounted to an offensive strategy in which one or more columns of regular troops, augmented by small bodies of civilian irregulars and Indian auxiliaries, would drive into Indian territory in an effort either to force the Indians to battle or to destroy Indian homes and food supplies, thereby compelling them to sue for peace. These were the principles inherited from antebellum campaigns and passed down by experienced soldiers by word, deed, and memory. They were also the principles that Dennis Mahan occasionally related to his students at the Military Academy.[9]

Mahan's approach to Indian warfare was reinforced in the minds of officers by the Army's experience in the Civil War. Many soldiers emerged from the rebellion convinced that the best way to win a "peoples" war was to strike at the foundation of resistance—the enemy population. Now, with the rebellion crushed, these officers were prepared to apply the same strategy of destruction to undermine the American Indians' physical and moral ability to resist.[10]

While Mahan's lectures on Indian warfare represented the most direct way in which the academy prepared its charges for frontier duty, it was not the only way. In his teachings on conventional warfare,

Mahan stressed the value of reconnaissance, security, skirmishing, and other aspects of *petite guerre* that, coincidentally, were also valuable in Indian warfare. Moreover, tactical instruction at West Point focused not upon the maneuver of large formations, but rather on small, company-size units, the level at which most frontier operations were conducted. Of course, the basic principles of small-unit tactics taught at the Military Academy regarding raids and ambushes, camp and march security, and outpost duty were to a large extent applicable to unconventional as well as conventional warfare.

Although the textbooks employed at the academy contained virtually no references to Indian warfare per se, they did in fact convey concepts that were highly relevant to the subject. Throughout the nineteenth century, standard West Point texts like Mahan's *Out-Post* and Col. J. B. Wheeler's *A Course of Instruction in the Elements of the Art and Science of War for the Use of the Cadets of the United States Military Academy* endorsed the use of winter operations, night marches, and dawn raids to surprise enemy encampments. Thus Mahan wrote that

> winter and bad weather are most favorable [for launching a surprise attack], as the enemy's sentinels and outposts will then, in all probability, be less on alert. ... The best positions are those where the enemy is inclosed in a defile, or village, and has not taken the proper precautions to secure himself from an attack. By seizing the outlets of the defile by infantry, in such cases, and making an impetuous charge of cavalry into it, the enemy may be completely routed.

Wheeler offered similar advice, and though neither text mentioned Indians specifically, the tactics well described any number of the Army's frontier operations. Winter campaigns, night marches, and dawn raids would all become standard operational techniques employed by the Army on the frontier with great effect.[11]

Occasionally, the academy supplemented these generic tactical discussions with more specific treatment of frontier warfare. A case in point occurred in the late 1870s, when the Army's lackluster performance during the Sioux and Nez Perce campaigns prompted the academy's commandant, Maj. Gen. John Schofield, to conclude that the school should provide "more extended instruction in the cavalry service required by our young officers on the frontier." Although the content of the "extended instruction" is not known, a clue to its nature can be gleaned from the fact that the Army posted an experienced frontier campaigner, Medal of Honor recipient Capt. Edward S. Godfrey, to West Point in 1879 to serve as the school's instructor of horsemanship and cavalry tactics. Moreover, it is likely that other frontier veterans

COUNTERINSURGENCY DOCTRINE, 1860–1941

Dismounted skirmish drill given to cadets at West Point helped prepare young officers for frontier combat.

assigned to West Point as instructors and commandants passed on their hard won lessons to cadets, at least informally.[12]

The academy addressed Indian warfare in one other part of its curriculum, the law course. International law as taught at West Point approached the subject of Indian warfare in somewhat the same manner as it did the treatment of guerrillas and actively hostile civilian populations in civilized warfare. On the one hand, it maintained that the laws of war did not apply to aboriginal peoples—just as they did not apply to guerrillas—for the simple reason that "savages" did not abide by those laws. This meant that soldiers were free to employ the harshest measures necessary to subdue them.

Yet academy textbooks also taught that principles of humanity and Christian charity demanded that soldiers employ stringent measures only when they were absolutely necessary. In fact, West Point encouraged the nation's young officers to respect the civil rights of aboriginal peoples and to treat native prisoners well, for by doing otherwise they risked descending to the level of their enemies. The result was the adoption of a dual approach to frontier warfare identical to that established in General Orders 100. The destruction of property and food supplies, the imposition of communal punishments, and the execution of particularly incorrigible individuals were all acceptable, just as they were in counterguerrilla warfare against a civilized foe, if such measures were compelled by military necessity. The wanton slaughter of Indian men, women, and children was not. The vast majority of officers followed this creed, and while a few exterminationists existed in the Army, such individuals were a distinct minority.[13]

The Military Academy thus imparted to its students an intellectual foundation from which to approach their frontier duties. But beyond this it did not go. There was little time in the academy's already cramped curriculum to explore Indian warfare in greater depth, nor did there appear to be a pressing need to do so, as the Army's casualties were remarkably low during the Indian wars. Besides, experienced soldiers recognized that these small conflicts, like most forms of guerrilla warfare, were highly localized affairs, in which unique factors of geography, climate, and culture weighed heavily upon the conduct of the campaign. Given this diversity, Mahan's approach of laying down a few broad principles relevant to most Indian war situations made sense.[14]

Perhaps West Point's greatest omission lay not in the realm of strategy, but in fieldcraft. Officers newly posted to the West often were unequipped to survive on the open plains, arid deserts, and rugged mountains. They had to learn how to follow a trail and how to maintain their mounts over long and difficult journeys. Finally, they had to learn the peculiar habits of the Indians with whom they had to deal. Indeed, subjects of this nature formed to a great extent the very heart of frontier service, as actual combat with Indians was rare.

Officers obtained this type of information largely through experience and conversations with frontier veterans. Although such informal methods were irregular at best, they should not be discounted. Frontier service had been the Army's primary duty since the foundation of the Republic, and many officers served ten, twenty, or more years on the frontier. Inadequate pensions and slow promotion rates in the postwar Army further facilitated the retention and transmission of experience. By the time of the last major Indian "war," the Ghost Dance uprising of 1890–1891, the average age of a first lieutenant was forty-five and that of a captain fifty. The Army thus had a solid cadre of long service veterans which it could tap to teach its younger officers the tricks of the frontier trade. By word and deed, these men passed along a portion of their experience to each succeeding generation of Indian fighters.[15]

While personal experience and word of mouth were the primary mediums through which the Army sought to preserve frontier lessons, the Army also provided some written guidance on certain aspects of frontier service. One of the War Department's many responsibilities in

One of the Army's many duties on the frontier was protecting civilian transportation and commerce.

relation to the settlement of the American West lay in the organization of civilian wagon trains. Local commanders were required to make sure that Western emigrants did not venture forth on their journey across the Plains without adequate supplies, equipment, and knowledge. In an effort to meet this obligation, the War Department asked an experienced frontier officer, Capt. Randolph Marcy, to prepare a manual on the ways and means of traveling across the Great Plains. Marcy agreed, and in 1859 he published *The Prairie Traveler* under the authority of the War Department.

The Prairie Traveler was nothing less than the Baedeker of the American West. It described in detail the primary trails and wagon routes and how to travel them. It also provided a treasure trove of information about the practical aspects of crossing the Plains, including what to bring and how to pack it, how to repair a wagon and make camp, first aid, hunting and tracking techniques, and the nature and habits of Indians.

But *The Prairie Traveler* was much more than a guidebook; it was also a primer on the conduct of military operations on the Great Plains. Recognizing that West Point's conventionally focused curriculum did not provide sufficient training in the many practical aspects of "border service," Marcy prepared the manual explicitly "to establish a more uniform system of marching and campaigning in the Indian country." In addition to providing many useful tips on traveling and fieldcraft, the manual discussed military march and camp procedures, weaponry and equipment, and native cultural and martial practices. It described measures that columns could take to protect themselves against guerrilla action and endorsed the use of Indian guides.[16]

In analyzing the military problems of the frontier, Marcy not only tapped his own experience but looked abroad, citing French and Turkish operations in North Africa. During the first half of the century both of these nations had waged pacification campaigns against nomadic tribesmen, and Marcy believed that French and Turkish experiences were sufficiently analogous to America's situation on the Great Plains to merit study. Based on his readings of several French tracts, Marcy derived three lessons from these foreign campaigns: first, that overdispersion stripped a counterguerrilla Army of initiative, increased its vulnerability, sapped morale, and impeded training; second, that mobility was at a premium, and that one way to increase the utility of infantry formations was to mount them on mules; and third, that the best way to come to grips with an elusive, nomadic foe was to employ mounted forces in a night march for the purpose of surprising the enemy in his encampment at dawn. This last point was, in Marcy's opinion, the key to successful offensive action against tribal irregulars, be they Arab or American Indian. Ultimately, Marcy's message was very much like Mahan's in that he urged soldiers to adapt themselves to the conditions in which they were operating by combining conventional "discipline with the individuality, self-reliance, and rapidity of locomotion of the savage."[17]

The Prairie Traveler was perhaps the single most important work on the conduct of frontier expeditions published under the aegis of the War Department. It was not, however, the only such work. Over the next several decades a few officers, either on their own or with the sponsorship of the department, produced guides on various aspects of frontier service. In 1881 2d Lt. Edward Farrow published a manual titled *Mountain Scouting* as a companion to *The Prairie Traveler*. In the same year Lt. Gen. Philip H. Sheridan directed Capt. W. P. Clark to prepare a manual on Indian sign language, a subject of great utility to frontier officers. *The Indian Sign Language*, published in 1885, discussed not only sign language, but also contained some insights into Indian culture and military methods. The following year, one of the Army's leading counterguerrilla experts, General Crook, put pen to paper on two occasions for the purpose of disseminating what he regarded to be the lessons of his Indian warfare experiences. Both "The Apache Problem," published by the *Journal of the Military Service Institution of the United States,* and *Resume of Operations Against Apache*

Indians, 1882 to 1886, published by the Army, provided significant insights into Crook's fighting and pacification techniques.[18]

Semiofficial works like these, together with other articles that occasionally appeared in military journals, played an important role in disseminating information on the practical side of frontier campaigning. That most of these works focused upon fieldcraft rather than tactics reflected the fact that, like most guerrilla, colonial, and small war campaigns, the Indian wars were to a large extent wars against nature. Weather, terrain, and the elusiveness of the enemy, rather than combat, posed the greatest challenges to the Army, and the writings of officers reflected that fact.

So, too, did Army regulations, which contained only a modicum of frontier information. Their utility was enhanced somewhat by changes on the conventional battlefield that were leading the Army to adopt more flexible tactical formations. By happy coincidence, those formations were equally suitable for the type of skirmishing that typified frontier operations. For example, the Army's basic infantry manual during the post–Civil War period, Emory Upton's *A New System of Infantry Tactics for Double and Single Rank Adapted to American Topography and Improved Fire-Arms,* advocated that soldiers make greater use of cover, aimed fire, and extended order formations, all of which were fully compatible with Indian warfare. In fact, frontier conditions reinforced these trends, and Brig. Gen. John Gibbon credited the Army's frontier experience with facilitating the adoption of more modern, open order formations throughout the Army.[19]

The frontier's influence was somewhat more evident in the Army's cavalry manuals. The first U.S. Army manual to incorporate the lessons of the frontier was Brig. Gen. Philip St. George Cooke's *Cavalry Tactics,* officially adopted by the War Department in November 1861. Cooke's *Tactics* differed in two respects from previous manuals. First, it included a short chapter on "Special Service of Cavalry in the West," which discussed march, camp, and security procedures. Second, Cooke replaced the standard two-rank formation with a single rank that was more suitable for irregular warfare. When the Army replaced Cooke's *Tactics* with Upton's *Cavalry Tactics* in the early 1870s, it retained both the discussion of frontier procedures and the single-rank formation in the new manual. The Army also added a second type of formation, mounted skirmish order, which, like the single-rank line, was designed primarily for employment in partisan and Indian warfare. By the end of the century the U.S. Army was the only "European" power to employ the single-rank cavalry formation, despite the warnings of traditionalists who argued that the formation was unsuited to conventional warfare.[20]

THE CONSTABULARY YEARS, 1865–1898

Mahan's teachings, Marcy's writings, and Cooke's and Upton's tactics, in combination with the personal experiences of veteran soldiers, provided the basis upon which the Army waged the Indian wars of the late nineteenth century. Taken together, they supplied the Army with an overall philosophy, a basic tactical system, and a body of practical fieldcraft that was extremely valuable. Yet they did not constitute a fixed doctrine for Indian warfare, and it remained for frontier officers to devise innovative solutions to their own Indian problems by combining conventional forces with slightly unconventional techniques to frame the contest in terms most favorable to the Army.

U.S. Army Counterguerrilla Operations on the Western Frontier

One of the first ways in which officers endeavored to overcome their irregular opponents in the trans–Mississippi West was by employing the traditional column method. As in the Second Seminole War, however, commanders soon found that the vastness of the terrain and the nomadic nature of Plains tribes often made it impossible for solitary columns to strike with effect. The Army, therefore, turned to multiple columns, which converged on a given area in an effort to prevent the Indians from escaping. Although this technique met with some success, more often than not the Indians still managed to outmaneuver their pursuers and slip the trap. The converging column method was also dangerous, as coordination between columns was difficult and each was exposed to being defeated in detail. The most notable example of this occurred in 1876, when the Sioux and Cheyenne first repulsed one of three converging columns (General Crook's) before annihilating a portion of a second (Lt. Col. George A. Custer's) at Little Big Horn.[21]

As in the antebellum period, the primary purpose of the converging columns was to destroy the Indians' food supply in the hope that the deprivations caused by the loss of food and shelter would break their morale and compel them to surrender. Commanders therefore tried to time their expeditions for late summer and early fall to disrupt end-of-season hunts and destroy winter food stocks. When this was not possible, they struck in early spring, before enough new grass had appeared to strengthen the Indians' ponies after a long and sparse winter. Neither of these methods proved entirely satisfactory, however, as the tribesmen usually retained sufficient mobility to evade Army columns. Consequently, the Army took to launching its major offensives during the winter, when the Indians were most vulnerable. Winter campaigns also had the advantage of transforming the Army's traditional weakness—its ponderous logistical tail—into a strength, for it

Counterinsurgency Doctrine, 1860–1941

A unit of Apache Indian scouts camps near the Mexican border in 1883.

was the Army's ability to assemble large quantities of food, clothing, and animals which allowed it to campaign at a time when the Indians were relatively dormant. The winter campaign was a classic example of Mahan's dictum that the way to defeat the Indians was by adapting the Army's conventional strengths to the circumstances at hand to frame the struggle in terms most favorable to the Army.[22]

Despite some significant successes, however, winter campaigning was not a panacea. Weather and terrain made it difficult, dangerous, and expensive, and the politico-military situation did not always afford the Army the luxury of waiting for the onset of winter before undertaking operations. Besides, attacks on Indian encampments inevitably resulted in casualties among Indian women and children, while many more died of starvation, disease, and exposure brought on by the campaign. Deaths among Indian noncombatants brought down upon the Army the wrath of Eastern newspapers and philanthropists who chastised it for waging barbaric campaigns of extermination. The Army resented such criticism, considering it both unfair and hypocritical. The criticism embittered many officers who, like future generations of American soldiers, were dismayed to discover that the public was often critical of military action during small wars, when the nation's security was not at stake but in which the Army was brought into direct conflict with a hostile civil population.[23]

Public criticism notwithstanding, converging columns and winter campaigning were the mainstays of Army operations on the Western frontier. Yet neither method could have worked had the Army not adapted to frontier conditions in many other ways. The essence of a successful Indian campaign, wrote veteran Indian campaigner General Miles, was to "find, follow, and defeat" the enemy wherever he might be. Over the course of its service on the frontier, Army officers adopted innovative measures for the conduct of each of these three phases.[24]

The first challenge of an Indian campaign was locating the small bands of raiders and nomadic tribesmen as they flitted across the vast Western landscape. Typically, local commanders attempted to monitor the indigenous population's activities through patrols. These patrols were usually conducted by company-size formations and took the form of an armed reconnaissance, sometimes staying out for weeks or months at a time. Indeed, scouting assumed such importance with the frontier Army that it employed the term *scout* as a noun to describe any type of patrol or reconnaissance mission.[25]

The vast majority of scouts were uneventful, in part because the average soldier was neither familiar enough with the terrain nor sufficiently trained in the art of tracking to locate the Indians. Consequently, in 1866 the War Department obtained congressional authorization for the inclusion of up to 1,000 Indian scouts as part of the regular establishment of the Army. The scouts proved highly effective both as individual guides and as forward reconnaissance units. They provided the Army with a knowledge of tracking, local geography, and Indian habits that was truly invaluable. Rare was the column of regular soldiers that successfully made contact with a band of hostile Indians without the aid of at least a few Indian guides.[26]

One of the leading exponents of Indian scouts was General Crook. Crook used his scouts not only as guides but as combat auxiliaries. Although he usually employed scouts in combination with regular troops, he also sent them on independent missions. Crook attributed his success to proper leadership. He carefully selected young, aggressive, and open-minded officers who, in the opinion of one observer, were not so much "Indian fighters" as "Indian thinkers." Recognizing the highly individualistic and personal nature of Indian warrior culture, Crook insisted that his officers build a personal bond with their scouts, based on mutual trust and respect. Above all, he demanded that officers not stifle the scouts' individuality. Not only did the Indians know their business better than their white superiors, he maintained, but their very

COUNTERINSURGENCY DOCTRINE, 1860-1941

The Army used soldiers, civilians, and Indians to fill its need for qualified scouts.

value stemmed from their "wildness." Imposing conventional drill and discipline upon them would only rob them of the very characteristics that made them so valuable. As frontier veteran Capt. John Bigelow observed, "General Crook makes of his Indian auxiliaries, not soldiers, but more formidable Indians."[27]

Crook's idea of using Indians in a combat role was not unique, and several other officers also employed natives successfully as auxiliaries. Nevertheless, professional opinion remained divided on this score. Many officers, including General Sheridan, believed that Indians were not sufficiently reliable to serve as combat auxiliaries, and consequently most commanders elected to employ their scouts primarily to find, rather than fight, the enemy.[28]

Assuming the Army had an idea of where the Indians were, the next hurdle—following them—was no easy task. The tribesmen moved so quickly that one officer estimated the chances of catching them to be less than twenty to one if they enjoyed a 24-hour head start. Mobility was the key to following the Indians, and the Army pursued it with a vengeance. It jettisoned much of the impediments normally carried on conventional operations, including bayonets, knapsacks, sabers, and even artillery. By the 1880s the load carried by an American cavalry horse on campaign was forty-two pounds lighter than the weight typically carried by horses in European armies. The most notable way in which the Army modified its logistical system to frontier conditions, however, was by substituting pack mules for wagons.[29]

Pack mules moved faster and traversed difficult terrain more readily than wagons, and consequently they offered a partial remedy for the Army's mobility problem. Marcy and Farrow recognized the mule's utility and included packing in their campaign guidebooks, but it was Crook who elevated packing into a science. Crook considered the mule essential to any counterguerrilla campaign, and his writings on the subject became the foundation of Army pack logistics doctrine in the twentieth century.

General Crook

Dispensing with wagons altogether proved impractical, however, as pack trains were more expensive and less efficient than conventional methods of transportation. Consequently, the Army employed wagons for routine hauling and reserved the mules for active service with flying columns of cavalry. The typical expeditionary force was thus divided into two parts: a heavy section of wagons escorted by infantrymen, which bore the bulk of the supplies, and a lighter strike force of cavalry and pack animals, which ranged ahead in search of the enemy. Should the cavalry require resupply or suffer a reverse, it could fall back upon the reserves of the infantry and wagon column. Conversely, should the cavalry require reinforcement to overcome a particularly difficult obstacle, it could hold its position until the infantry arrived.

The utility of the pack mule made a deep impression on the Army. By the end of the century the mule had become a standard element in its logistical approach to irregular operations, so much so that the Military Academy acquired a mule train for the purpose of instructing cadets in the fine art of packing. Thereafter, wherever the Army went on its small war assignments, from Cuba to China, the Philippines, and Mexico, the mule was sure to follow.[30]

While the mule won wide acceptance as a partial substitute for the wagon, the Army had a more difficult time deciding upon the best type of horse for frontier operations. Army horses were larger and heavier than the ponies of the Plains Indians and were therefore both faster and stronger than their Indian counterparts, at least in theory. In practice, Indian ponies often proved superior to cavalry horses because they were accustomed to subsisting on native plants, while the Army horse required premium fodder to maintain its health and stamina. This, coupled with the fact that most Indians had several ponies, gave them a significant advantage over the typical cavalryman who, for reasons of economy, was issued only one horse. Cavalry officers were faced with the choice of tying themselves down to the slow moving grain wagons or cutting loose and grazing their horses off the land in Indian fashion, thereby risking the health of their mounts. The solution, at least in the minds of some officers, was for the Army to replace its costly "high technology" horses with hardy native ponies. This idea was never officially adopted, in part because the scrawny range pony did not fit the image many officers had of what a proper cavalry mount should be. On the other hand, many commanders did adapt to the challenge. Some found that they could acclimate their horses to frontier conditions through careful management, and manuals like Marcy's and Cooke's helped them do so. Other officers abandoned their prejudices and purchased local animals for their units. An equally innovative approach involved swapping animals between regiments. An example of this occurred in 1875, when the 6th U.S. Cavalry replaced the 5th U.S. Cavalry in Arizona. Upon arrival in the Southwest, the 6th traded its Kentucky- and Missouri-bred horses for the 5th Cavalry's California mustangs, which were fully acclimated to Arizona conditions and accustomed to grazing on native plants.[31]

The mobility requirements of the frontier also affected the Army's organization and force structure. During the late nineteenth century, the U.S. Army maintained its cavalry regiments at greater strength than its infantry regiments and sheltered the cavalry from force structure reductions. Moreover, unlike European armies, which contained "heavy" shock cavalry designed to overthrow enemy formations by massed charges, all American cavalry units were "light" cavalry, designed for the conduct of raids and reconnaissances. Nevertheless, the Army never had enough cavalry to meet frontier demands, and like counterguerrilla commanders during the Civil War, several officers followed Marcy's advice and mounted a portion of their infantry on native ponies and mules in an effort to gain greater mobility. The most notable example of this was the 5th U.S. Infantry, a regiment that operated as mounted infantry between 1877 and 1881.[32]

Cavalry, often operating in small company-size units, was the Army's primary offensive weapon during the conquest and pacification of America's inland empire.

By adapting its logistical system and force structure to the requirements of the frontier, the Army achieved a degree of mobility that, if still inferior to that of the Indians, was sufficient to keep them on the run and eventually wear them down. Defeating the enemy was in some ways less difficult for the Army, especially if he could be taken unaware in his encampment. To achieve this, officers followed the suggestions of West Point textbooks and employed night marches and dawn raids. They supplemented these tactics with ruses, leaving camp fires burning at night after the troops had moved, or deliberately hanging back to give the Indians the impression that they had given up the chase, thereby lulling them into a false sense of security.[33]

To be successful, tactics such as these required training and preparation, which were not easy to achieve given the heavy burdens of frontier service. Although few soldiers reached the level of individual proficiency exhibited by Indian warriors, many commanders endeavored to increase the overall efficiency of their commands. Not only did they tailor their training regimens to the type of small-unit marching and skirmishing typical of frontier conditions, but the most successful field commanders habitually put their men through intensive rounds of rifle, riding, and endurance training before undertaking a campaign. The successes achieved by these men, as well as the litany of failures racked up by less ably prepared troops, convinced officers of the benefits of improved training, and during the last decades of the century the Army took significant steps to improve the level of skill of its soldiers, especially in the areas of physical fitness and marksmanship.[34]

One of the most progressive thinkers in this regard was General Miles. During the winter of 1873–1874, he opened a "military gymnasium" at Fort Leavenworth, Kansas, where he introduced his men to a rigorous course of calisthenics, field exercises, and long-range marksmanship. Later, during the Geronimo campaign, he instituted another rigorous program, requiring that the cavalry in the Department of Arizona be capable of marching up to two hundred miles in forty-eight hours. The successful conclusion of the Geronimo campaign in 1886 brought no relaxation in Miles' efforts. The following year he initiated a series of training maneuvers explicitly intended to hone the irregular warfare skills of the troops in his department. He divided his command into two forces: "raiders" and "pursuers." The raiders simulated Indians and bandits, while the pursuers played the cavalry's traditional role. During the exercises, troops practiced skills frequently required in Indian warfare, including stealth and deception, long-distance marching, skirmishing, signaling, navigation, fieldcraft, scouting, and security. One participant, 2d Lt. John J. Pershing, found the exercises to be excellent training.[35]

In addition to improving the performance of their commands, several officers experimented with the idea of pooling their best men into elite counterguerrilla organizations. One experiment along these lines occurred in 1868, when Sheridan created a fifty-man scout unit under the command of Maj. George Forsyth. Sheridan had employed two such units four years earlier in the Shenandoah Valley to counter rebel guerrillas, and he thought that the experiment was worth repeating against his new irregular opponents. Like Blazer's and Young's Scouts, Forsyth's unit was handpicked and specially armed. Unfortunately, the parallels were all too close, for like Blazer's organization, Forsyth's Scouts were doomed to have a short, meteoric career. No sooner had Forsyth taken to the field than his unit was severely mauled by Sioux and Cheyenne warriors in a desperate fight at Beecher's Island, and it never again undertook independent operations.[36]

Major Forsyth's unfortunate experience did not stop other commanders from experimenting with special counterguerrilla units. Both Generals Crook and Miles employed such units during the 1870s and 1880s, teaming their best soldiers with units of Indian scouts to form small, mobile strike forces. Although Crook found even his best men to be inferior to his native scouts, Miles put great stock in the idea that carefully chosen troops could at least approximate the level of skill

Captain Lawton's mixed column of cavalry, scouts, and pack mules on Geronimo's trail

exhibited by native warriors. In 1886 he attempted to prove it by forming an elite force of cavalry, mounted infantry, and Indian auxiliaries under the command of Capt. Henry W. Lawton and Army surgeon Capt. Leonard Wood. Miles sent the unit into Mexico for the purpose of apprehending the Apache renegade Geronimo. After four months and 4,000 miles, two-thirds of Lawton's original complement had dropped out. Although Lawton never caught his quarry, his relentless pursuit

Geronimo (standing to the right of the horse) *and his Apache warriors shortly after their surrender to Brig. Gen. Nelson A. Miles in March 1886*

contributed to Geronimo's decision to surrender. Miles considered the experiment a success, as did Lawton and Wood, who in later years formed similar units for counterguerrilla work in the Philippines.[37]

Pulling all of these adaptations together—finding the enemy with Indian scouts, following him with flying columns of light cavalry, mounted infantry, and mules, and defeating him with aggressive, small-unit tactics—was easier said than done. Not all commanders could do it, but the Army possessed enough talented, experienced, and resourceful officers and men who could and did rise to the occasion. By flexibly adapting conventional structures to fit unconventional situations, the Army managed to find, follow, and defeat the American Indians of the trans–Mississippi West.[38]

The Army and Indian Pacification

The conquest of the American West was not just a question of bullets and mules. It was, in fact, a complex politico-military problem that went beyond the physical subjugation of the indigenous inhabitants. The status of Native Americans was an anomalous one. Most Indians were not considered to be American citizens since they owed their political allegiance to their respective tribes rather than to the United States. Although the United States claimed suzerainty over tribes living in what it considered to be its territorial boundaries, it generally accorded the Indians sovereignty over their lands and internal affairs. Relations between the United States government and the various tribes were governed by treaties and agreements, which over time were progressively redrawn so as to circumscribe increasingly the power, autonomy, and geographical extent of the tribes. Throughout, the United States sought to achieve two goals. The first was to open as much Western land as possible to white settlement with a minimum of bloodshed. The second was eventually to assimilate Native American peoples into American culture and society. Together, these goals formed the foundation on which the Army based its pacification activities in the West. Unfortunately, the two goals were not necessarily compatible, nor did everyone, Indian or white, share them.[39]

Responsibility for the formulation and administration of the nation's Indian policy after the Mexican War resided with the Department of the Interior's Indian Bureau. Nevertheless, the Army was intimately involved in many aspects of Indian affairs. In addition to providing the muscle needed to enforce government policies, Army officers negotiated treaties with the Indians, disbursed annuities when Congress considered the Indian Bureau too inept to do so, and assisted in the administration of Indian reservations. Sometimes the government turned over particularly difficult reservations to the Army. More frequently, officers served as Indian agents under Interior Department control. The latter practice was widespread prior to 1870, a year in which Army officers accounted for no fewer than thirty-one of the fifty-two Indian agents and superintendents in the Division of the Missouri.

The situation changed somewhat thereafter, when Congress reacted to an Army-perpetrated massacre of Piegan Indians in Montana by banning officers from serving in civil posts. Nevertheless, the government continued to turn reservations over to the Army in emergencies, and in 1892 Congress officially lifted the ban on officers serving as Indian agents. Some of the Army's most distinguished frontier soldiers served in some capacity as Indian administrators, including Philip H. Sheridan, George Crook, William B. Hazen, Frank D. Baldwin, Ranald S. Mackenzie, and Adna R. Chaffee. Still others, like John J. Pershing and Hugh L. Scott, gained firsthand knowledge of Indian affairs by serving as commanders of companies of Indian scouts and soldiers, and virtually every frontier officer was concerned to one degree or another with what was commonly referred to as the "Indian question."[40]

Most officers believed the government's Indian policy to be a miserable failure. They deplored the way in which the government broke its promises to the Indians and chafed at the shortsightedness and corruption that characterized the administration of Indian affairs. Federal Indian policy represented a schizophrenic blend of ignorance, apathy, greed, altruism, and, perhaps most of all, expediency. That this was true was largely due to deep divisions within the body politic. Many Westerners believed the final solution to the Indian question was genocide. Eastern philanthropists talked of achieving a "conquest by kindness" rather than by bullets, in which the preacher, the teacher, and the social worker would achieve the cultural, rather than physical, extermination of the Indian race. The government muddled along a middle course, refusing to sanction all-out war, while doing virtually everything in its power—sometimes by design but more often by incompetence—to ensure that conflict was all but inevitable. The Army was the inevitable loser in this process. If it killed Indians, it was chastised by Easterners. If it failed to kill Indians, it was hanged in effigy by Westerners.[41]

The sad and sometimes confused state of the nation's Indian policy was greatly exacerbated by flaws in its administration. Interagency coordination on frontier-related matters was poor. General Sherman complained that government agencies constantly embarked upon projects that required military protection without consulting the Army, and it was not unknown for the Indian Bureau to negotiate treaties without informing local commanders. Although a certain amount of miscommunication and bureaucratic rivalry is normal in government, the relationship between the Indian Bureau and the Army was particularly poor. The lack of coordination between the civil and military agents of pacification inevitably robbed the Army of the initiative and forced it into a reactive mode that placed it at a great disadvantage. The Indians were aware of the bureaucratic disconnect and sometimes exploited it, using the civilian-controlled reservations as base camps and sanctuaries, knowing that the reservation agents, either out of kindheartedness or jealousy for their own authority, often denied the Army the right to enter the reservations in pursuit of marauding warriors.[42]

The military's solution to this problem was to urge Congress to transfer responsibility for Indian affairs back to the War Department where it had resided prior to 1849. It argued that the Indian Bureau was riddled with corruption, naivete, and incompetence, and it blamed many of the injustices that drove the Indians to war on the avarice and blunders of the bureau's agents. In contrast, the Army held that military officers were not only honest and capable administrators, but were also well acquainted with the Indian character. Most important, placing Indian affairs under the War Department would cut through the bureaucratic mess that entangled the management of Indian affairs and guarantee the full coordination of the political and military aspects of pacification, something the Army believed was desperately needed.[43]

The Indian Bureau and its supporters among Eastern philanthropists did not agree. Playing upon the nation's traditional antimilitarism, the bureau's defenders argued that military men had neither the skills nor the proper mindset to be entrusted with bringing civilization to the Indians. "Will you send professional soldiers, sword in one hand, musket in the other, and tactics on the brain, to teach the wards of the nation agriculture, the mechanical arts, theology, and peace?" queried the commissioner of Indian affairs. The debate coursed through Washington for years, but in the end the bureau won the argument.[44]

The fact that the military's influence over federal Indian policy was distinctly limited did not deter officers from paying serious attention to the subject and, when opportunity presented itself, of doing something about it. Leading frontier commanders, including Generals Miles, Gibbon, Pope, Howard, and Crook, wrote insightful commentaries on Indian affairs that were widely distributed in the form of reports, books, and journal articles. Although each officer approached the Indian question slightly differently, several themes dominated the Army's approach to the problem.

Most officers began their analysis from the premise that force was the *sine qua non* of Indian pacification. This view stemmed less from vindictiveness than acceptance of the brutal fact that government policy ultimately entailed the destruction of the Indians' traditional way of life, something many Native Americans were unwilling to accept without a fight. Before any progress could be made, reasoned Army leaders, it would first be necessary to break the Indians' will to resist. Many officers believed that it would be more effective, more humane, and more forthright simply to conquer the Indians outright and compel their compliance than to draw the process out through a series of misguided concessions, broken treaties, and desultory warfare, all of which created a tremendous amount of suffering and expense without changing the result.[45]

Conquest, however, was only the beginning of the Army's prescription for pacification. Most officers who wrote on the Indian question believed that the Indians' acculturation would be a long and gradual process. Cultures were complex entities that took centuries to evolve, wrote Lt. Col. Elwell S. Otis in his 1878 book, *The Indian Question*, and it would be naive to expect that the Indians would be able to make the transition into the "white man's" world overnight. General Gibbon agreed. Like many academics of his day, he maintained that human progress was evolutionary in nature and that there were several well-defined stages through which all human societies had to pass before they could progress to the next level of development. These stages were defined by the way man obtained his sustenance, beginning with primitive hunter-gatherers and gradually moving up the evolutionary scale to include herders, farmers, and finally, modern agriculturists and industrialists. If the Indians were going to be assimilated into modern American culture, they would first have to progress through the intermediary stages of development. Any attempt to skip a stage and propel them into sedentary forms of agriculture and industry before they had had a chance to develop the social and cultural infrastructure necessary to sustain that level of development would, in Gibbon's opinion, be doomed to failure.[46]

The nomadic tribes of the Great Plains were a case in point. For years the Indian Bureau had tried to turn them into farmers without success. Nor would it succeed, Gibbon argued, because the Indians were unready for that stage of development. Most of the Plains tribes were still in the hunter-gatherer stage, and thus their most natural course of development was to become herders, not farmers. General Pope, the commander of the Department of the Missouri, concurred in this assessment, and during the mid-1870s he put the pastoral theory to the test by authorizing Colonel Mackenzie to use the proceeds from the sale of captured Indian ponies to purchase cattle and sheep for the Kiowa and Comanche Indians at Fort Sill, Oklahoma. The tribesmen did not take to shepherding, nor did they like the taste of mutton, but the cattle program was a great success, thereby vindicating, at least in part, the pastoralist approach.[47]

Treating each tribe according to its particular level of cultural development was only one of the theories espoused by Army officers concerning Indian pacification. Some officers believed that acculturation could best be achieved by organizing the nomadic Plains tribes into military colonies similar to the cossacks of Russia. Each "colony" would be under the control of an officer and would supply the army with a steady source of irregular auxiliaries. Over time, the Army would gradually introduce the "colonists" to a more civilized and sedentary lifestyle, thereby achieving acculturation in a practical and less culturally disruptive way than the government's usual methods. The idea had merit but was never implemented, largely because Eastern philanthropists were appalled by the thought of building the road to civilization upon a foundation of military virtues.[48]

The demise of the cossack idea did not prevent the Army from endeavoring to promote assimilation through military service, at first in a limited way through the Indian scouts, and later more directly through the establishment of companies of Indian soldiers. In 1891 Secretary of War Redfield Proctor and Commanding General John Schofield added a company of Indian soldiers to fourteen of the Army's thirty-five regiments as an experiment in using the Army as a school for the assimi-

An Indian company practices saber exercises.

lation of the American Indian. In addition to introducing the Indians to a good dose of discipline, the Army provided its native soldiery with classes in English and some civilian job training as well. The experiment lasted until 1897, when the Army, unable to recruit enough Indians to keep the program alive, disbanded the last company of regular Indian soldiers. Ultimately, the experiment failed because the Indians found formal Army life unappealing and incongruous with their traditional cultural values.[49]

Another concept espoused by the Army was the replacement of trading posts with government-operated trading houses. Trading posts were privately owned commercial institutions established under government license. They acted as the primary means of economic exchange between the two societies. They were established under the theory that honest trade would not only foster good relations, but also expose the Indians to Western goods and methods in such a way as to further eventual assimilation. In reality, private stores cheated Indians and acted as focal points for friction between the two races. By operating the trading posts itself, as the War Department had done under the old factory system, the government would ensure that the Indians were treated fairly. Moreover, it would also gain greater control over the flow of arms and alcohol onto the reservations, thereby transforming the posts from flash points into centers of honest commerce and "civilization." Unfortunately, the Indian Bureau and the civilian contractors who owned the trading posts blocked this suggestion.[50]

Whereas cattle ranches, Indian soldiers, and government trading houses were some of the unique methods Army officers proposed to facilitate assimilation, military officers recognized that such measures were only stations along the road to civilization. They agreed with civilian philanthropists that land and education were the ultimate solutions to the Indian question. In the estimation of many officers, the private ownership of agricultural land would not only provide the Indians with an economic base, but would also foster a spirit of individualism that would help break down the old tribal institutions that officers regarded as obstacles to the integration of Native Americans into white culture. Likewise, officers placed great faith in the notion that education would solve many of the Indians' problems by driving out ignorance and opening the gates to the intellectual and material bounty of Western civilization. In this, the Army's approach to pacification was quintessentially American, for individualism, education, and the ownership of private property were the sacred tenets of the American creed. Nothing could have been more Jeffersonian than advocating that the Indians be transformed into a community of small farmers, the spiritual bedrock of American democracy.[51]

The Army's limited role in the formulation of Indian policy prevented it from having much of an impact upon the course of Indian pacification. Nevertheless, officers endeavored to put their ideas into practice whenever they had the opportunity to do so. Schofield's attempt at using the Army as a socializing agent and Pope's and Mackenzie's introduction of cattle ranching to the Comanches were only some of the ways the Army dabbled in this area. During the 1860s Brig. Gen. James H. Carlton established a military-controlled reservation at Bosque Redondo, New Mexico, to protect the Navajos from persecution by their white neighbors. General Howard, the former director of the Army's Freedmen's Bureau, played a similar role keeping the peace with the Apaches ten years later. So, too, did many other officers who, during the Army's many years on the frontier, performed their constabulary duties as humanely and fairly as possible. Capt. Adna R. Chaffee, one of the Army's toughest Indian fighters, campaigned just as hard for the Indians while serving as an Indian agent in 1879–1880 as he had against them in the field, moving aggressively to stamp out corruption on the reservation and improve the Indians' irrigation system. Another veteran campaigner, Capt. Frank D. Baldwin, was no less vigorous in defending Indian rights while serving as an Indian agent between 1894–1898, while 1st Lt. Richard H. Pratt established a major school for Indians at Carlisle Barracks, Pennsylvania. But perhaps the best example of the Army's approach to the Indian question was General Crook's pacification of the Apaches during two tours as commander of the Department of Arizona, in 1871–1875 and 1882–1886.[52]

Crook enjoyed one significant advantage that was the envy of many of his fellow officers. Due to the seriousness of the Apache problem, he was able to persuade the government to give him extended control over several reservations during his tours as departmental commander. This enabled him to implement a more unified civil and military pacification effort than was normally possible in view of the incessant infighting between the War Department and the Indian Bureau.

Like his fellow officers, Crook regarded pacification as a two-stage process. The first was to break the Apaches. The second, beginning while the first was still in progress, was to remold them gradually in the white man's image. He approached the first stage in much the same way as he had undertaken the pacification of West Virginia during the Civil War. In Arizona, as in West Virginia, he spent a considerable amount of time familiarizing himself with the land and the temper of its inhabitants. Having acclimated himself and his troops, he launched a relentless campaign, in which small, mobile columns adopted the guerrillas' own tactics of surprise and ambush. Crook took a hard line toward his irregular opponents and the population that supported them, putting their property and foodstuffs to the torch just as readily as he had when his adversaries had been secessionists.[53]

Yet Crook recognized that pacification entailed more than just bloodshed, and he skillfully wove political measures into his Apache campaigns. Like American commanders during the Mexican and Civil Wars, he began his operations with promises of good treatment for those who acquiesced to his rule and of stiff penalties for those who did not. He also followed Mexican and Civil War precedents by ordering his soldiers to conduct themselves in a manner that would enhance his pacification efforts. He directed his subordinates to redress Indian grievances, to treat Indian prisoners well, and to avoid killing women and children whenever possible.[54]

Crook extended his control over the Apache in a variety of ways. He met all the key tribal leaders and endeavored to persuade them to help maintain order. He made extensive use of spies, whom he termed "confidential Indians" and "secret service scouts" and through whom he monitored the pulse and temper of the tribe. When crimes were com-

An officer of the 10th Cavalry supervises Apache laborers digging an irrigation canal at the San Carlos Indian Agency, Arizona, in 1886.

mitted, he employed Indian scouts and policemen to apprehend the criminals and Indian juries to convict them, thereby further integrating the Indians into his system of control, as well as introducing them to concepts of American jurisprudence. He supplemented this system by issuing all Apache males metal identification tags and introducing a program of daily roll calls through which he was able to verify the identity and location of every warrior.[55]

Through all that he did, Crook endeavored to promote the disintegration of tribal bonds and loyalties. He adopted a divide-and-conquer strategy, employing Indian collaborators to infiltrate hostile bands to persuade at least a portion of the people to surrender. This, reported Crook, "at once divided the hostiles into two parties and broke up the band. The fact that this had been effected through the personal efforts of their own people, had an effect not only of a peculiarly demoralizing nature upon the hostiles, but also upon all others of the tribe, and rendered their subsequent management anywhere, an easy matter."[56] Having divided the Indians, Crook sent Indian scouts to conquer the still recalcitrant factions, noting that the employment of scouts was "not merely a question of catching them better with Indians, but of a broader and more enduring aim—their disintegration."[57]

While Crook busied himself with subjugating the Apaches, he did not neglect the second phase of his pacification program, for he recognized that the "most permanent and satisfactory way" of resolving the Apache problem was "to raise and elevate the condition of the Indian himself." During his years in Apacheria, Crook governed the tribesmen with a paternalistic blend of firmness, fairness, patience, and tact. The single most important element of his program was that of compensated labor. Crook put the Indians to work building irrigation canals and planting crops. Work projects of this nature not only kept what would otherwise have been idle and potentially mischievous hands busy, but also set the Apaches on the road toward "civilization." He reinforced these endeavors by establishing a complementary economic relationship between the Indians and the Army, paying the tribesmen to raise hay and cattle, which the Army then purchased for its own use. In this manner, he sought to demonstrate to the Apaches in an immediate and materialistic way the advantages of cooperation. He supplemented his economic program by establishing educational institutions on the reservations, hoping that, as the Apaches gained in prosperity and knowledge, they would gradually cast off their "primitive" tribalism and assimilate into mainstream American culture.[58]

Crook achieved much during his two tours in Arizona, but like most of the Army's other ventures into the political aspects of Indian pacification, the long-term effects were limited. The problems were too great, and the Army's control over the reservations too brief to make a significant impact on the course of the government's Indian program. Besides, while Army officers may have had a more realistic understanding of the Indian situation than many Eastern philanthropists, their approaches were stained by the same virulent ethnocentrism that weakened the government's Indian policy as a whole. Nevertheless, the Army's long experience in wrestling with the Indian question endowed it with an important legacy, a loose body of principles, assumptions, and beliefs concerning the pacification of "less developed" peoples. Included among these were the necessity of close civil-military coordination of a pacification campaign (preferably under military control), the establishment of a firm-but-fair paternalistic government, and the introduction of economic and educational reforms to uplift a benighted people. These principles would guide the actions of Army officers when the nation asked them to shoulder the "white man's burden" once again, in Cuba, Puerto Rico, and the Philippines.

COUNTERINSURGENCY DOCTRINE, 1860–1941

The New Professionalism and the Legacy of the Constabulary Army

By the time Crook stepped down as commander of the Department of Arizona in 1886 the Indian wars were virtually over. The Army continued to perform constabulary duties in the West for the remainder of the century, arresting criminals, evicting white squatters and rum runners from Indian lands, and quelling an occasional small uprising. Yet the days of the old constabulary Army were clearly numbered. The nation and the world were changing, and astute Army officers recognized that the Army would have to change with them if it was to survive the pacification of the frontier.

Many officers believed that the Army's long spell of constabulary service had rendered it ineffective as a conventional military force. As reform advocate 1st Lt. John Bigelow explained, an army's true function was to prepare for war.

Other work than waging war may incidentally devolve upon an Army without derogating from its efficiency, but when other work is its only work, and the only one for which it is fitted, the so-called Army is but a police force. Preserving the peace is not preparing for war, and to prepare for war should in time of peace, be the constant effort of our Army.[59]

The increasing scope and complexity of modern, conventional warfare made it imperative, reformers argued, that the American officer corps become a truly professional body dedicated to the study and practice of the science of war. To achieve this end, the Army's "young Turks" instituted a host of reforms during the late nineteenth and early twentieth centuries, all of which were designed to make the Army a more effective, modern, and thoroughly professional institution. They published professional journals to promote the study of war, pushed through reforms in Army administration, and introduced more realistic and comprehensive troop-training programs. Finally, they established educational institutions to indoctrinate the officer corps in the new military intellectualism. The most important of these academies was the School of Application for Infantry and Cavalry at Fort Leavenworth, a school, in the words of one officer, "whose teachings were turning the army away from a mere Indian police force to its true function, the art of war."[60]

Indian warfare received little consideration in all this. It was, after all, a dying mission. Nor did broader questions of irregular warfare and pacification receive much attention. Both were out of the conventional mainstream. Moreover, the new professional ethos appeared in the minds of many officers to leave little room for such subjects. In elevating officership to the status of a profession, many officers insisted that they must devote themselves exclusively to purely military subjects to the exclusion of all others, especially those tainted by politics.[61]

Nevertheless, it would be a mistake to conclude that the conventional thrust of the professionalism movement led the Army to ignore the lessons of its constabulary past or rendered it unfit for the conduct of future irregular operations. The Army was the "child of the frontier," and like a child grown to adulthood, its experiences during its formative years lingered on to shape some of its most basic attitudes and philosophies. The "old Army" bequeathed to its turn-of-the-century heir a deep appreciation for the value of mobility; a rich heritage of small-unit leadership that stressed self-reliance; aggressive, independent action and open order tactics; a near obsession with individual marksmanship that at times approached the status of a cult; and a force structure unusually strong in cavalry. Even the push that emerged during the 1880s and 1890s to improve the level of training of the individual soldier, while clearly oriented toward the conventional battlefield, owed a heavy debt to the frontier experience.[62]

Although the thrust of the reform movement was incontrovertibly toward conventional warfare, there were a few officers who applied the tools of the new professionalism to preserve and consolidate the lessons of the Army's constabulary past and to study less conventional subjects. During the 1880s officers like Farrow and Clark published useful frontier manuals, while the Army's new professional journals printed a variety of articles recounting Indian campaigns, explaining frontier fieldcraft, and debating Indian policy.

Yet, the writings of individual officers were not the only way in which the Army distilled and passed on its frontier experiences. General Miles' 1887 counterguerrilla maneuvers were one example of how commanders occasionally applied progressive techniques—in this case realistic field exercises—for the purpose of improving the Army's unconventional warfare skills. Another medium was the Army's grassroots educational institution, the post lyceum. During the late nineteenth century the Army encouraged post commanders to establish lyceums for the purpose of furthering the educational and professional development of their junior officers. The lyceums became forums in which officers applied the new tools of the professionalization movement—map exercises, colloquia, and group study sessions—to analyze military problems. Although conventional warfare topics naturally dominated lyceum discussions, participants also examined subjects pertaining to the frontier.

During the winter of 1897–1898, for example, 1st Lt. J. Franklin Bell, a future chief of staff of the Army, led the lyceum at Fort Apache, Arizona, in considering problems in Indian warfare. Bell crafted the problems to reflect the type of situation that troops at Fort Apache would most likely face should they be called upon in an Indian emergency. The scenarios postulated that a band of reservation Indians had rustled some cattle from a nearby rancher and refused to make reparations, causing a confrontation which neither the Indian police nor the scouts were capable of resolving. Bell required that, in solving the problems, the officers not only formulate military plans, but also outline how they would attempt to negotiate a peaceful resolution to the situation before resorting to force.[63]

The lyceum at Fort Grant, Arizona, adopted a similar approach. During 1896–1900 it featured discussions of such frontier-related topics as the conduct of convoys, outpost duty, Indian scouting, and a "Historical Sketch of Indian Warfare," the latter presented by a veteran Indian campaigner, Col. E. V. Sumner. The officers at Fort Grant also undertook problems relating to the administration of Indian scouts, the transfer of government supplies to Indian reservations, and the protection of reservations from white encroachment.[64]

Frontier lyceums studied constabulary-related subjects up to the end of the century because those subjects were still relevant to the missions of the posts concerned. The Army's institutions of higher learning, such as the School of Application for Infantry and Cavalry, concerned themselves with more universal subjects and were less likely to devote much attention to constabulary matters. Nevertheless, even Leavenworth was not entirely oblivious to the subject of irregular warfare. In fact, in 1897 the school conducted three counterguerrilla field exercises. One revolved around the protection of a convoy against partisan attack, another considered the defense of a rail line from raids by partisan cavalry and guerrillas, while a third involved a battalion-size sweep to root out forty partisans hidden in a forest. (The last proved to be somewhat of a disappointment, as half of the "partisans" escaped the dragnet.)[65]

Nor was the rest of Leavenworth's conventionally oriented curriculum necessarily irrelevant to irregular warfare concerns. Although the school eventually evolved into an institution dedicated to the higher arts of war and staff duty, during its first two decades Leavenworth's curriculum consisted largely of instruction in small-unit tactics and "minor operations," much of which was equally applicable to conventional and unconventional warfare. So too were some of the principles taught at the School of Application. Arthur Wagner, a veteran of several Indian campaigns and one of Leavenworth's top instructors during 1886–1898, emphasized to his students, as Mahan had done years before, that good soldiers adapted conventional tactics to the terrain and the nature of their opponents. The Army's educational system focused upon conventional warfare, he explained, because this was the type of warfare that it believed was both the most dangerous and the most likely for the future. But the "normal formations" prescribed by the Army were intended only to provide its officers with a common base from which they would be expected to develop their own, situation-specific solutions. This was a lesson that officers could apply with profit to all forms of warfare.[66]

Wagner wrote two major textbooks during his tenure at Fort Leavenworth: *The Service of Security and Information*, first published in 1893, and *Organization and Tactics*, which came out the following year. Neither volume discussed irregular warfare in any depth. *Organization and Tactics* confined its discussion of irregular warfare to a review of the role of partisan cavalry during the Civil War. *The Service of Security and Information*, on the other hand, covered subjects like reconnaissance, patrol, and security, all of which had been of prime importance to the Army during its long service on the frontier. Wagner pointed out to his readers that "many of the features of the service of security and information are common to both hemispheres and to all armed forces, whether savage hordes or highly organized armies." He also included a chapter on Indian scouting, in which he described native techniques, as well as the typical methods employed by a company of Indian scouts. Wagner's message was that the Indians' skill in reconnaissance was a learned rather than innate quality, and that, with proper training, American soldiers could emulate Indian methods and apply them with equal faculty in both conventional and unconventional settings.[67]

Another textbook that combined the new professionalism with the best lessons of the nation's irregular warfare experiences was Capt. John Bigelow's *The Principles of Strategy* (1894). Bigelow, a frontier veteran and West Point instructor, discussed the nature of Indian warfare and recounted some of the stratagems commonly employed by the Army, including night marches and surprise attacks. He also included a discussion of the most suitable march and combat formations for irregular warfare, echoing Miles' dictum that the proper march formation for irregular operations provide four things: all-round security, efficiency of command and administration, mutual support, and celerity of movement. Bigelow believed that some form of square formation best met these criteria. Miles had employed a square against the Sioux in

1876, and Bigelow explained how the 7th U.S. Cavalry routinely marched in a loose, rectangular formation that provided all-round security while in Indian country. He further described how both the French and British had employed squares as march and combat formations against irregular opponents in Africa. Although squares of this nature were clearly obsolete in modern warfare, Bigelow included them as examples of old ideas that were still of great utility in waging small wars against poorly armed, but highly mobile and impetuous, natives.[68]

In recounting the Army's experience on the frontier, Bigelow outlined the three most common approaches to countering Indians: chasing them, surprising them, and wearing them down. "What decides the campaign . . .," he concluded, "is not so much [the Indians'] physical exhaustion from long marches or scanty nourishment as their mental weariness from constant watching and devising and planning, and their final despair of ever thoroughly resting or returning to wives, children, and sweethearts, unless it be as prisoners." He offered as an example of this principle Miles' campaign against Geronimo, in which the Army wore the renegades down by combining a relentless pursuit with the "novel stratagem" of removing the Chiricahua population from the zone of operations, denying Geronimo a base of moral and logistical support.[69]

Bigelow heartily endorsed the "hard war" policies that Generals Sherman and Sheridan had adopted against Southern insurrectionists and Indians alike. He approved of Sheridan's destruction of the Shenandoah and Loudoun valleys to root out guerrillas and deny the rebels access to vital supplies, just as he approved of Miles' scheme of population removal. Enemy civilians were a decisive objective in warfare, Bigelow maintained, and therefore armies were entitled to deprive them of their rights, privileges, comforts, and even sustenance for the purpose of breaking their will to resist. He also recommended that commanders create dissension among the enemy population and exploit the resulting division by recruiting disaffected elements as auxiliaries, just as Crook had done in Apacheria.[70]

Coercion was a tricky instrument, however, and Bigelow cautioned officers to use it carefully. Should a people be willing to endure hardship, the application of pressure might only embitter them and stiffen, rather than weaken, their resistance. Consequently, he concluded that inflicting inadequate suffering was a cruel mistake. On the other hand, he recognized that public opinion, national and international law, and the personal scruples of the commander would affect the degree to which the Army could chastise a hostile population. Moreover, he conceded that to be effective a pacification campaign must include at least some positive inducements, for "the maintenance of military despotism in the rear of an invading army must generally prove a waste of manpower." He therefore concluded that no hard and fast rules were possible, and that officers must govern their pacification campaigns largely by their judgment of the particular situation, the temper and nature of the population, and the climate of opinion both at home and abroad.[71]

Bigelow ended his consideration of irregular warfare and pacification by examining Britain's operations in the Southern colonies during the American Revolution as a case study of a counterinsurgency campaign. He derived two principal conclusions from this study. First, an occupying army should not expect to receive much assistance from the population unless it can clearly demonstrate an ability to protect the people from guerrilla intimidation; and second, relatively undisciplined units of militia and partisans posed a serious threat to regular armies. Partisans, he warned, had become more dangerous since the American Revolution due to advances in weapons technology and explosives. He stressed the importance of march security to protect columns from "bushwhackers," and recounted with approval how the Army had combined blockhouse lines and rapid repair techniques to keep vital railroads open during the Civil War, despite the best efforts of rebel partisans to shut them down.[72]

The Principles of Strategy was a well-known textbook and is perhaps the best example of how Army officers sometimes employed the new intellectualism to capture the broad lessons of a half century of irregular warfare experience. Through a combination of formal and informal methods, the Army managed to preserve some key principles that would shape its approach to counterinsurgency situations into the next century. These included a general counterguerrilla strategy built upon aggressive small-unit action, relentless pursuit, and the destruction of enemy resources in an effort to destroy his will to resist. In terms of pacification, the Army continued to abide by the twin principles of moderation and retaliation laid down by international law and General Orders 100, to which were added a philosophy concerning the management of benighted peoples gained from a century of service on the frontier.

Finally, it should be noted that the Army's approach to pacification was also influenced by broader trends in American society as a whole. America in the late nineteenth century was becoming a more organized and rationalistic society, a society that was increasingly fascinated by science and the potential application of its methods to the questions of everyday life. Politically, this trend was represented by the Progressive movement—a loose confederation of political and social reformers who strove to harness the new forces of social organization for the betterment of society. Central to progressivism was the notion that informed and enlightened professionals, be they doctors, engineers, or bureaucrats, could improve society from the top down by applying their specialized knowledge to create more rational and efficient institutions.

Army officers shared the Progressive values of their society, and, indeed, the military reform movement was itself a part of the Progressive impulse, as it attempted to apply rational principles to improve the management and organization of violence. But progressivism had an even more profound influence upon the Army's approach to the nonviolent applications of military force. Not only did it endow the officer corps as a whole with an underlying philosophy about social organization and reform, but it also provided a rationale for those officers who were disposed to taking a more active role in social and political affairs.

These "Armed Progressives" challenged the traditionally narrow conception of officership that espoused a rigid separation of military from nonmilitary affairs, maintaining instead that the Army's expertise in human leadership and management made it an ideal instrument for social engineering. Reconstruction played virtually no role in the thinking of the Army's new breed of social activists, it being relegated to the position of an increasingly dim, if unpleasant, memory. Rather, progressivism's philosophy of government by enlightened experts dovetailed quite nicely with the Army's own brand of firm, yet benevolent, paternalism that it had applied on the frontier. As Col. Elwell Otis, the first commandant of the School of Application for Infantry and Cavalry and the author of *The Indian Question*, advised the West Point graduating class of 1882:

> Be not deceived and accept the foolish delusion . . . that the soldier's obligations only begin when summoned to meet a foreign enemy or to put down armed resistance which has overthrown civil power. . . . A soldier is now expected to exert himself within proper limits to preserve and organize peace. He should labor, in unison with the citizen and philanthropist, to impress and extend our civilization. So vast is the field of operations of our small army, and so scattered are the troops, it is possible, if not extremely probable, that in a few short years, whatever may be your age and rank, you may be obliged to administer affairs wherein considerable knowledge of civil matters may be necessary.[73]

Otis could not have guessed how right he would be.

Notes

[1] Allan Millett and Peter Maslowski, *For the Common Defense* (New York: Free Press, 1984), p. 248.

[2] James Sefton, *The U.S. Army and Reconstruction, 1865–77* (Baton Rouge: Louisiana University Press, 1967), p. 9; Robert Coakley, *The Role of Federal Military Forces in Domestic Disorders, 1789–1878* (Washington, D.C.: U.S. Army Center of Military History, Government Printing Office, 1988), pp. 268–341; Paul Pierce, *The Freedmen's Bureau* (New York: Haskell, 1971).

[3] Richard Zuczek, "State of Rebellion: People's War in Reconstruction South Carolina, 1865–77" (Ph.D. diss., Ohio State University, 1993), pp. 534–36.

[4] Sherman quote from Millett and Maslowski, *Common Defense*, p. 246. Miles quote from Nelson Miles, *Serving the Republic* (New York: Harper & Brothers, 1911), p. 111. Harry Pfanz, "Soldiering in the South During the Reconstruction Period, 1865–77" (Ph.D. diss., Ohio State University, 1958), pp. 488, 497, 536; Peter DeMontravel, "The Career of Lieutenant General Nelson A. Miles From the Civil War Through the Indian Wars" (Ph.D. diss., St. Johns University, 1983), pp. 130–31, 134; Edward Coffman, *The Old Army* (New York: Oxford University Press, 1986), p. 240; William Ulrich, "The Northern Military Mind in Regard to Reconstruction, 1865–72: The Attitude of Ten Leading Union Generals" (Ph.D. diss., Ohio State University, 1959), pp. 207, 365; Joseph Dawson, *Army Generals and Reconstruction: Louisiana, 1862–77* (Baton Rouge: Louisiana State University, 1982), pp. 1, 262; Sefton, *Reconstruction*, pp. 252–53.

[5] Robert Utley, *Frontier Regulars: The United States Army and the Indian, 1866–1890* (New York: Macmillan, 1973), pp. 3–4; Robert Utley, *The Indian Frontier of the American West* (Albuquerque: University of New Mexico Press, 1984), p. 4.

[6] John Gibbon, "Our Indian Question," *JMSIUS* 2 (1881): 117–18; Nelson Miles, "Rising From the Ruins of War," *Cosmopolitan* 50 (April 1911): 658. Quote from Thomas Leonard, *Above the Battle: War Making in America From Appomattox to Versailles* (New York: Oxford University Press, 1978), p. 215.

[7] Larry Roberts, "The Artillery With the Regular Army in the West From 1866 to 1890" (Ph.D. diss., Oklahoma State University, 1981), p. 17; Utley, *Frontier Regulars*, pp. 16–18, 47–48; Raymond Welty, "The Western Army Frontier, 1860–70" (Ph.D. diss., University of Iowa, 1924), pp. 33, 77, 102, 122–23, 378–79; Wooster, *Indian Policy*, p. 15; Utley, *Frontiersmen in Blue*, p. 348; Neil Thompson, *Crazy Horse Called Them Walk-a-Heaps* (St. Cloud, Minn.: North Star Press, 1979), p. 127.

[8] Roberts, "Artillery in the West," p. 21; Utley, *Frontier Regulars*, pp. 23–25; Coffman, *Old Army*, p. 371; Albert Brackett, "Our Cavalry: Its Duties, Hardships, and Necessities at Our Frontier Posts," *JMSIUS* 4 (1883): 397–400; Wesley Merritt, "Some Defects in Our Cavalry System," *United Service* 1 (October 1879): 559–60; James Hutchins, "Mounted Riflemen: The Real Role of Cavalry in the Indian Wars," in *Probing the American West*, ed. K. Ross Toole (Santa Fe: Museum of New Mexico Press, 1962), pp. 79–85; Ltr, O. O. Howard to Military Division of the Pacific, 19 Jan 1878, in Joseph Sladen, Service With General Howard, Nez Perce War, Correspondence Among Howard, Sheridan, Terry, and Miles, Assessments of the Performance of the 1st U.S. Cavalry Regiment, 1877, box 3, Sladen Family Papers, U.S. Army Military History Institute (MHI), Carlisle Barracks, Pa.

[9] Perry Jamieson, *Crossing the Deadly Ground: U.S. Army Tactics, 1865–1899* (Tuscaloosa: University of Alabama Press, 1994), p. 37; Vetock, *Lessons Learned*, p. 24; Griess, "Mahan," pp. 306–07; Brinsfield, "Military Ethics," p. 37; Wooster, *Indian Policy*, pp. 56–57; Ambrose, "Mahan," p. 35; Smith, "West Point and the Indian Wars," Sep 93, pp. 18–22; Mahan, "Composition of Armies," lithographic text, 1836, pp. 33–36, Welker Papers.

[10] Sheridan, *Memoirs*, p. 488; Paul Hutton, "General Philip H. Sheridan and the Army in the West, 1867–88" (Ph.D. diss., Indiana University, 1981), pp. 20, 54, 294; Wooster, *Indian Policy*, p. 127.

[11] Quote from Mahan, *Out-Post*, pp. 166–68. J. B. Wheeler, *A Course of Instruction in the Elements of the Art and Science of War for the Use of the Cadets of the United States Military Academy* (New York: Van Nostrand, 1893), pp. 271–80 (see also 1879 edition); *Centennial of the U.S. Military Academy*, 2:107, 131; Griess, "Mahan," pp. 312–13.

[12] Quote from Wooster, *Indian Policy*, p. 57; Smith, "West Point and the Indian Wars," Sep 93, pp. 11, 14–18.

[13] Vattel, *Law of Nations*, p. 348; Woolsey, *International Law*, pp. 230–32; George B. Davis, *The Elements of International Law* (New York: Harper & Brothers, 1903), p. 215; John Schofield, "Notes on 'The Legitimate in War,'" *JMSIUS* 2 (1881): 2; Sherry Smith, "Civilization's Guardians: Army Officers' Reflections on Indians and the Indian Wars in the Trans–Mississippi West, 1848–1890" (Ph.D. diss., University of Washington, 1984), p. 303; Utley, *Frontier Regulars*, p. 53; Thomas Dunlay, *Wolves for the Blue Soldiers* (Lincoln: University of Nebraska Press, 1982), pp. 47, 204.

[14] Ambrose, "Mahan," p. 100; Griess, "Mahan," p. 223; Utley, *Frontier Regulars*, p. 420; Swift, "Services of Graduates," pp. 570, 579; Robert Utley, "The Contribution of the Frontier to the American Military Tradition," in *Harmon Memorial Lectures in Military History* 19 (Boulder, Colo.: U.S. Air Force Academy, 1977), p. 6; Wooster, *Indian Policy*, p. 12.

[15] Coffman, *Old Army*, p. 230; Peter Karsten, "Armed Progressives: The Military Reorganizes for the American Century," in *Building the Organizational Society*, ed. Jerry Israel (New York: Free Press, 1972), p. 217.

[16] Quote from Randolph Marcy, *The Prairie Traveler, A Hand-book for Overland Expeditions* (Williamstown, Mass.: Corner House, 1978), pp. xi–xii, and see also editor's notes, 41–42, 55–57, 64–70, 92, 98, 111, 155, 183, 196–229.

[17] Marcy, *The Prairie Traveler*, pp. 201–05, 224; Randolph Marcy, *Thirty Years of Army Life on the Border* (New York: Harper & Brothers, 1866), pp. 67–71, 77. Quote from Dunlay, *Wolves for the Blue Soldiers*, p. 76.

[18] Edward Farrow, *Mountain Scouting* (New York, 1881), pp. 76, 85–86, 148, 227, 230, 239, 243–48; W. P. Clark, *The Indian Sign Language* (Philadelphia: L. R. Hamesly, 1885), pp. 5–6; George Crook, "The Apache Problem," *JMSIUS* 7 (1886): 257–69; George Crook, *Resume of Operations Against Apache Indians, 1882 to 1886* (Washington, D.C.: War Department, 1886).

[19] Stephen Ambrose, *Upton and the Army* (Baton Rouge: Louisiana State University Press, 1964), pp. 62–64; Virgil Ney, *Evolution of the U.S. Army Field Manual, Valley Forge to Vietnam* (Combat Operations Research Group, CORG Memorandum 244, January 1966), p. 43; William Crites, "The Development of Infantry Tactical Doctrine in the U.S. Army, 1865–1898" (Master's thesis, Duke University, 1968), pp. 29, 34, 89; Jamieson, *Deadly Ground*, p. 44.

THE CONSTABULARY YEARS, 1865–1898

[20] Philip St. George Cooke, *Cavalry Tactics*, 2 vols. (Philadelphia: J. B. Lippincott, 1862), 2:67–71; E. Lisle Reedstrom, *Apache Wars* (New York: Sterling Publishing, 1990), pp. 148–51; Fred Ward, "Single or Double Rank for Cavalry," *Cavalry Journal* 12 (1899): 139; James Parker, "Cavalry in Extended Order Formation," *Cavalry Journal* 7 (1894): 61.

[21] Swift, "Services of Graduates," p. 526; Williams, *The History of American Wars From Colonial Times to World War I*, pp. 312–15.

[22] Weigley, *American Way of War*, pp. 159–62; Carl Rister, *Border Command: General Phil Sheridan in the West* (Norman: University of Oklahoma Press, 1944), pp. 92–96; Paul Hutton, ed., *Soldiers West: Biographies From the Military Frontier* (Lincoln: University of Nebraska Press, 1987), pp. 51, 182–85, 216–19; Utley, *Indian Frontier*, pp. 71, 84, 92; Jamieson, *Deadly Ground*, pp. 37–38.

[23] Hutton, "Sheridan," pp. 150–52, 344–45, 351; Hutton, *Soldiers West*, pp. 86–87, 173, 417, 439; Richard Ellis, *General Pope and U.S. Indian Policy* (Albuquerque: University of New Mexico Press, 1970), p. 240; Thomas Leonard, "The Reluctant Conquerors," *American Heritage* 27 (August 1976): 35.

[24] Utley, *Frontier Regulars*, p. 285.

[25] Dunlay, *Wolves for the Blue Soldiers*, p. 77; Welty, "Western Army," pp. 336–37.

[26] Dunlay, *Wolves for the Blue Soldiers*, pp. 2, 11, 44, 50–51, 55–56, 106.

[27] Indian thinkers quote from Utley, *Frontier Regulars*, p. 55. Bigelow quote from Dunlay, *Wolves for the Blue Soldiers*, pp. 93–95.

[28] Utley, *Frontier Regulars*, p. 54; Hutton, "Sheridan," pp. 423, 532; Crook, *Autobiography*, p. 214; John Bourke, "Crook in Indian Country," *Century Magazine* 4 (March 1891): 657; Dunlay, *Wolves for the Blue Soldiers*, pp. 11, 24, 46, 61–63, 67; Joyce Mason, "The Use of Indian Scouts in the Apache Wars, 1870–86" (Ph.D. diss., Indiana University, 1970), p. 359.

[29] Brackett, "Our Cavalry," pp. 385–86; Archibald Forbes, "The U.S. Army," *North American Review* 135 (1882): 144–45.

[30] Crook, *Autobiography*, p. 213; H. W. Daly, *Manual of Pack Transportation* (Washington, D.C.: Government Printing Office, 1910), pp. 11–12, 17–18; Hugh Scott, *Some Memories of a Soldier* (New York: Century, 1928), pp. 91, 387; Welty, "Western Army," p. 294; Forbes, "U.S. Army," p. 144; *Centennial of the U.S. Military Academy*, 1:400, 403.

[31] Marcy, *The Prairie Traveler*, p. 111; William H. Carter, *The Life of Lieutenant General Chaffee* (Chicago, 1917), pp. 77–78; James Hutchins, Use of Range-Bred Horses by the U.S. Cavalry, 11 Mar 61, Guy V. Henry Papers, MHI.

[32] G. W. Baird, "General Miles' Indian Campaigns," *Century Magazine* 42 (1891): 359; Julius Penn, "Mounted Infantry," *JMSIUS* 12 (November 1891): 1128, 1136; Weigley, *Towards an American Army*, pp. 69–70; Utley, *Frontier Regulars*, pp. 12, 16–17.

[33] Hutton, *Soldiers West*, pp. 50, 182–83, 185, 218–19; Crook, *Autobiography*, pp. 38, 46, 48, 177; Clarence Clendenen, *Blood on the Border: The U.S. Army and the Mexican Irregulars* (London: Macmillan, 1969), p. 68; Alice Baldwin, *Memoirs of the Late Frank D. Baldwin, Major General, U.S. Army* (Los Angeles, 1929), p. 92; John Bigelow, *The Principles of Strategy, Illustrated Mainly From American Campaigns* (New York: Greenwood Press, 1968), pp. 103–04.

[34] John Bourke, "Crook in Indian Country," p. 656; Smith, "Civilization's Guardians," pp. 149, 181; Wooster, *Indian Policy*, p. 38; Russell Gilmore, "'The New

Courage': Rifles and Soldier Individualism, 1876–1918," *Military Affairs* 40 (October 1976): 98–99; Edward Coffman, "Army Life on the Frontier, 1865–98," *Military Affairs* 20 (Winter 1956): 197; Welty, "Western Army," p. 327; Rister, *Border Command*, p. 96; Clendenen, *Blood on the Border*, pp. 66–67.

[35] Miles, *Serving the Republic*, pp. 141, 143, 221; DeMontravel, "Nelson A. Miles," p. 199; Donald Smythe, *Guerrilla Warrior: The Early Life of J.J. Pershing* (New York: Charles Scribner's Sons, 1973), p. 16; War Department, *War Department Annual Report, 1888* (Washington, D.C.: Government Printing Office, 1888), 1:125–27; George MacAdam, "The Life of General Pershing," *Worlds Work* 37 (January 1919): 291–92.

[36] Thomas Crittenden, "Marches," *JMSIUS* 1 (1879): 37–38; Brackett, "Our Cavalry," p. 395; Hutton, *Soldiers West*, pp. 62, 65.

[37] Crook, *Resume of Operations*, p. 21; Utley, *Frontier Regulars*, pp. 397, 402; DeMontravel, "Nelson A. Miles," pp. 307–14.

[38] Utley, *Frontier Regulars*, p. 178.

[39] Felix Cohen, *Handbook of Federal Indian Law* (Washington, D.C.: Department of the Interior, 1945), pp. viii–xi, 34, 40–41, 66–67, 94, 153–55, 170; Wilcomb E. Washburn, *Red Man's Land—White Man's Law: A Study of the Past and Present Status of the American Indian* (New York: Charles Scribner's Sons, 1971), pp. 53–59, 73, 79, 173, 182; Utley, *Frontier Regulars*, pp. 7–8.

[40] War Department, Quartermaster General's Office, *Outline Description of U.S. Military Posts and Stations in the Year 1871* (Washington, D.C.: Government Printing Office, 1872), pp. 194–95; Utley, *Frontier Regulars*, pp. 141, 197; Wooster, *Indian Policy*, p. 145; Hutton, *Soldiers West*, p. 237; Smythe, *Guerrilla Warrior*, p. 24; Smith, "Civilization's Guardians," p. 181.

[41] Ellis, *General Pope*, p. 240; Leonard, "Reluctant Conquerors," p. 35; Hutton, *Soldiers West*, pp. 86–87; Hutton, "Sheridan," pp. 150–52, 344, 351.

[42] Wooster, *Indian Policy*, p. 39; Raymond Welty, "The Indian Policy of the Army, 1860–70," *Cavalry Journal* 36 (July 1927): 374; Welty, "Western Army," pp. 127–28, 155; Ellis, *General Pope*, p. 233.

[43] Swift, "Services of Graduates," p. 572; Welty, "Indian Policy," p. 375; DeMontravel, "Nelson A. Miles," p. 356; Smith, "Civilization's Guardians," pp. 283, 291, 295–96; Ellis, *General Pope*, pp. 33, 38, 39–46, 199–201; Gibbon, "Our Indian Question," p. 117.

[44] Wooster, *Indian Policy*, pp. 81–82. Quote from Richard Ellis, "The Humanitarian Generals," *Western Historical Quarterly* 3 (April 1972): 170.

[45] Welty, "Indian Policy," p. 371; Marcy, *The Prairie Traveler*, p. 211; Utley, *Frontier Regulars*, p. 201; Brinsfield, "Military Ethics," p. 40; Dunlay, *Wolves for the Blue Soldiers*, p. 83; Sheridan, *Memoirs*, pp. 115–16; Baldwin, *Memoirs of Frank Baldwin*, p. 94; DeMontravel, "Nelson A. Miles," pp. 190–91, 248, 324; Scott, *Memories*, pp. 112–20; Hutton, *Soldiers West*, pp. 119, 197, 387; Nelson Miles, "My First Fights on the Plains," *Cosmopolitan* 50 (May 1911): 801–02.

[46] Elwell Otis, *The Indian Question* (New York, 1878), p. 222; Gibbon, "Our Indian Question," pp. 113, 115; Miles, *Serving the Republic*, pp. 197, 202–06; Nelson Miles, "Our Indian Question," *JMSIUS* 2 (1881): 285; Ellis, *General Pope*, p. 234.

[47] Hutton, *Soldiers West*, p. 184; Ellis, "Humanitarian Generals," pp. 176–77.

[48] Dunlay, *Wolves for the Blue Soldiers*, pp. 191–92; H. C. Cushing, "Military Colonization of the Indians," *United Service* (September 1880): 370–75.

[49] Michael Tate, "Soldiers of the Line, Apache Companies in the U.S. Army, 1891–97," *Arizona and the West* 16 (Winter 1974): 343–64; W. Bruce White, "The American Indian as Soldier, 1890–1919," *Canadian Review of American Studies* 7 (Spring 1976): 15–23.

[50] Welty, "Indian Policy," p. 375.

[51] Otis, *Indian Question*, pp. 158, 196–97, 257–58, 266–67, 270–77; Crook, *Autobiography*, p. 229; Miles, *Serving the Republic*, pp. 200–206; Gibbon, "Our Indian Question," pp. 113–15; C. E. Wood, "Our Indian Question," *JMSIUS* 2 (1881): 149–53; H. O. P., "Dodge's 'Our Wild Indians,'" *JMSIUS* 3 (1882): 287; John Carpenter, *Sword and Olive Branch: Oliver Otis Howard* (Pittsburgh, 1964), pp. 267–68; Richard Pratt, "Violated Principles, The Cause of Failure in Indian Civilization," *JMSIUS* 7 (1886): 46–60.

[52] Gerald Thompson, *The Army and the Navajo: The Bosque Redondo Reservation Experiment, 1863–68* (Tucson: University of Arizona Press, 1976), pp. ix–x, 158–65; Paul Wellman, *Death in the Desert* (New York: Macmillan, 1935), p. 94; Carter, *Chaffee*, pp. 66, 84–89; Hutton, *Soldiers West*, pp. 231, 233, 237–38; Oliver Howard, *My Life and Experiences Among Our Hostile Indians* (Hartford, Conn., 1907), pp. 186–225; Ernest Wallace, *Ranald S. Mackenzie on the Texas Frontier* (College Station: Texas A&M University Press, 1993), pp. 170–71.

[53] Utley, *Frontier Regulars*, p. 387; Smith, "Civilization's Guardians," p. 293; Hutton, *Soldiers West*, p. 119; Crook, *Autobiography*, p. 181; Donald Rattan, "Counterguerrilla Operations: A Case Study," in U.S. Army Office of Chief of Information, *Special Warfare, U.S. Army* (U.S. Army, 1962), pp. 47–49; John Gates, "General George Crook's First Apache Campaign," *Journal of the West* 6 (April 1967): 310–18.

[54] John Bourke, *On the Border With Crook* (Lincoln: University of Nebraska Press, 1971), pp. 142–43; Crook, *Resume of Operations*, p. 2. Crook employed a similar approach during the Sioux campaign of 1876. See John Bourke, "Mackenzie's Last Fight With the Cheyennes: A Winter Campaign in Wyoming and Montana," *JMSIUS* 11 (1890): 29–49.

[55] Crook, *Resume of Operations*, pp. 4–5; Wesley Merritt, *Merritt and the Indian Wars* (London, 1972), p. 19; Bourke, *On the Border*, pp. 213, 219.

[56] Crook, *Resume of Operations*, p. 9.

[57] Quote from Utley, "Contribution of the Frontier," p. 7; Crook, *Autobiography*, pp. 213–14; Crook, "Apache Problem," p. 267.

[58] Quote from Crook, *Resume of Operations*, p. 2. Crook, "Apache Problem," pp. 267–68; Utley, *Frontier Regulars*, p. 388; Bourke, *On the Border*, pp. 213–18, 225–29; Crook, *Autobiography*, p. 229.

[59] Quote from Brackett, "Our Cavalry," p. 406. Ambrose, *Upton*, p. 106.

[60] Allan Millett, *The General, Robert L. Bullard and Officership in the U.S. Army, 1881–1925* (Westport, Conn.: Greenwood Press, 1975), p. 75.

[61] Millett and Maslowski, *Common Defense*, pp. 255–58; Weigley, *Towards an American Army*, pp. 272–92.

[62] Russell Weigley, "The Long Death of the Indian-Fighting Army," in *Soldiers and Civilians: The U.S. Army and the American People*, ed. Garry Ryan and Timothy Nenninger (Washington, D.C.: National Archives and Records Administration, 1987), pp. 27–37; Samuel Huntington, "Equilibrium and Disequilibrium in American Military Policy," *Political Science Quarterly* 76 (December 1961): 490; Thompson, *Crazy Horse*, pp. 123–24; Gilmore, "New Courage," pp. 98–99.

[63] George Rodney, "Shall Subordinate Officers Learn the Business of Generals?" *Cavalry Journal* 15 (1905): 538, 542.

[64] Records of the Officers Lyceum, 1896–1902, Records of the U.S. Army Continental Commands, pt. 5, Fort Grant, Arizona, Record Group (RG) 393, National Archives and Records Administration (NARA), Washington, D.C.

[65] U.S. Infantry and Cavalry School, *Annual Report, June 30, 1897*, app. B, Department of the Military Art, Exercise 3 (pp. 18, 19, 29); Exercise 5 (p. 24); and Exercise 6 (p. 28).

[66] Timothy Nenninger, *The Leavenworth Schools and the Old Army* (Westport, Conn.: Greenwood Press, 1978), pp. 1, 25–26, 30–31, 36, 43, 87, 92; Arthur Wagner, *Organization and Tactics* (Kansas City: Franklin Hudson Publishing Company, 1906), pp. vii–viii.

[67] Quote from Arthur Wagner, *The Service of Security and Information* (Kansas City: Hudson-Kimberly Publishing Company, 1903), preface to 1893 edition, and see also pp. 242–48.

[68] Bigelow, *The Principles of Strategy*, pp. 21–26, 82, 103–04, 139, 149; Miles, *Serving the Republic*, p. 151; DeMontravel, "Nelson A. Miles," p. 159.

[69] Bigelow, *The Principles of Strategy*, pp. 149–51.

[70] Ibid., pp. 228, 232–33.

[71] Quote from John Gates, *Schoolbooks and Krags* (Westport, Conn.: Greenwood Press, 1973), pp. 83–84. Bigelow, *The Principles of Strategy*, pp. 228, 232–33.

[72] Bigelow, *The Principles of Strategy*, pp. 31, 114–15, 119, 257–58.

[73] Quote from Heath Twichell, *Allen: The Biography of an Army Officer, 1859–1930* (New Brunswick, N.J.: Rutgers University Press, 1974), p. 24. Jack Lane, *Armed Progressive: General Leonard Wood* (San Rafael, Calif.: Presidio Press, 1978); John Gates, "The Alleged Isolation of U.S. Army Officers in the Late Nineteenth Century," *Parameters* 10 (September 1980): 32–45; Howard Gillette, "The Military Occupation of Cuba, 1899–1902: Workshop for American Progressivism," *American Quarterly* 25 (1973): 410–25.

4

CUBA AND THE PHILIPPINES 1898-1902

In October 1898 the 3d U.S. and 14th Minnesota Volunteer Infantry regiments suppressed a minor Indian uprising at Leech Lake, Minnesota. Government forces suffered twenty casualties during this constabulary operation, yet the event passed largely unnoticed. Six months earlier the United States had gone to war with Spain, and the nation's attention was riveted to the process of carving out new empires rather than policing old ones. In a "splendid little war" of only eight months duration, the United States successfully invaded Cuba, Puerto Rico, and the Philippines, although by the time peace was declared in December 1898, it controlled only small portions of those islands. In the treaty of Paris, Spain ceded to the United States the islands of Guam and Puerto Rico and relinquished its claim to Cuba, placing it under American control. Spain also sold the Philippines to the United States for $20 million. With little preparation or forethought, the United States found itself responsible for the governance of over ten million Cubans, Puerto Ricans, Filipinos, and Guamanians.

Because the United States had acquired Spain's former colonies by force of arms, the Army initially governed these territories until Congress and the president provided for their ultimate disposition. Washington sought to replace the military governments in the two territories actually ceded to the United States—Puerto Rico and the Philippines—with civilian officials as soon as possible. In Puerto Rico, civilians replaced uniformed administrators in the spring of 1900, but an insurrection against American authority in the Philippines delayed full implementation of civilian rule there until 1902.[1]

The situation was somewhat different in Cuba. Cuba had been in a state of revolt against Spain since 1895, and prior to the outbreak of the

Spanish-American War, Congress had opined that Cuba should be a free, independent country. There were, however, many Americans who felt otherwise, especially after American soldiers had gone ashore. After much deliberation, Washington opted against annexation, but not until it had given Cuba a crash course in American-style government. Because of the uncertain and transitory nature of American rule in Cuba, Washington kept the military government there in place until the termination of Cuba's period of tutelage in 1902.

Virtually every officer in the Army served in either Cuba, Puerto Rico, or the Philippines between 1898 and 1902, and the experiences they gained in nation building, pacification, and, in the case of the Philippines, counterguerrilla warfare, became the models on which the Army would base its approach to these issues for the next forty years. After reviewing the philosophical basis upon which the Army approached its overseas duties, this chapter examines the Army's experiences in the two largest occupations, those of Cuba and the Philippines.[2]

The Army's Approach to Overseas Nation Building

Although each of the territories of which the United States found itself in control at the end of 1898 was unique, they all shared a common heritage of exploitative colonial rule that had produced oligarchical societies in which a small class of wealthy, hispanicized planters and merchants held sway over masses of poor, uneducated, subsistence farmers and agricultural laborers. Socioeconomic mobility and democracy were virtually unknown in Spain's former colonies, where patron-client relationships dictated socioeconomic affairs, and politics was regarded as little more than a vehicle through which elements of the ruling classes competed among themselves for the spoils that political power could offer.

President William McKinley believed that the United States had a duty not just to liberate the "benighted" peoples of Spain's former colonies, but to guide them toward obtaining the fruits of Western—and particularly American—civilization. He therefore directed that the Army conduct its occupations as benevolently as possible with an eye toward establishing prosperous, self-governing (though perhaps not independent) democratic societies. The president refrained, however, from providing the Army with concrete guidance on how it was to achieve these goals, leaving the War Department and its proconsuls in the field to formulate occupation policies as they saw fit. Though individual officers did not always agree on specific methods and programs, several broad concepts shaped the Army's approach to its nation-building duties.[3]

The Army based its occupation policies upon the principles of international law and General Orders 100 of 1863. Fundamental to these legal doctrines was the notion that an occupier had a moral obligation to protect the people under its control from undue hardship and to provide them with basic governmental services. In pursuit of these goals, the laws of war discouraged commanders from radically altering the laws and customs of an occupied territory unless military necessity mandated such changes. These prescriptions were based on a combination of ethics and enlightened self-interest, as it was generally recognized that a contented population was easier to control than a hostile one, and that civil upheaval merely hindered the successful prosecution of military operations. Only if the occupier contemplated annexation of the occupied territory did the laws of war sanction the introduction of significant changes in the subject society, although even then such alterations were to be undertaken with prudence.

Most regular officers were well acquainted with these concepts, as both the laws of war and Lieber's code were an integral part of the Army's educational curriculum during the latter half of the nineteenth century. Standard textbooks such as Henry Halleck's *International Law* (1861), Theodore Woolsey's *Introduction to the Study of International Law* (1864), George B. Davis' *Outlines of International Law* (1888), and William E. Birkhimer's *Military Government and Martial Law* (1892) all relayed the same basic principles and illustrated them with examples from European and American conflicts. Consequently, it was no accident that when the time came to formulate occupation policy in 1898 the Army republished General Orders 100 and adopted procedures patterned upon those first employed by the Army in Mexico during the 1840s.[4]

While the basic tenets of international law and Lieber's code served as the framework for American occupation policy, Army officers were also influenced by several other intellectual and historical precepts. From American society at large, they brought with them a deep faith in America's political and economic system, a system that they generally believed the rest of the world would do well to emulate. Other elements that made up the typical Army officer's intellectual baggage included Protestant ethics, racist attitudes, social Darwinistic theories, and vague notions of the white man's burden, all of which were prevalent in turn-of-the-century America. To these the officer corps added its own particular conservative creed based upon a respect for authority, a fondness for efficiency and order, and a high regard for such public virtues as honesty, honor, and self-sacrifice. Finally, the Army's approach to "uplifting" benighted peoples was heavily influenced by its own experience in "civilizing" the American Indian and by the reform impulses of contemporary American progressivism. From the former, the Army derived lessons in benevolent paternalism and the firm-but-fair approach to governing "less civilized" peoples. From the latter, it drew a rough blueprint for social engineering in which well-meaning experts, in the guise of Army officers, would bestow upon a grateful society a host of social, political, and economic reforms designed to produce a more efficient and honest government and a more modern, rational, and organized society.[5]

In bringing reform to Spain's former colonies, the Army not only implemented the Progressive impulse, but blazed new trails in government activism that Progressives at home were destined to follow. On the other hand, while progressivism and the military's own "can do" spirit inspired the aggressive way in which it tackled nation-building tasks, there were other American values that acted as equally strong constraints upon Army activities. Thus, while the Army provided free emergency assistance to the needy, it preferred that recipients be made to work for their dole. In economic matters, the Army's activities were both shaped and limited by the standards of laissez-faire capitalism, while its respect for private property, one of the most sacrosanct of American tenets, prevented officers from dabbling in schemes of land redistribution and agrarian reform that might have helped redress some of the deepest social and economic inequities of the islands, just as similar attitudes had limited federal action during Reconstruction.

Insightful officers realized that drastic changes were necessary to transform the exploitative oligarchies of Spain's former colonies into open societies, but they wanted change to be a quiet, evolutionary process, one in which the government would provide as much of a level playing field as possible without infringing upon anyone's personal or property rights. After that, it would be up to the people to pull themselves up "by their bootstraps" in the finest American tradition. Whether such a program could succeed, given the socioeconomic conditions of the islands, remained to be seen. Nevertheless, it is questionable whether the Army could have taken a more activist stand than it did under the prevailing values and philosophies of turn-of-the-century America.[6]

One thing upon which all officers agreed was that educational reform was the key to the success or failure of the entire nation-building program. Not only did they consider public education to be vital for the maintenance of efficient public and private institutions, but they regarded it as the fount of individual self-improvement, economic prosperity, and social mobility. Public education was the ultimate solution to breaking down the economic and political domination of the old colonial oligarchies and opening the island societies up to an ever-increasing level of social and political democracy. By planting the seed of universal public education, the Army believed it was laying the groundwork for a gradual evolution in the political, social, and economic structure of Spain's former colonies.

Achieving such changes was not simply a matter of teaching the inhabitants reading, writing, and arithmetic. Rather, education's greatest mission was to inculcate civic virtues. Both Secretary of War Elihu Root and his uniformed subordinates believed that the most difficult obstacle to introducing American-style democracy was the absence of any sense of civic responsibility among the majority of Spain's former subjects. Centuries of colonial government had imbued them with the notion that government was naturally corrupt and exploitative and that its prime purpose was to dole out patronage and protect the existing sociopolitical structure. This heritage, combined with the excitable temper supposedly exhibited by Latin cultures, were the primary causes, in Root's opinion, for the "continual revolutions" that wracked Latin American countries. Only by inculcating a sense of civic responsibility and self-control could the islanders be saved from themselves.[7]

Root believed that it would take years—if not generations—of "tuition under a strong and guiding hand" to instill a sense of civic virtue in America's insular wards because "it is a matter not of intellectual apprehension, but of character and of acquired habits of thought and feeling."[8] The Army's frontier veterans concurred in this assessment, for they fully appreciated the difficulties inherent in trying to alter an alien culture. But while they believed that achieving a change in values was the *sine qua non* of the entire nation-building process, they were also cognizant of the fact that such changes could not be achieved by riding roughshod over the customs and traditions of the indigenous population. The *Army and Navy Journal* advised its readers in 1899,

We must rid ourselves of the prejudices of race, of religion and of social customs and the disposition to deal as "niggers" with people we consider inferior because they are different, and thus plant in their breasts the seeds of undying prejudice and race antagonisms. . . . Putting Cubans, Porto Ricans [*sic*], or Filipinos into panatoons and pantalettes and teaching them the catechism does not transform them into Americans, and interference with their customs and habits of living is only to be tolerated when the change is so obviously an improvement that this will in the end be so recognized by the subjects of reform.[9]

Root agreed, informing his subordinates to

bear in mind that the government which they are establishing is designed not for our satisfaction or for the expression of our theoretical views, but for the happiness, peace, and prosperity of the people . . . and the measures adopted should be made to conform to their customs, their habits, and even their prejudices, to the fullest extent consistent with the accomplishment of the indispensable requisites of just and effective government.[10]

Rather than rushing to impose contemporary American institutions for which the people were unprepared, the nation's military leaders preferred to work through intermediary stages, much as they had proposed for the American Indian. The Army's theory of nation building thus rested upon an ability to respect native customs while gradually inculcating new values that would be more supportive of modern, democratic institutions. In practice, it proved to be an almost impossible task.

The Military Government of Cuba, 1898–1902

Cuba was in shambles when Maj. Gen. John R. Brooke officially took control of the island from departing Spanish officials in January 1899. Three years of rebellion and eight months of war had left the country impoverished. Commerce was at a standstill, agriculture in disarray, and many homes and villages had either been abandoned or destroyed. Driven by poverty and unemployment, bandits roamed freely throughout the countryside. Nor did the political situation offer much solace. Although Cuba's political and administrative institutions were woefully inadequate for the task, many Cubans were anxious to obtain the independence for which they had sacrificed so much, and the presence of 50,000 guerrilla fighters of the Cuban Army of Liberation outside of Havana gave weight to their sentiments. The outbreak of an insurrection against American authority in the Philippines under similar circumstances gave Brooke, who had only 11,000 American soldiers at his disposal, further cause for caution. With Washington still undecided over annexation, Brooke felt constrained to adopt a moderate path, establishing American control without taking any action that would irrevocably commit the United States to any particular course of action in regard to Cuba's future.

Brooke's first task was to establish the machinery of military government. For the most part he preferred to rule through civil, rather than military, channels. Cubans, assisted by U.S. military and civilian personnel, headed most of the departments of the central government. In the countryside, Brooke created four geographical departments headed by general officers who wielded much authority, but whose civil affairs role gradually diminished as the Army established native provincial governors who were responsible directly to Havana. Nevertheless, while the Army governed largely through native officials, there never was any doubt that it was the Americans who were making all of the policy decisions.

Having created the framework of government, Brooke defused the potentially explosive situation around Havana by getting the Cuban revolutionary army to demobilize. He achieved this by paying the soldiers' wages, handing out bonuses for surrendered arms, and giving several thousand discharged veterans jobs either in the military government or in the newly formed Rural Guard, which, with American advisers, was given primary responsibility for maintaining law and order in the countryside.[11]

Over the course of his year-long tenure as governor, Brooke provided efficient government services to Cuba. He maintained law and order, gave wartime refugees emergency assistance, enforced new sanitation codes, and built roads, sewers, and schools. Following legal precedent as well as the evolutionary principles of nation building widely espoused throughout the Army, he instituted incremental changes in Cuban law and government, rather than trying to rapidly make over Cuba on the American model. Nevertheless, his cautious approach attracted criticism from ambitious subordinates who wished not only to have his job, but to use it to promote more aggressive measures aimed at furthering the Americanization, and possibly annexation, of Cuba. These criticisms eventually influenced the McKinley administration which, while it had finally decided against annexation, firmly believed that the soon-to-be independent island would benefit from a greater dose of American values and methods. Consequently, in December 1899 Secretary Root replaced Brooke with one of the Army's leading Armed Progressives, Maj. Gen. Leonard Wood.

Wood brought a new spirit to the governorship, one that embraced a greater degree of government activism for the purpose of uplifting and reforming Cuban society. Though mindful of the obstacles inherent in trying to instill foreign values and institutions into an indigenous culture, a combination of personal ambition, ethnocentrism, and a philosophical commitment to the Progressive creed drove Wood to bestow upon Cuba as many of the fruits of American civilization as possible before Washington ended the occupation. Building upon many of Brooke's initiatives, Wood turned Cuba into a "workshop for American progressivism." Between 1900 and 1902 he spent $15 million on public works, paving streets, erecting buildings, and refurbishing harbors.

In doing so, he not only improved the island's economic infrastructure, but put thousands of unemployed men to work, thereby helping to dissipate potential social unrest. In line with the military's prevailing philosophy that education and the inculcation of Western values held the key to political, cultural, and economic regeneration, Wood established Cuba's first public library and built thousands of schools, organized according to the laws of the state of Ohio and partially staffed with American-trained Cuban teachers. He continued Brooke's efforts in health and sanitation reform, attacking dangerous diseases and overhauling Cuba's medical and mental health care systems. Finally, the military government gradually modernized and liberalized Cuba's legal and administrative system. It attacked graft and corruption and established more vigorous local governments in the belief that democracy naturally developed first at the grass-roots level. Though still adhering to many Spanish forms, the Army introduced several key American legal concepts, such as *habeas corpus* and trial by jury, while crafting municipal charters that would have gladdened the heart of many an urban reformer at home.[12]

The U.S. Army achieved much before it handed the reins of government over to the Cuban Republic and set sail for home in May 1902. Wood was hailed as the very embodiment of a modern major general, one who could not only destroy nations, but build them. Yet many of the Army's achievements proved superficial. No sooner had the Americans left than matters rapidly began to deteriorate. The roads were not maintained, public services declined, and democratic institutions decayed. Rather than transform Cuba, all the Army had really done was to impose a thin veneer of American-style institutions for which there was very little support from within Cuban society itself.

Many factors contributed to the failure of the Army's nation-building programs to take root. Part of the problem was that Wood had attempted to move too quickly. Nor had the Army always been successful in adhering to its enlightened policy of respecting native culture. Ethnocentrism proved to be a powerful force, and all too often American soldiers used their position of authority to impose their moral and ethical values upon a resentful people. But cultural arrogance on the part of American officials was not the only problem. Traditions of patronage, corruption, and authoritarianism created an unfavorable climate for political reforms that required a certain level of civic responsibility to flourish. Even the most fundamental concepts, such as *habeas corpus* and trial by jury, quickly withered in Cuba because they did not fit easily into traditional Roman law. A similar fate befell many of the Army's health and sanitation programs, which the Cubans readily abandoned as soon as the Army had withdrawn. Ultimately, history and culture conspired to make Cuba infertile ground for many transplanted institutions, regardless of their particular merits. Cultural barriers on both sides thus contributed to the demise of many of the Army's best-intentioned works.

The Army had unwittingly contributed to the shallowness of the institutions it planted in Cuba, for its top-down management style had given the indigenous population very little say over fundamental policy decisions. Moreover, frustration with corrupt and incompetent native officials had eventually led Wood to consolidate power in the hands of the central government to ensure that his programs were carried out as intended. This response, while both understandable and perhaps inevitable, undermined efforts to establish independent local governments and grass-roots democratic institutions. Moreover, the prevailing conservatism of American social and political philosophy ended up strengthening, rather than weakening, the power and position of the traditional elites, to whom American soldiers and politicians with middle- and upper-class values instinctively turned for the provision of stable political and economic leadership. Despite a greater openness to embrace government activism, neither American politicians nor their military proconsuls were any more willing than their Reconstruction-era predecessors to fundamentally alter existing patterns of land and property ownership, patterns that perpetuated conditions of poverty and exploitation throughout much of rural Cuba. In the end, the educational reforms proved to be too modest, the economic conditions in the islands too oppressive, and the newly transplanted democratic institutions too weak and unfamiliar to allow the type of bootstrap social, political, and economic "revolution" that American officers had hoped would occur. Instead, the old social and political culture, in which patron-client relationships governed the way people lived, worked, and voted and government posts were regarded as sinecures, continued to shape the reality of insular life despite the veneer of republican institutions erected by the United States.[13]

America's first venture into overseas nation building thus proved to be a disappointment. Nor did it prove any easier in Puerto Rico and the Philippines, where civilian colonial administrators labored for decades to create stable and economically prosperous democratic societies on the American model.[14] In fairness, it should be remembered that Army leaders had always recognized that the new institutions they brought to the tropical isles could never survive unless accompanied by a corresponding change in cultural values, something they believed would take generations to achieve. Time, however, was a luxury the Army did not have. The continuous agitation of the Cubans, Filipinos, and Puerto Ricans for greater independence received a receptive hearing from many Americans. Steeped in the principles of liberty and self-determination, much of the American public felt uncomfortable at the prospect of maintaining the type of lengthy stewardship necessary to fundamentally change Cuban society, if such a change was possible at all. Nor was an antimilitaristic nation any more willing to trust the long-term tutelage of Cubans to uniformed officers than it had been in the case of the American Indian. Even in the Philippines and Puerto Rico, the U.S. government moved rapidly to create local civilian self-rule, albeit under American governors. Under such circumstances, Army officers found that they had very little leverage.

Ultimately, the nation's soldier-administrators had but two methods they could use in uplifting America's insular wards. Persuasion and incrementalism, though the more enlightened strategy, proved frustrating, time consuming, and offered no guarantee of success. Compulsion, while certainly quicker and easier, often bred hostility and rejection. These were the horns of a dilemma on which American officials, both within the military and without, were destined to find themselves in many of the country's future nation-building endeavors.

The Philippine War, 1899–1902

The Army's efforts at nation building in Cuba and Puerto Rico were relatively peaceful affairs. Such was not the case in the Philippines, an archipelago of 7,000 islands and over seven million people divided among a patchwork of tribal, linguistic, and religious groups, many of which disliked the other. (*Map 2*) At the time Spain ceded the Philippines to the United States in December 1898, the Army actually controlled only the colony's capital city, Manila. The remainder of the archipelago was dominated by Filipino revolutionaries, primarily of the Tagalog tribe, who, with some assistance from the United States, had seized the opportunity provided by the Spanish-American War to rise up against their Spanish overlords. Unlike Cuba, where the United States had been able to persuade the indigenous rebel forces to disband, the Filipino revolutionaries refused to acknowledge American authority over the islands. Instead, under the leadership of Emilio Aguinaldo, they proclaimed their own government and surrounded Manila with an army. In February 1899 fighting erupted on the outskirts of Manila, while Filipino fifth columnists staged an abortive uprising inside the city itself. The Philippine War was on, a war that would last over three years and cost the United States $400 million and over seven thousand casualties.[15]

MAP 2

Operations during the Philippine rainy season were particularly difficult.

Aguinaldo initially opted to fight a conventional war, but by November 1899 U.S. forces under the command of Maj. Gen. Elwell Otis had crushed his army and forced him to flee into the mountains of northern Luzon. Rather than surrender, Aguinaldo abandoned the conventional approach in favor of guerrilla warfare. The switch was a well-considered one. The Philippine Islands were a labyrinth of rice paddies, mountains, jungles, and dense stretches of towering cogon grass pierced only by rough trails and a few primitive roads. In this arena, the Filipino guerrillas enjoyed numerous advantages over their American opponent, not the least of which were their familiarity with the terrain and people and their acclimation to the region's tropical climate. Moreover, several Filipino commanders had employed guerrilla tactics in an unsuccessful revolution against Spain in 1896–1897 and were therefore somewhat experienced in the intricacies of this type of warfare. The revolutionary command reinforced this capability by issuing instructions explaining the hit-and-run philosophy of guerrilla warfare and the tactical methods to be employed in waging it.[16]

Aguinaldo organized his forces into a number of highly autonomous regional commands, each of which included a core of full-time "regular" guerrillas backed by part-time militiamen. Together, these forces waged a war of ambushes, raids, and surprise attacks

Soldiers of the Philippine insurgent army on a firing line

designed to keep the Americans off-balance. Although some guerrillas wore uniforms, many did not, and even those who did freely changed into civilian clothes and hid their weapons to disguise their true identity from American patrols. This "chameleon act," whereby the guerrillas transformed themselves into obsequious "amigos" in the blink of an eye, made them difficult to counter, especially given the Army's lack of familiarity with Filipino language and customs.[17]

Complementing the guerrillas in the field was a clandestine civil-military organization or infrastructure that acted as a shadow government in the villages, enforcing insurgent edicts, raising recruits, collecting supplies and "taxes," and gathering intelligence on American activities. In some areas the infrastructure was based on secret societies that dated back to Spanish days, like the revolutionary Katipunan society, or mystic religious sects like the Colorum. Since many of the leaders of the resistance were from the middle- and upper-class elite (*principales*), they were able to exploit the oligarchical nature of Philippine society and the system of patron-client relationships upon which it was based to further the movement's influence over the people. Using a complex mixture of genuine nationalism, paternalism, xenophobic propaganda, superstition, and terror (including the assassination of "Americanistas"), the leaders of the resistance maintained their control over the population despite their inability to defeat the American Army in the field.[18]

In fact, military victory was never the aim of Filipino leaders after 1899. Instead, they hoped to undermine America's will to continue the struggle by harassing U.S. military forces. The Filipinos were well aware that many Americans opposed the government's adventure in imperialism, and they consciously played to this audience, timing their offensives to coincide with the presidential election of November 1900 in the hope that a disenchanted electorate would replace McKinley with the avowed anti-imperialist, William Jennings Bryan.[19]

Thus the U.S. Army faced a formidable challenge in the Filipino resistance movement, incorporating as it did many of the characteristics of a modern guerrilla movement, including a politico-military organization, military and paramilitary units, and a strategy of political and guerrilla warfare. Although poorly armed and lacking a revolutionary ideology to mobilize fully the masses in its support, the movement's dexterous employment of patriotic appeals, terror, propaganda, and patron-client relationships enabled it to keep the insurrection alive for several years.

Counterinsurgency Techniques of the Philippine War

Faced with the task of conquering and civilizing a "savage" foe, the Army's senior leadership naturally turned to those principles that had long guided the old frontier constabulary. The Filipinos, wrote Brig. Gen. Theodore Schwan in the fall of 1899, "are in identically the same position as the Indians of our country have been for many years, and in my opinion must be subdued in much the same way, by such convincing conquest as shall make them realize fully the futility of armed resistance, and then win them by fair and just treatment."[20]

Achieving a "convincing conquest" over an irregular foe in a strange land required the Army to demonstrate the same type of adaptability with which it had approached irregular warfare on the western frontier. In this it was highly successful, despite the fact that most junior officers had never seen combat prior to 1898. The key to the Army's successful performance during the war stemmed from two factors. At the junior officer level, officers demonstrated a willingness to learn by trial and error that enabled them to adjust their methods according to the situations that they faced, much as Wagner and other prewar instructors had hoped they would. At the senior levels of command, most division, department, brigade, and regimental commanders were old Army hands who brought to the islands experience in either the Civil or Indian Wars, if not both. While neither experience was directly applicable to the situation in the Philippines, both endowed the Army with important legacies that would shape the conduct of the war. From the Civil War, veterans and young officers alike drew inspiration and guidance from Lieber's code and Sherman's deeds, both of which had been emblazoned in the Army's collective consciousness. From the frontier, the men who directed the operational level of the Philippine War brought with them a mind-set that was accustomed to conducting small-unit constabulary operations from dispersed posts and that encouraged adaptability, individual initiative, and aggressiveness. These attributes contributed much more to the Army's success than did the transference of any specific techniques of Indian-fighting or prairie fieldcraft, few of which could be directly applied in the Philippine's tropical jungles. By blending old concepts with techniques adapted to the situation at hand, the old frontier Army successfully adjusted to the demands of overseas constabulary service.

One feature of frontier service that had applicability to the Philippines was the necessity of dispersing one's forces for the purpose of protecting the population, maintaining a presence in troubled areas, and providing bases for prompt, offensive action. Although Otis underestimated the depth of Filipino opposition, ascribing the resistance that followed the destruction of the Filipino Army to the work of bandits and the machinations of a few unprincipled leaders, he nevertheless recognized that true pacification could only be achieved by controlling the people and isolating them from the militants. Consequently, he responded to Aguinaldo's switch from conventional to guerrilla warfare by dispersing his forces as well. As on the western frontier, the dispersal was not undertaken without significant costs in terms of logistics, administration, communications, and security, but the Army's senior leadership, accustomed to such deployments, instinctively recognized the necessity. As the Army spread its control over the archipelago, the number of posts grew exponentially from several dozen at the outbreak of the guerrilla phase in December 1899 to 639 two years later.[21]

Dispersion did not mean, however, the adoption of a defensive posture. Rather, the Army used its many posts as bases from which to launch an aggressive campaign reminiscent of its counterguerrilla operations of the previous century. Col. William E. Birkhimer expressed the Army's basic strategy in words that could just have easily been spoken by Miles or Crook twenty years before.

The object was to make things as uncomfortable as possible for the enemy, thus pursuing the policy which alone, apparently, will break down the rebel resistance, namely, the wearing-out policy; pounding away until the bandit chiefs get tired of living in hiding in the far distant mountains, and the people wearying of their importunate demands for money and their impotent military efforts, withdraw their material and moral support for them.[22]

The insistence with which field commanders pushed their subordinates into taking the offensive rested partially on the belief that psychological factors played an especially important role in irregular warfare. "Savage" races were particularly excitable, went the conventional wisdom, and the worst thing soldiers could do was to show any sign of weakness or hesitancy, for such displays would only encourage the inhabitants to redouble their efforts. On the other hand, a clear and convincing display of military superiority and confidence by the Army, it was believed, would dispirit the impressionable natives and speed their eventual submission.[23]

Operationally, the Army conducted itself in much the same way as it had against irregular opponents during the Civil and Indian Wars. Although it occasionally engaged in large-scale cordon-and-sweep campaigns, the most common operation of the Philippine War was the "hike," a combination of what would later be termed *reconnaissance-in-force* and *search-and-destroy* missions. Similar to the "scout" of the Plains wars, most hikes featured small columns of fifty to a hundred men that combed the countryside for signs of guerrillas and their base camps (*cuartels*), which were destroyed on discovery. In performing these missions, the Army demonstrated the same willingness to adapt to unconventional conditions which it had shown on the Plains and which the advocates of the "new" military science like Bigelow and Wagner found so admirable. It quickly modified conventional tactics to take advantage of Filipino weaknesses and developed new march, camp, and outpost procedures to meet the exigencies of guerrilla and jungle warfare. Within a few months after the Filipinos had switched to guerrilla warfare, many American commands were already operating at night, laying ambushes and launching expeditions for the purpose of surrounding and surprising an insurgent encampment or village at dawn. Raids of this nature were commonly referred to as "roundups" and quickly became standard throughout the Philippines.[24]

Army commanders soon discovered that mobility was just as important in this irregular conflict as in those of the past, and they pursued it with the same aggressiveness. By the winter of 1899 commanders had begun to jettison heavy packs and other impediments, establish mule pack trains, and employ indigenous means of transport like water buffalos (*carabaos*) and native bearers (*cagadores*). The search for mobility also led the Army to increase the number of cavalry serv-

An infantry unit on a hike. Forces of this size were the standard operational element during the war; below, *American infantrymen on patrol riding native ponies.*

ing in the Philippines and to create special detachments of mounted infantry and scouts. Virtually every infantry regiment in the Philippines raised such detachments. As in the Civil and Indian Wars, these units consisted of handpicked men who were accorded elite status and spared routine chores. They bore the brunt of the counterguerrilla war, acting in reconnaissance, strike, and mobile reserve capacities, functions in which they quickly developed an expertise.[25]

One of the best methods of opposing partisan forces, opined one West Point text, was to employ "forces of a similar character," and most officers readily agreed.[26] Old frontier hands recognized that the native soldiers' familiarity with the terrain, people, and language of the region gave them an edge over American troops in constabulary operations. They also appreciated, as had Crook and Bigelow, that the recruitment of native auxiliaries facilitated the implementation of a divide-and-conquer strategy, especially since the Filipino insurgents, like the American Indian before them, found it particularly demoralizing to learn that their own people had turned against them. European employment of native soldiers in overseas colonies, the relative inexpensiveness of native troops as opposed to American soldiers, the baleful effects that tropical service had on the health of white soldiers, and serious manpower shortages also contributed to the Army's willingness to employ Filipino soldiers.

Although the Army began recruiting Filipino auxiliaries before the outbreak of the insurrection, it moved cautiously. Operating in an unfamiliar environment against enemies whose true allegiances were not always readily apparent, prudence dictated that only the most reliable individuals be enrolled in American service. This not only slowed recruitment, but meant that the Army frequently restricted enlistments to groups deemed especially loyal. Most notable among these were the Macabebes, a tribe whose long-standing hatred for the largely pro-revolutionary Tagalog tribe was well known.

Recruiting Macabebes and similar groups had the additional benefit of undermining Filipino unity by exploiting preexisting fractures in Filipino society. This advantage was not obtained without cost, however. As in America's previous irregular conflicts, local auxiliaries were prone to committing acts of brutality that contravened the achievement of pacification. Indeed, it was primarily for this reason that Otis restricted the growth of Filipino troops. Eventually, however, the Army decided that the advantages to be gained by employing Filipinos outweighed the drawbacks, and by the end of the war the government had at its disposal over fifteen thousand native auxiliaries organized into units of light infantry (Philippine Scouts), paramilitary police

A detachment of Macabebe scouts in American service

(Philippine Constabulary), and local police, not to mention a number of volunteer militia organizations.[27]

The adaptations which the Army made in the Philippines and the aggressiveness with which it operated made it a highly capable and dangerous opponent. Yet it soon found that relentless military activity was not sufficient to overcome the guerrillas. Most hikes failed to come to grips with the enemy as the guerrillas' superior intelligence system kept them well informed of American activities. The more astute officers realized relatively early in the war that they would have to crack the insurgents' clandestine infrastructure if they were ever to have a chance at apprehending the guerrillas and breaking their control over the population. Toward this end, local commanders began establishing networks of secret agents as early as the winter of 1899, and by the spring of 1900 the practice was becoming increasingly common.

As the war progressed, the Army devoted an ever-increasing amount of attention to intelligence and counterinfrastructure activities. It used Philippine Scouts, spies, and informants to gather information and identify suspects. It conducted frequent roundups of villages suspected of harboring guerrillas, created a special agency to translate captured guerrilla documents, and employed a number of techniques to

American infantrymen advance in standard single-file formation down a Filipino road.

monitor the movement and activities of the population. Included among these techniques were the issuance of identity cards and travel passes, the compilation of census records, and the development of intelligence files bearing, when available, photographs of key insurgent leaders.[28]

As in the Mexican and Civil Wars, military commissions and provost courts played an integral role in the battle against the guerrilla infrastructure, and consequently it was the local provost officer who often bore primary responsibility for intelligence and counterinfrastructure operations. Some officers, like 1st Lt. William T. Johnston and Maj. Edwin F. Glenn, developed reputations as specialists in this line of work. They shuttled around the Philippines, undertaking especially difficult cases and giving seminars in their methods. The Army gradually augmented its local intelligence efforts by creating regional and eventually "national" systems, yet the real heart of the Army's intelligence effort remained at the local level. This decentralized approach worked well, given the fact that the resistance movement was itself largely decentralized in nature.[29]

Pacification: The Policy of Attraction

By blending a recognition for the need to control and protect the population with an aggressive counterguerrilla and intelligence campaign, the Army performed ably with regard to the military aspects of the Philippine War. Yet, achieving a "convincing conquest" was only half of the Army's strategy for winning the conflict. U.S. military and political authorities had recognized from the start that political affairs would play an important role in achieving the final pacification of the Philippines—a point President McKinley made clear in the winter of 1898 when he directed General Otis to "win the confidence, respect, and admiration of the inhabitants of the Philippines."

In executing these instructions, Otis, a graduate of the Harvard Law School, an expert on the Indian question, and one of the Army's Armed Progressives, was influenced by the same set of factors that shaped Army policies in the Caribbean. While the principles of contemporary progressivism provided inspiration, Otis' basic formula for dealing with the Filipinos—"simply to keep scrupulous faith with these people and teach them to trust us"—was clearly a legacy of the frontier. Similarly, Otis followed the course laid out by Birkhimer's *Military Government and Martial Law*, which noted that in the Mexican and Civil Wars the United States had endeavored to avoid resorting to the harshest of measures permitted by the laws of war because "by a policy of forbearance it was hoped ultimately to convert the people, including the insurgents, into loyal citizens." Such a policy seemed natural, for as Brig. Gen. J. Franklin Bell explained, "Government by force alone cannot be satisfactory to Americans. It is desirable that a Government be established in time which is based upon the will of the governed. This can be accomplished satisfactorily only by obtaining and retaining the good will of the people." A confluence of enlightened self-interest, historical precedent, genuine humanity, progressive reform impulses, and traditional American ideals lay behind the Army's commitment to benevolent pacification in the Philippines.[30]

As the Army spread out over the Philippine archipelago, Otis and his commanders in the field followed these precepts closely. Ordering their men to respect the people and their customs, they imposed strict discipline, forbidding looting and wanton destruction and punishing those who committed such crimes. They paid in cash for supplies requisitioned from the populace, in an effort to win its favor and counter

The policy of attraction: American soldiers feeding Filipino children.

the mistrust engendered by insurgent propaganda. They opened schools staffed with soldier volunteers, built roads, refurbished markets and other public facilities, and inaugurated a general effort to sanitize towns across the Philippines. Finally, the Army established municipal governments under native officials that were largely based upon Spanish traditions, both to provide basic governmental services to the community and to demonstrate America's commitment to political autonomy for the Philippines at the local level.[31]

Maj. Gen. Arthur MacArthur, who succeeded Otis as military governor and commander of the Department of the Philippines in May 1900, continued his predecessor's campaign of benevolent pacification. As Otis had done, MacArthur instructed his subordinates to release Filipino soldiers soon after their capture. He instituted a generous amnesty program, offering thirty pesos to anyone who voluntarily surrendered a rifle. Although the Army could have brought every Filipino combatant and every civilian who actively aided the resistance before a military commission as insurgents, guerrillas, and war rebels, it preferred to try only the major leaders and those suspected of committing major crimes. Even those who were placed on trial had little to fear, as reviewing officials in Manila habitually overturned death sentences and reduced prison terms handed out by local

American soldiers detailed as teachers with their Filipino students

military commissions. Indeed, the Army treated guerrillas so leniently that common bandits hastened to claim that they too were guerrillas, deserving similar treatment.[32]

As in the Caribbean, the nation's Asian proconsuls firmly believed that public education was the ultimate solution to the problem of transforming societies, and consequently they moved ahead with an aggressive education program despite the continuance of hostilities. By August 1900 the Army had established no fewer than 1,000 schools and had spent $100,000 on pedagogical supplies and facilities. General MacArthur justified such endeavors as not only a step in the long-term elevation of Philippine society, but also as "an adjunct to military operations, calculated to pacify the people and procure and expedite the restoration of tranquility throughout the archipelago." He considered the "rapid extension of educational facilities as an exclusively military measure."[33]

The Army's many pacification programs placed heavy burdens on small-unit commanders who, without the benefit of additional staff, had to oversee local governments and orchestrate civil affairs activities while attending to routine administrative and operational duties. Many had neither the ability nor the desire to do all these things, and under such leaders the management of civil affairs invariably suffered. On the other hand, there were many officers, perhaps the majority during 1899–1900, who put in an honest effort in the hope that, by demonstrating to the Filipinos the benefits of American rule, they could hasten the end of the insurrection. Such men often supplemented the general policies emanating from Manila with programs of their own. Maj. Henry T. Allen not only established schools in his district but also solicited schoolbooks by making a private appeal through a New York newspaper. Others detailed their surgeons to look after the local populace because they, like Col. Cornelius Gardener, believed that "just mere pills will be more effective than bullets in undermining the insurgent leaders' authority."[34]

Yet, extraordinary measures were not necessary to make benevolent pacification work. American officials liked to talk about how new roads, schools, and governments were making mass conversions among the populace, but in fact what lay at the heart of the policy was much simpler than that. As Capt. John R. M. Taylor, the author of the Army's official history of the Philippine War, conceded, it was not the allure of democratic ideology or even the promise of a bright and prosperous future that won over the people in the barrios. Rather, it was the local garrison commander's force of character that won or lost the day. Where he spoke with authority and governed like a benevolent patron, he acted in ways which the people could understand and respect. Only when they were convinced that the American officer had the character, the will, and the means to protect them did they begin to submit themselves to American authority. In this sense, pacification was a very personal affair, in which the "allegiance of whole communities was transferred from the guerrillas to a young American, not because he represented principles of which they knew nothing, of which it was impossible for them to know anything, but because he was a man."[35]

While overburdened young officers wrestled with the many military and civil aspects of pacification in the backcountry, the McKinley administration decided to enhance the appeal of American rule even further by moving to replace the military government in Manila with a civilian one. In the fall of 1900 Washington transferred legislative powers in the Philippines from the military to a body of civilian commissioners, thereby splitting authority in the islands. Full civilian government was instituted throughout most of the archipelago in mid-1901, when William Howard Taft assumed the post of governor general, although the Army retained control over a few of the most recalcitrant areas for an additional year.

The civilian government complemented the Army's pacification efforts in many ways. Building upon Army initiatives, it passed a variety of legislation designed to improve the economic and social conditions on the islands. It instituted civil courts, revamped municipal governments, and created new provincial-level governments as well. The civilian commissioners were also instrumental in promoting the development of the Federal Party, a political organization of Filipino collaborators whose mission was to spark a "counterrevolution" that would mobilize the population in support of American rule.[36]

For all of its good work, Army officers deeply resented the establishment of civilian government in the Philippines prior to the termination of the insurrection. Most officers held the principle of unity of command to be sacrosanct and objected vehemently to the intrusion of civilians into an active theater of operations. Although the new civilian government remained under the overall control of the War Department in Washington, relieving some of the friction that had characterized the management of Indian affairs, personal and bureaucratic rivalries inevitably arose between soldiers and civilians, neither of whom particularly trusted the other. The Army further complained that the shift to civilian rule was premature and that it needlessly complicated military operations by imposing not only a new layer of bureaucracy, but peacetime restrictions, such as *habeas corpus*, which were inappropriate during an insurrection. The progressive establishment of civilian rule in 1900–1901 had less to do with a well-considered pacification strategy, they argued, than with domestic politics, for by shifting power to civilians the government deflected a certain amount of criticism of the war and created the impression that all was going well in the Philippines. And this, the Army knew, was not entirely true.[37]

The Army's benevolent policies had achieved some positive results during the early stages of the war, especially in those parts of the archipelago that had never been firmly committed to the rebellion. Indeed, the war was only a few months old when Filipino resistance leaders openly began to worry that America's "policy of attraction" might undermine the commitment of the population to the insurgent cause. Yet, by the spring of 1900 it was already becoming evident that the policy of attraction was not powerful enough to win the war by itself.

There were several reasons why this was the case. To begin with, U.S. military authorities were never able to stamp out completely instances of unauthorized foraging, drunkenness, and disorderly conduct among their own men—actions that, no matter how minor, created an undercurrent of tension between Americans and Filipinos. Filipino-American relations were further complicated by linguistic and cultural barriers, not to mention the virulent racism which Americans of all ranks brought with them from their parent society. Some officers

Army bands frequently put on concerts for the local population as part of the policy of attraction.

recognized the corrosive effects of what Brig. Gen. Thomas M. Anderson called "good natured condescension," but they were unable to change those attitudes. The best they could do was to enforce strict discipline to minimize the potential ill effects of racially or criminally motivated conduct.[38]

Although racist attitudes and individual misconduct doubtlessly aggravated relations between soldiers and Filipino civilians, such behavior did not prove fatal to the pacification campaign, if for no other reason than the conduct of Filipino guerrillas was often equally deplorable. As in the American Army, many Filipino commanders demanded impeccable conduct on behalf of their men. Yet loose supervision, an irregular commissary, tensions between differing Filipino social and tribal groups, and in some cases outright banditry, all reduced guerrilla relations with the population to a level that was not much better than Filipino-American relations.

Ironically, another reason why U.S. benevolence failed to win over the population was the guerrillas' willingness to use intimidation, violence, and terror in their dealings with civilians. "Nothing that we can offer in the way of peace or prosperity weighs against their fear of assassination which is prosecuted with relentless vigor against any one giving aid or information to the government," lamented Brig. Gen. Samuel S. Sumner. Although the Army endeavored to protect the population from terrorism, the rebel infrastructure was often too deep, the people too afraid, and the Army's resources too slim to accomplish this effectively. Moreover, the meekness with which the Army punished insurgents—setting prisoners free and engaging in cumbersome legal procedures in which superior authorities often downgraded court sentences—appeared to the ordinary Filipino as the epitome of folly compared to the swift, uncompromising justice meted out to Americanistas by the guerrillas. Until the Americans could convince the people that they were strong enough to protect their friends and punish their enemies, the Filipinos saw little reason to risk their lives for "Uncle Sam."[39]

Perhaps the most important reason why the policy of attraction failed to end the war was that American officials had made a twin miscalculation. On the one hand, Otis greatly underestimated the depth of the rebellion. Like Lincoln during the Civil War, he made the mistake of believing that the rebellion rested solely upon a small coterie of self-interested oligarchs, unscrupulous demagogues, and bandit chieftains. These few individuals, he thought, had duped and terrorized the people into following them in their misguided quest for independence. Overthrow the leaders and demonstrate to the masses the benefits of American rule and the revolt, Otis and his subordinates believed, would quickly collapse. Although Otis was correct in thinking that much of the revolutionary leadership came from the dominant social classes and that large segments of the Filipino population were not truly committed to independence or any other ideology, he miscalculated the appeal and power of the resistance movement. Some Filipinos, including much of the educated elite that provided the bulk of the insurgency's leadership, were truly nationalistic in sentiment, while others found it difficult to overcome their suspicions of American intentions, no matter what protestations of goodwill the Americans might make. Moreover, the very political inertness of the mass of Filipino people and their subordination to their socioeconomic betters meant that they would follow their leaders almost instinctively, regardless of the temptations American officials dangled in front of them. General Bell put the case rather bluntly:

The common *hombre* is dominated body and soul by his master, the *principale*. He is simply a blind tool, a poor down-trodden ignoramus, who does not know what is good for him and cannot believe an American. We cannot appeal to him direct. It is impossible. You can no more influence him by benevolent persuasion than you can a fly. He is going to do whatever he is told to do by his master or his leaders, because he is incapable of doing anything else.[40]

American promises of moderate political reforms, economic growth, and good government made little impression upon the peasant, who could not quite fathom how all this had any immediate relevance to his day-to-day existence. Schools seemed like a nice idea, but many of the other programs that touched him, such as enforced vaccinations and stringent sanitary codes, violated traditional norms and appeared rather Draconian. Some elements of the upper classes found the American program more appealing, for it corresponded with many of their own aspirations, and the program did in fact win converts to the American cause. Yet, the majority of the leaders of the resistance saw no reason why they could not achieve modernization on their own without the help of the United States. Consequently, the rebellion would drag on until the leaders of the resistance were given some compelling incentives to discontinue their activities. When the policy of attraction failed to provide such incentives, the U.S. Army was forced, as it had been in the Mexican and Civil Wars, to turn to more severe methods to crush the insurgency.

Pacification: The Policy of Chastisement

Officers in the field began to pressure authorities in Manila to adopt less benign measures almost immediately after the Filipinos adopted guerrilla warfare. They were well aware that the laws of war took a dim view of this form of conflict. Moreover, textbooks, such as Birkhimer's *Military Government and Martial Law*, made clear that should a population repay an occupier's benevolent deeds with "overt acts or secret plottings," then the military was entitled to take vigorous repressive measures. Among the suitable responses enumerated by GO 100 and military texts were the imposition of fines and communal punishments, the destruction of private property, the exile of individuals and the relocation of populations, imprisonment, and, in the case of guerrillas and their closest civilian allies, execution. During the course of the war the Army eventually resorted to all of these options.[41]

The shift toward more repressive forms of pacification did not occur all at once. Some officers adopted a policy of burning homes and villages in retaliation for Filipino ambuscades during the first days of the war, but instances were relatively rare in 1899 because Otis clearly frowned on such activities. His replacement, General MacArthur, was

The policy of chastisement: A company of the 44th U.S. Volunteer Infantry forms up after destroying a barrio.

more willing to consider stern measures, but he too wanted to give the policy of attraction a chance. Moreover, he was keenly aware that a major change in the direction of Army policy was impolitic during an election year, for it would fuel anti-imperialist criticism and jeopardize the McKinley administration's chances of reelection in November. Consequently, he carefully delayed taking any significant steps toward stiffening Army policy until after the fall vote.[42]

While officials in Manila delayed, officers in the field acted. As the year 1900 progressed, a growing number of local commanders took matters into their own hands, tempering Manila's lenient policies with increasingly punitive measures. One of the first to make the transition was Major Allen. In early 1900 Allen won high praise from his superiors for his adherence to the policy of attraction. Yet, after only a few months he came to the realization that benevolence was not working, for the people regarded American leniency as weakness and were overawed by the guerrillas' ability to strike down their foes. Like Sherman before him, Allen reluctantly came to the conclusion that people were motivated "by fear more than by any other impulse and that I propose to profit by that fact." He decided to stiffen the policy of attraction with what he called the "policy of chastisement." He banned the importation of food into rebel controlled areas and launched punitive campaigns in which he put villages and crops to the torch, punishing the hostile population while destroying the rebels' logistical base.[43]

The policy of chastisement manifested itself in many forms during 1900 as local commanders, impatient with Manila's reluctance to take decisive action, implemented on their own authority the more punitive clauses of General Orders 100. As their predecessors had done in prior conflicts, American field commanders held local officials responsible for insurgent activities and punished communities for failing to notify the Army of the presence of guerrillas. They fined villages for damage done to public property and burned both individual homes and entire villages in retaliation for guerrilla actions. In some districts Army officers supplemented these measures by establishing Draconian curfews that authorized the killing of any man found near a telegraph line or out on the roads at night.[44]

Degrees of retaliation varied greatly from district to district, depending upon the temperament of the commander and the particular politico-military situation in which he found himself. Some commanders held to fairly high standards throughout the conflict. On the island of Mindanao, for example, Maj. E. F. Taggart refused to destroy captured stocks of guerrilla uniforms "for fear that some [clothes] of innocent persons might be among them." Most officers were not so accommodating. Sgt. Mark Evans estimated that by June 1900 the Army had already burnt between 10 to 15 percent of the houses in the province of Bataan, and as the war dragged on other areas received similar treatment.[45]

By the fall of 1900 the policy of attraction had clearly given way to a new and sterner one, if not in theory, then in practice. Even those who had been strong supporters of benevolence now believed that the "milk and water" system of pacification would have to be discarded if the Army was to crush the insurrection, and they clamored for Manila to send a clear signal authorizing the hard war approach.

They did not have long to wait. Once the election was safely behind him, MacArthur formally embraced the policy of chastisement. On 20 December 1900, he issued a proclamation that officially put into effect those sections of General Orders 100 authorizing stern measures against guerrillas and civilian insurgents. He exiled a group of prominent Filipino leaders, terminated the policy of automatically releasing prisoners (although he still exchanged prisoners for guns), and authorized commanders to destroy towns harboring guerrillas and confiscate the property of rebel sympathizers. The Manila command likewise loosened the restraints over the judicial system by authorizing provosts to arrest and detain suspects without evidence and by permitting many condemned prisoners to be executed.[46]

The clear thrust of all of these programs was to give commanders in the field the tools they needed to strike not at the guerrillas in the field, who were kept at bay by the Army's vigorous tactical initiatives, but at the clandestine infrastructure that lay at the heart of the insurrection. Of special interest to MacArthur were the upper classes, for they were the ones who provided much of the insurgent leadership and who, by their status and economic power, dominated Philippine society at large. By making them feel the costs of the war directly—by placing them in jail and threatening them with prosecution as war rebels, by confiscating their property and destroying their crops—MacArthur and his subordinates planned to undermine the Filipino people's will to resist. Thus the Army countered the guerrilla's terror with some intimidation of its own to make "compliance with insurgent demands . . . as dangerous as a refusal."[47]

MacArthur coupled the announcement of the new policies with a fresh offensive. The initiative could not have been better timed. The rainy season had passed, and MacArthur had on hand 70,000 veteran troops, the highest troop level of the war. Moreover, McKinley's reelection had proved a severe blow to the morale of Filipino nationalists whose hopes for independence had been riding on a Bryan victory in November. Disheartened by the election results and wearied by two years of war, the leaders of the rebellion now had to face a new and vigorous offensive aimed directly at them. The number of arrests increased and the number of executions soared. So too did the amount of property destruction, as officers demonstrated an increasing willingness to burn barrios tainted by association with the insurrection.

Indeed, devastation, not just selective retaliatory burnings but the complete destruction of sections of countryside, soon became a hallmark of the counterinsurgency campaign. The scope and intensity of Army incendiary operations varied throughout the archipelago depending on the degree of resistance and the inclinations of local commanders. In their most extreme form they entailed the obliteration of entire areas deemed to be under guerrilla control or strongly sympathetic to the resistance. In such sectors the Army put to the torch homes, villages, storehouses, orchards, crops, livestock, boats, and even fishing nets. By destroying entire areas, field commanders hoped to give the surrounding regions an object lesson in American power that would encourage insurgent collaborators to reconsider their position. More important, devastation was part of a wider military strategy to beat the guerrillas into submission by eliminating all food and shelter in their base areas.[48]

In many cases the Army linked its incineration campaigns with measures designed to increase its control over the civilian population and to deny the guerrillas access to the villages upon which they had always depended for information, recruits, and supplies. U.S. forces imposed land and sea blockades to prevent the movement of food to and from insurgent-dominated regions. In some areas, American commanders confiscated all the food in a district, then doled it out to the local inhabitants to ensure that they would have little left over to pass on to the starving guerrillas in the hills. In others, they regulated the flow of food into the countryside by limiting the amount of hemp or other cash crops each peasant could deliver into town for sale. As conditions worsened in the countryside, refugees flowed into American-controlled towns, and in some cases villagers volunteered to build stockades to keep out the increasingly desperate bands of guerrillas and bandits.[49]

Beginning in late 1900, commanders in several parts of the Philippines also began to experiment with a technique known as concentration, in which they relocated the population to a location where the Army could more readily protect the people from guerrilla intimidation, as well as prevent them from giving the rebels material aid. One early advocate of concentration compared it to the nation's policy of concentrating American Indians on reservations, for it had the same effect of increasing government control and making clear the distinction between friend and foe.

Concentration came in various shapes and sizes, as commanders tailored it to local circumstances. Sometimes the Army forced the people to relocate, but in most cases it made relocation "voluntary." The Army gave people little incentive to stay behind, however, as it made life miserable for those who did by classifying them as enemies and destroying their homes and crops. In one particular section of Cavite Province the Army rounded up all the families of insurgents and relocated them to a town where they could be watched. On the island of Marinduque the Army took a dual approach, first attempting to deport all males of military age, and then concentrating the entire civilian population. On the island of Mindanao, Brig. Gen. William A. Kobbe and Colonel Birkhimer experimented with a type of reverse concentration, in which they expelled all males of military age from towns along the Tagaloan River. Patterns of concentration were equally diverse in the other provinces where the Army employed population relocation during 1900 and 1901.[50]

Regardless of the way in which it was done, the Army treated concentration with extreme delicacy. Stories of the horrible conditions in Spanish concentration camps in Cuba had been one of the factors that had motivated the American people to support the war with Spain. President McKinley had roundly criticized Spain's "cruel policy of concentration." Consequently, Army commanders did not launch any significant concentration campaigns until after the November 1900 elections, and even then they employed euphemisms such as "colonies" and "zones of protection" to masquerade the true nature of their activities. The issue was so sensitive that when Maj. Gen. Adna R. Chaffee forwarded to Adjutant General of the Army Brig. Gen. Henry C. Corbin a plan for a major concentration campaign in southern Luzon in December 1901, he requested that Corbin "hand it to the Secretary to read and then destroy it. I don't care to place on file in the Department any paper of the kind, which would be evidence of what may be considered in the United States as harsh measures or treatment of the people."[51]

Although the Army's methods were severe, its actions generally fell within the parameters permitted by the laws of war. MacArthur insisted that his subordinates stay within the bounds of General Orders 100. Prisoners were still to be well treated, looting and other transgressions by the soldiery punished, and the people treated as kindly as circumstances and their behavior warranted. Yet there is no doubt that as the war progressed American servicemen acted in increasingly callous and sometimes brutal ways. Such behavior was perhaps inevitable, given the circumstances. Deployed in small, isolated detachments under the command of inexperienced junior officers, surrounded by an alien and untrustworthy population with whom they could not communicate, and frustrated by their inability to come to grips with an elusive foe, American soldiers felt the war's corrosive effects both on their morale and their morals. The overly benign policies that had emanated out of Manila during the early stages of the war had unwittingly contributed to the growing harshness by spawning a backlash among the frustrated soldiery.[52]

As their forbearers had done during the Civil War, American soldiers in the Philippines redressed what they regarded as the government's unwarranted leniency by adopting a rough justice of their own. Although they usually treated Filipinos who surrendered on their own accord relatively well, they did not always spare guerrillas met on the field of battle. Moreover, some commanders freely shot unarmed men who ran at the approach of an American column since, in the words of Maj. George S. Anderson, "they probably all deserved it." Soldiers were particularly ill disposed to show leniency after one of their comrades had been murdered. Under such circumstances it was not unknown for columns to deny quarter, summarily execute prisoners, and engage in indiscriminate acts of killing and destruction.[53]

American soldiers and their Filipino auxiliaries also employed torture and other coercive measures to extract information from captured guerrillas and their civilian allies. Only a small percentage of all Filipinos taken prisoner or interrogated by the U.S. Army underwent any form of physical or mental abuse. On the other hand, practices such as forcing large quantities of water down the throats of uncooperative natives (the "water cure"), hanging suspects by ropes (the "rope cure"), denying prisoners food or water, penning prisoners in overcrowded cells, and administering dunkings and beatings occurred more frequently than American authorities cared to admit. Officially, the Army condemned the water cure, which fell under GO 100's proscription of torture. Unofficially, many officers winked at the practice, and military courts proved exceedingly reluctant to punish officers charged with applying coercive methods. As the war progressed the number of incidences of abuse grew as officers, disenchanted by the failure of benevolent policies, came to believe that the "cure" was the only effective way to uproot the guerrilla infrastructure. Even well-known champions of the policy of attraction, like Col. Arthur Murray, eventually conceded that the water cure "might be a good thing if judiciously administered in occasional doses, provided that the antis [anti-imperialists] at home did not find it out."[54]

Although officers can justly be criticized for giving in to the frustrations of the guerrilla campaign and employing unsavory interrogation methods, many of those techniques did not differ materially from the "third degree" commonly practiced by police departments in the United States during the late nineteenth and early twentieth centuries. In beating, grilling, and otherwise abusing certain captives, the Army was imitating law enforcement procedures widely employed in the United States at the same time.[55]

For the most part the campaigns of the winter of 1900 and spring of 1901 were highly successful. With their troops relentlessly hounded by mobile columns of soldiers and Philippine Scouts, their civilian infrastructure picked apart by increasingly effective American intelligence and judicial systems, and portions of the countryside in flames, one major guerrilla commander after another surrendered during the spring of 1901. By the time the United States announced the formation of a civilian government under Taft in July 1901, only two major guerrilla leaders remained at large, General Miguel Malvar, whose base of operations included the provinces of Batangas and Tayabas in southern Luzon, and General Vincente Lukban, who made his home on the island bastion of Samar. Other areas remained troubled, but it was clear that MacArthur's offensive, backed by extensive coercive measures, had turned the tide of the Philippine War.

The task of bringing the war to a close fell upon General Chaffee, who replaced MacArthur as commander of the Department of the

Men of the 35th U.S. Volunteer Infantry demonstrate the water cure.

Philippines in mid-1901. As a young officer, Chaffee had served under Sheridan in the Shenandoah Valley in 1864 and was well aware of how the Army had treated guerrillas and their civilian allies in the past. He had participated in the great sweep of December 1864 when Sheridan's cavalry had put much of the Loudoun Valley to the torch in an effort to root out Mosby's Partisan Rangers. What had been good for American secessionists, Chaffee held, was certainly good for Asians who, in his opinion, placed so little value upon human life that they could be brought to their senses only by a strong demonstration of force. Chaffee not only approved of the use of extreme measures, but replaced squeamish officers with those who were not afraid to "make a wilderness" out of guerrilla-infested regions. The most notable example of this occurred in the fall of 1901 when Chaffee shuffled the command system to place several noted "hardliners" in command of those few provinces that were still in a state of rebellion. He assigned General Bell to overcome Malvar's guerrilla army in Batangas, and Brig. Gen. Jacob H. Smith to oversee the reduction of the island of Samar.[56]

The final campaigns in Batangas and Samar represented the culmination of the policy of chastisement. Like the majority of their colleagues, Bell and Smith had come to the conclusion that the United States had made a great mistake in not making the Filipino people feel

Counterinsurgency Doctrine, 1860–1941

American soldiers and Filipino civilians witness a formal surrender ceremony.

the burdens of war during the early part of the insurrection. Rather than bringing about the end of the rebellion, such "coddling" had only encouraged the unrepentant natives to continue the struggle. Believing, as Sherman had, that "a short and severe war creates, in the aggregate, less loss and suffering than a benevolent war indefinitely prolonged," they set out to create conditions that would keep "the minds of the people in such a state of anxiety and apprehension that living under such conditions will soon become unbearable."[57]

Both Smith and Bell waged particularly ruthless campaigns of concentration and mass destruction. On Samar, Smith established "colonies" along the coast while sending columns of soldiers, marines, and scouts to devastate the island's interior. In southern Luzon, Bell set out "to destroy everything I find outside towns[;] all able-bodied men will be killed or captured." After concentrating several hundred thousand people in "zones of protection," he put the province of Batangas to the torch.

Of the two campaigns, Bell's was better organized and quickly won acclaim throughout the Army as a model counterinsurgency operation. Smith's operations were less well coordinated and were tainted with murky allegations of atrocities that eventually led the Army, under great public pressure, to court-martial him. Nevertheless, both men had been successful despite the human suffering caused by their methods. Smith captured General Lukban in February 1902, and the majority of insurgents on Samar capitulated soon thereafter, while Malvar surrendered to Bell in April. With the last two major figures of the resistance movement in captivity, the United States declared the Philippine War to be officially over on 4 July 1902.[58]

The Legacies of the Philippine War

"It is evident that the insurrection has been brought to an end both by making a war distressing and hopeless on the one hand and by making peace attractive," concluded Secretary of War Root in his official report upon the conclusion of the war. As in the Civil War, the Army had ultimately adopted a carrot-and-stick approach in which it alternately enticed and beat a hostile population into submission. But it had not settled upon any set mix of "positive" and "negative" incentives, preferring to allow local commanders to respond to situations as they saw fit.[59]

One thing most officers firmly believed, however, was that positive incentives alone could not overcome a strong rebellion. "You can't put down a rebellion by throwing confetti and sprinkling perfumery," wrote Maj. Gen. Loyd Wheaton in 1900, and by the end of the Philippine War there were few American soldiers who would have argued with him. For many if not most, the principal lesson of the war had been that decisive military action and the policies of chastisement, rather than policies of attraction, were the ultimate keys to a successful counterinsurgency campaign. Indeed, most officers believed, like Col. Robert L. Bullard, that "our aversion and long failure to use the justifiable and necessary severity against insurgents prolonged the war."[60]

The students and, at least in Chaffee's case, the veterans of Sherman's and Sheridan's campaigns realized that ultimately the followers of Emilio Aguinaldo had laid down their arms for the same reason that the followers of Jefferson Davis had—because they had been beaten and were no longer willing to endure the pain and suffering that continued resistance would bring. It was only when they had been pushed to the brink that the policy of attraction had played a significant role in bringing about the end of the insurrection, for at this point benevolence helped to reconcile the remaining insurgents to defeat. This was especially so because, by accident rather than by design, America's program of moderate political reforms, economic growth, and education, appealed to the conservative leaders of the Filipino insurrection.[61]

That the policy of attraction had failed to win the war did not mean that American authorities dismissed its usefulness entirely. Most Army leaders recognized that benevolent policies had a positive role to play. They realized that personal misconduct on the part of American soldiers could only exacerbate what was already a delicate situation, and that morality, military efficiency, and simple prudence demanded that the Army maintain strict discipline. They conceded that benevolence had won some adherents among the Filipino population and that it was therefore a useful tool in promoting the fragmentation and disintegration of the resistance movement. Besides, insofar as the war had been "a contest for the adherence of the people of the archipelago," most officers understood that good conduct and constructive U.S. programs contributed to American success, while destructive acts, if not carefully controlled, made the guerrilla cause more attractive.

But the hard school of experience had led them to doubt that benevolence alone could subdue a strong insurgent movement, and it was foolish, if not inhumane, they believed, to blindly adhere to such policies and not to avail themselves of the sterner measures permitted by General Orders 100 and the laws of war. "Doubtless there will continue to be Americans who think that the milk and water policy is best, because that is the system that we would like to apply," wrote Major Allen. But in reality, he said, the best policy was to treat "the good man very well indeed and the bad man very harshly."[62]

The Army thus emerged from the Philippine War in much the same way as it had entered it—dedicated to the mixed policy of benevolence and retaliation that had been laid out in the texts of Halleck, Lieber, Birkhimer, and Bigelow, but without a fixed formula for the mixture. Pacification had proved to be more alchemy than science. And it was perhaps for this reason that the Army continued to shy away from writing a formal doctrine on the subject. Textbooks employed by the Army changed very little as a result of the Philippine experience. Judge Advocate General George B. Davis' *The Elements of International Law* (1903), which replaced Davis' *Outlines of International Law* as a West Point textbook, differed from the earlier work only in that it contained a new section justifying the practice of "laying waste a portion of the territory of the enemy." The changes in Colonel Birkhimer's *Military Government and Martial Law* were more extensive and more important, given the fact that the Army would use it as a text and reference work for decades. Birkhimer expanded coverage of such issues as the governance of occupied areas, pacification, and guerrilla warfare and illustrated these topics with examples from the Philippine War. Yet he did not materially alter any of his previous interpretations. He praised what he regarded as America's traditional approach of trying to win the confidence of a hostile population while giving his

Soldiers and civilians intermingle in the Philippines.

approval to the employment, when necessary, of such measures as the taking of hostages, the levying of fines and other forms of communal punishments, destruction, concentration, and the execution of particularly recalcitrant guerrillas and their civilian aides. Birkhimer's work stood as an endorsement of the Army's dual approach to pacification in the Philippines.[63]

Operationally, the Army learned, or at least reaffirmed, several useful lessons as well. Its leaders emerged from the conflict convinced of the importance of separating the population from the guerrillas through a combination of population control and counterinfrastructure measures. The importance of mobility, scouting, march security, native auxiliaries, and aggressive, small-unit action were well understood. The officer corps especially appreciated the important roles that military commissions and intelligence networks played in counterinsurgency operations, although the question of torture remained a gray area. Although the Army officially condemned it, several officers defended the practice, and textbooks employed at West Point after the war, while forbidding torture and discouraging coercion, conceded that it was sometimes useful to rough up uncooperative civilians to gain information.[64]

The veterans of the Philippine War passed on the lessons they had learned in terms of fieldcraft, tactics, and pacification through articles in professional journals and, to a lesser extent, military textbooks. Postwar editions of Wagner's *The Service of Security and Information*, for example, incorporated Philippine situations to illustrate tactical points and to reassert Wagner's prewar contention that good soldiers adapted their methods to the circumstances in which they found themselves. Wagner discussed modifications American officers had made to standard skirmish, outpost, and march formations to deal with jungle conditions and briefly described Filipino ambush techniques. Since *The Service of Security and Information* was widely used in the Army's educational system, these lessons made their way into the lexicon of Army tactical doctrine.[65]

Yet as important as these writings were in distilling and passing on doctrinal lessons, the discussions were limited, and the Army's official manuals and drill regulations contained only a few references to jungle and guerrilla warfare. This was partially due to the Army's belief that the war had largely vindicated prewar small-unit tactical doctrine, only minor modifications being required to meet the peculiar aspects of Philippine service. Moreover, the successful outcome of the war had reaffirmed the military's traditional view that guerrilla warfare, while often frustrating and sometimes dangerous, was not in and of itself capable of producing victory. The Army, therefore, continued to relegate the study of partisan operations to the fringes of military science.[66]

There was, however, another reason why some of the Army's actions went unrecorded. The Philippine War had been an unpopular war, both at home and within the Army itself. Most soldiers were reluctant to expose the seamier side of the war to public scrutiny or even to record the lessons of these experiences. Indeed, it was somewhat dangerous to do so, as allegations of abuse and torture led to the convening of a Senate investigation and a flurry of courts-martial at the end of the war. Even the commanding general of the Army, veteran Indian fighter Nelson Miles, publicly accused his subordinates of committing atrocities. All of this discouraged a full airing of the Philippine experience.

One of the most serious casualties in this process was the *Telegraphic Circulars*, a compilation of the orders that General Bell had issued during the final Batangas campaign. The pamphlet was a gem reminiscent of Crook's *Resume of Operations Against Apache Indians* in that it contained not only Bell's orders, but also a discussion of his counterinsurgency philosophy. Although the pamphlet was inserted into the record by a congressional committee investigating the war, the Army itself did not distribute it beyond the archipelago, allegedly because of the sensitivity of the subject matter. Similarly, the Army declined to publish its own official record of the Philippine War, Capt. John R. M. Taylor's *The Philippine Insurrection Against the United States*, which reviewers alternately lambasted either as too candid about sensitive issues or as a whitewash of American conduct. Consequently, the Army was compelled to rely upon the memories of its soldiers to preserve many of the lessons from the war, just as it had during the previous century of Indian warfare. This was a precious asset, for the next twenty years were destined to be some of the most active ones for the Army in terms of pacification and small war operations, and it would be the veterans of the insurrection in the Philippines who would guide the Army through these many and diversified challenges.[67]

Notes

[1] Guam was initially administered by the Navy.

[2] The military government of Puerto Rico offers few insights that can not be gained by studying the larger occupations, and consequently it will not be discussed here. For information on Puerto Rico, see P. E. Pierce, "Puerto Rico, A Short History of the Military Occupation and Government by the United States," *JMSIUS* 49 (1911): 74–89, 232–47; F. W. Mansfield, "Puerto Rico," *JMSIUS* 27 (1900): 30–52; "The American Army," *Outlook* 74 (July 1903): 643–45; War Department, *Annual Reports of the War Department for the Fiscal Year Ending June 30, 1900* (Washington, D.C.: War Department, 1900), vol. 1, pts. 3 and 13 (hereafter cited as *WDAR* accompanied by the fiscal year covered in the volume); *WDAR*, 1899, vol. 1, pts. 3 and 6; *WDAR*, 1901, vol. 1, pts. 3 and 13.

[3] David Healy, *The United States in Cuba, 1898–1902: Generals, Politicians, and the Search for Policy* (Madison: University of Wisconsin Press, 1963), pp. 55–56; Gillette, "Occupation of Cuba," pp. 412–13.

[4] Davis, *Outlines of International Law*, pp. 248–49; War Department GO 101, 18 Jul 1898; Healy, *United States in Cuba*, p. 55; War Department, *Correspondence Relating to the War With Spain*, 2 vols. (Washington, D.C.: Government Printing Office, 1902), 2:858–59.

[5] Gates, "Alleged Isolation," pp. 32–45; Allan Millett, *The Politics of Intervention: The Military Occupation of Cuba, 1906–1909* (Columbus: Ohio State University, 1968), p. 13.

[6] Gillette, "Occupation of Cuba," pp. 410, 423–25; Millett, *Politics of Intervention*, p. 14; Robert Bacon and James Scott, eds., *The Military and Colonial Policy of the United States: Addresses and Reports by Elihu Root* (Cambridge, Mass., 1916), pp. 164–68; Lane, *Armed Progressive*, p. 97.

[7] W. Cameron Forbes, *The Philippine Islands*, 2 vols. (New York: Houghton Mifflin, 1928), 1:423; Richard Brown, "Social Attitudes of American Generals, 1898–1940" (Ph.D. diss., University of Wisconsin, 1951), pp. 78–79; Bacon and Scott, *Military and Colonial Policy*, pp. 164–65, 168.

[8] Bacon and Scott, *Military and Colonial Policy*, pp. 165–69.

[9] *Army and Navy Journal* (15 July 1899): 1097.

[10] *WDAR*, 1901, vol. 10, pt. 1, p. 8.

[11] Louis Perez, *Army Politics in Cuba, 1898–1956* (Pittsburgh: University of Pittsburgh Press, 1976), pp. 6–7.

[12] Healy, *United States in Cuba*, pp. 179–86; *WDAR*, 1901, vol. 10, pt. 1, p. 8; Gillette, "Occupation of Cuba," pp. 410–25; Scott, *Memories*, pp. 232–49; Lane, *Armed Progressive*, pp. 91–99.

[13] Gillette, "Occupation of Cuba," pp. 414, 418–22; Lane, *Armed Progressive*, pp. 95, 100–104; Healy, *United States in Cuba*, pp. 147, 183–84, 186–88; Millett, *Politics of Intervention*, p. 43.

[14] Norman Owen, ed., *Compadre Colonialism: Studies on the Philippines Under American Rule* (Ann Arbor: University of Michigan Press, 1971), pp. 4, 25–26; Glenn May, *Social Engineering in the Philippines* (Westport, Conn.: Greenwood Press, 1980), pp. 180–81; John Gates, "The Limits of Power: The U.S. Conquest of the Philippines,"

in *Great Powers and Little Wars: The Limits of Power*, ed. A. Hamish Ion and E. J. Errington (Westport, Conn.: Praeger, 1993), pp. 136–41.

[15] Brian Linn, *The U.S. Army and Counterinsurgency in the Philippine War, 1899–1902* (Chapel Hill: University of North Carolina Press, 1989), p. 3.

[16] Glenn May, *Battle for Batangas* (New Haven, Conn.: Yale University Press, 1991), pp. 99, 169; Linn, *Counterinsurgency in the Philippine War*, pp. 12–17; Charles J. Crane, "The Fighting Tactics of Filipinos," *JMSIUS* 31 (1902): 496–505; Gates, *Schoolbooks*, pp. 157–58; John R. M. Taylor, "The Spanish Campaign in the Philippines," *JMSIUS* 33 (1903): 139.

[17] Twichell, *Allen*, p. 109; William Scott, *Ilocano Responses to American Aggression, 1900–1901* (Quezon City, Philippines: New Day Publishers, 1986), p. 59; Thaddeus Sexton, *Soldiers in the Sun* (Harrisburg, Pa.: Military Service Publishers, 1939), p. 239; John R. M. Taylor, *The Philippine Insurrection Against the United States*, 5 vols. (Pasay City, Philippines: Eugenio Lopez Foundation, 1971), 5:142–45, 581–91, 596–97.

[18] Glenn May, "Why the United States Won the Philippine-American War, 1899–1902," *Pacific Historical Review* 52 (1983): 365–66, 369; Linn, *Counterinsurgency in the Philippine War*, pp. 17–18, 167; Glenn May, "Resistance and Collaboration in the Philippine-American War: The Case of Batangas," *Journal of Southeast Asia Studies* 15 (March 1984): 69–90.

[19] Gates, *Schoolbooks*, pp. 163–64.

[20] Quote from May, *Battle for Batangas*, p. 95. Gates, *Schoolbooks*, p. 113; Wooster, *Indian Policy*, pp. 198–99.

[21] Taylor, *Philippine Insurrection*, 2:285, 288; War Department, *Report of Major General E.S. Otis, USA, Commanding General of the Philippines, Military Governor* (Washington, D.C.: Government Printing Office, 1900), pp. 194, 252, 364 (hereafter cited as *Otis Report*); Gerald Early, "The U.S. Army in the Philippine Insurrection, 1899–1902" (Master's thesis, U.S. Army Command and General Staff College, 1975), pp. 79–80; *WDAR*, 1900, vol. 1, pt. 8, pp. 68, 322–25, 331–32; Gates, *Schoolbooks*, p. 108; *Correspondence Relating to the War With Spain*, 2:1070.

[22] Quote from *WDAR*, 1901, vol. 1, pt. 6, p. 306. *Otis Report*, p. 252.

[23] *Otis Report*, pp. 127, 131; Cirs 3 and 12, in *Telegraphic Circulars and General Orders, Regulating Campaign Against Insurgents and Proclamations and Circular Letters Relating to Reconstruction After the Close of War in the Provinces of Batangas, Laguna, and Mindoro, Philippine Islands, Issued by Brigadier General J. Franklin Bell, Batangas, Philippine Islands* (HQ, 3d Separate Brigade, 1902), Adjutant General's Office (AGO) 415839, Records of the Adjutant General's Office, RG 94, NARA (hereafter cited as *Telegraphic Circulars*).

[24] Wagner, *Service of Security*, p. 14; Millett, *Bullard*, p. 142; Sand-30, "Trench, Parapet, or 'the Open,'" *JMSIUS* 30 (July 1902): 481; Ewing Booth, *My Observations and Experiences in the U.S. Army* (1944), p. 47; Charles J. Crane, *The Experiences of a Colonel of Infantry* (New York: Knickerbocker Press, 1923), pp. 502–07; Edgar Raines, "Major General J. Franklin Bell, U.S.A.: The Education of a Soldier, 1856–1899," *Register of the Kentucky Historical Society* 83 (Autumn 1985): 341–43; James Parker, "Some Random Notes on the Fighting in the Philippines," *JMSIUS* 27 (November 1900): 317–40; Louis Hamilton, "Jungle Tactics," *JMSIUS* 37 (1906): 23–28; *Otis Report*, p. 198; Ltrs, John L. Jordan to mother, 28 Apr 1900 and 11 Jul 1900, Spanish American War Survey (SPAWS), 38th Infantry, MHI; Ltr, George Gelbach to father, 31 May 1900, SPAWS, 46th Infantry, MHI; Ltrs, Samuel Lyon to

wife, 30 Jul 1900, 15 Nov 1900, and 27 Nov 1900, Samuel Lyon Papers, MHI; Linn, *Counterinsurgency in the Philippine War*, p. 112; *WDAR*, 1900, vol. 1, pt. 5, p. 191; John Nankivell, *History of the Twenty-Fifth Regiment, U.S. Infantry* (1927), p. 112; Glenn May, "Filipino Resistance to American Occupation: Batangas, 1899–1902," *Pacific Historical Review* 48 (1979): 547.

[25] *WDAR*, 1900, vol. 1, pt. 4, pp. 280–81, 657; Thomas Crouch, "The Making of a Soldier: The Career of Frederick Funston, 1865–1902" (Ph.D. diss., University of Texas at Austin, 1969), pp. 389–90, 395; Allan Marple, "The Philippine Scouts: A Case Study in the Use of Indigenous Soldiers, Northern Luzon, the Philippine Islands, 1899" (Master's thesis, U.S. Army Command and General Staff College, 1983), pp. 53–54, 68–70, 74, 79, 90; Parker, "Random Notes," pp. 327–28, 336–39; Senate, Philippine Committee, *Hearings Before the Committee on the Philippines*, 57th Cong., 1st sess., 1902, S. Doc. 331, pt. 2, p. 882; J. A. Augur, "The Cavalry in Southern Luzon," *Journal of the U.S. Cavalry Association* 13 (1903): 530, 532; *WDAR*, 1900, vol. 1, pt. 8, pp. 346–47; Kirby Walker, "Cavalry Experiences From 1898–1901," *Journal of the U.S. Cavalry Association* 13 (1902): 42.

[26] Davis, *Outlines of International Law*, p. 242.

[27] Marple, "Philippine Scouts," pp. 5–6, 93–96; Louis Seaman, "Native Troops for Our Colonial Possessions," *North American Review* 171 (1900): 847, 859–60; J. N. Munro, "The Native Scout Organization," *Cavalry Journal* 20 (1910): 178–79; John Ward, "The Use of Native Troops in Our New Possessions," *JMSIUS* 31 (1902): 797–98, 804; *WDAR*, 1902, vol. 1, pt. 9, p. 234; *Otis Report*, pp. 13, 204, 365; *Correspondence Relating to the War With Spain*, 2:969; *WDAR*, 1901, vol. 1, pt. 5, p. 39; *WDAR*, 1900, vol. 1, pt. 8, p. 14.

[28] William Kobbe, Service in the Philippines, p. 160, William A. Kobbe Papers, MHI; *Otis Report*, pp. 131, 134; Millett, *Bullard*, p. 139; *WDAR*, 1900, vol. 1, pt. 8, pp. 260, 332; Charles J. Crane, "The Filipinos' War Contribution," *JMSIUS* 29 (1901): 270; Fred Brown, *History of the Ninth U.S. Infantry, 1799–1909* (R. R. Donnelly, 1909), pp. 359–60, 364; Linn, *Counterinsurgency in the Philippine War*, p. 42.

[29] Brian Linn, "Intelligence and Low Intensity Conflict in the Philippine War, 1899–1902," *Intelligence and National Security* 6 (1991): 90–114; William T. Johnston, A Brief Record of Services Since 1898, c. 1902, 4625ACP91, RG 94, NARA. Ltrs, Chaffee to Corbin, 25 Oct 01 and 9 Dec 01, both in Henry C. Corbin Papers, Library of Congress (LC). D. H. Boughton, "How Soldiers Have Ruled in the Philippines," *International Quarterly* 6 (September 1902–March 1903): 227–28; William Bisbee, *Through Four American Wars* (Boston: Meador Publishing Co., 1931), p. 261; U. G. McAlexander, *History of the Thirteenth Regiment, U.S. Infantry* (Fort McDowell Regimental Press, 1905), pp. 190–92, 196.

[30] McKinley quote from *Correspondence Relating to the War With Spain*, 2:859. Otis quote from Gates, *Schoolbooks*, p. 149, and see also p. 83. Bell quote from ibid., p. 215. Birkhimer quote from William Birkhimer, *Military Government and Martial Law* (Washington, D.C.: James Chapman, 1892), p. 236. *Otis Report*, pp. 111, 122, 242; *WDAR*, 1900, vol. 1, pt. 8, pp. 80, 235, 257–65.

[31] U.S. Congress, Senate, Philippine Committee, *Charges of Cruelty, etc., to the Natives of the Philippines*, 57th Cong., 1st sess., 1902, S. Doc. 205, pp. 34–38; Virginia Mulrooney, "No Victor, No Vanquished: U.S. Military Government in the Philippine Islands, 1898–1901" (Ph.D. diss., University of California, Los Angeles, 1975), pp. 168–79, 234–35.

[32] Linn, *Counterinsurgency in the Philippine War*, pp. 21, 51; Gates, *Schoolbooks*, pp. 139, 216–17; Sexton, *Soldiers in the Sun*, pp. 247–48; *WDAR*, 1901, vol. 1, pt. 5, p. 38; *WDAR*, 1901, vol. 1, pt. 4, p. 141.

[33] First quote from Gates, *Schoolbooks*, p. 199, and see also pp. 137–39. Second quote from Forbes, *Philippine Islands*, 1:422–23.

[34] Quote from Linn, *Counterinsurgency in the Philippine War*, p. 128. Millett, *Bullard*, p. 147; *WDAR*, 1900, vol. 1, pt. 4, pp. 657, 668, 794, 798; Senate, Philippine Committee, *Charges of Cruelty*, 57th Cong., 1st sess., 1902, S. Doc. 205, p. 40; Gates, *Schoolbooks*, pp. 113–14; Twichell, *Allen*, p. 112.

[35] Taylor, *Philippine Insurrection*, 2:306.

[36] Gates, *Schoolbooks*, pp. 196, 219.

[37] Mulrooney, "No Victor, No Vanquished," pp. 200–204, 210–21; *WDAR*, 1902, 9:188, 216, 222; James Blount, *The American Occupation of the Philippines, 1898–1912* (New York: G. P. Putnam's Sons, 1912), pp. 382, 385, 393.

[38] Taylor, *Philippine Insurrection*, 5:775. Quote from Thomas Anderson, "Our Rule in the Philippines," *North American Review* 170 (1900): 282.

[39] Sumner quote from Linn, "Intelligence in Low Intensity Conflict," p. 10. Taylor, *Philippine Insurrection*, 5:228–29, 647–48, 797–98.

[40] Quote from *Telegraphic Circulars*, p. iii. *WDAR*, 1900, vol. 1, pt. 8, pp. 259–60.

[41] Davis, *Outlines of International Law*, p. 242; Birkhimer, *Military Government* (1892), pp. 75–82, 233–36; Bigelow, *The Principles of Strategy*, pp. 228–33; Senate, Philippine Committee, *Charges of Cruelty*, 57th Cong., 1st sess., 1902, S. Doc. 205, pp. 19, 37; Mercur, *Art of War*, pp. 244–45.

[42] *Otis Report*, pp. 80, 90; *Correspondence Relating to the War With Spain*, 2:1175–78; Sexton, *Soldiers in the Sun*, pp. 247–48; Crane, *Experiences of a Colonel*, p. 321; Leon Wolff, *Little Brown Brother* (Garden City, N.Y.: Doubleday, 1961), p. 237; Stuart Miller, *'Benevolent Assimilation': The American Conquest of the Philippines, 1899–1903* (New Haven, Conn.: Yale University Press, 1982), pp. 69, 182–83.

[43] Ltrs, Allen to wife, 16 Apr 1900 and 20 Apr 1900 and quote from 25 Apr 1900, box 7; Ltrs, Allen to Adj Gen, Military District of Albay, 15 Apr 1900 and 21 May 1900, box 32; Ltr, Maj J. C. Gilmore to Allen, 26 May 1900, box 32. All in the Henry Allen Papers, LC.

[44] Nankivell, *Twenty-Fifth Regiment*, p. 103; William C. Brown Diary, 1 Jun 1900, William C. Brown Papers, MHI; *Correspondence Relating to the War With Spain*, 2:1123; Sexton, *Soldiers in the Sun*, pp. 243–44; Ltr, Lt Samuel Lyon to wife, 30 Jul 1900, Samuel Lyon Papers, MHI; *WDAR*, 1900, vol. 1, pt. 8, p. 162; Scott, *Ilocano Responses*, pp. 31, 33; Linn, *Counterinsurgency in the Philippine War*, p. 46.

[45] Quote from *WDAR*, 1901, vol. 1, pt. 6, p. 313, and see also pp. 312–15. David Fritz, "The Philippine Question: American Civil/Military Policy in the Philippines, 1898–1905" (Ph.D. diss., University of Texas at Austin, 1977), p. 428; Charles D. Rhodes Diary of the Philippine Insurrection, p. 9, Charles D. Rhodes Papers, MHI; *WDAR*, 1900, vol. 1, pt. 5, p. 317; William C. Brown Diary, 1 Jun 1900, Brown Papers; Senate, Philippine Committee, *Hearings Before the Committee on the Philippines*, 57th Cong., 1st sess., 1902, S. Doc. 331, pt. 3, pp. 2893–94.

[46] Gates, *Schoolbooks*, pp. 187–93, 206–07; John H. Parker, Conditions in the Philippines in October 1900, p. 6, attached to Ltr, Theodore Roosevelt to Root, 24 Nov 1900, box 162, Elihu Root Papers, LC; U.S. Congress, Senate, Philippine Committee, *Conditions in the Philippines*, 56th Cong., 2d sess., 1901, S. Doc. 167, pp. 201–04;

Forbes, *Philippine Islands*, 1:107; Taylor, *Philippine Insurrection*, 2:279–80; Richard Welch, *Response to Imperialism: The United States and the Philippine-American War, 1899–1902* (Chapel Hill: University of North Carolina Press, 1979), p. 37.

[47] Quote from Gates, *Schoolbooks*, p. 207. May, *Battle for Batangas*, p. 149.

[48] *WDAR*, 1901, vol. 1, pt. 4, pp. 140–41; Elkanah Babcock, *A War History of the 6th U.S. Infantry* (Kansas City, Mo.: Hudson-Kimberly, 1903), p. 85. Ltrs, Henry to Seton, 6 Aug 1900; Henry to mother, 7 Dec 1900; Henry to mother, 19 Feb 1901; all in Henry Papers. HQ, Island of Marinduque, GO 1, 8 Dec 1900, 4th District Department of Southern Luzon (DSL), unregistered correspondence, 2458, Records of U.S. Army Overseas Operations and Commands, RG 395, NARA; Linn, *Counterinsurgency in the Philippine War*, pp. 60, 117; Frederick Presher Diary, vol. 1, p. 98, SPAWS, 1st Cavalry, MHI; *WDAR*, 1902, 9:432–33, 438–43, 447–49, 454–56, 461–62, 595, 605, 616–17; Ltr, Lt Charles Clifton, in *The Rensselaer*, 3 Apr 02, SPAWS, 43d Infantry, MHI; W. A. Damon, Record of Events, Co. 'E,' 2d Infantry, p. 4, SPAWS, 2d Infantry, MHI; Brown, *Ninth Infantry*, pp. 562, 571.

[49] Brown, *Ninth Infantry*, p. 600; *WDAR*, 1902, 9:432; Joseph Schott, *The Ordeal of Samar* (New York: Bobbs-Merrill, 1964), p. 77; Clarence Tenney, Official History of the 46th Regiment, pp. 78–79, SPAWS, 46th Infantry, MHI.

[50] Tenney, Official History of the 46th Regiment, pp. 78–79; Brown, *Ninth Infantry*, pp. 562, 571–73; *WDAR*, 1902, 9:594–95, 603–06; Senate, Philippine Committee, *Hearings Before the Committee on the Philippines*, 57th Cong., 1st sess., 1902, S. Doc. 331, pt. 2, pp. 554–56, 2443–44; Scott, *Ilocano Responses*, pp. 34, 142–44; Taylor, *Philippine Insurrection*, 5:200, 287; *WDAR*, 1901, vol. 1, pt. 5, p. 37; May, *Battle for Batangas*, pp. 246–47; *Historical Sketch of the Twentieth United States Infantry, 1861–1919* (1920), p. 41; HQ, Island of Marinduque, GO 10, 7 Feb 01, 2458, RG 395, NARA; Irving Heaslip, Hike Book, pp. 43, 46, 68, SPAWS, 2d Infantry, MHI; Kobbe, Service in the Philippines, pp. 273–75, Kobbe Papers.

[51] First quote from Welch, *Response to Imperialism*, p. 138. Second quote from Ltr, Chaffee to Corbin, 10 Jan 02, box 1, Corbin Papers.

[52] "Insular Notes," *JMSIUS* 29 (1901): 448; Ltr, George Gelbach to father, 30 Nov 1900, SPAWS, 46th Infantry, MHI; Frederick Palmer, The Real Situation in the Philippines, c. 1900, Kobbe Papers.

[53] U.S. Congress, Senate, Philippine Committee, *Trials or Court-Martial in the Philippine Islands in Consequence of Certain Instructions*, 57th Cong., 2d sess., 3 March 1903, S. Doc. 213, pp. 14–15. Anderson quote from Senate, Philippine Committee, *Charges of Cruelty*, 57th Cong., 1st sess., 1902, S. Doc. 205, p. 21. Ltr, William Eggenberger to mother, 25 Mar 01, SPAWS, 3d Infantry, MHI; Ltrs, George Gelbach to father, 31 May 1900, and to brother, 16 Jun 1900, both in SPAWS, 46th Infantry, MHI; Wolff, *Little Brown Brother*, p. 318; Schott, *Ordeal of Samar*, pp. 80, 84; Russell Roth, *Muddy Glory: America's 'Indian Wars' in the Philippines, 1899–1935* (W. Hanover, Mass.: Christopher Publishing, 1981), pp. 53–54; B. O. Flower, "Some Dead Sea Fruit of Our War of Subjugation," *Arena* 27 (June 1902): 650; Nankivell, *Twenty-Fifth Regiment*, pp. 102–03; Miller, *Benevolent Assimilation*, p. 188; Fritz, "Philippine Question," pp. 439–40; Blount, *American Occupation*, pp. 200–201; Ltr, Allen to Col Clarence R. Edwards, 8 Apr 02, box 7, Allen Papers.

[54] Murray quote from Ltr, Arthur Murray to Henry Allen, 21 May 02, box 7, Allen Papers. Richard Welch, "American Atrocities in the Philippines: The Indictment and the Response," *Pacific Historical Review* 43 (1974): 235–36; May, *Battle for Batangas*, pp.

147, 257–59, 262; Augustus Blocksom, "A Retrospect and Prospect of War," *JMSIUS* 35 (1904): 215; Frederick Presher Diary, vol. 1, p. 95, SPAWS, 1st Cavalry, MHI; Charles Clifton questionnaire, SPAWS, 43d Infantry, MHI; Ltr, Samuel Lyon to wife, 13 Jan 01, Lyon Papers; Henry Graff, *American Imperialism and the Philippine Insurrection* (Boston: Little, Brown & Company, 1969), pp. 74–81, 97–107; Blount, *American Occupation*, pp. 204–05; Senate, Philippine Committee, *Hearings Before the Committee on the Philippines*, 57th Cong., 1st sess., 1902, S. Doc. 331, pt. 3, pp. 1979, 2061–63, 2236, 2243, 2251, 2896.

[55] The term *third degree* referred broadly to the use of intense physical or psychological pressure for the purpose of extracting a confession. There has never been a formal definition as to exactly what measures constituted the third degree, but beatings, the deprivation of food and sleep, long interrogations, and other actions taken to terrorize, intimidate, or demoralize the subject generally fall within its parameters. Ernest Hopkins, *Our Lawless Police* (New York: Viking, 1931), pp. 189–211, 324–25, 328–29; Samuel Walker, *A Critical History of Police Reform* (Lexington, Mass.: D. C. Heath, 1977), pp. 15–16, 58, 132–35.

[56] Carter, *Chaffee*, pp. 45, 47, 66, 84, 89; Ltr, Chaffee to Corbin, 18 Dec 01, Corbin Papers.

[57] First quote from Edward Filiberti, "The Roots of U.S. Counterinsurgency Doctrine," *Military Review* 68 (January 1988): 54, and see also p. 56. Second quote from Roth, *Muddy Glory*, pp. 84–85.

[58] Quote from May, *Battle for Batangas*, pp. 253–56. Herbert White, "The Pacification of Batangas," in *Centennial of the U.S. Military Academy*, 1:789; *WDAR*, 1902, 9:228–36, 263–75; *Telegraphic Circulars*.

[59] Forbes, *Philippine Islands*, 1:107.

[60] First quote from Stanley Karnow, *In Our Image: America's Empire in the Philippines* (New York: Ballantine Books, 1979), p. 179. Second quote from Robert Bullard, Why Has the Philippine War Lasted So Long? c. 1901, p. 4, box 9, Robert Bullard Papers, LC.

[61] May, *Battle for Batangas*, pp. 99–100; May, "Filipino Resistance," pp. 553–54; Taylor, *Philippine Insurrection*, 5:315–18; Norman Owen, "Winding Down the War in Albay," *Pacific Historical Review* 48 (1979): 581–82, 587.

[62] First quote from Taylor, *Philippine Insurrection*, 2:304. Second quote from Ltr, Allen to wife, 10 Feb 01, box 7, Allen Papers. Third quote from Gates, *Schoolbooks*, p. 200.

[63] Fort Leavenworth and other Army schools used Birkhimer's work as a textbook during the early twentieth century, while the Office of the Judge Advocate of the Army continued to rely on it as late as 1943. Davis, *Elements of International Law*, p. 304. Quote from William Birkhimer, *Military Government and Martial Law* (Kansas City, Mo.: Frank Hudson, 1904), p. 204, and see also pp. 101–11, 120, 124, 202–04, 310, 312. Dan Campbell, William E. Birkhimer, Colonel, 28th U.S. Volunteer Infantry, A Brief Sketch, 4 Aug 43, pp. 21–23, William E. Birkhimer Papers, MHI; John Clous, "Military Government and Martial Law," *JMSIUS* 38 (1906): 147.

[64] Charles D. Rhodes, "The Experiences of Our Army Since the Outbreak of the War With Spain: What Practical Use Has Been Made of Them and How May They Be Further Utilized To Improve Its Fighting Efficiency," *JMSIUS* 36 (1905): 216; Celwyn Hampton, "The Experiences of Our Army Since the Outbreak of the War With Spain: What Practical Use Has Been Made of Them and How May They Be Further Utilized

To Improve Its Fighting Efficiency," *JMSIUS* 36 (1905): 414; Parker, "Random Notes," pp. 317–40; John H. Parker, "The Last Phase of the Philippine Rebellion and the Problems Resulting Therefrom," *Review of Reviews* 21 (October 1901): 562–67; James Parker, "Notes on Field Duties. The Attack by Ambush," *JMSIUS* 32 (1903): 374–75; Crane, "Fighting Tactics," pp. 496–505; Filiberti, "U.S. Counterinsurgency Doctrine," pp. 51–61; Hamilton, "Jungle Tactics," pp. 23–28; Charles J. Crane, "Paragraphs 93, 97, and 88, of General Orders 100," *JMSIUS* 32 (1902): 254–56; E. J. McClernand, "Our Philippine Problem," *JMSIUS* 29 (1901): 327–32; Wagner, *Service of Security*, p. 100.

[65] Wagner, *Service of Security*, pp. 17–18, 34–35, 66–67, 101, 105.

[66] Ibid., preface to 1903 edition; Birkhimer, *Military Government* (1904), pp. 78, 308.

[67] *Telegraphic Circulars*; Gates, *Schoolbooks*, pp. 287–88; Taylor, *Philippine Insurrection*, 1:xi; Fritz, "Philippine Question," pp. 16–18; James Biedzynski, "Frank McIntyre and the Philippines" (Ph.D. diss., Ohio University, 1990), pp. 103–18.

5

THE IMPERIAL CONSTABULARY YEARS 1900-1913

America's victory over Spain in 1898 inaugurated a new era in the nation's history. Pursuing the status of a great power, the United States arbitrated international disputes, established a protectorate over the Republic of Panama, built a canal across the isthmus, and sent a fleet of warships around the world to herald America's coming of age. In 1904 President Theodore Roosevelt issued a "corollary" to the Monroe Doctrine, in which he declared that the United States had the right to intervene in the internal affairs of any nation in the Western Hemisphere when public discord or mismanagement adversely affected American interests. The burden of carrying out his ambitious policies fell upon the military. While the Navy cruised the seas, occasionally landing marines and sailors to protect American lives and property, the Army undertook a host of constabulary duties in the newly created empire and adjacent areas. Its experiences added steadily to a growing store of knowledge and informal doctrine about the conduct of small wars and interventions.

The Peking Relief Expedition, 1900–1901

The twentieth century hardly had begun when an American force was dispatched to China. Although the expedition was small in military terms, it revealed the nation's growing role in the world. The expedition marked the Army's first overseas contingency operation and its first venture in coalition warfare since the American Revolution. In addition to being a historic watershed, the China experience also seems to have influenced how the expedition commander, General Chaffee, would eventually approach the problem of pacifying the Philippines. (*Map 3*)

COUNTERINSURGENCY DOCTRINE, 1860–1941

During the last half of the nineteenth century, Japan and a number of Western powers sought to carve up the ailing Chinese empire into a series of colonies, protectorates, and spheres of influence. This predatory behavior eventually sparked a wave of nationalistic and xenophobic sentiment in China that took the form of an antiforeign and anti-Christian movement known to westerners as the Boxer movement. Chinese authorities had little success in suppressing the Boxers, in part because elements of the imperial court sympathized with their goals. In June 1900 a large force of Boxers entered the imperial capital of Peking, burning churches and killing Chinese Christians. Many Chinese Christians and most foreigners took refuge behind the walls of the city's legation quarter, where foreign embassies and residences were located. Since the Chinese government was reticent to protect them, the leaders of the foreign diplomatic community in Peking called on their governments for aid, a request that assumed additional urgency after the Chinese government openly sided with the Boxers and declared war on all the nations that had legations in Peking, including the United States. The United States responded by earmarking nearly 15,000 men from garrisons in the United States, Cuba, and the Philippines for service in China. Time was of the essence, however, and ultimately only a few thousand American soldiers and marines actually reached China in time to participate in the campaign. In June an international force of 2,100 men (including 100 U.S. marines but no American soldiers) under the command of British Admiral Sir Edward Seymour failed to break the siege of Peking's foreign community. A second force of 19,000 European, Japanese, and American troops (the latter commanded by General Chaffee and numbering 2,500 soldiers), successfully relieved the legation quarter in August 1900. A year of parleying followed, during which China agreed to a huge indemnity and accepted serious limitations on its sovereignty.[1]

Meanwhile, the allies divided Peking into several zones, each ruled by one of the foreign powers that had participated in the expedition. Decisions affecting the entire city were made by committee. The American zone consisted of several square miles and roughly 50,000 inhabitants. General Chaffee and his second in command, Brig. Gen. James H. Wilson, were well prepared for the job of civil administration. Chaffee had served a stint as an Indian agent, while Wilson had exercised military government responsibilities during Reconstruction. More importantly, both men came to China fresh from significant military government duties in Cuba. Together, they set about governing the American zone in much the same way as the Army was administering Havana, San Juan, and Manila. They restored law and order, first by using American troops and military courts, and later by reestablishing

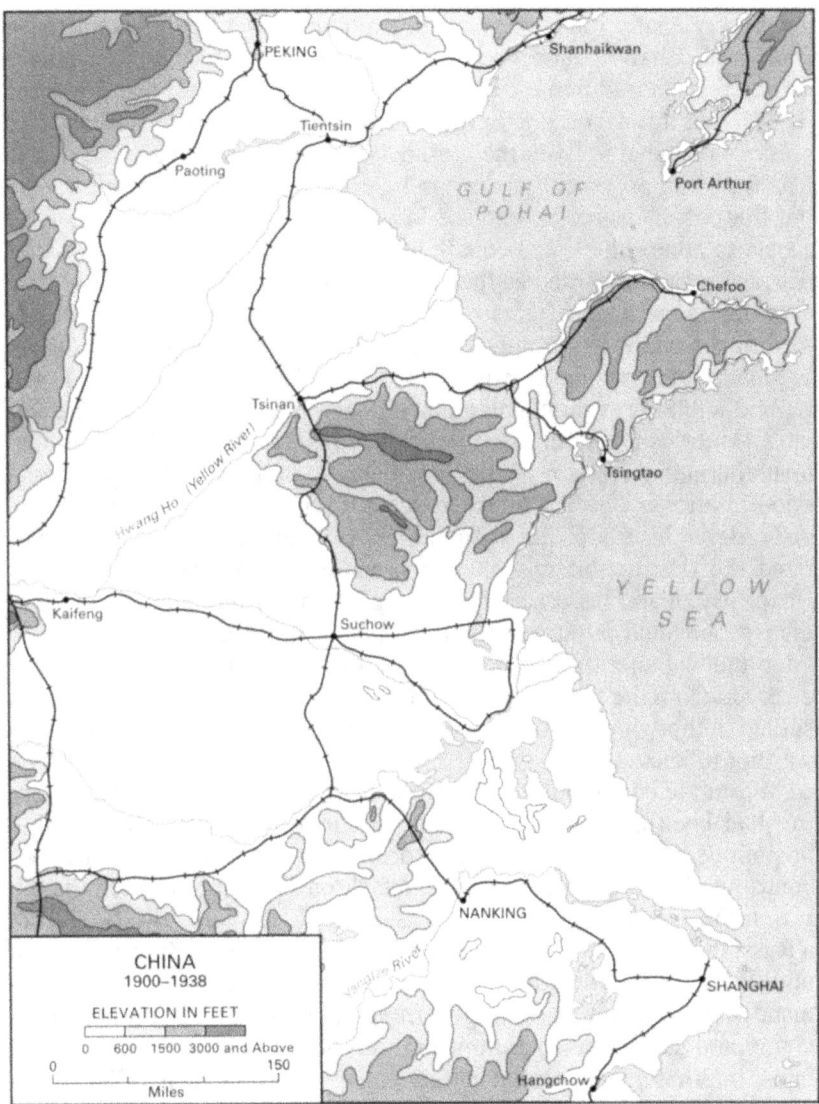

MAP 3

Chinese police and judicial institutions. They imposed a rigorous regimen of sanitation and inoculated the population against disease. They repaired roads and public buildings, installed street lighting, established hospitals and schools, opened charity kitchens to feed the destitute, and closed gambling houses and opium dens. Although some of these measures—especially those relating to sanitation—were enforced with an iron hand, Chaffee endeavored to rule as benignly as possible, taking care to respect traditional customs. The American quarter was governed so well that it was not long before people began to flock to it from other sections of the city. Even the criminals preferred American rule due to Chaffee's ban on executions, a ban he eventually had to rescind to stop the flow of undesirables into the U.S. zone. With the exception of the Japanese zone, which was equally well managed, the American quarter was universally regarded as the best-run section of Peking.[2]

Most American officers were appalled by their first experience in coalition warfare. The conduct of the other powers—especially Russia, France, and Germany—was exceedingly brutal. They looted and burned without restraint, and gunned down thousands of Chinese civilians. American conduct, by contrast, was restrained. Mindful that unadulterated terrorism would only delay the restoration of peace and good relations, Chaffee imposed strict discipline. He forbade looting and ordered his troops not to fire unless fired upon. Although he authorized the destruction of homes and villages suspected of harboring Boxer irregulars, he generally refrained from participating in the vindictive raids and punitive operations that typified coalition operations after the capture of Peking. Thanks to his efforts, the U.S. Army emerged from the Boxer affair with its reputation enhanced rather than sullied, although personal misconduct on the part of American soldiers was not unknown.[3]

From the beginning of the multinational effort, command and control had been a recurring problem that greatly complicated coalition operations and logistics. Poor coordination and miscommunication contributed directly to a disastrous attack on Tientsin, in which the 9th U.S. Infantry suffered 20 percent casualties. Later, "friendly fire" from a Russian battery caused fifteen American casualties at Yang-ts'un. Not until Peking had fallen did the coalition institute a single, overall command, and even then the U.S. government, jealous of its national sovereignty and suspicious of European motives, refused to place its forces under international control. Consequently, while American officers recognized the utility of combined command in operations of this nature, they made no effort to craft a doctrine for multinational operations. Nor would such a system be easy to achieve, as demonstrated by World War I. During that conflict the same countries that had participated in the China expedition were unwilling to commit themselves to a combined command until late in the war.[4]

Other than giving the Army some expeditionary experience and an opportunity to observe the workings of foreign armies, the Peking

U.S. troops guard Boxer prisoners at Tientsin; below, *American soldiers on police detail during the occupation of Peking.*

A Chinese village lies in ruins after a visitation by allied forces.

Relief Expedition had little impact on Army doctrine. With the Philippine War in full swing, the War Department withdrew most American troops from China in the fall of 1900. Chaffee and the remaining troops left the following spring. Only a 150-man detachment from the 9th Infantry stayed behind to guard the American legation in Peking, a duty that it performed until the Marine Corps assumed that function in 1905. Nevertheless, the expedition had made an impression on at least one important Army officer, General Chaffee. During his stay in China, Chaffee noted the harshness with which the European powers approached Asian warfare, as well as what he perceived to be the relatively low status accorded to individual human life by oriental society. From these observations he drew the conclusion that while brutality and wanton destruction had no place in the conduct of war, stern measures were necessary in subjugating rebellious Asians. Benevolence of the kind he had shown to the conquered people of Peking was possible once the enemy had been subjugated, but it was folly to attempt to win a war over such a people by kindness alone. These ideas were not new to Chaffee, a man familiar with the exigencies of irregular warfare. Rather they reinforced in his mind the traditional view that stubborn rebels and "semi-civilized" peoples must be managed with a firm hand. It was a lesson Chaffee applied when he left China for the Philippines in mid-1901.[5]

Policing the Philippines, 1902–1907

By July 1902 Chaffee's hard war policies had succeeded in crushing the last major bastions of Filipino resistance. But the Army's role in the Philippines did not end with his victories over Malvar and Lukban. Three and a half years of war and insurrection had left many areas in shambles—homes destroyed, crops ruined, and populations uprooted. The chaos of war was further aggravated by disease, which swept through the Philippines killing tens of thousands of Filipinos and the carabao they relied upon for agricultural labor. Such conditions proved fertile ground for *ladrones*—organized bands of bandits that plundered and terrorized the countryside.

Although many *ladrones* were little more than brigands, a few aspired to higher ideals. Some were genuine insurgents who refused to accede to U.S. authority. Others fought to redress perceived injustices in Filipino society or were members of mystical and often fanatical religious sects that preached the coming of a new era, free of American devils. Taken together, these roaming bands posed a significant threat to the internal stability of the Philippines for several years after the "official" termination of the insurrection. Not only did the *ladrones* employ the same guerrilla techniques used by Aguinaldo and his commanders, but they also maintained quasi-political structures that resembled those established during the war. The religious cults were usually based upon secret societies, while even the bandits had sophisticated intelligence and support networks among the population. Some *ladrones* were "social bandits" of the "Robin Hood" variety who enjoyed a genuine popularity among the people, while others had extensive contacts with town merchants and municipal officials through whom they marketed stolen goods. All freely used terror to strengthen their control over the population and to punish informers. Moreover, unlike the insurgents of 1899–1902, who were usually under the firm control of middle- and upper-class Filipinos, the *ladrone* movements of the postwar period were often peasant-based and hostile to the basic socioeconomic order. Deep ethnic, regional, and social fissures in Philippine society fueled many of these movements and gave them a strong flavor of civil and class warfare. When mixed with religious mysticism and its promise of a socialistic paradise, some of the postwar resistance movements achieved both a mass base and a revolutionary fervor that the earlier insurrection had lacked and that U.S. authorities found difficult to uproot.[6]

Civil and military officials alike recognized that the ultimate solution to the problem of postwar banditry was to eliminate the social and economic conditions that bred it. Consequently, the civil government followed the course charted by the Army, sponsoring a host of economic, educational, and governmental programs designed, in the words of one provincial governor, to win the "heart and mind" of the Filipino people. Nevertheless, while American officials hoped that economic development would eventually eliminate social unrest, many reluctantly agreed with Brig. Gen. Henry T. Allen that "the only immediate remedy is killing and for the same reason that a rabid dog must be disposed of. Education and roads will effect what is desired, but while awaiting these, drastic measures are obligatory."[7]

As chief of the Philippine Constabulary, Allen bore primary responsibility for completing the pacification of the Philippines. Governor Taft had created the Constabulary in July 1901 to give the civil government its own counterinsurgency capability. Relying on the Army to perform this function after peace had been restored was impolitic, Taft believed, because it would indicate that many parts of the Philippines were not truly pacified, thereby strengthening the hands of his two major critics—the anti-imperialists at home and Army officers who advocated a return to military government until stability had been entirely restored. Better, reasoned Taft, to create a "civil" counterinsurgency force that was made up of natives whose activities would arouse less public scrutiny and that could be safely controlled by the civil government without having to rely upon the military. By the time the U.S. government proclaimed the war to be over in mid-1902, the Constabulary numbered around 5,000 men and was put to work dousing the remaining embers of the insurrection.[8]

Although the Philippine Constabulary was an arm of the civil government, the U.S. Army profoundly influenced it during its formative years. Allen, who served as the organization's chief until 1907, staffed the Constabulary's officer corps almost entirely with officers and NCOs from the Army. Constabulary service was credited toward service in the Regular Army, and it was common for Constabulary officers to return to the Army after a few tours with the police organization. In fact, rather than being a dead-end assignment, Constabulary service attracted ambitious officers who sought to enhance their reputations with some combat duty during peacetime. No fewer than twenty-five Constabulary officers went on to achieve general officer rank in the U.S. Army.[9]

In picking his subordinates, Allen used the same criteria that Crook had employed in selecting officers to lead his Indian Scouts. He sought

The Philippine Constabulary

bright, ambitious, and physically robust men who could not only withstand the rigors of bush service, but who were also sensitive to the local sociopolitical environment. Whether in the American Southwest, the Caribbean, or the Philippines, the leaders of America's native auxiliaries all agreed that the successful leader of native troops had to exhibit the traits of a paternal strongman, sufficiently aloof from his charges to gain their allegiance while demonstrating a genuine concern for their welfare and a respect for their cultural idiosyncracies.[10]

Using the organization and administration of the U.S. Army as a guide, Allen and his handpicked assistants crafted the Constabulary into a capable organization. They trained their "soldiers" as light infantrymen, using the Army's own drill regulations as the basis for tactical instruction. Supplementing this instruction were lessons from the Philippine War compiled in the *Manual for the Philippine Constabulary*, first published in 1906. The manual's discussions of small-unit, irregular operations were similar in many ways to those that had long graced the pages of Mahan, Marcy, Wagner, and Bigelow. The guide prescribed vigorous action in battle and described various counterambush techniques. It recommended that columns operate at night and during the rainy season, when they had the best chance of catching their irregular opponents off guard. Like its predecessors, the book suggested various techniques to deceive the enemy, such as doubling back, padding equipment to dampen noise, and relocating campsites at night to foil surprise attacks.[11]

But the manual was more than a tactical supplement for irregular warfare. It contained a great deal of information pertaining to the Constabulary's police functions, describing court and legal matters, arrest procedures, and the collection of evidence. It directed constables to monitor closely the mood of the population and gave tips on how to accomplish this end. Officers were required not only to know Spanish, but also to learn the dialects and customs of the regions where they were posted. More than mere policemen, the government regarded the constables as key agents in civilizing the islands. Consequently, the manual enjoined Constabulary officers to employ minimal force and to conduct themselves "with justice and kindness," so as to win the population's allegiance.[12]

Although the Constabulary bore primary responsibility for pacifying the postwar Philippines, it could not do the job alone. It lacked the manpower, the administrative and logistical infrastructure, and to some degree the combat skills required to deal with the larger and more virulent insurgent movements. Consequently, during the five years that followed Malvar's surrender, the Philippine government was compelled to call upon the U.S. Army on numerous occasions for assistance in maintaining order and suppressing banditry. In most cases support came in the form of the Philippine Scouts, whose cultural attributes made them more suitable for peacetime pacification work than regular soldiers. By mid-1903 no fewer than thirty of the Scouts' fifty companies were serving with the Constabulary. U.S. Army regulars, on the other hand, participated in only a half-dozen counterinsurgency operations during 1902–1907. Nevertheless, the campaigns in which regulars participated were usually the most difficult and dangerous of the period.[13]

In setting out to restore order and tranquility to the troubled districts of the Philippines, American security forces applied the same blend of carrot-and-stick policies that had become standard fare in

Moro soldiers of the U.S. Army's Philippine Scouts in 1904

American pacification campaigns. On the one hand, Constabulary and Army officers exhorted their men to treat the population kindly, banned torture, and initiated such civil activities as building roads, providing free medical care, and establishing work programs. On the other, they vigorously prosecuted the military campaign. In the process they followed Constabulary Chief Allen's old formula of stiffening the policy of attraction with the policy of chastisement. Indeed, Constabulary operations during the immediate postwar period were sometimes ugly affairs, in which quarter was neither expected nor given. Villages and crops were burnt, suspects tortured despite Constabulary regulations, and *ladrone* leaders gunned down by special assassination squads.[14]

Operationally, the counterguerrilla campaigns of the postwar years were virtually identical to those conducted during the Philippine War. Roundups, cordon-and-sweep operations, and hikes proved to be the mainstay of the security forces' tactical arsenal, while spies and informants helped root out *ladrone* infrastructures. Perhaps the major difference in tactics between the campaigns of 1899–1902 and those that followed stemmed from the *ladrone*'s greater reliance on hand to hand combat. This was especially true of religious insurgents like the red-clothed *pulahans* of Samar and the Visayas, who used mass charges by sword-wielding fanatics to overcome their foes. This contrasted sharply with Aguinaldo's guerrillas, who had been more apt to carry firearms and who had exhibited less determination in driving home machete (*bolo*) attacks. To counter the new threat, American forces developed special march and camp procedures designed to provide all-round security. The Army also adjusted to the threat of fanatical charges by outfitting the regulars with special weapons, most notably repeating shotguns and heavy-caliber revolvers. Financial considerations limited the Scouts and Constabulary to older, slower-firing black powder weapons that made them somewhat more vulnerable. On the other hand, the single-shot shotguns with which the Constabulary was equipped were more suited to close-in jungle fighting than the Army's standard long-range rifles.[15]

Perhaps the most drastic and effective counterinsurgency measure employed by U.S. security forces during the postinsurrection years was concentration. In 1903 the Philippine government passed a law permitting the use of concentration in *ladrone*-infested areas, provided that officials gave the concentrated populations adequate food, shelter, and health care. Between the end of the Philippine War and 1907, American security forces imposed concentration or other population relocation programs in nearly a dozen Philippine provinces.

As in the war, the manner in which concentration was applied varied widely. In Albay, for example, Col. Harry H. Bandholtz, a veteran of several concentration campaigns during the Philippine War, concentrated nearly 125,000 people in towns and camps that, despite government efforts, were wracked by "disease and suffering for want of food and ordinary living accommodations." In the province of Cavite, the government concentrated about a third of the population, partially relocated another third, and left the remainder alone, preferring instead to concentrate the food supply in protected areas rather than the people themselves. The Constabulary also created "death zones" in Cavite, where anyone found by the troops was liable to be shot.[16]

Using a mixture of civil enticements, concentration, and aggressive action in the field, the Constabulary, backed by the regulars and the Scouts, consolidated America's victory in the Philippine War through a series of hard campaigns between 1902 and 1907. By 1908—the first year in which the Constabulary did not have to call upon either the Army or the Scouts for support—the work was largely done. Although the Philippine Constabulary would continue to combat the last vestiges of the *ladrones* and *pulahans* for several more years, the Regular Army's role in pacifying the Philippines had finally come to an end.

THE IMPERIAL CONSTABULARY YEARS, 1900–1913

Governing the Moros, 1900–1913

There was one exception to the Army's general disengagement from Philippine internal affairs after 1907, and this had to do with the management of a portion of the Philippines colloquially referred to as "Moroland." Moroland consisted of the large island of Mindanao and the Sulu archipelago, the Philippine Islands' southernmost appendage. This area differed significantly from the rest of the Philippines in that it was dominated by a Muslim people, the fiercely independent Moros, who had never submitted fully to Spanish rule. In recognition of the special difficulties involved in pacifying the Moros, the government charged the Army with responsibility for governing them until 1914.

Not only religious beliefs differentiated the Moros from other Filipinos. Moro laws, customs, and language (of which there were a variety of dialects) differed fundamentally from those of the Christianized north. Slavery and piracy were common features of Moro life, while politically Moroland was divided into a bewildering patchwork of feuding tribes and clans, each led by a hereditary chieftain (*dato*) and linked by a complex web of familial and semifeudal ties. Moreover, the Moros were a xenophobic and warlike people whose religious fervor only intensified their dislike for outsiders in general and Christians in particular. It was not uncommon for Moros, either as individuals or in small groups, to launch murderous rampages against infidels with the assurance that death for the *juramentado*, as the religious kamikaze was called, guaranteed his entry into paradise.

In approaching the "Moro question," military leaders were greatly influenced by the Army's experiences with the "Indian question" of the previous century. Many of the officers who played a role in shaping Moro policy shared General Otis' belief that cultural change could only be achieved by evolution rather than revolution and that the best way to guide a warlike and "primitive" race through the progressive stages of civilization was by exercising a strong, paternal hand. They urged that the Army be given exclusive control over the Moros, not only because it had the prerequisite experience to do the job, but also to avoid the type of bureaucratic muddle that had plagued pacification efforts during the Indian and Philippine Wars. They were quite determined not to repeat what they considered to have been the tragic flaws of America's Indian policy—divided authority, vacillating policies, corrupt officials, and unrealistic expectations.[17]

Although the frontier experience had endowed the officer corps with a broad philosophy concerning the management of aboriginal peoples, Army leaders still had to formulate a specific policy for governing

A Moro warrior in full armor

the Moros. Two approaches suggested themselves. The United States could either strengthen the sultan of Sulu—the titular head of Islam in the Philippines—and rule Moroland indirectly, as the British and Dutch did in their Malaysian colonies, or it could attempt to rule directly. Ultimately, American officials opted for direct rule. Neither the sultan nor any other *dato* had sufficient prestige to rule all of Moroland, and any effort to elevate one Moro leader over his peers would undoubtedly have resulted in civil war. If violence was inevitable, reasoned officers, it made more sense to establish direct American rule than to uphold some native autocrat. Besides, the notion of ruling through a despotic Asian potentate was distasteful to Americans. As on the Great Plains, officers believed that progress toward political and economic democracy could only be achieved by replacing tribalism with individualism—a goal that appeared incompatible with the perpetuation of despotic *datos*.[18]

The American colonial government in Manila took the first step toward asserting direct control by announcing the formation of Moro Province in 1903. Mimicking the system used by Spain and the Netherlands in governing Asian Muslims, Manila endowed the province's governor with special powers, including direct command over all military forces in the area. Since all three provincial governors between 1903 and 1913 were general officers, and many of the province's lower-ranking officials were soldiers as well, Moro Province became the domain of the Army. This politico-military form of government was designed to give provincial authorities the unity of effort and the muscle that the Army believed were essential for the civilization of a "savage" race.

Army officers were not so naive, however, as to believe that they could rule the Moros without the assistance of the traditional ruling class. Throwing out the *datos* would only create confusion and resentment, and for this reason the Army chose a gradual approach in tune with its evolutionary philosophy. Rather than imposing a democratic system for which the people were unprepared, General Wood, the former governor of occupied Cuba and the first governor of Moro Province, crafted a paternal system of government that blended Moro traditions with Western institutions. He divided the province into districts and appointed American officers as their governors. He further subdivided the districts into tribal wards, each of which was headed by the principal *dato* of the region. Lesser *datos* served as deputies. Although the *datos* continued to govern at the local level, they did so now as American civil servants who had to conform their behavior to American-dictated standards. The tribal ward system thus tapped the *datos*' power and prestige but circumscribed their authority and laid the groundwork for their ultimate demise as autonomous, hereditary chieftains. Though not flawless, the system proved a practical compromise between modernization and tradition that served America's long-term interests without overly disrupting Moro society.[19]

General Wood

Having established a basic governmental framework, Army officers introduced the same set of institutional reforms that were now standard features of the American way of pacification. They cleaned the streets (where there were streets), inoculated the population, and provided free medical care. They regularized the administration of government, courts, and taxes; established schools; and where civilian teachers were not available, detailed soldiers to serve as instructors. They introduced a number of measures designed to enhance both the prosperity of Moro Province in general and the socioeconomic standing of the individual Moro in particular. They built roads and improved harbors. They established experimental farms and agricultural colonies to promote diversification and modernization. Finally, they distributed small plots of public land to homesteaders in an effort to promote the development of that class of independent yeoman farmer that Americans have traditionally regarded as the bedrock of a democratic society.[20]

Of all of their endeavors, officers considered the promotion of education and commerce to be the most important. Education, however, was a long-term proposition, and consequently the Army regarded economic development as the primary engine for the immediate pacification of the Moros. From the beginning, garrison commanders encouraged the development of marketplaces near their posts, both to meet the needs of the troops and to foster better relations with the Moros. The business generated by the soldiers and the security that they offered local merchants provided a conducive environment for economic growth, and soon the markets became thriving centers of trade and "civilization." In September 1904 the district governor of Zamboanga, Maj. John P. Finley, systematized the marketplace concept by creating the first Moro Exchange—a cooperative market and commodity exchange complete with storage facilities and accommodations for those bringing their wares to market. General Wood enthusiastically embraced the exchange concept, and by 1910 the Army had established thirty-two such markets. In 1911 Moro Governor Brig. Gen. John J. Pershing supplemented the largely coastal-based exchanges with a new kind of government-controlled market, the Industrial Trading Station, which he established deep in the interior of Moroland. He complemented the expanded trade network by building more roads and by stationing small detachments of Scouts and Constabulary in the backcountry. These outposts became islands of security and influence that, together with the markets, greatly enhanced the pacification of the province.[21]

While roads, markets, clinics, and schools formed the basis of the Army's nation-building campaign, ultimately the success or failure of the Army's activities rested on the ability of officers in the field to win the trust and confidence of the Moros. "The personal equation in the government of a semibarbarous people such as this is everything," wrote General Wood. Consequently, the Army attempted to fill civil posts in Moro Province with officers known for their intelligence, character, tact, and prior pacification achievements.

Officers of this caliber were rare, and many of those who served in the province—especially those assigned to military units as opposed to civil posts—were ill suited for the work. The Army's efforts to select appropriate people for pacification service was complicated by its personnel system, which routinely rotated individuals and units in and out of Moroland. The average tour of an officer in a civil post was only fourteen months, an inadequate time in which to build any lasting rapport with the inhabitants. The Army realized that frequent rotations

Major Scott, district governor of Moro Province's Sulu archipelago, and the sultan of Jolo

harmed its pacification efforts, yet it was unable to solve the problems created by a system designed to meet the larger needs of the Army and not the narrow mission of pacification. Congress dealt the Army's efforts to maintain at least a modicum of continuity in Moro civil posts a final blow in 1912 when it mandated that officers spend four out of every six years with their regiments. The "Manchu Law" convinced Pershing that the Army was an inappropriate tool for long-term pacification work. It was one of the factors that led to the termination of the Army's reign in Moro Province in December 1913.[22]

The most important functionaries in Moro Province were the U.S. officers who served as district governors, for they were the pointmen of the pacification campaign. These officials supervised local nation-building activities, adjudicated disputes, enforced the laws, and punished recalcitrants. In many respects they became *datos* themselves, political strongmen who ruled through a mixture of charisma and acumen, backed by the ever-present threat of force. It was a difficult and often frustrating task. The most successful were those who were open-minded enough to learn the local language and customs and who endeavored to achieve their ends by working through, rather than against, the indigenous culture. In governing Moro Province, Army officers strove to find that delicate and often illusive balance between modernization and tradition. They tailored nation-building activities so as not to violate native beliefs, and they made extensive efforts to soften changes in policy to avoid unnecessary conflict. Some district governors, like Majs. Hugh L. Scott and Robert L. Bullard, complemented their efforts to build good relations with the natives by holding orientation programs for units newly posted in the province. Even General Wood, whose ethnocentrism sometimes led him to impose American concepts too quickly in Moroland as it had in Cuba, recognized that certain aspects of Moro society had to be respected if the United States was to succeed in pacifying the province.[23]

Yet for all of the Army's efforts to avoid conflict, violence occurred, necessitating the presence of approximately five thousand troops in the province between 1902 and 1913. Although traditional banditry, piracy, personal rivalries, and intertribal conflicts caused much of the violence, America's soldier-governors also contributed, either through unwise actions or, more often, through the adoption of policies which attempted to move the Moros too fast down the road of "progress." Nevertheless, a certain amount of conflict was probably inevitable, given the basic differences between the two cultures.[24]

Most of the serious fighting in Moroland occurred between 1903 and 1906 as the United States moved to consolidate its hold over the region during Wood's governorship. A veteran of the Indian wars, Wood was imbued with the old Army ethos that the best way to subjugate an aboriginal foe was through a short, sharp campaign. During his tenure, the Army employed the type of slash-and-burn methods that it had used in earlier counterguerrilla operations, destroying the forts, homes, and crops of those who resisted U.S. authority. Where the opposition was particularly obstinate, the Army occasionally resorted to the techniques of population relocation and concentration.[25]

The Moros certainly were dangerous, but they never posed a serious military threat to American authorities. They were poorly armed and even poorer shots. Although they staged ambushes and fanatical attacks, they were not as fond of making mass charges as the *pulahans* to the north. Instead, the Moros preferred to fight from fixed fortifications, called *cottas*. These works were vulnerable to American firepower, and by taking to their *cottas*, the Moros facilitated their own conquest.

Regiments newly arrived in Moroland were given briefings in Moro tactics and trained in the best ways to counter them. As it had done elsewhere in the Philippines, the Army modified conventional procedures to meet jungle conditions and the threat of ambush. Following advice given by Bigelow in *The Principles of Strategy*, military commanders in Moro

American soldiers stormed the Moro cotta *of Fort Bacolod in April 1903 by using bamboo poles to bridge the fort's deep moat.*

Province resurrected the time-honored square formation and successfully employed it to fend off Moro sword attacks. Night marches for the purpose of making surprise dawn raids on hostile camps and *cottas* were standard tactics during the Army's constabulary operations there. Where the terrain was suitable, the Army maintained garrisons of mounted troops both for their mobility and for their psychological effect on the population. It also endeavored to deter *juramentados* by burying dead fanatics with a pig, an act of defamation that Moros believed prevented the passage of the warrior's soul to heaven.[26]

Chasing bandits and renegades through steaming tropical jungles was enervating work that required a level of stamina and skill for which not all Americans were prepared. As in the past, the Army responded to the special demands of irregular warfare by creating groups of specialists from within its own ranks. In addition to permanently assigning a few men of each company to reconnaissance and point duty, field commanders also created specialized units in Moro Province, designated provisional, or provo, companies.

General Wood was the leading exponent of the specialist approach. As a young surgeon, he had served in such a unit created by General Miles for the purpose of catching Geronimo. Wood shared Miles' opinion that a body of highly skilled, physically fit regulars could beat

Counterinsurgency Doctrine, 1860–1941

Men of the 23d U.S. Infantry's elite provo company cross the Rio Grande River, Mindanao Island, in 1904.

native irregulars at their own game, and when in 1904 he was confronted by an especially elusive opponent of American authority, *Dato* Ali, he naturally turned to the lessons of his frontier experiences. In August he created four provisional companies, one from each of the four regular regiments under his command. Standards in the provo companies were tough. To qualify, soldiers had to be able to swim 100 yards without clothes, 75 yards with clothes, and 50 yards in heavy marching gear. They also had to meet certain standards of health and physical conditioning and demonstrate proficiency in handling a native boat, first aid, signals, and marksmanship. Unlike line companies, which were often reduced to half strength from illness and expired enlistments, provo companies were always kept up to full strength. Assignment to provo units was permanent, and the soldiers who joined them quickly developed a special esprit de corps. There was even an elite within the elite, as one squad within the company always took the point. The provisional companies carried the brunt of the *Dato* Ali campaign, and it was a provo unit under the command of Capt. Frank R. McCoy that finally killed the elusive chieftain. Provo units remained in use in Moroland until the end of the Army's rule there.[27]

Perhaps the thorniest aspect of Moro warfare was not killing Moros but keeping them alive. The problem stemmed from the Moro warriors'

U.S. artillery bombards Dato *Ali's fort at Siranaya, Mindanao Island.*

habit of bringing their women and children with them into their *cottas*, a practice that inevitably resulted in high civilian casualties, especially given the Moros' proclivity for fighting to the death. American officers usually attempted to persuade the defenders of a *cotta* either to surrender or to send out their women and children before a battle. More often than not, the Moros refused to do either, and the Army was compelled to assault the fort with the civilians inside. The resultant noncombatant casualties generated a storm of public disapproval back home that resembled the criticism leveled at the Army during the Indian wars. Similar too was the Army's response to such criticism, for while officers deeply regretted civilian casualties, they considered such losses as the unfortunate price of victory in a struggle for which the Moros, rather than the soldiers, were responsible.

Nevertheless, public scrutiny did affect Army operations. On the one hand, it made commanders more cautious and gave them an added incentive to try and minimize civilian casualties, either through negotiation or by besieging, rather than assaulting, Moro strongholds. Some operations were even canceled, due to the administration's fear that its political opponents would convert stories of civilian deaths into political capital. On the other hand, the situation also led officers to cover up operations that might otherwise have aroused public condemnation. General Wood did just that in 1904 when he made sure that no journalists were present before embarking upon a punitive expedition in the Taraca region of Mindanao that "laid waste" the countryside.[28]

Through a combination of punitive campaigns, "*cotta*-busting," provo units, and diplomacy, Wood broke the back of Moro resistance by the end of 1906. Operations to stamp out banditry and piracy continued, and occasionally a small punitive campaign was needed to put a recalcitrant *dato* in his place, but Wood had secured American sovereignty. As in the rest of the Philippines, the Constabulary and Scouts carried the main burden for maintaining order in Moro Province after 1906. They were well adapted to the demands of the work, somewhat more mobile than regulars, and, from a political standpoint, infinitely more discreet—an important consideration, given the sensitivity of both Moro and American publics to military activities. For the most part, therefore, the Army confined its regulars in the post-1906 period to garrisoning towns, conducting practice marches, and assisting the auxiliaries during particularly difficult operations. As conditions stabilized, the possibility of transferring Moro Province from military to civilian control grew stronger, an event that finally occurred in December 1913.[29]

By and large, the Army wrote a creditable record in the subjugation and pacification of the Moros. Building upon their previous experiences on the western frontier, in the Caribbean, and in other parts of the Philippine archipelago, American officers applied the well-worn creed of firm-but-fair treatment to establish a paternal regime that attempted to uplift the Moros without completely disregarding their political, economic, and religious heritage. Although relations had not always been smooth, many Moros regretted the departure of the soldier-administrators, whom they considered to be more sensitive to their concerns than the Christian Filipinos who increasingly dominated provincial affairs after the Army's departure.

But while the Army had succeeded in "pacifying" the Moros, it had been much less successful in "civilizing" them. Social, economic, and political changes came with painful slowness to Moroland, while a lack of resources and the Moros' own suspicion of Westernized education meant that few Moro children ever attended school during the period of military rule. The Army could leave Moro Province justifiably proud of its achievements, yet mindful of the tremendous difficulties inherent in pacification and nation building. It was a lesson the Army was destined to learn and relearn during the imperial constabulary years.[30]

The Second Cuban Intervention, 1906–1909

While the Army worked to complete the pacification of the Philippines, President Theodore Roosevelt saddled it with another major constabulary mission in September 1906, when he ordered troops to resume nation-building activities in Cuba. The island was in the throes of a revolution that had begun when the opposition Liberal Party refused to accept the results of an election rigged by the ruling Moderate Party. Both sides appealed for American aid, but in the end Roosevelt decided to take control of Cuba himself, a decision that represented a victory for the liberals. He opted for this course because he wanted to avoid embroiling the United States in another frustrating guerrilla conflict like the Philippine War. By pledging to act as an honest broker, the president hoped to defuse rather than suppress the insurrection. In this he was successful. The "revolutionaries" welcomed the intervention, and U.S. military forces were able to occupy the country without incident. Secretary of War William Howard Taft, whom Roosevelt put in temporary charge of the island until a full-time American administrator could be found, offered a blanket amnesty to all insurgents and, with the help of U.S. Army and Marine Corps officers, successfully disarmed and disbanded the insurgent military forces. By the end of October the immediate crisis had passed, and occupation officials could devote themselves to the job of rebuilding the Cuban political system.[31]

In organizing the second occupation, Secretary Taft selected civilian Charles Magoon, former governor of the Panama Canal Zone, to head the provisional government of Cuba. To command U.S. military forces on the island, Taft appointed Brig. Gen. Frederick Funston, a veteran of the Philippine War who also had served as a volunteer in the Cuban revolutionary movement prior to the Spanish-American War. Funston's command was designated the Army of Cuban Pacification. Although both the provisional government and the Army of Cuban Pacification operated under the rubric of the War Department, the division of authority violated the Army's cherished creed of unified command and military control during an occupation. Fortunately, civil-military relations were relatively harmonious, in large part because the occupation was essentially peaceful.

The absence of open warfare notwithstanding, banditry plagued certain sections of the country. President Roosevelt insisted that Cuban security forces shoulder the entire burden of policing the island, lest clashes between Cubans and American soldiers spark an insurrection against U.S. authority in Cuba and a storm of public anger at home. Therefore, the 6,000 soldiers and marines of the Army of Cuban Pacification maintained a low profile, acting more as a deterrent than as an active agent in the island's pacification. Its passive posture, however, did not mean that it lacked a positive role in helping the provisional government to achieve its objectives. General Bell, Funston's successor, exhorted his men to be on their best behavior, imposed strict limits on fraternization, and forbade officers to become involved in partisan politics. Meanwhile, the Army took steps both to discourage insurrectionary plotting should the populace come to resent America's presence in Cuba and to prepare itself for active operations, should deterrence fail.[32]

The Army made its presence felt most demonstrably through practice marches. As in the Philippines, practice marches served the dual purpose of familiarizing the troops with the countryside while showing the flag in a nonconfrontational way. The Army also launched an elaborate mapping program. Previous experience had made officers painfully aware of the importance of good maps to offset the superior topographical knowledge that guerrillas usually enjoyed. Consequently, the Army sent out numerous parties to map every inch of the island. Not only did the surveyors compile an impressive amount of information, but their activities also had a positive effect, signaling Cubans who might be tempted to rebel that they would have no place to hide.

In a quieter manner, Bell concentrated his mobile counterguerrilla forces in areas deemed to be the most potentially dangerous. Plans were drawn up to supplement the initial occupation force with significant numbers of cavalry, often the Army's most effective counterguerrilla agent. The Army of Cuban Pacification also applied a lesson from the Philippine experience by establishing an extensive intelligence network of spies, informers, and local intelligence officers, all under the supervision of a central intelligence office in Havana. The network gathered information on the social, political, and economic situation in Cuba, amassed an impressive amount of data on the physical features of the island, and compiled dossiers on all politically active Cubans. The Army rounded off its preparations by assigning Capt. John W. Furlong to prepare a counterinsurgency guide for commanders should the Cubans revolt against the occupation.[33]

Furlong's work, "Notes on Field Service in Cuba," identified three primary missions for American forces during a potential insurrection—identifying, isolating, and destroying the enemy. The first and most important mission was to create a first-rate intelligence organization to identify and eliminate the clandestine civil-military infrastructure that an insurgent movement would doubtlessly establish. Having served as a provost and intelligence officer in southern Luzon during the Philippine War, Furlong was well aware that guerrilla warfare tends to be highly contingent upon local factors. Thus, while he encouraged the creation of a "national" intelligence system, he emphasized that the heart of intelligence operations was at the local level. In fact, the Army of Cuban Pacification had already divided Cuba into military districts, each with its own intelligence office, with just this thought in mind. Should the Cubans rise in revolt, the district intelligence offices were expected to break the insurgents' clandestine civil-military command and control structure by bribing informers, translating captured documents, and interrogating suspects. Although Furlong's guide forbade torture, it encouraged American interrogators to employ "police methods" in questioning suspects, a term that was hardly benign. Furlong also counseled American interrogators that "the accused should not be allowed to sleep until he confesses all he knows," and that captured insurgent leaders should be placed on a strict regimen of hard labor and bread-and-water diets until all the insurgents in the area surrendered. Should these measures fail to uproot the local infrastructure, he advised trying suspected insurgent leaders before military commissions, citing his own experience that the accused often confessed to avoid a death sentence.

While the Army's intelligence and judicial systems were busy cracking the hypothetical insurgency's command, control, and supply system, the soldiers in the field were to execute the other major missions of the counterinsurgency war—separating the population from the guerrillas and destroying the insurgent combat forces. Furlong believed the former mission could best be accomplished by concentrating the civilian population and destroying the food supply in the countryside, just as Bell had done in Batangas. To defeat the guerrillas in the field, Furlong prescribed an active campaign in which mobile columns would relentlessly hound the insurgents. If all went well, the campaign would be short, sharp, and decisive—the type of conflict the Army desperately wanted so as to avoid a long, enervating guerrilla war.[34]

Armed with a blueprint for the conduct of a counterinsurgency campaign, the Army of Cuban Pacification proceeded to take the preliminary steps needed to implement the plan, including an active training program. Training in Cuba focused on "minor tactics," small-unit maneuvers characteristic of counterguerrilla operations such as the conduct of patrols, camp and outpost security, convoys, and ambushes. Field exercises similar to General Miles' old game of "raiders and pursuers" were common, as were exercises simulating the protection of railroads from guerrilla attack, the relief of beleaguered outposts, the interception of mounted raiding forces, and the conduct of counterguerrilla patrols. Many of these exercises were conducted at night, using pack trains for mobility—standard U.S. counterinsurgency procedures for nearly a half century. These measures, in conjunction with frequent practice marches, transformed the Army of Cuban

A one-room schoolhouse built by the Army of Cuban Pacification during the second Cuban occupation

Pacification into a potentially strong counterguerrilla force.[35]

While the Army prepared for the possibility of active operations, the provisional government undertook the difficult task of reforming Cuba's political system. Magoon was fortunate in having the assistance of officers who had served in similar administrations in Asia and the Caribbean; indeed, Army officers filled a considerable number of posts in his technically civilian government. Yet the task he and his assistants faced was formidable. In the four years since the end of the first occupation (1898–1902), many of General Wood's achievements had failed to bear fruit. Political reforms had withered on the vine, roads had fallen into disrepair, and sanitary measures had been neglected.

Using Cuban revenues (most of America's nation-building activities prior to World War II were funded not by the American taxpayer, but by the indigenous peoples themselves via taxes and tariffs), Magoon launched an ambitious program of civic action crafted in the tradition of American progressivism. He improved Cuba's educational facilities and filled the new schoolhouses by hiring more faculty and introducing mandatory attendance for children. He attacked deficiencies in Cuba's health and sanitation systems with such vigor that by 1909 the island had one of the lowest death rates in the world. With the

Road-building projects, like this one in Cuba, were an integral part of all U.S. Army nation-building and pacification endeavors.

assistance of the U.S. Army Corps of Engineers, he increased paved-road mileage on the island by 125 percent, halving the cost of transporting sugar and tobacco to market in the improved areas. The provisional government spent large sums on these and other public works projects, not only to improve Cuba's long-term infrastructure, but also to provide relief during the growing season, when unemployment and public discontent traditionally peaked. U.S. military advisers supported the government's quest for internal order by endeavoring to create a nonpartisan paramilitary force, the Rural Guard, that was similar in many respects to the Philippine Constabulary. Most important, the Magoon administration revamped Cuba's political order, crafting under the guidance of Col. Enoch Crowder a set of legal and constitutional reforms designed to put Cuba back on the democratic track. After holding free elections under the new rules, U.S. officials judged the island sufficiently stable to return governmental authority to the Cubans. The Army of Cuban Pacification withdrew in January 1909.[36]

The War Department achieved many positive things in Cuba between 1906–1909. Yet in the end America's second foray into Caribbean nation building was no more successful than the first and for essentially the same reasons. Turn-of-the-century Americans were ideologically too conservative to undertake the type of sweeping reforms necessary to address the fundamental socioeconomic problems facing Cuban society. The Army's bootstrap approach to development—sponsoring public education and providing "workfare" programs for the unemployed—only scratched the surface of the problems of social stratification and rural poverty. Moreover, as during the first occupation, the Army failed to change Cuba's political culture. In consequence, many of the new, progressive institutions introduced by the War Department, including the majority of Colonel Crowder's reforms, were doomed to fall on infertile soil, while those that survived often mutated in ways that America's social engineers had not intended.[37]

In fact, most Army officers familiar with Cuban society disapproved of the provisional government's tendency to focus on short-range solutions to Cuba's political problems. Real change, they recognized, could not be achieved without a fundamental overhaul of Cuba's political culture, something that would take many years to achieve. Yet neither the nation's political leaders nor the public at large was willing to make such a commitment. Army officers left Cuba in 1909 with little confidence that they had achieved any lasting improvements, and rightly so, as the country gradually fell under the spell of corrupt and dictatorial regimes.[38]

The Imperial Constabulary Mission and Army Doctrine

The imperial constabulary mission had a mixed impact upon the Army. On the one hand, fighting ill-armed Filipinos and building roads in Moroland may have sharpened the leadership skills of the Army's junior officers. But these and other constabulary experiences greatly interfered with the Army's ability to prepare itself, both organizationally and intellectually, for modern warfare. Even the finest officers of the time, including Generals Wood and Pershing, openly worried about the diversion and pressed for a reorientation of Army training toward conventional operations. The outbreak of World War I dramatized their concerns and reinforced the Army's traditional inclination to relegate constabulary functions to a distinctly secondary status.[39]

The harsh methods that were sometimes necessary in pacification, and the public criticism that followed, also served to dampen the Army's interest and to discourage frank analysis of its experiences. Army leaders, for example, deemed it "inadvisable" to publish Captain Furlong's primer on counterguerrilla warfare in Cuba because of the sensitivity of the subject matter. Similarly, as late as 1938 the chief of the Chemical War Service opposed the publication of an examination of whether the use of nonlethal gas could have prevented civilian casualties during some of the Army's assaults on Moro strongholds because "discussion of these actions may revive public attention to military operations that might well remain forgotten." Such squeamishness stifled the development of a formal small wars doctrine.[40]

Another reason why imperial policing had only a marginal impact upon tactical doctrine was that the Army's conventional small-unit tactics had proved sufficiently adaptable for counterguerrilla work to obviate any major change. Consequently, both the 1905 *Field Service Regulations* and the 1911 *Infantry Drill Regulations* confined their discussions of irregular, "minor," warfare to reviewing the nature of guerrilla conflicts and enumerating some of the countermeasures that had proved effective in the past. Neither manual, however, provided details on the conduct of counterguerrilla operations, preferring instead to follow Mahan and Wagner in encouraging readers to apply innovatively the general principles contained within their pages.[41]

Although the Army did not develop formal doctrines for waging small wars, neither did it completely ignore the subject. At Leavenworth, Philippine veterans occasionally instructed their students in methods designed to defeat charging fanatics and partisans, while the U.S. Military Academy continued to instruct its pupils in the management of pack trains and pack artillery. Moreover, several officers encouraged their colleagues to examine recent small war campaigns to gain insights into this type of warfare. Capt. Matthew F. Steele's Leavenworth lectures included discussions of European colonial campaigns, while Col. Arthur Wagner published a reading list for officers that, while heavily oriented toward conventional operations, included a section on "minor wars." Included were histories of the Seminole and Plains Indian wars, the Boxer Rebellion, and works on Britain's colonial campaigns in Africa and Asia.[42]

As in the nineteenth century, many of the most practical and immediate lessons from the Army's experiences were preserved through less formal methods. One of the most important was the development of "field service notes"—short articles or pamphlets written by veteran officers detailing campaign experiences. Such notes usually blended tactical, operational, and logistical advice with information on the terrain, climate, and inhabitants of the area in question. The notes, which were either published in professional journals or distributed internally within the Army, served as primers on some of the Army's more exotic postings.[43]

Army leaders supplemented this informal transmission system by permitting local commanders to modify conventional training programs for local conditions. The Army of Cuban Pacification's counterguerrilla training program was by no means an exception. Troops in Moro Province likewise trained to meet local conditions, while units stationed in the Panama Canal Zone received special training in jungle and guerrilla warfare based upon lessons derived from conflicts in the Philippines and European experience in Africa.[44]

Another way in which the Army attempted to encourage the accumulation of expertise for imperial constabulary duty was through the "colonial army" system, inaugurated by Army Chief of Staff General Leonard Wood in 1912. Under this system, certain regiments were permanently assigned to overseas garrison and constabulary work. The Army hoped that the system would reduce the costs associated with rotating units to and from the United States and produce colonial garrisons that were fully acclimated and trained to meet local conditions. In the Philippines, for example, such special knowledge included "training and acquiring knowledge of the native population that would be of service in quelling a native uprising or insurrection."

In practice, the colonial army system did not work well. From the beginning, short, congressionally mandated tour lengths undermined the anticipated benefits. Moreover, as the threat of internal insurrection receded, the Army in the Philippines increasingly neglected counterguerrilla training in favor of measures designed to protect the islands from external threats. Ironically, the policy of making native auxiliaries the first line of defense against internal upheaval merely accelerated this trend, for if pacification was truly the responsibility of the Constabulary, there seemed little reason for the Army to devote much of its precious training time preparing for the remote possibility of another insurrection. Nevertheless, the colonial army system represented an attempt by the Army's senior leadership to keep alive those skills it had found to be valuable in successful constabulary operations.[45]

While the Army attempted to preserve some of the tactical and operational lessons of the imperial constabulary experience, it did not neglect the other half of the constabulary equation—pacification and military government. As the Army moved from one constabulary mission to the next, several officials, including Secretary of War Root, urged the military educational system to better prepare the nation's officers for overseas duty. Col. Charles W. Miner, commandant of the General Service and Staff College (as the Leavenworth school was then known), and his assistant Colonel Wagner responded by expanding Leavenworth's curriculum to include such topics as the geography of potential intervention sites, the government of occupied territories, the treatment of civilian populations, the use of military commissions, "guerrilla warfare," and concentration. By 1909 Leavenworth's course in martial law and military government was considered to be the most exhaustive of its kind in the world.[46]

West Point matched Leavenworth's curricular changes stride for stride. In 1906 one of the Army's most experienced constabulary warriors, Col. Hugh L. Scott, returned from his tour as a district governor in Moro Province to assume the superintendency of West Point. Scott shared Root's conviction that the Army's young officers needed to be better prepared for assuming the many civil functions characteristic of imperial constabulary duty. To accomplish this, he moved to increase the amount of liberal arts instruction at the academy, especially in the areas of history, geography, economics, and political science. Although the academy's curriculum continued to be heavily technical in focus, Scott had taken the first step toward providing the type of intellectual training that American officers required to meet the increasingly complex politico-military challenges of the modern world.[47]

The Army also encouraged officers to study Spanish. The movement to promote Spanish actually began prior to the Spanish-American War, when several officers, including 1st Lt. Matthew F. Steele, argued against replacing Spanish with German at West Point. Steele maintained that Spanish was a much more practical language for officers to master than German, given the likelihood of "future contingencies" under the Monroe Doctrine. His foresight quickly became evident, and after 1902 the Army dramatically increased its support of Spanish-language instruction. Field commanders in Cuba and the Philippines directed their subordinates to study Spanish, while the Military Academy devoted increased attention to it as well. Meanwhile, Leavenworth not only created a Department of Spanish in 1904, but made the study of the language mandatory in 1906, while French and German remained only electives. For the next several decades, Spanish remained an integral part of the curriculums of both institutions in recognition of its utility in civil-military missions in the Western Hemisphere.[48]

One of the more vocal proponents for the study of pacification in the Army's educational system was Lt. Col. Robert L. Bullard. A veteran of the Philippines, Moro Province, and Cuba, Bullard wrote a series of articles during the first decade of the twentieth century analyzing the Army's experiences in those campaigns. The most important, "Military Pacification," appeared in the January 1910 edition of the *Journal of the Military Service Institution of the United States*.[49]

Bullard defined pacification as "all means, short of actual war, used by the dominating power in the operation of bringing back to a state of peace and order the inhabitants of a district lately in hostilities." Since unadulterated repression was unpalatable to a democratic nation like the United States, he urged the Army to adopt enlightened and benevolent policies when undertaking pacification or nation-building tasks. Though he shared the racial prejudices of the day, he stressed that troops on pacification duty had to have "sympathy with the people," for there was "no greater marplot, no worse troublemaker than the officer or soldier to whom 'all coons look alike.'" He recommended that officers learn the language, customs, and history of the indigenous population so that they might avoid doing anything that ran counter to the inhabitants' core cultural and religious beliefs. Following the tenets of international law and the Army's traditional notion of the evolutionary nature of cultural development, he counseled against trying to revolutionize backward societies overnight. Rather, soldiers on pacification assignments had to exercise patience and tact as they alternately enticed and prodded benighted peoples down the "road of progress."[50]

Although Bullard stressed the importance of benevolence in a successful pacification program, he never forgot that force had an equally legitimate role to play. Persuasion alone was usually insufficient to quell an uprising or to govern a less civilized people, he argued, and consequently force—applied not in passion but as the result of reasoned calculation—was indispensable for the successful prosecution of a pacification campaign. Like Bigelow and Bell, Bullard believed that being too gentle could prove to be just as harmful as being too harsh, and he endorsed the employment of punitive measures, trials by military commissions, and concentration, for "without them there is no pacification." In the final analysis, Bullard echoed Jomini in concluding that pacification could only be achieved through "a judicious mixture of force and persuasion, of severity and moderation."[51]

"Military Pacification" was one of the most significant pieces written by an American officer on the subject prior to World War II. Its importance lay not so much in charting new ground, but in giving cogent expression to widely shared views regarding the lessons of the Army's experiences. Yet, while Bullard urged the Army to take the pacification mission seriously, he stopped short of advocating the development of a formal doctrine on the subject. Pacification, he wrote, was "largely personal," for it depended "more upon the wisdom, tact, personality, and disposition of the officials applying it than upon any defined governmental policy or definite legislative acts." Although officers needed a general philosophy and a set of guiding principles, Bullard, like Bigelow, believed that no hard and fast rules were possible. The Army agreed, and neither in its classrooms nor in its official publications did it attempt to dictate a formula for subduing and governing foreign populations. Rather, official doctrine, as expressed in the *Rules of Land Warfare* (1914) compiled by pacification veteran and former "water cure" enthusiast Col. Edwin F. Glenn, reaffirmed the principles of GO 100 and the Army's traditional carrot-and-stick philosophy, while declining to prescribe specific programs.[52]

Army leaders did, however, put the lessons of the past to practical use, as evidenced by the war plans written at the Army War College during the decade between 1904 and 1914. Most of these plans concerned peacetime contingency operations to protect American lives, property, and interests abroad. By far the most detailed dealt with the nation's revolution-wracked southern neighbor, Mexico.

No one in the U.S. Army was particularly eager to take on the job of restoring order in Mexico, a country of 15 million people whose animosity toward "gringos" transcended political affiliations. Although the Mexican government only had a little over 30,000 regulars under arms, American military planners believed they would need between 400,000 to 550,000 men to pacify the country. The Army based these figures on studies of the Philippine and Boer Wars, Mexico's long history of irregular conflict, and the fact that the Mexicans were both better armed and imbued with a much deeper hatred of Americans than the Filipinos. Occupying Mexico would be easy, a matter of a few months, the Army imagined, but it would take three to four years to pacify the country. These estimates were enough to frighten any American politician, and based on them President William Howard Taft prudently decided against intervening in Mexico's domestic troubles.[53]

Although never used, the Army's approach to intervention in Mexican affairs reflected its internal civil-military operational doctrine. Its plans envisioned a two-phase campaign—an initial period of conventional military operations aimed at the capture of Mexico City and the destruction of organized Mexican forces; "and a second period of pacification, during which our military forces are employed, incidentally, in stamping out guerrillas, and principally in an extensive occupation of municipalities for the restoration of law and order and the resurrection or creation of civil government."[54]

Military operations during the second phase were to be characterized by small, mobile columns of mounted troops and pack mules which would wage a "merciless crusade against bandits and guerrillas" in the finest tradition of Generals Crook, Miles, and Bell. Military courts and an elaborate intelligence network would reinforce the Army's efforts in the field and strike at the guerrillas' politico-military infrastructure. In accordance with what had now become standard

American practice, the Army hoped to place "the dirty job of re-establishing order in the provinces" squarely upon a native constabulary that it planned to organize soon after the occupation began. Not only would such a corps of native auxiliaries be perfectly suited for performing counterguerrilla tasks, but, as Capt. Andrew J. Dougherty explained, "a force of Rural Guards can clean up a band of insurgents or ladrones as a police measure without exciting comment; whereas, should the same thing be done by regular troops every newspaper will have columns about the latest insurrection."[55]

The Army complemented its plans for the military suppression of Mexican irregulars with plans for reestablishing civil government. The core of these plans, "A Study of the Pacification of Mexico and Establishment of Civil Government," was developed by a committee of four officers at the Army War College, all veterans of America's overseas constabulary operations. Essentially, the planners wanted to replace Mexico's corrupt and inefficient administration with an efficient, modern bureaucracy, while carefully retaining as many indigenous legal and institutional forms as possible to minimize the danger of the Mexican body politic rejecting the transplanted organs of Anglo-Saxon efficiency. To accomplish this, most burdens were to fall on field commanders, who would be urged "to be as mild and humane as the necessities of the situation permit" to "convince the mass of inhabitants that our purpose is just and our desire is to be as humane as possible." "Arbitrary or needless use of any armed force" would be proscribed and the confidence of the people won by courting the Catholic Church, respecting local customs, and initiating a series of programs designed to improve socioeconomic conditions throughout the country. Included among these were the construction of roads and other infrastructure facilities and the institution of reforms in charitable, penal, health, and educational systems. Free medical care was to be provided to the masses, "but as few governmental acts can be more vicious and more debasing to the public morale than wholesale gratuities," the planners espoused a program of public works to reduce Mexico's unemployment rolls.[56]

Although the Army's social engineers continued to prefer "workfare" to "welfare," they also recognized that fundamental changes would have to be effected in Mexico's basic socioeconomic structure if the traditional American slate of progressive reforms was going to have a chance of succeeding. Committee members judged the underlying cause of poverty and unrest in Mexico to be its system of peonage and therefore declared "it is the policy of our administration to discourage peonage and to assist in every legitimate way the building up of a middle class in Mexico." To accomplish this task, the committee proposed that the Army distribute land to the peasantry, both by parceling out vacant public lands and by breaking up some of the largest private estates. Nevertheless, the committee was not optimistic about the Army's chances of overhauling Mexico's socioeconomic structure. Fundamental reform takes time, yet military governments were by their very nature of short duration, and "hence measures of reform that might be undertaken with great advantage to the country may have to be put aside because the time indispensable to their inception and to their prosecution to a successful finish is denied." Besides, noted one committee member,

it is their government, not ours (except for the moment), and if organic or radical change be desirable, the right and duty of making them belong to the people of the country, not to the United States. And it may well be doubted if great changes imposed by us, even though theoretically in the direction of reform, would serve any good purpose or last long after our departure. In national, as in private life, people must, to a great extent, work out their own salvation and build their own careers.[57]

In the end, the best the Army could hope to do was to repeat what it had done in Cuba—give the Mexicans an object lesson in good government in the hopes of inspiring them to emulation. But nobody was particularly confident that the Army would be able to work any lasting changes in Mexican society.

The skepticism and ambivalence exhibited by the authors of the Mexican pacification study reflected the attitudes of the Army as a whole. Ten years of nation building in Asia and the Caribbean had tarnished the optimism with which many officers had embraced social engineering and international activism at the turn of the century. Perhaps the best indicator of how the Army felt about the overseas constabulary mission is the degree to which it increasingly tried to avoid it. In 1905, when the Roosevelt administration was considering sending troops to China to break a Chinese boycott of American goods, General Wood begged the president to give the mission to the Army and not the Marine Corps. Such bellicosity was short lived. In 1906 the Army General Staff was wary about intervening in Cuba out of fear of becoming embroiled in another Philippine-type guerrilla war. In 1911 the Army counseled against participating in another international intervention in China. The following year it balked twice more at undertaking interventionist missions. Chief of Staff Wood labeled President Taft's suggestion that the Army intervene in yet another Cuban revolution "extreme and foolish," while Secretary of War Henry Stimson objected to Taft's order to send soldiers to intervene in a revolution in Nicaragua on the grounds it was an inappropriate mission for the U.S. Army. The Army represented the full power of the nation, he argued, and therefore using soldiers to intervene in the affairs of other nations would have a much greater negative impact on public opinion at home and abroad than if Taft sent in marines. Taft agreed and sent marines rather than soldiers into both Cuba and Nicaragua.

The Army's attitude reflected the lessons it had learned about such operations: they were messy, trying, and institutionally unrewarding. While the Army realized that it had to be prepared to meet such contingencies, it did not seek them out. Better to let the Marine Corps do it. And the marines did take up the constabulary mission, not so much because they wanted to but because they lacked the institutional strength to avoid it. The Marine Corps quickly became the government's instrument of choice to execute contingency operations for the protection of American interests overseas, and the corps soon earned the nickname "State Department troops" for its efforts. It was an appellation the U.S. Army was happy to let the marines have.[58]

Notes

[1] Victor Purcell, *The Boxer Uprising* (London: Cambridge University Press, 1963), pp. 124–25, 248–52, 260–61; Chester Tan, *The Boxer Catastrophe* (New York: Columbia, 1955), pp. 71–73.

[2] Michael Hunt, "The Forgotten Occupation: Peking, 1900–01," *Pacific Historical Review* 48 (1979): 518; War Department, Adjutant General, "Extracts From the Report of Major General Adna R. Chaffee, Commanding U.S. Troops in China, on Military Operations in China," in *Reports on Military Operations in South Africa and China* (Washington, D.C.: Government Printing Office, 1901), p. 340 (hereafter cited as *Chaffee Report*); Carleton Waite, *Some Elements of International Military Cooperation in the Suppression of the 1900 Antiforeign Rising in China With Special Reference to the Forces of the United States* (Los Angeles: University of Southern California Press, 1935), pp. 33–34.

[3] *Chaffee Report*, pp. 332, 334, 345, 502, 577; *WDAR*, 1900, vol. 1, pt. 9, pp. 113, 138–39; *WDAR*, 1901, vol. 1, pt. 6, pp. 510–12.

[4] At Tientsin, coalition commanders committed the 9th Infantry into making an attack without first reconnoitering the ground. The 9th Infantry advanced into a swamp, where heavy Chinese fire pinned it down for the remainder of the day. Seventeen Americans (including the regiment's commander, Col. Emerson H. Liscum) were killed and seventy-one wounded. At Yang-ts'un, the problem was interoperability. The Russian battery commander obtained the range to a Chinese target from a British officer, who expressed the distance in yards. The Russian, however, assumed the numbers were in metric. He fired his guns accordingly, with the result that the shells fell short into American lines. Purcell, *Boxer Uprising*, p. 259; Richard O'Connor, *The Spirit Soldiers* (New York: G. P. Putnam's Sons, 1973), p. 223; Benjamin Pope, "The Causes of the Boxer Uprising and the Battle of Tientsin," in *Monographs of the World War* (Fort Benning, Ga.: Infantry School, c. 1922–23), pp. 660–65.

[5] Hunt, "Forgotten Occupation," p. 529.

[6] Twichell, *Allen*, p. 137; War Department, *Philippine Commission Annual Report* (hereafter cited as *PCAR*), 1904 (Washington, D.C.: Government Printing Office, 1905), 3:67–68; ibid., 1905, 10:50, 212; George Coats, "The Philippine Constabulary, 1901–17" (Ph.D. diss., Ohio State University, 1968), pp. 198–200; Charles Elliott, *The Philippines to the End of Commission Government* (Indianapolis: Bobbs-Merrill Company, 1917), pp. 21, 24.

[7] First quote from *PCAR*, 1904, 1:387. Second quote from Ltr, Allen to Luke Wright, 19 Nov 02, box 7, Allen Papers.

[8] Coats, "Philippine Constabulary," p. 5; Forbes, *Philippine Islands*, 1:203; James Woolard, "The Philippine Scouts: The Development of America's Colonial Army" (Ph.D. diss., Ohio State University, 1975), pp. 89–91.

[9] Sexton, *Soldiers in the Sun*, pp. 283–84; Harold Elarth, *The Story of the Philippine Constabulary* (Los Angeles: Globe Printing, 1949), pp. 15–16.

[10] Eben Swift, "Peon or Soldier," *JMSIUS* 30 (1902): 229; Ward, "Uses of Native Troops," p. 799; Ltr, Allen to Corbin, 24 Mar 03, box 8, Allen Papers.

[11] Richard Smith, "Philippine Constabulary," *Military Review* 48 (May 1968): 73–80; Philippine Constabulary, *Manual for the Philippine Constabulary, 1907*

(Manila: Bureau of Printing, 1906), pp. 122, 125–30.

[12] Quote from *Manual for the Philippine Constabulary, 1907*, pp. 145–46, and see also pp. 23–26, 37.

[13] Twichell, *Allen*, p. 131; Coats, "Philippine Constabulary," p. 397.

[14] Vic Hurley, *Jungle Patrol* (New York: E. P. Dutton, 1938), p. 50; Twichell, *Allen*, p. 143; Stanley Hyatt, *The Diary of a Soldier of Fortune* (New York: John Lane, 1909), p. 331; *WDAR*, 1903, vol. 1, pt. 3, p. 248; Coats, "Philippine Constabulary," pp. 62–63, 246, 253, 274–76; Fritz, "The Philippine Question," pp. 533–34; *PCAR*, 1905, vol. 12, pt. 3, pp. 92–93, 97–98; *PCAR*, 1905, vol. 19, pt. 1, pp. 402–03; *WDAR*, 1905, vol. 1, pt. 3, pp. 292–93.

[15] *WDAR*, 1903, vol. 5, pt. 1, pp. 33–34, 141; Hurley, *Jungle Patrol*, pp. 144–45, 283–84; Elarth, *Story of the Philippine Constabulary*, p. 22; Coats, "Philippine Constabulary," pp. 115, 141–44; Hamilton, "Jungle Tactics," pp. 23–28; Ltr, Capt Stacey to Maj H. L. Leonhaeuser, 21 Apr 05, General Correspondence, Department of the Visayas, 3412, RG 395, NARA.

[16] *WDAR*, 1902, vol. 10, pt. 1, pp. 205–10; *WDAR*, 1903, vol. 5, pt. 1, p. 141; *WDAR*, 1905, 3:262–64, 285–96. Quote from *PCAR*, 1904, 1:365–66. *PCAR*, 1905, 10:52–58, 210–13; *PCAR*, 1905, 12:138; Elliott, *The Philippines*, pp. 25, 29, 31–34; Twichell, *Allen*, pp. 138–40; Roth, *Muddy Glory*, pp. 104–11; Owen, "War in Albay," p. 580; Blount, *American Occupation*, pp. 417–18; Coats, "Philippine Constabulary," pp. 59, 71–72, 92, 95, 122, 124, 132, 141, 160–81, 263, 311–51.

[17] George Jornacion, "The Time of the Eagles: U.S. Army Officers and the Pacification of the Philippine Moros, 1899–1913" (Ph.D. diss., University of Maine, 1973), pp. 29, 48, 62, 70, 252, 277, 293–94; Peter Gowing, *Mandate in Moroland* (Quezon City: Philippine Center for Advanced Studies, 1977), pp. 38, 49, 104–05, 151; *WDAR*, 1902, vol. 1, pt. 9, pp. 560, 563, 565; John Finley, "Race Development by Industrial Means Among the Moros and Pagans of the Southern Philippines," *Journal of Race Development* 3 (January 1913): 353, 360.

[18] Scott, *Memories*, p. 273; Samuel Tan, "Sulu Under American Military Rule, 1899–1913," *Philippine Social Sciences and Humanities Review* 32 (March 1967): 103–04; *WDAR*, 1902, vol. 1, pt. 9, p. 561; Gowing, *Mandate in Moroland*, p. 115; *PCAR*, 1904, 1:6–8.

[19] Herman Hagedorn, *Leonard Wood* (New York: Harper & Brothers, 1931), pp. 8, 39; Ltr, Wood to Taft, 7 Oct 03, box 33, Leonard Wood Papers, LC; Senate, Philippine Committee, *Hearings Before the Committee on the Philippines*, 57th Cong., 1st sess., 1902, S. Doc. 331, pt. 2, pp. 2121–29; Jornacion, "Time of the Eagles," pp. 56–57.

[20] *WDAR*, 1900, vol. 1, pt. 5, pp. 255–68; Tan, "Sulu Under American Rule," pp. 116–18; Gowing, *Mandate in Moroland*, pp. 57–62, 134–38, 201, 217–18; Robert Bullard, "Preparing Our Moros for Government," *Atlantic Monthly* 97 (March 1906): 385–94; Ltr, John McAuley Palmer to Governor of Moro Province, 18 Jan 08, box 1, John McAuley Palmer Papers, LC; Ltrs, Edwin F. Glenn to Tasker Bliss, 10 Feb and 15 Mar 09, pp. 19997, 20044, Tasker Bliss Papers, LC.

[21] Senate, Philippine Committee, *Hearings Before the Committee on the Philippines*, 57th Cong., 1st sess., 1902, S. Doc. 331, pt. 2, p. 5; *WDAR*, 1900, vol. 1, pt. 5, p. 260; *WDAR*, 1901, vol. 1, pt. 6, p. 262; Atherton Brownell, "Turning Savages Into Citizens," *Outlook* 96 (September–December 1910): 922–23, 928; Finley, "Race Development," pp. 346–53; John Finley, "The Mohammedan Problem in the Philippines," *Journal of Race Development* 5 (April 1915): 353–63; Smythe, *Guerrilla Warrior*, pp. 145, 150,

152; Gowing, *Mandate in Moroland*, pp. 127, 228–30; Ltr, Pershing to Bell, 2 Apr 11, box 371, John J. Pershing Papers, LC.

²² Quote from *PCAR*, 1904, 1:11–12. Other factors that led toward the termination of military rule in Moro Province included the desire of civil authorities to place the province on a more normal governmental footing, the military's wish to consolidate its forces to better defend the Philippines from external attack, and the civil government's desire gradually to turn the job of governing the Philippines over to the Filipinos, a movement that gained momentum after the election of Woodrow Wilson as president in 1912. Gowing, *Mandate in Moroland*, pp. 248–49; Jornacion, "Time of the Eagles," p. 230; *WDAR*, 1902, vol. 1, pt. 9, p. 566.

²³ Bullard, "Preparing Our Moros," p. 388; Scott, *Memories*, pp. 307, 313, 321; Brownell, "Savages Into Citizens," p. 931; Sydney Cloman, *Myself and a Few Moros* (Garden City, N.Y.: Doubleday, 1923), p. 40; Gowing, *Mandate in Moroland*, p. 322; Smythe, *Guerrilla Warrior*, p. 149; Robert Bullard Diary, bk. 2, pp. 183–87, box 1, Robert Bullard Papers, LC.

²⁴ Richard Kolb, "Campaign in Moroland: A War the World Forgot," *Army* 33 (September 1983): 52; Gowing, *Mandate in Moroland*, pp. 4, 56–67, 132, 139–45, 170, 231, 332–33; Samuel Tan, "The Muslim Armed Struggle in the Philippines, 1900–41" (Ph.D. diss., Syracuse University, 1973), p. 54; Bacon and Scott, *Military and Colonial Policy*, p. 324; Scott, *Memories*, pp. 289, 320; Robert Bullard, "Road Building Among the Moros," *Atlantic Monthly* 92 (December 1903): 825.

²⁵ Gowing, *Mandate in Moroland*, p. 151; C. C. Bateman, "Military Road Making in Mindanao," *JMSIUS* 33 (1903): 192; C. C. Smith, "The Mindanao Moro," *Cavalry Journal* 17 (1906): 288; Bullard Diary, 29 Nov 03, bk. 2, pp. 179–80, box 1, Bullard Papers; Ltr, Hobbs to sister, 17 Apr 05, and Horace Hobbs, History of the 3d Squadron, 14th U.S. Cavalry Regiment, pp. 18–19, both in Horace Hobbs Papers, MHI; Charles D. Rhodes, Diary of Pirate-Hunting in the Sulu Archipelago, pp. 28–29, Rhodes Papers; Tan, "Sulu Under American Rule," p. 67; Ltr, Wood to Maj H. J. Slocum, 29 Aug 04, box 34, Wood Papers.

²⁶ Gowing, *Mandate in Moroland*, pp. 94–96; I. B. Holley, *General John M. Palmer, Citizen Soldiers, and the Army of a Democracy* (Westport, Conn.: Greenwood Press, 1982), pp. 154, 161–62, 173; Lieutenant L. B., "The Regular and the Savage," *Lippincott's Magazine* 74 (December 1904): 732–36; Robert Bullard Notebook 12, pp. 89–94, box 4, Bullard Papers; John J. Pershing Notebook 11, Apr 03, box 1, Pershing Papers; R. O. Van Horn, "Notes on Field Service in the District of Cotabato, Mindanao, PI," *Infantry Journal* 2 (1906): 119, 125–26; Rhodes, Diary of Pirate-Hunting in the Sulu Archipelago, pp. 29, 36, Rhodes Papers; Robert Bullard, "Field Service," *JMSIUS* 48 (January–February 1911): 73–74; John J. Pershing, Field Notes Among the Moros, Pershing Papers; Millett, *Bullard*, p. 174; Hobbs, History of the 3d Squadron, 14th U.S. Cavalry Regiment, Hobbs Papers; John Palmer, Report on a Scheme for a Well Balanced Army, 31 Oct 11, p. 7, War College Division (WCD), 6358–41, Records of the War Department General Staff, RG 165, NARA.

²⁷ *WDAR*, 1905, vol. 1, pt. 3, p. 312; H. S. Howland, "Field Service in Mindanao," *Infantry Journal* 2 (October 1905): 36, 78–79; Jornacion, "Time of the Eagles," p. 145; Holley, *John Palmer*, p. 173.

²⁸ Robert Bullard, "Among the Savage Moros," *Metropolitan Magazine* 24 (June 1906): 268; Gowing, *Mandate in Moroland*, pp. 160–63, 236; Donald Smythe, "Pershing and Counterinsurgency," *Military Review* 46 (September 1966): 85–92; Eli

Helmick Autobiography, p. 144, Eli Helmick Papers, MHI; Smythe, *Guerrilla Warrior*, pp. 169–73; Hagedorn, *Leonard Wood*, p. 43; Bullard Diary, 7 Apr 04, bk. 3, pp. 9–10, Bullard Papers.

[29] Coats, "Philippine Constabulary," p. 372; Donald Smythe, "Pershing and the Disarmament of the Moros," *Pacific Historical Review* 31 (1962): 241–56; Wayne Thompson, "Governors of the Moro Province: Wood, Bliss, and Pershing in the Southern Philippines, 1903–13" (Ph.D. diss., University of California, San Diego, 1975), pp. 202, 211.

[30] Gowing, *Mandate in Moroland*, pp. 337–40; Tan, "Armed Struggle," pp. 102–03.

[31] Millett, *Politics of Intervention*, pp. 40–41, 58–61, 68, 80; *WDAR*, 1906, 1:454–55, 528–30; David Lockmiller, *Magoon in Cuba: A History of the Second Intervention, 1906–09* (Chapel Hill: University of North Carolina Press, 1938), p. 67.

[32] HQ, Army of Cuban Pacification, GO 17, 3 Nov 06; Millett, *Politics of Intervention*, pp. 122–23; Robert Bullard, "The Army in Cuba," *JMSIUS* 41 (September–October 1907): 154.

[33] Bullard, "Army in Cuba," p. 156; Allan Millett, "The General Staff and the Cuban Intervention of 1906," *Military Affairs* 31 (Fall 1967): 113–19; Cuba, Army War College (AWC) 11, 3 Sep 06, AWC Monographs, Reports, Studies, RG 165; Ltrs, Bell to Roosevelt, 30 Aug and 22 Sep 06, Theodore Roosevelt Papers, LC; Millett, *Politics of Intervention*, pp. 66–67, 125, 130–31.

[34] Quote from Rpt, Furlong to Chief of Staff, Military Information and Intelligence Office, 26 May 08, p. 10, WCD, 4352, RG 165, NARA. John W. Furlong, Notes on Field Service in Cuba, 2 Nov 07, pp. 30–41, 45–49, WCD, 4352, RG 165, NARA; Millett, *Politics of Intervention*, pp. 14–15, 91.

[35] 28th Inf, Problems 1 and 2, atchmt to Proceedings of a Board of Officers Convened Pursuant to the Following Order, 9 Aug 07; 15th Cav, Santa Clara, Cuba, Field Exercises Numbers 1, 2, and 3, Sep 07; 15th Cav, Problems in Connection With Practical Instruction in Field Training; Ltr, Col Parker to Adj Gen, Army of Cuban Pacification, 27 Aug 07; Ltr, Col Parker to Chief of Staff, Army of Cuban Pacification, 19 Dec 07; Ltr, Lt Overton to Adj Gen, Army of Cuban Pacification, 4 Sep 07. All in Records of the Army of Cuban Pacification (ACP), 2029, RG 395, NARA. James Parker, *The Old Army Memories* (Philadelphia: Dorrance & Company, 1929), pp. 400–401; HQ, Army of Cuban Pacification, GO 50, 23 May 07; Cir 11, Camp Ciego de Avila, 20 Sep 07, General Orders and Special Orders, Post of Ciego de Avila, Cuba, ACP, RG 395, NARA.

[36] Lockmiller, *Magoon in Cuba*, pp. 90, 100, 111–15, 133; Millett, *Politics of Intervention*, pp. 125, 198–200, 206.

[37] The evolution of Cuban security forces into a corrupt and repressive institution best illustrates how U.S.-imposed institutional reforms sometimes had unintended consequences. See Millett, *Politics of Intervention*, pp. 198–200, 222–38, 260–67; Allan Millett, "The Rise and Fall of the Cuban Rural Guard, 1898–1912," *Americas* 29 (October 1972): 191–96, 200–202, 206–12; Freddy Polk, "Building Armies for Democracy: U.S. Attempts To Reform the Armed Forces of Cuba (1906–09) and Nicaragua (1927–33)" (Master's thesis, Command and General Staff College, 1987), pp. 1–4, 45–50, 90; Perez, *Army Politics in Cuba*, pp. xv–xvi, 23, 29–30.

[38] Bullard Notebook 15, pp. 38–39, box 4, Bullard Papers; Millett, *Politics of Intervention*, pp. 154–56, 205, 213–15.

[39] Millett and Maslowski, *Common Defense*, p. 317; Frank Vandiver, *Black Jack: The*

THE IMPERIAL CONSTABULARY YEARS, 1900–1913

Life and Times of John J. Pershing, 2 vols. (College Station: Texas A&M University Press, 1977), 1:419; *WDAR*, 1913, 1:22.

[40] Ltr, Adj Gen to Brig Gen Thomas Barry, 5 Dec 07, ACP, 4192, RG 395, NARA; Millett, *Politics of Intervention*, p. 141. Quote from Smythe, *Guerrilla Warrior*, p. 203.

[41] War Department, *Field Service Regulations*, 1905 (Washington, D.C.: Government Printing Office, 1905), pp. 206–09, 210, 217; War Department, *Infantry Drill Regulations, 1911* (Washington, D.C.: Government Printing Office, 1917), pp. 139–40.

[42] *Annual Report of the Infantry and Cavalry School and Staff College, 1904–05*, pp. 4, 11, 17; *Annual Report, U.S. Infantry and Cavalry School, U.S. Signal School, and Staff College, 1906*, p. 12; Lecture, Joseph Dickman, "Modern Improvements in Fire Arms and Their Tactical Effects," General Service and Staff College, 20 Sep 02, p. 9, U.S. Army Command and General Staff College (CGSC) Library, Fort Leavenworth, Kans.; Lecture 5, Malin Craig, "Cavalry on the Offensive," in *Course in Organization and Tactics*, Infantry and Cavalry School and Staff College, 30 Nov 04, pp. 18–19, CGSC Library; *Annual Report, U.S. Military Academy, 1910*, p. 39 (hereafter cited as *Annual Report, USMA, 1910*); Carol Reardon, "The Study of Military History and the Growth of Professionalism in the United States Army Before World War I" (Ph.D. diss., University of Kentucky, 1987), p. 248; "From the U.S. Military Academy, April 1903," *Cavalry Journal* 14 (1903): 150–55.

[43] Hamilton, "Jungle Tactics," pp. 23–28; Parker, "Notes on Field Duties," p. 374; Hugh Wise, "Notes on Field Service in Samar," *Infantry Journal* 4 (July 1907): 3–58; Philip Reade, "The Cargador in Mindanao," *JMSIUS* 37 (1905): 114–20; C. C. Bateman, "Military Taming of the Moro," *JMSIUS* 34 (1904): 259–66; Van Horn, "Field Service," pp. 115–27; Howland, "Field Service," pp. 36–80; Furlong, Notes on Field Service in Cuba, 2 Nov 07; Pershing, Field Notes Among the Moros, Pershing Papers; Cir, HQ, Department of the Visayas, 20 Oct 06, sub: Distribution of Capt Frank R. McCoy's "Notes on Field Service in the Cotabato Valley," Dept of the Visayas, Island of Samar, Second District, RG 395, NARA; Ltr, Maj Hutton to Military Secretary, Department of the Visayas, 3 Dec 06, sub: Submits Information for the Compilation of "Notes" on Service in Samar, Dept of the Visayas, Island of Samar, Second District, General Correspondence, RG 395, NARA.

[44] Rhodes, Diary of Pirate-Hunting in the Sulu Archipelago, pp. 4–6, 21, 24, Rhodes Papers; James Collins, "The Battle of Bud Bagsak and the Part Played by the Mountain Guns Therein," *Field Artillery Journal* 15 (November–December 1925): 569–70; Dana T. Merrill, Notes on Jungle Warfare, c. 1912–16, Joseph A. Harmon Papers, MHI.

[45] Quote from Memo, Brig Gen M. M. Macomb, Chief, WCD, for Chief of Staff, Army (CSA), 2 Apr 15, sub: Policy To Be Followed in Returning Troops From Foreign Service, WCD, 9047–1, RG 165, NARA. *WDAR*, 1903, 3:136–37; *WDAR*, 1911, 1:13; *WDAR*, 1912, 1:23, 94–98; *WDAR*, 1916, 1:48; Ltr, Harbord to Wood, 6 May 09, vol. 3, p. 272, James Harbord Papers, LC; Forbes, *Philippine Islands*, 1:227; Elliott, *The Philippines*, p. 163; Memo, Brig Gen Joseph Kuhm, Chief, WCD, for CSA, 7 Jul 17, sub: Training of Cavalry in the Philippine Islands and Policy To Be Pursued in Determining Force To Be Kept in Those Islands, w/atchmts, WCD, 8438–16, RG 165, NARA.

[46] Bacon and Scott, *Military and Colonial Policy*, p. 389; F. M. Beall, "Custom of War in Like Cases," *Infantry Journal* 3 (January 1907): 96; Bullard, "Army in Cuba," p. 157; *WDAR*, 1903, 1:104; *Annual Report, General Service and Staff College, 1903–04*, pp. 74, 94, 132; *Annual Report of the Army Service Schools, 1909*, p. 67;

Nenninger, *Leavenworth Schools*, p. 102; Army Staff College, Department of Law, *Law Theses of the Staff Class*, vol. 2, *1910–11* (1911); U.S. Infantry and Cavalry School, *Annual Report, 1898*, app. A—Department of Law, p. 1; Lecture 14, W. B. Reynolds, "Intervention," Mar 1898, in *Infantry and Cavalry School Lectures*, 1893–1898.

[47] *Annual Report, USMA, 1910*, p. 13.

[48] R. G. Hill, "The Proper Military Instruction for Our Officers; the Method To Be Employed; Its Scope and Full Development," *JMSIUS* 20 (1897): 470; Matthew Steele, "Proper Military Instruction," *JMSIUS* 20 (1897): 430–31; HQ, Division of the Philippines, GO 134, 21 Jun 02; *WDAR*, 1902, 9:205; Robert Doherty, "Foreign Language Study at U.S. Service Academies: Evolution and Current Issues" (Ed.D. diss., Columbia University Teachers College, 1983), pp. 22, 24, 26; *Annual Report, USMA, 1902*, p. 7; *Annual Report, USMA, 1907*, p. 16; *Annual Report, USMA, 1912*, p. 21; *Annual Report, USMA, 1920*, p. 23; *Annual Report, General Service and Staff College, 1903–04*, pp. 95–96; *Annual Report of the Command and General Staff School, 1930–31*, p. 6; Nenninger, *Leavenworth Schools*, p. 102.

[49] Robert Bullard, "Military Pacification," *JMSIUS* 46 (January–February 1910): 1–24.

[50] First quote from Bullard, "Military Pacification," p. 4, and see also pp. 5–6, 12–13, 20. Second quote from ibid., p. 14. Third quote from Robert Bullard, "The Military Study of Men," *Infantry Journal* 8 (November–December 1911): 320.

[51] First quote from Bullard, "Military Pacification," p. 17, and see also pp. 18–19. Second quote from ibid., p. 4.

[52] Quote from Bullard, "Military Pacification," p. 3; *Field Service Regulations*, 1905, pp. 206–08, 210, 217; War Department, *Rules of Land Warfare* (Washington, D.C.: Government Printing Office, 1917), pp. 21–24, 64–65, 105–17, 130–34; Army Staff College, Department of Law, *Military Government, Papers Prepared by the Class of 1908* (Fort Leavenworth, Kans., March 1908), pp. 23–24.

[53] Harry Ball, *Of Responsible Command: A History of the Army War College* (Carlisle Barracks, Pa.: Alumni Association of the U.S. Army War College, 1983), pp. 95, 126; George Ahern, A Chronicle of the Army War College, 1899–1918 [Washington, D.C.: Army War College, 24 Jul 19], pp. 34, 50, 52, 58; Lecture, "Military Monograph on Mexico," in *AWC Course 1909–10*, vol. 14, pp. 355–58, MHI; Parker, *Old Army*, p. 410; Memo, Brig Gen A. L. Mills, Chief, WCD, for CSA, 13 Feb 12, WCD, 6474–25, RG 165, NARA; Maj Melvin W. Rowell, The Military Strength for Armed Intervention in Mexico, 4 Mar 16, WCD, 6474–372, RG 165, NARA.

[54] Rowell, Intervention in Mexico, p. 1.

[55] First quote from C. A. Flagler, A Study of the Pacification and the Establishment of Civil Government in the Area Occupied by the 4th Field Army, 1914, pp. 52–53, and see also pp. 32, 57, WCD, 8334–3, RG 165, NARA. Second quote from Parker, *Old Army*, p. 413. Third quote from A. J. Dougherty, Strength of Rural Guards Necessary for Occupation of Mexico, 1911, p. 1, Military Intelligence Division (MID), 5761–149, RG 165, NARA.

[56] All quotes from Francis Kernan, A Study of the Pacification of Mexico and Establishment of Civil Government in the Area Occupied by the First Army, 1914, pp. 6, 11–12, 36, and 9, respectively, and see also pp. 3–5, 10, 13–14, 36–37, WCD, 8334–1, RG 165, NARA. George Read, A Study of the Pacification of Mexico and Establishment of Civil Government in the Area Occupied by the Second Field Army, 1914, pp. 21, 29–32, 35, 42, WCD, 8334–2, RG 165, NARA.

THE IMPERIAL CONSTABULARY YEARS, 1900–1913

[57] First quote from Read, A Study of Pacification, p. 42. Second and third quotes from Kernan, A Study of Pacification, pp. 43–44 and p. 17, respectively.

[58] Thompson, "Governors of Moro Province," pp. 21, 75. Quote from Ball, *Responsible Command*, p. 126. Richard Challener, *Admirals, Generals, and American Foreign Policy* (Princeton, N.J.: Princeton University Press, 1973), pp. 285–86; Memo for CSA, The Role of the Army for the Protection of Foreigners in China . . ., 14 Nov 11, AWC, 6790-15, RG 165, NARA; Allan Millett, *Semper Fidelis: The History of the United States Marine Corps* (New York: Macmillan, 1980), pp. 150, 164, 174, 261.

6

MILITARY INTERVENTIONS DURING THE WILSON ADMINISTRATION 1914-1920

Though the Army might disdain international constabulary duty, it could not avoid such work altogether. The nation's growing overseas interests prohibited the Army's disengagement from world affairs. This was especially true during Woodrow Wilson's tenure as president of the United States from 1913 to 1920. Wilson fervently believed that the United States had a moral obligation to spread its concepts of individual freedom, self-government, and political democracy to the world at large. A humanitarian idealist who disliked soldiers and abhorred violence, Wilson's evangelical idealism nevertheless led him to embrace the use of force as a means to achieve his greater ends. As he explained, "If I cannot retain my moral influence over a man except by occasionally knocking him down, if that is the only basis upon which he will respect me, then for the sake of his soul I have got occasionally to knock him down. If a man will not listen to you quietly in a seat, sit on his neck and make him listen."[1]

Woodrow Wilson sat on a lot of necks during his eight years as president. Driven by a curious mixture of moral imperialism and pragmatic self-interest, Wilson deployed naval and Marine forces to Cuba, Haiti, the Dominican Republic, Russia, Mexico, Honduras, and Guatemala, not to mention China and Nicaragua, where he inherited deployments initiated by his predecessor. Though the Marine Corps proved to be his instrument of choice, the Army did not escape its share of duty. In addition to sharing China garrison duty with the marines, the Army participated in military interventions in Mexico (1914, 1916), north Russia (1918–1919), Siberia (1918–1920), and Panama

(1918–1920). All five of these operations proved trying experiences in which the Army fulfilled its specific and limited objectives while failing to achieve the president's long-term goals. These interventions highlighted for American soldiers the difficulties in coordinating politico-military policy during contingency operations. They also reaffirmed the officer corps' already widespread impression regarding the disagreeable nature of foreign constabulary duty.[2]

Vera Cruz, 1914

"I am going to teach the South American republics to elect good men!" Wilson proclaimed, and it was no idle remark. High on his list of prospective pupils was Mexico, a country mired in a seemingly endless cycle of poverty, revolution, and oppression. Convinced that social and political justice were impossible under the latest usurper of the Mexican presidency, Victoriano Huerta, Wilson became obsessed with the notion of ousting Huerta and redirecting the Mexican Revolution along liberal, constitutional channels. After diplomatic pressure failed to achieve these ends, the president turned to more forceful measures. He provided 10,000 rifles to Huerta's leading opponent, Venustiano Carranza, and when this gesture failed to produce results, sought an excuse to intervene directly in Mexican affairs. On 9 April 1914, a patrol of Huerta's soldiers arrested several American sailors in the Mexican port of Tampico. (*Map 4*) The incident gave Wilson the pretext for which he was looking. Although Mexican authorities quickly released the sailors and apologized for the incident, the president was determined to exploit the episode. The United States admiral on the scene demanded that Mexico affirm its apology by firing a 21-gun salute to the American flag. When Huerta refused, Wilson made his move.[3]

On 21 April U.S. marines seized the wharves at Vera Cruz, the maritime gateway to Mexico City. The action was designed to weaken Huerta, both by blocking the delivery of foreign arms bound for his army and by denying him access to the important revenues generated from the city's dockside customs house. Much to the president's chagrin, the Mexicans refused to accept the indignity. Although the majority of the city's garrison obligingly withdrew, a motley assemblage of policemen, released convicts, naval cadets, and patriotic citizens opened fire on the wharves, making the marines' position on the docks untenable and compelling them to occupy the entire town. Assisted by naval gunfire, approximately 6,000 U.S. sailors and marines seized the rest of the city the following day. By the time the fighting had stopped, over a hundred and thirty Americans and several hundred Mexicans lay dead or wounded.[4]

The president was devastated by the news. He had hoped to discomfit Huerta without loss of life on either side. Instead, he was in possession of a city of 40,000 hostile people and perilously close to the outbreak of an all-out war he did not want. Both the Army and the Navy clamored for Wilson to take the next step and initiate a full occupation of Mexico as envisioned by the official war plans. Although mindful of the hardships to be incurred in pacifying Mexico, the nation's military leaders believed that war was now inevitable and that it would be the height of folly to give Mexico the time to mobilize and concentrate its forces. Like their counterparts in Europe, America's military leaders of 1914 believed that war plans and mobilization timetables were finely crafted mechanisms that had to be executed completely and without interruption once they had been put into motion. Failing to do so—to delay the call-up of reserves and impede the planned deployment of men and materiel—would create chaos in the rear echelons and court disaster at the front. The die was cast, they argued, and it was time for the politicians to step aside.

Wilson, however, refused to step aside. He agreed to replace the naval assault force in Vera Cruz with Army troops in preparation for a thrust on Mexico City but declined to authorize the drive itself. War was not what the president wanted, and he rejected the military's pleas for action and its dire predictions of disaster. Rather than becoming the launch point for the subjugation and pacification of Mexico, Vera Cruz was merely to be a fulcrum from which Wilson could exercise additional pressure on the Huerta regime. It was a limited role of which the nation's military leaders did not approve.[5]

Wilson's stubborn adherence to the notion of a limited intervention threw the Army's war plans into disarray, so much so that Brig. Gen. Tasker H. Bliss, the commander of U.S. forces along the Texas-Mexican border, roundly denounced the War College's failure to develop flexible plans for contingencies short of a full-scale intervention. The criticism was justified, yet in fairness to the Army it should be pointed out that the nation's war planners had indeed considered the problem. In the spring of 1911 the president of the War College, Brig. Gen. William W. Wotherspoon, had urged Army Chief of Staff Leonard Wood to have the State Department clarify American objectives in the event of an intervention in Mexico. He pointed out that while the Army had a plan for the occupation of all of Mexico, it could not prepare for lesser contingencies unless it knew what those contingencies might be. Unfortunately, neither the nation's diplomats nor Presidents Taft and

Map 4

Wilson provided such guidance, and consequently, the Army had never bothered to develop plans for the type of limited contingency it now faced. It would not be the last time that such operations would be bedeviled by poor civil-military communication.[6]

On 30 April Maj. Gen. Frederick Funston led approximately 4,000 soldiers ashore at Vera Cruz to relieve the Navy, which left behind 3,000 marines—nearly half the U.S. Marine Corps—to assist him. Although the Navy wished to retain control of the marines, President Wilson saw the wisdom of a unified command and followed the precedents established in earlier joint operations by placing the marines under Funston's command.[7]

With the city secured, Funston turned to the thorny question of civil administration. Mexican law prohibited its citizens from working for an occupying power, and this made it difficult for the military to employ its traditional method of incorporating indigenous officials into the occupation regime. Using the Army's administration of the Philippines as an example, Funston established a civil administration staffed with veterans of the Army's previous governments in the Philippines, Cuba, and Puerto Rico. In addition to the usual departments like education, finance, and public works, he created an Office of Civil Affairs whose head served as his chief adviser on civil matters. He did not, however, reestablish Mexican civil courts, not only because most native judges refused to serve, but also because he realized that the Mexican government would not recognize the judgments handed down by occupation courts after the Americans had left. The Army therefore encouraged civil plaintiffs to settle their disputes out of court, while confining the activities of U.S. military courts to the adjudication of criminal cases.[8]

Having established the basic machinery of government, Funston followed precedent by inaugurating a vigorous civil affairs campaign, both to demonstrate America's benevolent intentions and to establish precedents he hoped the Mexicans would emulate after the Americans had gone. There was much to be done. Vera Cruz's government was notably corrupt and inefficient. The sorry state of municipal affairs was best illustrated by the city's trash disposal system, which relied entirely upon the appetites of the huge, black vultures that adorned city edifices. Like Hercules in the Augean stables, Funston threw himself into the work. He imposed strict sanitary codes, established refuse collection services, paved streets, installed sidewalks, began vaccination programs, improved the prisons, reformed the city's finances, and eliminated government corruption. At his direction schools were reopened, new teachers recruited, and a teacher's institute established to improve the overall quality of instruction. He launched a campaign against vice,

Street improvements instituted by the U.S. Army in Vera Cruz in 1914

banning gambling and the sale of marijuana and cocaine, and regulating, but not prohibiting, prostitution. At times Funston's reforms strayed into the realm of the puritanical, as in the case of his banning bullfighting and cockfighting, prohibitions that violated deeply rooted traditions. For the most part, however, he tried to respect native institutions as called for by Army doctrine. By the time he was done, the city was virtually unrecognizable. Governmental administration was efficient, while the death rate had dropped by 25 percent. Even the vultures had left town for better pickings elsewhere. Funston reinforced his civic program by enforcing strict discipline among his men, so much so that nearly half the garrison had been court-martialed by the end of the occupation. "This government is too pious . . . to suit me," grumbled one marine, Maj. Smedley Butler.[9]

The most important item of tactical doctrine to emerge from the Army's Mexican sojourn was a pamphlet compiled by the headquarters of the Vera Cruz expedition titled "Memorandum in Reference to the Methods To Be Employed in the Capture and Occupation of Latin-

American Cities." The essay was prompted by the recognition that any campaign to pacify Mexico or any other Latin American country would most likely entail episodes of urban irregular warfare similar to the Navy's recent experience. The pamphlet prescribed methods for fighting in cities and became the basis for U.S. Army tactical doctrine on the subject for years to come, as the Army periodically reissued the work whenever intervention into a Latin state was imminent.[10]

While Army officers in Vera Cruz busied themselves with administering the city and developing street-fighting doctrine, pressure continued to mount on the Huerta regime. Defeated by Carranza in the field and denied access to the customs revenues from Vera Cruz, Huerta resigned from the presidency in mid-July. Although the intervention had only been one factor in Huerta's downfall, Wilson was elated by the success of his experiment in the limited use of military power. But the euphoria was short-lived. Carranza ignored Wilson's call for elections, insisting instead that the United States evacuate Vera Cruz immediately. After hesitating for two months, Wilson acceded to Carranza's demand and ordered American forces to withdraw in mid-September.

General Funston promptly protested the evacuation order on the grounds that a quick departure would undermine all the good work he had accomplished. He proposed that the United States retain control over the city through a transition period during which representatives from the Carranza regime could visit and learn American administrative methods. He also argued that it would be immoral for the United States to leave Vera Cruz without first being assured that Carranza would not retaliate against Mexican nationals who had worked for the U.S. military government as policemen, teachers, clerks, and maintenance workers. Washington accepted his proposals, but Carranza balked, and another two-month stalemate ensued. Ultimately, it was Carranza who backed down. With his domestic enemies closing in around him, he needed to gain control of Vera Cruz's valuable wharves and customs house, and on 9 November he issued a blanket amnesty for all Americanistas. Two weeks later, on 23 November 1914, Funston's expeditionary force loaded onto transports and sailed over the horizon, leaving the city to Carranza.[11]

Vera Cruz was the Army's first venture in the Wilson administration's brand of limited military intervention, and the experience had proved to be an uncomfortable one. Although the operation had contributed to Huerta's downfall, it had also highlighted underlying tensions between civil and military policy makers over the use of the Army as a tool of American diplomacy. Moreover, Wilson's success had been only superficial. Huerta was gone, but internecine warfare continued in

Mexico, with constitutional democracy and social justice a distant dream. No sooner had the Army departed than Carranza repudiated his pledge and purged everyone who had worked for the Americans during the occupation. As the Mexicans regained control over Vera Cruz, they ignored nearly all of Funston's reforms. They rapidly reintroduced corruption and inefficiency to government, neglected the sanitary codes, and allowed municipal facilities to deteriorate. Within a few months virtually every vestige of the Army's presence in Vera Cruz had been expunged—much to the relief of the vultures, which happily returned to their roosts.

Rather than help foster democracy, all Wilson had accomplished was to further alienate Mexicans of all political stripes, from Huerta supporters to Carrancistas, who resented the arrogance with which the United States had meddled in their internal affairs. Only one major Mexican political leader had openly supported the intervention—a revolutionary general named Francisco "Pancho" Villa. It was a name Americans were not soon to forget.[12]

The Mexican Punitive Expedition, 1916–1917

The withdrawal from Vera Cruz did not mark the end of Wilson's meddling in Mexico's internal affairs. Carranza was soon faced with a major insurgency in northern Mexico led by General Villa. Though he favored Carranza, President Wilson refused to acknowledge the Carrancista regime as the legitimate government of Mexico. Instead, he withheld formal recognition in the hope of pressuring Carranza to make more democratic reforms. Carranza struck back by applying a little pressure of his own. In the summer of 1915 he orchestrated a covert campaign of bandit raids and guerrilla attacks in southern Texas. Integral to this campaign was a document circulated in the borderland in early 1915 called the Plan of San Diego, after the Texas town in which it was said to have originated. The plan called for an insurrection by Hispanics, Indians, and blacks against United States authority in the American Southwest and the establishment of an independent republic there. Although fantastic in conception, it represented an attempt to tap the resentment which the Mexican-American majority in southern Texas felt toward the ruling Anglo minority.[13]

As summer faded into fall, the situation along the border became critical. Encouraged by the Mexican press and supported by Carrancista soldiers stationed along the banks of the Rio Grande, Mexican-American bandits and guerrillas waged a low-level insurgency against U.S. authority in southern Texas. Occasionally led by Carrancista officers, the raiders attacked U.S. Army outposts, looted ranches and stores, burnt bridges, and cut telegraph lines. By October 1915 twenty-eight U.S. soldiers and fourteen civilians had become casualties at the hands of Carranza's proxy war against the Wilson administration.[14]

Efforts to control the bandit problem were hampered by the U.S. government's refusal to declare martial law and by its inability to coordinate effectively the efforts of competing federal, state, and local law enforcement agencies. General Funston, the commander of the Army's Southern Department headquartered at Fort Sam Houston, Texas, initially responded to the crisis by spreading his troops out in penny packets in an effort to protect every small community. In doing so he overextended his forces to such an extent that many outposts were too weak either to defend themselves or to hunt the bandits aggressively. The general soon realized his error and reconcentrated his forces into fewer but stronger mixed detachments of infantry and cavalry. The infantry provided point defense and patrolled the local area at night while the cavalry performed long-range daytime patrols and special night operations. He then waged an aggressive constabulary campaign modeled on the Army's previous counterguerrilla operations.

Colonel Bullard, who commanded a regiment as part of Funston's border constabulary, likened the operation to the Philippine War, for in both cases the Army was confronted with elusive irregulars harbored by a restive population. Cognizant that they could not overcome the bandits without the assistance of the inhabitants, Philippine veterans urged their troops "to deal with both Mexicans and Americans with diplomacy and tact, to make them realize that the troops are their best friends and protectors, and thus to gain not only their sympathy, but their active co-operation."[15]

As the banditry continued, Funston also sought to apply some of the sterner lessons of the Philippines, requesting among other things that he be allowed to deny the bandits quarter. Washington recoiled at the suggestion, but it had little control over the many state and local organizations of Rangers, police, and vigilantes that waged a terror campaign of their own against the Mexican-American community. By the fall of 1915 nonfederal security forces had executed hundreds of Mexican-Americans, often with little or no judicial procedure. Nevertheless, the solution to the bandit problem ultimately proved to be political, rather than military. In October Wilson backed down and recognized Carranza as the de facto ruler of Mexico. The bandit raids ceased immediately. Carranza's proxy war had achieved its purpose.[16]

President Wilson solidified the deal with Carranza by allowing him to send troops through U.S. territory to reinforce the Mexican border town of Agua Prieta, which was besieged by Villista forces. The reinforcements inflicted a decisive defeat upon Villa and further consolidated Carranza's hold over the country. Yet the change in U.S. policy also bought Wilson a new and dangerous foe. Angered by the Agua Prieta affair, and perhaps hoping to spark a crisis that might ultimately topple Carranza, Villa attacked the town of Columbus, New Mexico, on the night of 8–9 March 1916. The raiders killed or wounded about thirty Americans and looted part of the town before being driven off with the loss of approximately a hundred and fifty. Goaded by Villa's raid, Wilson moved once again to intervene in Mexico's internal affairs.[17]

On 10 March the president ordered General Funston to organize a punitive expedition "with the sole object of capturing Villa and preventing any further raids by his bands." Army Chief of Staff Maj. Gen. Hugh L. Scott recognized the fallacy of the order. "Suppose he [Villa] should get on the train and go to Guatemala, Yucatan or South America. Are you going to go after him?" queried Scott of Secretary of War Newton D. Baker. Baker saw the point, and the War Department revised the orders so as to instruct the expedition's commander, General Pershing, to pursue Villa until either his "band or bands are known to be broken up" or "the de facto government of Mexico is able to relieve them of this work." Nevertheless, Wilson's earlier instructions had been widely publicized and gave American people the incorrect impression that the expedition's sole purpose was to "get" Villa personally. This unfortunate misapprehension contributed to the widespread belief that the expedition was a failure when it ultimately failed to capture the elusive guerrilla chieftain.[18]

The Army entertained no illusions about the hazards of the undertaking. The Mexican province of Chihuahua, where Villa made his home, was an arid plateau whose western fringes rose gradually into the Sierra Madre Mountains—a rugged jumble of narrow canyons, watered valleys, and jagged rock outcroppings 10,000 feet above sea level. Roads were poor, food and forage scarce, and the sparse population united in their dislike of "gringos." Clearly, finding Villa and his mounted guerrillas under such conditions would be difficult. Moreover, by inserting American troops into Mexico, Wilson once again risked sparking a general war between the two nations.

The president tried to minimize the threat of war in two ways. First, he ordered Pershing to avoid confrontations with Carrancista soldiers and officials at all costs. Second, he negotiated an agreement with the Mexican government permitting the United States to pursue bandits across the border into Mexico. Unfortunately, the United States misinterpreted the agreement, which in actuality applied only to *future* contingencies, not to incidents that had occurred prior to its consummation, such as the Columbus raid. The Carranza government therefore considered Pershing's expedition to be a violation of Mexican sovereignty and responded accordingly.[19]

The U.S. Army was thoroughly alarmed by the whole affair. It estimated that Carranza, Villa, and Mexico's various other revolutionary chieftains had 180,000 men under arms, and that there was a very real danger that they would put aside their internecine squabbles and unite to crush Pershing's force, which at its peak numbered no more than 12,000 men. To the Army's senior leaders, sending Pershing's tiny column into the midst of Mexico's revolutionary ferment seemed to be an ill-conceived half-measure *a la* Vera Cruz, an exercise in the limited use of force that they found distinctly unappetizing. In the words of a War College report written five days before Villa raided Columbus,

> In an armed intervention it is axiomatic that an overwhelming force used in vigorous field operations without costly pauses and directed straight and continuously at the organized field forces and centers of resources will most effectively and economically overcome organized resistance and make possible a more orderly and more economical period of pacification. . . . Our war plans accept this axiom. . . . To reject these plans, to use only a part of the plans, or to curtail the forces outlined in the plans, can but invite local disasters and delays, lengthening the period of military operations, and make more costly in lives and treasure both this period and the period of pacification.[20]

Army leaders still preferred an all-or-nothing approach when intervening in the affairs of other nations. Even General Bliss—the advocate of flexible plans for limited contingencies—was uncomfortable with Wilson's second experiment in limited interventionism. It was one thing to seize and hold a port, quite another to launch a column of troops deep into the interior of a hostile country. Moreover, catching Villa's mobile bands would take time, and the longer the operation lasted and the deeper Pershing drove into Mexico, the greater the chance for an incident that might escalate into a war between the two nations. Bliss therefore joined other senior military officers in urging the president to authorize preparations for the full-scale invasion and pacification of Mexico. Wilson refused, and the State Department, anxious not to antagonize Carranza further, rejected the War Department's request to pressure the Mexican government to permit Pershing to use Mexican railroads to keep his far-flung columns supplied. Pershing was to be on his own. Chief of Staff Scott was so infuriated by the administration's unwillingness to back Pershing that he later remarked, "I could have burned down the State Department with everybody in it."[21]

General Pershing began his difficult mission on 15 March 1916, when he led a mixed force of cavalry, infantry, and support troops across the border in what was termed a "hot pursuit" of Villa's nearly week-old trail. While the infantry guarded his line of communications and supply back to the United States, the cavalry, divided into three major and four minor columns, scoured Chihuahua in search of Villa's irregulars. It was grueling work reminiscent of the Indian campaigns of the previous century. Pershing—himself a veteran of the Indian wars and a graduate of General Miles' "raiders and pursuers" training course—was fortunate to have among his subordinates a large cadre of officers experienced in frontier and imperial constabulary work. These veterans of the Indian, Philippine, and Moro wars were well prepared to meet the physical and operational challenges inherent in chasing bandits and guerrillas over inhospitable terrain under the most adverse conditions. They performed exceedingly well. Under their guidance, the expedition pressed the chase in the finest constabulary tradition, marching light, traveling at night, and taking their adversaries by surprise in dawn raids. Their aggressive action soon forced Villa to scamper deeper into Mexico, dispersing his guerrillas as he went in the hope that they might better evade the hard-riding Americans.[22]

As the days progressed, however, the obstacles facing the Punitive Expedition steadily mounted. The Mexican population—motivated by admiration and fear of Villa and by hatred of Americans—aided Villa's escape. Mexicans sheltered the guerrillas and either withheld or passed erroneous information to Pershing's troopers. Meanwhile, the cavalry columns quickly outran their supply lines and were in desperate need of food, forage, and replacements. The Army unwittingly exacerbated their plight by issuing the cavalrymen paper vouchers rather than hard currency to purchase supplies from Mexican farmers. Although the Mexicans were always willing to trade supplies for cash, they were suspicious of the vouchers and refused to accept them, compounding the cavalry's resupply problems. One officer, Col. William C. Brown, spent $1,600 of his own money to procure supplies for his men.[23]

Pershing made every effort to overcome these obstacles. He sought to win the population's favor, or at least tolerance, by avoiding Mexican towns and insisting that his men take nothing from the people without compensation. At the same time, he gained War Department approval to issue hard currency to the cavalry columns for the procurement of food and forage. To overcome the paucity of local intelligence, Pershing established an elaborate information network under Maj. James Ryan, a former commander of Apache Scouts who had been court-martialed during the Philippine War for employing the water

Major Tompkins' cavalry column searches for Pancho Villa during the Punitive Expedition.

cure. The Punitive Expedition's intelligence office interrogated prisoners, recruited guides, interpreters, and informers, and organized a secret service of Mexican expatriates to get Villa. The organization performed valuable service during the campaign, though it never managed to apprehend the elusive general.[24]

There was one obstacle that Pershing could not overcome, however, and that was the growing hostility of the Carranza regime to his presence in Mexico. The deeper he pushed, the more antagonistic the Mexican government became. Despite the Army's best efforts to avoid a confrontation, Carrancista forces instigated a number of incidents in early April in which several American and Mexican soldiers were killed. Then, on 12 April, a large force of Mexican civilians and Carrancista soldiers attacked a column of the 13th U.S. Cavalry in the city of Parral, approximately 400 miles south of Columbus, New Mexico. The clash marked the turning point of the expedition. Pershing requested authorization to seize the entire state of Chihuahua as the precursor to the full-scale pacification of Mexico. Wilson demurred. War was exactly what he did not want, and instead he directed Pershing to fall back. After a month of rigorous campaigning, the hunt for Villa was effectively over.[25]

Washington instructed Pershing to consolidate his position so as to create an American-patrolled "Villa-free" zone in northern and western Chihuahua. The redeployment reflected a change in strategy by the Wilson administration, for while Pershing still prowled for guerrillas within the new zone, he realized that the president had effectively converted the Punitive Expedition from an anti-Villa operation into "something of a club that the administration can use over the Mexican government." Indeed, the expedition now became another Vera Cruz, with Wilson endeavoring to extort concessions from Mexico by occupying a portion of its territory.

At first the president merely requested that Carranza effectively police the border as the condition for Pershing's withdrawal. When Carranza demanded that the United States commit itself to a fixed withdrawal timetable, Wilson countered with additional conditions, insisting that the Mexican government guarantee religious toleration, protect the property rights of foreigners, and concede to the United States the right to provide humanitarian relief within Mexico. Carranza steadfastly refused to bow to these demands, and a stalemate ensued.[26]

Meanwhile the two sides engaged in brinkmanship. Carranza resurrected the Plan of San Diego, encouraged cross-border bandit raids, and organized a special covert brigade whose mission was to spark a Mexican-American insurrection in southern Texas. The United States responded in May by authorizing additional cross-border pursuits and by ordering a partial mobilization of the National Guard to protect the border. Meantime, Carranza poured troops into Chihuahua, boxing Pershing in from the south, east, and west and threatening his lines of communications. As tensions mounted, Pershing decided to test Carranza's intentions by sending a patrol to probe Mexican positions on his flank. He gave the patrol commander, Capt. Charles T. Boyd, strict instructions to avoid a confrontation with the Mexicans. Nevertheless, on 21 June the impetuous captain disobeyed orders and attacked a detachment of Mexican soldiers at the town of Carrizal. In the ensuing fight the Mexicans killed Captain Boyd and routed his command.[27]

The battle at Carrizal brought the United States and Mexico to the brink of war. But once again they refused to take the plunge. Although neither Wilson nor Carranza were willing to compromise, neither wanted war. The stalemate thus continued. Meanwhile, Pershing's command languished under the hot Mexican sun, hamstrung from making any progress against Villa by the combined efforts of Presidents Wilson and Carranza. "I feel like a man looking for a needle in a hay stack with an armed guard standing over the stack forbidding you to look in the hay," Pershing ruefully remarked. Frustrated by

U.S. Army Indian scouts who participated in the Punitive Expedition

Wilson's caution and Carranza's obstinacy, Pershing recommended that the expedition be recalled. However, the president preferred to keep him across the border as a thorn in Carranza's side. All Pershing could do was to patrol the occupied zone and wait for the diplomats to find a way out of the dilemma.[28]

In the meantime, Pershing registered some progress toward clearing the occupied area of Villistas. He reorganized his command into five geographical districts, each with its own intelligence network and cavalry regiment responsible for conducting an elaborate system of counterbandit patrols. Pershing also instituted a rigorous training program reminiscent of the one set up by the Army of Cuban Pacification.

Though the program included conventional warfare, much of the training focused upon the tactics and techniques to be employed against Mexican irregulars. Pershing drilled his command in the arts of countering ambushes, escorting convoys, scouting, raiding, and patrolling. Throughout, he emphasized the old axiom that good commanders modified doctrine to meet the exigencies of the moment. In the Mexican case, this translated into adopting a more aggressive and vigorous posture than would have normally been acceptable. Aggressiveness was fundamental, Pershing believed, to win not only the physical, but also the moral and psychological battle against his irregular foe, a doctrine entirely in keeping with the Army's tradition-

During the Punitive Expedition, the tried and true wagons of the old Army seem to have an edge over the newer forms of transportation.

al philosophy for dealing with "less civilized" races, whether Indian, Filipino, or Latin American.[29]

Army officers stationed along the Mexican border provided similar training to their troops as well, introducing their young soldiers to the time-honored skills of frontier service. In the process, the Army also experimented with new methods. It introduced more systematic training programs to improve the proficiency of the cavalry in their traditional skills, while applying new technology to the old problems of constabulary duty. The Punitive Expedition and related border operations represented the first time the U.S. Army employed aeroplanes, trucks, and armored cars in active operations. When 1st Lt. George S. Patton roared into a Villista hacienda in a motor car, pistols blazing, to gun down one of Villa's top lieutenants, he heralded the dawn of a new era in counterguerrilla warfare.[30]

While the Army relearned old constabulary skills and experimented with new ones during the fall and winter of 1916, Villa staged a resurgence. With Pershing safely tethered, the renegade general came out from hiding and inflicted several embarrassing defeats on Carrancista forces. Pershing longed to go after him, but the president refused. The United States was drifting toward entering World War I, and Wilson needed to extricate himself from the Mexican quagmire.

Fortunately, Carranza handed him the opportunity by decisively defeating Villa in a major battle in January 1917. With Villa weakened, Wilson dropped all his extraneous demands and pulled Pershing out of Mexico the following month. Two months later the United States declared war on Germany, and Pershing was on his way to France.

The U.S. Army performed extremely well in northern Mexico in 1916–1917, given the arduous circumstances under which it operated. It skillfully used constabulary-style tactics, while employing tact and discretion to minimize confrontations with the Mexican population. In the process it fulfilled its original mission by dispersing Villa's forces and killing three of his top generals, although it never managed either to get Villa or destroy his guerrilla band. While pleased with the Army's handling of the bandit problem, military leaders remained unhappy with Wilson's second venture into the realm of limited intervention. The president may have been correct in avoiding a war with Mexico, officers conceded, but his policies had placed Pershing in an untenable position, made worse by Wilson's decision to recast Pershing's mission from the pursuit of Villa into a means of pressuring Carranza. The limited application of force for diplomatic purposes was no more palatable to soldiers in 1917 than it had been in 1914. Nevertheless, it was a role that Wilson would insist the Army continue to play for the remainder of his presidency.[31]

Wilson and Russia

America's entry into World War I in April 1917 gave the Army its first taste of sustained conventional warfare after a half century of constabulary service at home and abroad. Yet even as America's soldiers entered the largest military conflict the world had ever known, they could not escape from performing the type of unconventional, politico-military operations that typify small wars and contingency operations. Nowhere was this more apparent than in Russia, where the Army became enmeshed in the murky world of the Russian Revolution and Civil War.

In the winter of 1917–1918 Bolshevik revolutionaries seized control of the Russian government and withdrew Russia from the Allied coalition. Its departure left the Allies in dire straits by permitting Germany to concentrate all its combat power on the Western Front. Desperate for some way to reestablish an Eastern Front against Germany, Britain and France proposed that the Allies seize the Russian ports of Murmansk, Archangel, and Vladivostok. Tons of Allied war materiel originally intended for the pre-Bolshevik government lay stockpiled in these ports, and the Allies were anxious that the supplies not fall into either German or Bolshevik hands. Next, Anglo-French planners proposed that the Allies clear the rail lines emanating out of these ports to open lines of communications with the Czech Legion—over 50,000 Czech and Slovak soldiers who had been fighting for Russia prior to the Bolshevik takeover but now found themselves at odds with the Communist, or Red, government. Once the ports and rail lines were secured, the British and French hoped to use the legion as a nucleus around which non-Communist, or White, Russian political and military organizations might coalesce to sweep the Bolsheviks from power and resume the war in the east.[32]

Army Chief of Staff General Peyton C. March strenuously objected to the Anglo-French scheme. France, not Russia, was the decisive theater of the war, and he opposed any diversion of Allied strength from Western Europe. Besides, the Army considered the political, military, and logistical problems of establishing a second front thousands of miles inside a nation wracked by political upheaval and civil war to be insurmountable. President Wilson concurred, for he had serious reservations of his own. He feared that the British and French would support any non-Communist regime that protected their own economic and political interests, regardless of whether it was committed to improving the lot of the Russian people. Although he had no love for the Bolsheviks, Wilson did not wish to support any White leader not dedicated to the establishment of a progressive, democratic society in Russia. Similarly, he worried that Japan, whose assistance was essential for the Far Eastern element of the plan, would use the intervention as an excuse to gain control over Siberia's vast natural resources. The president thus stood firmly behind the principles of national self-determination and territorial integrity.

In time, however, Wilson felt compelled to modify his position. Britain and France were adamant about the expedition, and he was loath to alienate them as their cooperation would be vital in reconstructing the postwar world. Besides, American participation would at least ensure that the United States had some leverage over the situation in Russia. Hence, in July 1918 the president announced that the United States would provide contingents for the two major multinational expeditions called for by the Anglo-French plan: the expedition in north Russia at Archangel and the expedition in Siberia at Vladivostok.[33]

The ambivalence with which Wilson undertook these twin operations was reflected in the instructions he gave the two men selected to command America's contribution to the operations in Russia, Col. George E. Stewart (north Russia) and Maj. Gen. William S. Graves

(Siberia). Wilson ordered them to remain strictly neutral in Russia's internal political squabbles and to confine their activities to the relatively passive tasks of guarding the military stockpiles and keeping communications open with the Czech Legion. Yet he also authorized them "to steady any efforts at self-government or self-defense in which the Russians themselves may be willing to accept assistance," including "such aid as may be acceptable to the Russians in the organization of their own self-defense." These instructions failed to address one crucial question—who were "the Russians" whom American forces were supposed to aid? Were they the Reds or the Whites? And if they were the Whites (as most presumed), which of the various anti-Communist factions were the Americans to aid? The president did not provide any guidance on these points, either before or during the interventions. The vague and somewhat conflicting orders placed his field commanders in a difficult position.[34]

The Allied intervention began in August 1918, when British and Japanese forces landed at Archangel and Vladivostok, respectively. The first U.S. Army troops arrived at both ports the following month. Despite the fact that they shared a common mission, there was no coordination between the Allied expeditionary forces in north Russia and Siberia. (*Map 5*) Nearly 4,000 miles of wilderness separated the two forces, while the political and military circumstances in which the two expeditions found themselves differed dramatically. Consequently, each of these interventions must be examined separately.

North Russia, 1918–1919

The mission assigned by the Allied Supreme War Council to the north Russia expeditionary force was to secure "bridgeheads into Russia from the north from which forces can eventually advance rapidly to the center of Russia." British Maj. Gen. Frederick C. Poole, the commander of Allied forces in northern Russia, intended to implement these instructions by pushing his troops 400 miles south of Archangel to Vologda and Viatka, where he planned to effect a linkage with the Czechs. Wilson had hoped that America's 5,500-man contingent would restrict itself to guarding Archangel and avoid direct participation in the Supreme War Council's offensive. But that was not to be. No sooner had the Americans disembarked than General Poole rushed them to the front as the spearhead of his anti-Bolshevik offensive.[35]

Colonel Stewart bore some of the responsibility for the subversion of Wilson's intentions, for he failed to stand up to Poole, preferring instead to comply passively with the British general's demands. In fact, Stewart showed little signs of leadership at all, and he so removed him-

The 339th U.S. Infantry disembarks at Archangel, September 1918. The regiment was equipped with poor quality Russian rifles, British clothing, and water-cooled Vickers machine guns that frequently froze up under arctic conditions.

self from operational matters that the British soon ignored him altogether and routinely ordered American units about without troubling to notify the American headquarters. Nevertheless, Washington must bear much of the blame for Stewart's predicament. Wilson's vague instructions and his decision to place the north Russia expeditionary force under foreign command, despite his misgivings about British intentions, left Stewart vulnerable to manipulation. Armed, clothed, and fed by the British and dispersed by them in penny packets along the entire front, the American force lacked the cohesiveness and autonomy needed to make it an effective tool of American policy.

Ironically, the president's one attempt to rectify the situation backfired when he ordered Stewart—over the strenuous objections of the War Department—to subordinate himself to the American ambassador to Russia, David R. Francis, who happened to be residing at Archangel. Francis was a strong anti-Communist, who believed Wilson was too timid in confronting the Communists. Rather than pull the Americans out of the front line, Francis assured General Poole that he favored a liberal interpretation of Washington's instructions and encouraged Stewart to commit his men to the British offen-

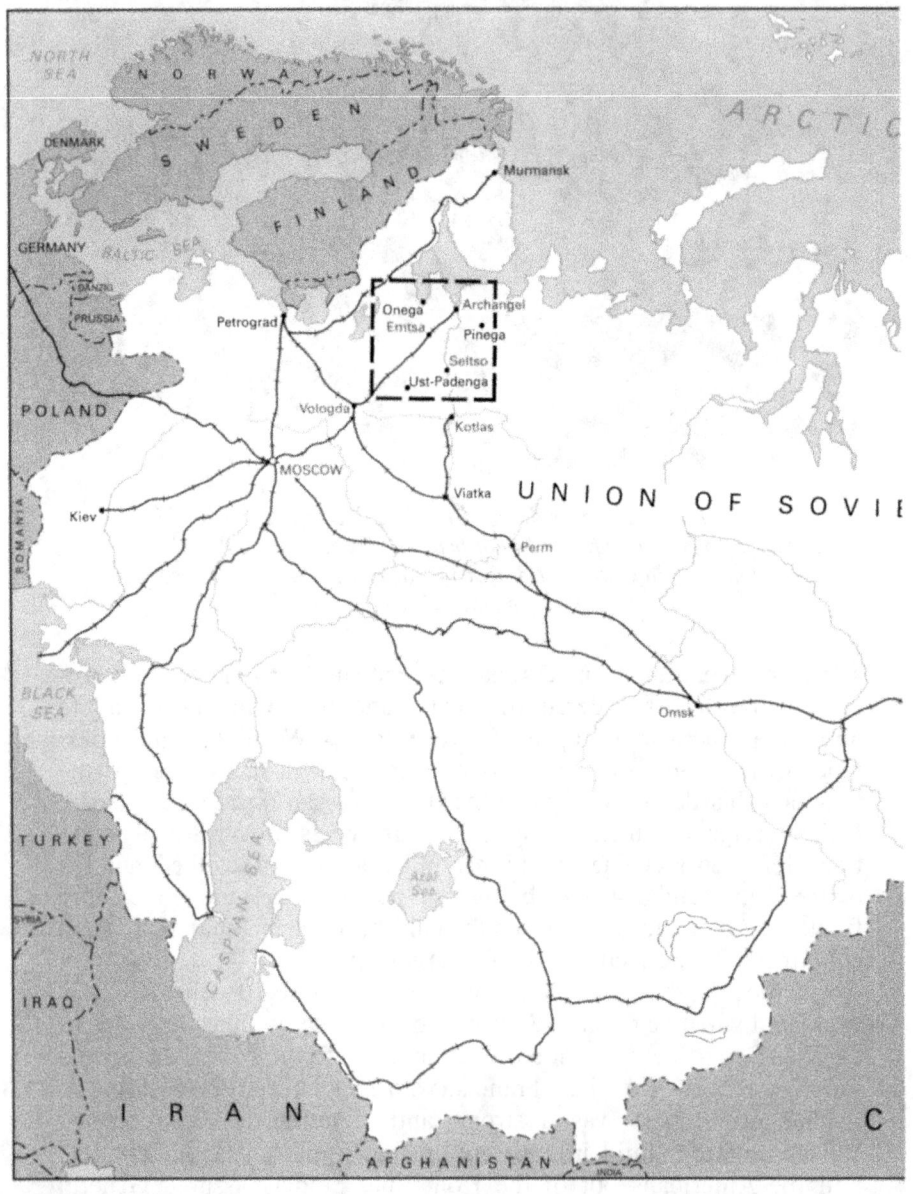

MAP 5

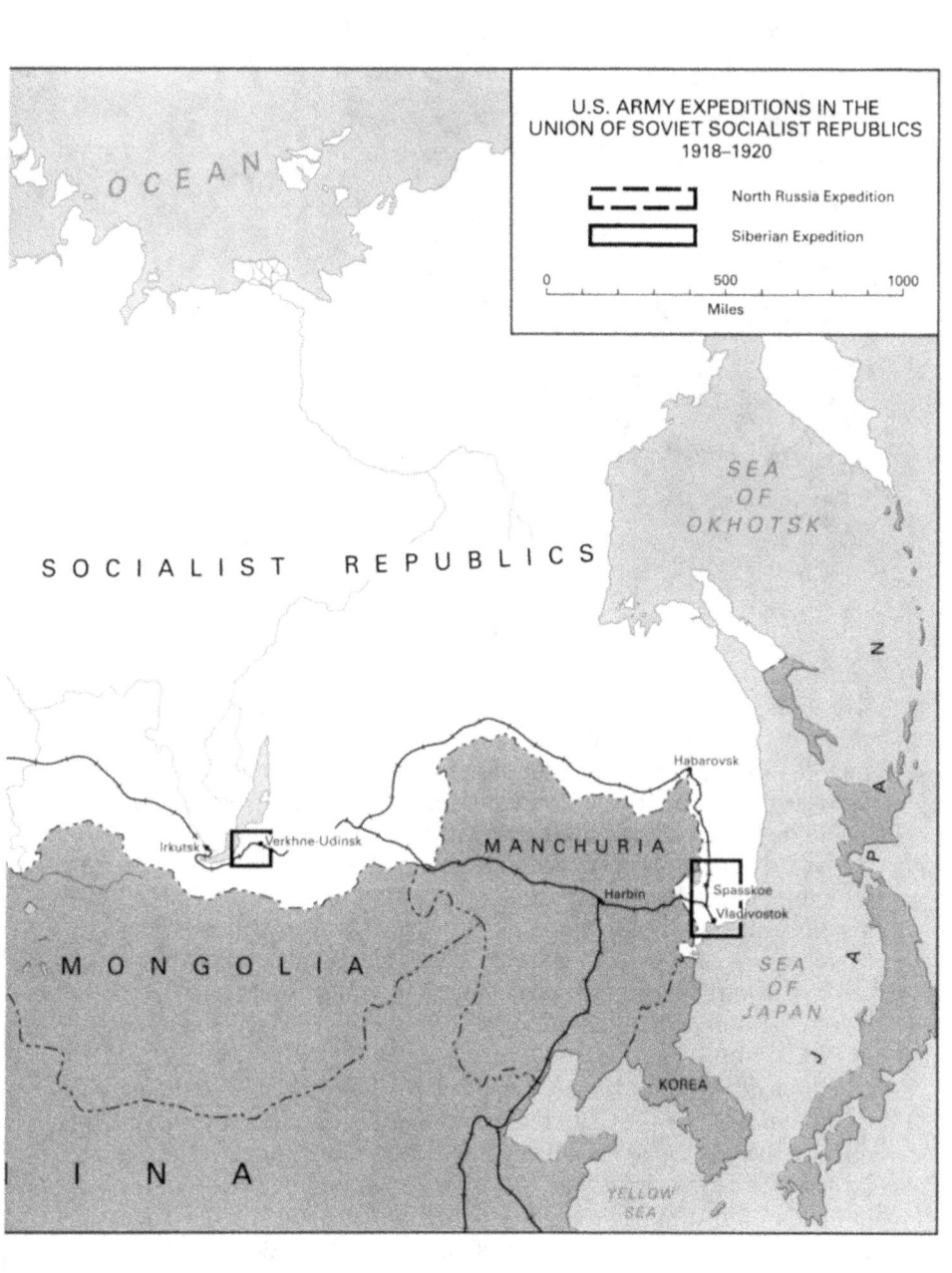

A small American outpost in north Russia

sive. Besides, Francis argued, there was little else the Americans could do; the Bolsheviks had already removed the majority of the supplies stockpiled at Archangel before the Allies had arrived. Since Stewart was charged with the mission of protecting those supplies, would he not be complying with his instructions if he pushed south to recover the misappropriated materiel? Subordinated to two strong-willed men, torn between vague and contradictory instructions from his government, and abandoned by the War Department (General March was so disgusted that he "washed [his] hands of the whole matter"), Stewart permitted the American contingent to become a direct—and, like the other allied forces, an unsuccessful—participant in Russia's civil war.[36]

Logistical problems and opposition from the more numerous Communist forces prevented the north Russia expedition from linking up with the Czechs or establishing an Eastern Front against the Central Powers before the Great War ended on 11 November 1918. But the termination of hostilities brought no relief to the soldiers in north Russia, for whom the enemy had always been the Bolsheviks and not the Germans. Disenchanted with the situation at Archangel, Washington wanted to withdraw the American contingent. But the onset of winter

An American convoy winds its way through northern Russia's heavily forested terrain; below, *American soldiers guard Bolshevik prisoners at Archangel.*

American soldiers share their rations with the children of Archangel.

weather made evacuation impossible, and the doughboys were compelled to fight for their lives against a series of Bolshevik counteroffensives during the long arctic winter that followed.

Meanwhile, the British moved forward with the second element of the intervention—the establishment of a non-Communist government designed to carry the anti-Bolshevik crusade forward into central Russia. The U.S. Army played virtually no role in this political effort that was largely mishandled by the Anglo-White leadership. Most British and White officers exhibited little sympathy for the peasants and workers on which Bolshevik power rested, and their propaganda campaigns proved heavy-handed and ineffective. In contrast, American soldiers, who were not only less class conscious but in many cases also of Slavic descent, usually worked well with the common man. In some localities U.S. officers ran successful public relations campaigns that won not only the affection, but also the material support of the local population. Nevertheless, such endeavors were not sufficient to overcome the overall ineptitude of the Allied civil affairs effort. As Ralph Albertson, a YMCA worker who accompanied the American contingent, recalled,

The expedition called for military skill and it called for leadership, sympathy, social skill. There was a sad failure to realize that an expedition of this sort is

American soldiers in winter camouflage clothing on patrol in north Russia

bound to run into social and political problems that are quite as important, perhaps more so, than mere military practice. The management of this campaign has ignored all social and political considerations that might have contributed to its success or failure and has blundered stupidly whenever these matters have forced themselves to the front.

This American blockhouse withstood several Communist attacks during the winter of 1918–1919.

Consequently, Albertson noted, "We failed to win their hearts or their confidence."[37]

Having failed to defeat the Bolsheviks on either the military or political fronts, there was little the Allied soldiers could do but to hold on to the enclave they had carved out of the arctic tundra until their home governments decided to withdraw them. Ignoring British pressure to stay the course, President Wilson acted as soon as the winter's ice and snow had melted sufficiently to make an evacuation possible. In mid-1919 the last American soldier bid farewell to Archangel. The British attempted to go it alone a bit longer, but by year's end they too elected to depart. Secretary of War Baker pronounced a suitable epitaph to the Allied intervention in north Russia, stating that "the expedition was nonsense from the beginning." For the U.S. Army, the north Russia expedition had dramatized once again the worst aspects of Wilson's penchant for ill-conceived politico-military interventions.[38]

Siberia, 1918–1920

Just about the time Colonel Stewart's north Russia expeditionary force landed at Archangel, a second, larger American expedition under the command of General Graves disembarked at Vladivostok, nearly

A camouflaged train of the Czech Legion

4,000 miles away. Like Stewart, Graves had instructions to use his 10,000-man expeditionary force to guard military stockpiles, secure communications with the Czech Legion, and assist in bringing stability to Russia without embroiling his force in partisan political and military struggles. The first two tasks were relatively easy, since the legion already controlled the port and the Trans-Siberian Railroad. The third task, however, proved to be impossible.

As in north Russia, both Allied and U.S. State Department representatives in Siberia endeavored to persuade Graves to commit American forces against the Bolsheviks. Graves, however, had both the rank and the mettle to stand up to these pressures, and he firmly adhered to the letter of Wilson's neutrality instructions. He forbid the transfer of arms to a non-Communist Russian force under British control. He not only declined to participate in any anti-Bolshevik operations, but refused to confiscate the weapons of suspected Communists. Instead, he released Red prisoners, forbade American soldiers to fire unless fired upon, and instructed his subordinates to avoid becoming entangled in partisan political questions.

Graves' determination to remain neutral also led him to refuse to subordinate himself to the senior Allied commander in Siberia, Japanese General Otani Kikuzo. Incredibly, President Wilson had agreed to place Graves under General Otani's command without informing either the War Department or Graves of this decision. Fortunately, Graves wisely declined to participate in the schemes of foreign powers.[39]

Yet his insistence on strict neutrality was not without its price. His subordinates were obliged to adhere to a policy of noninterference that was extremely difficult to maintain, especially on humanitarian issues. Moreover, many officers chafed at headquarters' restrictive rules of engagement, which they believed placed them in untenable positions. Finally, Graves' stance greatly aggravated relations with the other members of the multinational expedition, especially the British and Japanese, both of whom were committed to driving the Bolsheviks out of eastern Siberia. The non-Communist government in Siberia, led by Admiral Alexander Kolchak, was similarly annoyed by Graves' behavior.

Consequently, the Kolchak, Japanese, and British governments, aided by pro-Kolchak members of the U.S. State Department, all lobbied for Graves' removal. In Siberia the Japanese and their allies among the Russian Cossack troops that Kolchak had sent to control eastern Siberia orchestrated an anti-American propaganda campaign designed to turn the population against the United States and force the Americans to withdraw, giving Japan a freer hand in Siberian affairs. By 1919 tensions between the so-called Allies were so high that a number of incidents occurred between U.S. forces on the one hand and the Japanese and Cossacks on the other, including one clash between American and Japanese patrols. Graves was unshakable in his adherence to the letter of his instructions, however, and the War Department backed him up.[40]

One reason why Graves refused to provide more assistance to the Whites was that he was appalled by their conduct. Kolchak governed by force and intimidation, while the behavior of his Cossacks appeared to Graves to be nothing less than barbarous. Misdeeds by the Communists were not unknown, but they paled in comparison with the atrocities committed against the Russian peasantry by the non-Communists, who, with Japanese support, instituted a reign of terror over large areas of eastern Siberia.

General Graves realized that Kolchak's misrule alienated the mass of the Russian people and severely damaged their cause. A veteran of several counterinsurgency campaigns in the Philippines, he fully understood that a policy of unremitting repression would only undermine the Allies' position. His views were shared by the president, as well as other high-ranking constabulary veterans like Generals March and Bliss, all of whom believed that it was futile to attempt to stem the tide

One of the principal antagonists in Siberia, Cossack commander Ataman Semenoff, meets with General Graves (right).

of revolution with bayonets alone. As in north Russia, the American Expeditionary Force, Siberia (AEFS), actively attempted to win popular approval by following the Army's traditional creed of fair dealing and good conduct. Americans paid for everything they needed, occupied buildings only with the owner's consent, and detailed their doctors to attend local populations. AEFS soldiers organized local entertainment programs and delivered Christmas trees to brighten an otherwise bleak Siberian winter.[41]

Graves' good deeds, however, were insufficient to counteract the ill will generated by the actions of America's Allies. He lacked both the authority and the resources to correct their errors. Wilson's neutrality edict prevented him from instituting a full-fledged civil affairs/pacification campaign, nor is there any evidence that the non-Communists would have accepted such a program. Instead they demanded more guns, not more humanitarian assistance. Although President Wilson announced his intention to establish a civilian commission to organize the delivery of socioeconomic aid and advice to Russia, he never followed through, partly because he was unwilling to undertake a large aid program until he had found a Russian regime he deemed worthy of his support and partly because the proposal became ensnared in a battle for control between the Departments of State and Commerce. The bureaucratic donnybrook led the president to dump the idea altogether, assuring that what little civil aid the United States provided, largely through the works of private agencies, would be uncoordinated.[42]

As in north Russia, the end of World War I brought no relief to the Siberia expedition. The Czechs, whom the United States was committed to support, were still deep inside Russia. So too were the Japanese, against whose machinations Washington found the AEFS to be a useful counterweight. Moreover, as time passed the president found himself under growing diplomatic pressure to provide more direct assistance to Kolchak's regime at Omsk, 3,000 miles west of Vladivostok. Though he refused to provide the non-Communists with direct combat support, the president took a tentative step toward helping Kolchak in February 1919, when he ordered the AEFS to protect several sections of the Trans-Siberian Railroad, Kolchak's logistical lifeline. Theoretically, the soldiers were to keep the railroad open for all Russians to use, regardless of ideology. In reality, the line operated for the exclusive benefit of the non-Communists, since all of the railroad officials were Kolchak appointees.[43]

Graves realized that the arrangement dangerously compromised his nonpartisan position, and he immediately cabled the War Department "to ask if my policy in considering the Bolshevik trouble in Siberia an internal trouble in which I should take no part is the policy the Department desires me to continue to follow." No new guidance emanated from Washington until a few months later, when the president further eroded America's neutrality by ordering Graves to deliver a large quantity of arms to Kolchak, who in return promised to establish a progressive, democratic government in Russia. Graves, who knew the true mettle of Kolchak and his supporters, protested the order but complied when Washington overruled his objections.

Yet the situation remained muddled, for while the president had moved to prop up the Kolchak regime, he remained skeptical about its viability and refused to commit the United States entirely behind it. He not only declined to recognize Kolchak as the legitimate ruler of Russia, but insisted on maintaining the image of neutrality, informing the Senate only two weeks after authorizing the arms delivery that "the instructions to General Graves direct him not to interfere in Russian affairs." The president was strangely silent on how one could deliver arms to one faction and protect that faction's lines of communications at the expense of another and not interfere in Russian affairs. Nevertheless, that is what he expected Graves to do, and the general endeavored to comply as best he could.[44]

Graves implemented the president's new policy by establishing outposts along the Trans-Siberian and by threatening to hold local populations responsible for acts committed against the line by Red partisans. He also ordered villagers to turn in their firearms and promised to treat anyone found with a weapon as an enemy. In practice, he took a milder course. He refrained from resorting to harsh, collective punishments and treated all captives as legitimate prisoners of war. To some extent the Army's reputation for fair play yielded benefits, as the Bolsheviks preferred to attack those sections of the Trans-Siberian that were manned by the Whites and Japanese than those guarded by the more benevolent Americans. Nevertheless, Graves' position was precarious, for in protecting Kolchak's lifeline, he had crossed the threshold from being an observer to a participant in the Russian Civil War. By the spring of 1919 American garrisons along the Trans-Siberian found themselves drawn inextricably into a desultory game of cat and mouse against small groups of bandits and Communist partisans who sought to disrupt railroad traffic.[45]

The situation came to a head in the Suchan Valley, a mining district seventy-five miles east of Vladivostok. Suchan's coal was vital for the operation of the Trans-Siberian, and consequently General Graves had tried to cast a blanket of neutrality over the region by negotiating an agreement between White and Red leaders to keep their troops out of the area. The agreement quickly unraveled, as excesses by White forces on the outskirts of the district, as well as the rather callous labor practices of the mines' pro-Kolchak management, alienated the local population. Besides, the Suchan mines were too important a target for the Bolsheviks to ignore for long, and they soon initiated hostilities against American troops stationed in the region. After a slow start, the guerrilla campaign exploded when, on 25 June, Red partisans surprised a small American outpost at Romanovka, killing or wounding forty-four of the garrison's seventy-two men.[46]

The Romanovka raid compelled Graves to drop all pretense of neutrality and to wage an active campaign against the Communists in the Suchan region. His first step was to intern all males in the district who were not either manifestly pro-Allied or gainfully employed in the mines. Then, in July, he joined Japanese and Kolchak's forces in launching a coordinated sweep of the Suchan region. Cooperation between American and White forces was particularly close. Joint patrols were common, and local U.S. commanders routinely turned

The vital Suchan mining district in eastern Siberia, where the Army conducted counterguerrilla operations against Bolshevik partisans

Russian prisoners over to non-Communist authorities for disposition. Using traditional counterguerrilla methods, the Army first employed large-scale sweeps to disperse Communist concentrations before breaking down into progressively smaller patrols that scoured the countryside in search of Red guerrillas. In the process, Army commanders made frequent use of the time-honored tactic of making night marches for the purpose of surprising guerrilla encampments and searching villages for Communist collaborators and illicit arms.[47]

As in all of the Army's previous experiences in irregular warfare, tracking down the poorly armed but elusive partisans, rather than defeating them in battle, proved to be the real challenge of the campaign. The Communists enjoyed all of the advantages traditionally accorded to guerrillas, including mobility, familiarity with the terrain, a superior intelligence network that kept them apprised of Allied movements, and an ability to blend in with the surrounding population.

Intelligence was the key to overcoming these advantages, and the AEFS took special measures to obtain it. In addition to maintaining a central intelligence office at AEFS headquarters, General Graves had directed in 1918 that every post and detachment have an intelligence officer. These officers gathered information on the surrounding terrain as well as the local political, military, and economic situation, to include barometers of local sentiment and loyalties.

During 1918–1919 the 27th U.S. Infantry created battalion intelligence sections modeled closely upon the Czech Legion's highly successful intelligence system. Meanwhile the 31st U.S. Infantry, whose men patrolled the Suchan, established an intelligence school that gave selected NCOs an intense course in interrogation and investigatory techniques, scouting and reconnaissance, and small-unit tactics, as well as an introduction to Russian language, geography, and politics. The graduates of this school were designated "intelligence scouts" and played a key role in the Suchan counterinsurgency campaign, serving in small detachments as guides, interpreters, liaisons, and agents. With their help, Allied forces cleared the Suchan Valley of Communists in just two months, killing 500 guerrillas in the process.[48]

The Allied victory in Suchan was a Pyrrhic one, however, for the guerrillas had managed to wreck several key railway facilities, preventing the movement of coal to the main railroad line. Realizing that the mines had been crippled, and anxious to escape the partisan fray, Graves removed all American forces from the Suchan district in September 1919. The withdrawal virtually ended active U.S. participation in counter-Bolshevik operations. Minor clashes between American soldiers and Communist partisans continued through the remainder of the year along the Trans-Siberian Railroad, but they were the exception rather than the rule. Once out of the Suchan Valley, Graves sharply curtailed cooperation with the non-Communists and terminated the procedure of turning over Communist prisoners to government authorities. Some American commanders even went so far as to negotiate "live and let live" agreements with local Communists, although Graves frowned on the practice.[49]

Despite the Allies' deployment of about 160,000 men to Siberia, they could not keep the feeble and unpopular Kolchak regime afloat. In November 1919 the Bolsheviks crushed Kolchak's armies and captured his capital at Omsk. Two months later the admiral was dead, and with him the hopes for a non-Communist victory in Siberia. In February 1920 the Czech Legion began to evacuate Siberia via Vladivostok. American forces remained in position long enough to cover the legion's withdrawal and then withdrew also. The last American troops embarked at Vladivostok in June 1920, bringing to a close nearly two years of difficult service in Russia.

By every measure, President Wilson's interventions in Russia had failed. The Eastern Front had not been reestablished, the war supplies stockpiled in Russian ports had not been saved, and no popular, progressive, non-Communist government had been established. The Japanese continued to meddle in Siberian affairs for another two years in a futile effort to carve out a puppet state. Even the successful extrication of the Czech Legion had little to do with Graves' small expedition, as the legion's 50,000 hardened veterans were more than capable of fending for themselves. In the words of Chief of Staff March, the expeditions in Russia had been little more than "a military crime."[50]

Panama, 1918–1920

Just as it was about to commit U.S. troops to the two expeditions in Russia, the Wilson administration launched its longest and by far the smallest U.S. Army intervention into the affairs of a foreign country, this time in Panama. Panama had been an American protectorate since 1903, when President Theodore Roosevelt had helped engineer its successful revolution against its then parent state, Colombia. Since that time, the United States had built a canal across the isthmus on land ceded to it by Panama. It had also occasionally employed military forces based in the Canal Zone to influence Panamanian affairs, under provisions sanctified by treaty and clauses of Panama's own constitution. When in the summer of 1918 the Panamanian government threatened to postpone elections, American troops from the Canal Zone seized the cities of Panama and Colon and compelled the government to move ahead with the elections. While U.S. Army units maintained order in Panama's two principal cities, another 200 soldiers spread out over the rest of the country to monitor polling places. After the conclusion of the voting, the Army withdrew its troops back to the Canal Zone, all except for a small detachment of men in the city of David, the capital of Panama's Chiriqui Province.[51] (*Map 6*)

Chiriqui was Panama's richest province, the home of large plantations and cattle ranches, many of which were owned by American and European citizens. Unfortunately, the province also had a reputation for lawlessness and corruption. Cattle rustling and land disputes were common, with the foreign community obtaining little redress from the province's government. When in July 1918 the foreign community appealed to the United States for relief, the American minister to Panama asked Brig. Gen. Richard M. Blatchford, the commander of

U.S. forces in the Canal Zone, to keep the election-monitoring detail in David until the Panamanian government corrected the situation in Chiriqui. General Blatchford complied.[52]

The Chiriqui detachment was small, fluctuating between fifty and seventy men from the 33d U.S. Infantry, supplemented by a few soldiers from the Puerto Rican Regiment who acted as interpreters and intelligence officers. Nevertheless, the detachment was quite active during its first few months in the province. Under the leadership of Maj. Herbert E. Pace, American soldiers crisscrossed the countryside to demonstrate their presence and discourage the further persecution of foreigners. Although Major Pace had absolutely no police authority, he detached men to assist the Panamanian police force in the performance of its duties. This assistance, coupled with the appointment of a new police chief in the province, resulted in the arrest of nearly a hundred cattle thieves, many of whom had previously enjoyed virtual immunity from the law.[53]

In addition to assisting the Panamanian police, the Chiriqui detachment performed the State Department's bidding by gathering intelligence on conditions in the province and by intervening in local political and judicial proceedings on behalf of American landowners. But the detachment lacked any official authority over the provincial government and had to achieve its aims purely through persuasion. This naturally limited the detachment's ability to improve provincial affairs, once criminals and officials alike realized that the troops lacked the authority to use force. Corruption and petty criminality soon resumed, undisturbed by the detail's admonitions. It quickly became apparent that the only real leverage the detachment gave the United States over the Panamanian government was that derived from its physical presence inside Chiriqui.

As in 1914 and 1916, the Army chafed at having to play the heavy in the State Department's game of coercive diplomacy. The Panamanians liked the Army's presence even less, and they bombarded the U.S. government with demands for the detachment's withdrawal. The State Department ignored both sides, refusing to withdraw the troops until Panama had made some material progress in addressing American concerns in the province. Meanwhile, the soldiers at David languished. Lacking a clear mission and denied any authority to affect the situation, the detachment gradually fell victim to all the vices one might expect from sleepy garrison duty in a remote Central American town. By July 1919 discipline and morale had become so bad at David that the new commander of the Panama Canal Zone, Maj. Gen. Chase W. Kennedy, replaced the entire garrison and brought back the ener-

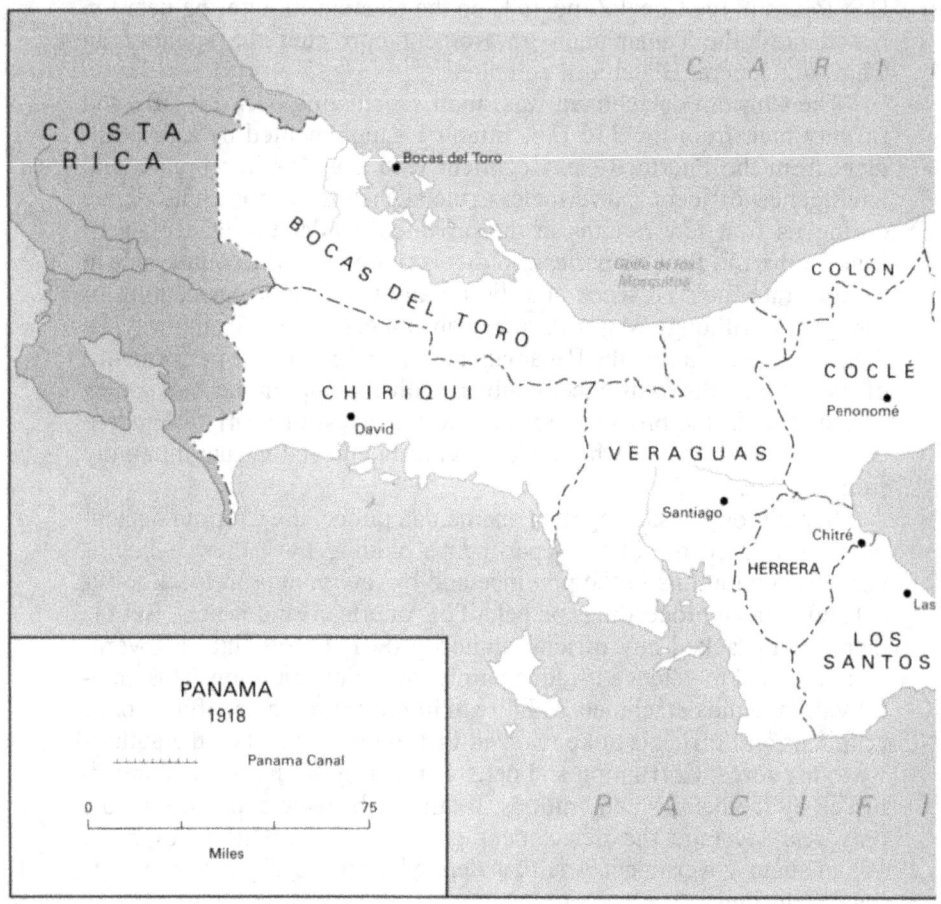

MAP 6

getic Major Pace, who had previously left Chiriqui, to revitalize the detachment.[54]

The change of personnel improved the administration of the detachment but could not alter the difficulty of the situation. When in early 1920 the population rallied behind a member of an influential anti-American family who had assassinated the reform-minded governor of the province, the frustrated major rashly issued a handbill declaring that the U.S. Army would remain in Chiriqui forever unless the Panamanians changed their ways. The handbill created a stir in Panama, embarrassing the State Department, which demanded that the Army replace Major Pace. Secretary of War Baker, however, refused to make

the major a scapegoat for what he regarded as the folly of the State Department's policy in Chiriqui. Pace may have been guilty of a momentary lapse of judgment, Baker conceded, but he was the best man the Army had for the job, and if the State Department did not like him, it should replace the military detachment with its own personnel. The department declined the offer, and Major Pace and his small band of soldiers, now down to about twenty men, continued their uncomfortable vigil in David.[55]

The standoff continued until August 1920, when General Kennedy saw an opportunity to extricate his men. Recent Panamanian elections had passed without incident, while the outstanding problems in

Chiriqui seemed relatively trivial. Moreover, a momentary lull in the Panamanian government's political offensive to oust the Americans gave Kennedy the chance to pull the detachment out with minimal loss of face. Last, but certainly not least, the American minister to Panama, who had steadfastly opposed the withdrawal of the troops, happened to be out of the country on leave. Seizing the moment, the War Department unilaterally withdrew the troops from Chiriqui before the minister returned, confronting the State Department with a *fait accompli*. After two years of uncomfortable and often frustrating duty, the last of the Army's interventions under the Wilson administration had come to an end.[56]

Army Doctrine and the Wilson Interventions

The military interventions of the Wilson administration had relatively little impact upon the development of military doctrine in those areas most closely identified with the small wars experience—irregular warfare, pacification, and civil affairs. True, the Army's two sojourns into Mexico had given it the opportunity to brush up on some old constabulary skills and experiment with new ones, while the Army's adventures in Russia had provided challenges in cold weather operations. Yet on the whole, the various forays abroad had produced few tactical innovations, and whatever lessons might have been derived were overshadowed by those of the Great War. Unlike the previous fifty years, when constabulary operations were the Army's bread and butter, the interventions of 1914–1920 affected a progressively smaller percentage of an Army thronged with young officers whose primary military experience was conventional combat on the Western Front.

The interventions under President Wilson made equally little mark on the development of civil affairs doctrine, primarily because their limited nature did not permit extensive civil activities. Within the narrow confines of their missions, American officers had applied their now time-honored nostrums to civil-military questions, but they neither developed new concepts nor modified the Army's traditional thinking.

The true significance of the experience under Wilson lay not in the realm of doctrine, but in matters of policy. Prior to 1914, the U.S. Army's constabulary operations on foreign soil had been all-or-nothing affairs, in which the Army occupied and administered the entire area in question. President Wilson added a new dimension to the Army's small wars experience, for he was the first American president to extensively employ limited force for the pursuit of equally limited diplomatic objectives. In the process, the interventions of 1914–1920 demonstrated both the utility and the limitations of using force as an instrument of foreign policy. Among the latter were the dangers of committing troops into nebulous politico-military situations without sufficient information, clear mission statements, or feasible objectives—as well as the difficulty of extracting such troops once they had been committed.[57]

Army leadership derived two principal lessons from the experience. The first was the need for greater coordination of civil and military policy both before and during an intervention. Never before had the Army had to cooperate with, and subordinate itself to, the State Department as extensively as during the contingency operations during the Wilson administration. It found the experience no more pleasant than its dealings with the Interior Department during the previous century. By championing closer civil-military coordination, Army leaders henceforth sought to wrest clear statements of mission and policy from their civilian superiors. The Army's experiences during 1914–1920 also reinforced the sense of caution and disenchantment toward overseas constabulary work that already existed in the officer corps, as a result of earlier travails in Cuba and the Philippines. Over the next two decades these lessons became cardinal tenets of Army thinking with regard to the execution of overseas contingency operations.

Notes

¹ Quote from Frederick Calhoun, "The Wilsonian Way of War: American Armed Power From Veracruz to Vladivostok" (Ph.D. diss., University of Chicago, 1983), p. 35. Edward Haley, *Revolution and Intervention: The Diplomacy of Taft and Wilson With Mexico, 1910–17* (Cambridge: Massachusetts Institute of Technology [MIT] Press, 1970), p. 138.

² U.S. Congress, House, Committee on Foreign Affairs, *Background Information on the Use of United States Armed Forces in Foreign Countries*, 91st Cong., 2d sess., 1970, pp. 55–56; Lester Langley, *The Banana Wars: United States Intervention in the Caribbean, 1898–1934* (Lexington: University of Kentucky Press, 1983); Calhoun, "Wilsonian Way of War," pp. 8–9; Richard Kolb, "'Restoring Order' South of the Border," *U.S. Naval Institute Proceedings* 110 (July 1984): 56–61. The Army contributed to the Marine Corps' intervention in Cuba between 1917–1922 by sending one man—Maj. Gen. Enoch Crowder, the 1906–1909 author of Cuba's electoral system. Crowder spent the years 1921–1922 directing political reforms in Cuba. The Army also staffed a number of international fact-finding, relief, and truce observation missions in Eastern Europe. Included among these were Col. William Haskell's Allied High Commission for Armenia, Maj. Gen. James G. Harbord's fact-finding mission to Turkey and the Caucus, Brig. Gen. Harry Bandholtz's Inter-Allied Military Commission to Hungary, a Baltic Military Mission to observe German troop withdrawals from Courland and Latvia, and a medical aid mission to Poland. On the last named event, see Alfred Cornebise, *Typhus and Doughboys: The American Polish Relief Expedition, 1919–21* (Newark: University of Delaware Press, 1982).

³ Quote from Marlin Forster, "U.S. Intervention in Mexico: The 1914 Occupation of Veracruz," *Military Review* 57 (August 1977): 89; Robert Quirk, *An Affair of Honor: Woodrow Wilson and the Occupation of Veracruz* (Lexington: University of Kentucky Press, 1962), pp. 20–25, 54–56, 60; Edward Haley, "Comparative Intervention: Mexico in 1914 and Dominica in 1965," in *Intervention or Abstention: The Dilemma of American Foreign Policy*, ed. Robin Higham (Lexington: University of Kentucky Press, 1975), pp. 42–43; Haley, *Revolution and Intervention*, pp. 131, 134.

⁴ Forster, "Intervention in Mexico," pp. 90–91; Jack Sweetman, *The Landing at Veracruz* (Annapolis, Md.: U.S. Naval Institute Press, 1968), pp. 103–15, 138, 140; Quirk, *Affair of Honor*, pp. 95–96.

⁵ Calhoun, "Wilsonian Way of War," pp. 72–73, 81.

⁶ Challener, *Admirals, Generals, and American Foreign Policy*, p. 395; Ltr, Brig Gen W. W. Wotherspoon to General Leonard Wood, 11 Apr 11, MID, 5761–114, RG 165, NARA.

⁷ Clendenen, *Blood on the Border*, p. 162; Calhoun, "Wilsonian Way of War," pp. 67–68; Quirk, *Affair of Honor*, pp. 106–07.

⁸ Quirk, *Affair of Honor*, pp. 105, 141; Sweetman, *Landing at Veracruz*, p. 139; Forster, "Intervention in Mexico," p. 93; Frederick Funston, *Report of Operations of U.S. Expeditionary Forces* (War Department, n.d.), p. 24; War Department Bulletin 24, Secy of War Garrison to Funston, 4 May 14, Records of the Judge Advocate General's Office, 99–415, RG 153, NARA; Guy Donnell, "U.S. Intervention in Mexico, 1914" (Ph.D. diss., University of Texas, 1951), pp. 241–42; Lecture, "Legal Principles," in

MILITARY INTERVENTIONS DURING THE WILSON ADMINISTRATION, 1914–1920

Command and General Staff School (CGS), 2d Year Course, 1931–32, lecture series on military government. Rear Adm. Frank Fletcher, Funston's predecessor, had responded to the vacuum of authority created by Mexico's anti-collaboration law by assuming direct control of local governmental machinery. He also recruited American civilians living in Mexico to oversee the effort. Funston acquiesced in the admiral's approach, and the two officers selected Robert Kerr, a civilian lawyer with extensive experience in Mexico, to serve as a civil governor under Funston's overall authority. Kerr proved to be a poor choice, for he was an outspoken critic of the Wilson administration, and Washington quickly removed him on this account. In his stead, Secretary of War Lindley M. Garrison directed that Funston establish a traditional military government with Funston at its head.

[9] Quote from Sweetman, *Landing at Veracruz*, p. 158. Funston, *Report of Operations*, pp. 38–39; Quirk, *Affair of Honor*, pp. 132, 144; Donnell, "Intervention in Mexico," pp. 249–53.

[10] HQ, U.S. Expeditionary Forces, Vera Cruz, Mexico, Memorandum in Reference to the Methods To Be Employed in the Capture and Occupation of Latin-American Cities, 10 Aug 14, WCD, 8699–2; Memo, Brig Gen Charles Treat, Chief, WCD, for Chief of Staff, Southern Department, 11 Nov 16, sub: Memo in Reference to the Methods To Be Employed in the Capture and Occupation of Latin-American Cities, WCD, 8699–7. Both in RG 165, NARA.

[11] Sweetman, *Landing at Veracruz*, p. 164; Forster, "Intervention in Mexico," p. 95; Quirk, *Affair of Honor*, pp. 160–65.

[12] Sweetman, *Landing at Veracruz*, p. 167; Quirk, *Affair of Honor*, pp. v–vi, 117, 171; Forster, "Intervention in Mexico," p. 95.

[13] Charles Harris and Louis Sadler, "The Plan of San Diego and the Mexican-U.S. War Crisis of 1916: A Reexamination," *Hispanic-American Historical Review* 58 (1978): 381–408.

[14] Ibid.

[15] Quote from Frank McCoy, "Patrolling the Rio Grande," *Military Historian and Economist* 2 (January 1917): 92. Robert Bullard, Mexican Bandit Service on the Lower Rio Grande, c. 1916, pp. 4–5, box 7, Bullard Papers.

[16] George Marvin, "Bandits and the Borderland," *World's Work* 32 (October 1916): 663; Harris and Sadler, "Plan of San Diego," pp. 391–92; Charles Cumberland, "Border Raids in the Lower Rio Grande Valley—1915," *Southwestern Historical Quarterly* 57 (January 1954): 301, 304–08.

[17] Clendenen, *Blood on the Border*, pp. 208–10; Haldeen Braddy, *Pershing's Mission in Mexico* (El Paso: Texas Western Press, 1973), p. 4.

[18] Quotes from Herbert Mason, *The Great Pursuit* (New York: Random House, 1970), pp. 69–70. Calhoun, "Wilsonian Way of War," p. 93; Robert Thomas and Inez Allen, The Mexican Punitive Expedition Under Brigadier General John J. Pershing, 1916–17 [Washington, D.C.: U.S. Army Center of Military History, 1954], pp. II-4, V-9.

[19] Haley, *Revolution and Intervention*, p. 206; Smythe, *Guerrilla Warrior*, p. 224.

[20] Quote from Calhoun, "Wilsonian Way of War," p. 90. George H. Cameron, "Lecture on the Mexican War Plan," AWC session 1915–16, Mar 16, WCD, 6474–377, RG 165, NARA.

[21] Memo, Maj Gen Bliss for CSA Hugh Scott, 10 Mar 16, sub: Expedition Into Mexico, WCD, 6474–374, RG 165, NARA; Calhoun, "Wilsonian Way of War," pp.

90–96. Scott quote from Mason, *Great Pursuit*, p. 144. As noted earlier, the Army did not take the prospect of pacifying Mexico lightly, believing that the task would last several years and require nearly a half million men to do the job. Any failure to be fully prepared, should Pershing's expedition spark a war, would add greatly to the pacification problem, and it was for this reason that the Army urged the president to prepare in earnest for the outbreak of war with Mexico. See Rowell, Intervention in Mexico; Memo, Brig Gen M. Macomb, Chief, WCD, for CSA, 13 Mar 16, sub: A Call for Volunteers, WCD, 6474–375, RG 165, NARA.

[22] Not only were approximately two-thirds of Pershing's officers veterans of the Philippine War, but his command included a surprising number of veterans of the Indian wars, many of whom were assigned key roles in the expedition. Constabulary service veterans who served with the expedition included General Pershing, expedition commander (Indian, Philippine, and Moro Wars); Lt. Col. DeRosey Cabell, expedition chief of staff (Geronimo campaign); Col. George Dodd, cavalry brigade commander (Indian and Philippine Wars) (and former commander of Indian Scouts); Col. James B. Erwin, cavalry column commander (anti-*pulahan* campaign); Lt. Col. Henry T. Allen, cavalry column commander (Philippine War) (and former chief of Philippine Constabulary); Col. William C. Brown, cavalry column commander (Indian and Philippine Wars) (and former commander of Indian Scouts); Col. Herbert J. Slocum, cavalry column commander (Indian, Philippine, and Moro Wars) (and former adviser to Cuban Rural Guard); Maj. Frank Tompkins, cavalry column commander (Philippines and Texas border patrol); and Col. Robert Howze, cavalry column commander (former commander of Indian Scouts and the Puerto Rican Regiment). Thomas and Allen, Mexican Punitive Expedition, pp. II-19, II-20; James Sandos, "Prostitution and Drugs: The U.S. Army on the Mexican-American Border, 1916–17," *Pacific Historical Review* 49 (1980): 624; Harry Toulmin, *With Pershing in Mexico* (Harrisburg, Pa.: Military Service Publishing Co., 1935), p. 97; Smythe, *Guerrilla Warrior*, p. 226; John Porter, "The Punitive Expedition," *Quartermaster Review* 12 (January–February 1933): 23; Clendenen, *Blood on the Border*, pp. 239–40, 358. On tactics, see Stuart Cramer, "The Punitive Expedition From Boquillas," *Cavalry Journal* 27 (November 1916): 213; S. M. Williams, "The Cavalry Fight at Ojos Azules," *Cavalry Journal* 27 (January 1917): 406; James Shannon, "With the Apache Scouts in Mexico," *Cavalry Journal* 27 (1917): 539–57; Frank Tompkins, *Chasing Villa: The Story Behind the Story of Pershing's Expedition Into Mexico* (Harrisburg, Pa.: Military Service Publishing Co., 1934), p. 126.

[23] Porter, "Punitive Expedition," pp. 24, 28; O. C. Troxel, "The Tenth Cavalry in Mexico," *Cavalry Journal* 28 (1917): 201.

[24] "Messages from Mexico," *World's Work* 32 (August 1916): 435; HQ, Punitive Expedition, GO 14, 31 Mar 16, Records of American Expeditionary Forces, 1917–20, RG 120, NARA; Richard McMaster, An Artilleryman in Mexico, 1916, Extracts from the Diary of Maj R. H. McMaster, 4th F.A., p. 8, Richard H. McMaster Papers, MHI; Clendenen, *Blood on the Border*, pp. 331, 333; Toulmin, *With Pershing in Mexico*, p. 113.

[25] Mason, *Great Pursuit*, p. 131; Porter, "Punitive Expedition," pp. 23–26; Smythe, *Guerrilla Warrior*, p. 246; Toulmin, *With Pershing in Mexico*, pp. 59–61; *WDAR*, 1916, 1:6–7.

[26] Quote from Calhoun, "Wilsonian Way of War," p. 115. Haley, *Revolution and Intervention*, pp. 208–11, 236.

[27] Thomas and Allen, Mexican Punitive Expedition, pp. I-9, I-10, IV-24–IV-28; *Annual Report, Commanding General, Southern Department*, Fiscal Year 1916, p. 15, 2480591, RG 94, NARA; Harris and Sadler, "Plan of San Diego," pp. 392–402; Cramer, "Punitive Expedition," pp. 200–227; Porter, "Punitive Expedition," p. 25; Joseph McDonough, "The Political and Military Background of the Mexican Punitive Expedition" (Master's thesis, Georgetown University, April 1957), p. 90.

[28] Calhoun, "Wilsonian Way of War," p. 98.

[29] Company Problems no. 3 & 4, 2d Battalion, 6th Infantry, 14 Sep 16; Ltr, Col Nicholson to Pershing, 10 Sep 16, sub: Field Exercises; Ltr, Maj M. W. Rowell to Commanding Officer, 11th Cav, 3 Sep 16, sub: Troop Problems—Tactical Exercises; Ltr, Lt Col Evans to Camp Commander, 4 Sep 16, sub: Field Problems; Ltr, Col S. R. H. Tompkins to Camp Commander, 7 Sep 16, sub: Problems; Ltr, Maj Wilcox to Division Adjutant, 21 Sep 16; Ltr, Maj Elleuill to Commanding General (CG), Punitive Expedition, 7 Sep 16; Memo, Maj S. Rutherford for Chief of Staff, Punitive Expedition, 3 Dec 16. All in 1207, Records of the Punitive Expedition, Records of American Expeditionary Forces, 1917–1920, RG 120, NARA. Rpt, CG, Punitive Expedition, to CG, Southern Department, 7 Oct 16, sub: Report of Operations of Punitive Expedition to June 30, 1916, box 32, Allen Papers; LeRoy Eltinge, *Psychology of War* (Fort Leavenworth, Kans.: Army Service Schools, 1911), p. 42; HQ, Punitive Expedition, GO 42, 17 Jun 16, RG 120, NARA.

[30] "Cavalry Training," *Cavalry Journal* 27 (1917): 508–17; George Patton, "Cavalry Work of the Punitive Expedition," *Cavalry Journal* 27 (1917): 426–33; H. S. Hawkins, "The Pistol Attack," *Cavalry Journal* 20 (October 1915): 179–82; DeRosey Cabell, "Field Training for Cavalry," *Cavalry Journal* 26 (October 1915): 197–202; Bullard, Mexican Bandit Service, p. 5; Harry Smith, "The Texas Bandit Problem," *Infantry Journal* 12 (March 1916): 845–52; McCoy, "Patrolling the Rio Grande," p. 90; James Parker, "Cavalry and Auto Trucks," *Cavalry Journal* 27 (1917): 348–60; "Here and There," *Infantry Journal* (January 1917): 407; John Madden, "Thanks to Villa," *Quartermaster Review* 1 (September–October 1921): 27–31; George Millard, "U.S. Army Logistics During the Mexican Punitive Expedition of 1916," *Military Review* 60 (October 1980): 58–68; Robert Sawyer, "Viva Villa," *Military Review* 41 (August 1961): 65–75; Toulmin, *With Pershing in Mexico*, pp. xiv–xv, 24–25, 113, 131–40; "Some Cavalry Lessons of the Mexican Punitive Expedition," app. A, in Tompkins, *Chasing Villa*, pp. 231–32.

[31] Villa continued to wage a low-level guerrilla war against Carranza until 1920 when he finally "surrendered" in return for a 25,000-acre ranch. The continued instability in Mexico meant that the border remained troubled as well. Between 1917 and 1919 the U.S. Army established an aerial border patrol and staged nearly a dozen cross-border punitive operations, including one last major clash with Villista forces in June 1919. Not till the Mexican revolution finally petered out in the early 1920s would the border return to a more normal, though never entirely tranquil, state. Mason, *Great Pursuit*, pp. 223–31, 236–37; Stacy Hinkle, *Wings and Saddles: The Air and Cavalry Punitive Expedition of 1919* (El Paso: Texas Western Press, 1967); Clendenen, *Blood on the Border*, pp. 337, 343–44.

[32] Carl Richard, "'The Shadow of a Plan': The Rationale Behind Wilson's 1918 Siberian Intervention,'" *Historian* 49 (1986): 83.

[33] Calhoun, "Wilsonian Way of War," p. 365; Richard Goldhurst, *The Midnight War: The American Intervention in Russia, 1918–20* (New York: McGraw-Hill, 1978), p. 78.

[34] Quotes from William Graves, *America's Siberian Adventure, 1918–20* (New York: Jonathan Cope and Harrison Smith, 1931), pp. 7–8. Edward Coffman, "The Intervention in Russia, 1918–21," *Military Review* 68 (September 1988): 62.

[35] Quote from Goldhurst, *Midnight War*, p. 86. Daniel Bolger, "Cruel Russian Winter," *Military Review* 67 (June 1987): 65; Benjamin Rhodes, *The Anglo-American Winter War With Russia, 1918–19* (New York: Greenwood Press, 1988), p. 42. An American engineer contingent also participated in Allied operations out of Murmansk. The Murmansk expedition is not covered in this text.

[36] Harry Costello, *Why Did We Go to Russia?* (Detroit, Mich.: Harry J. Costello, 1920), p. 22; Joel Moore et al., *The History of the American Expedition Fighting the Bolsheviki* (Detroit, Mich.: Polar Bear Publishing, 1920), pp. 44–45; Rhodes, *Anglo-American Winter War*, pp. 42–45. Quote from Coffman, "Intervention in Russia," p. 63.

[37] First quote from Ralph Albertson, *Fighting Without a War* (New York: Harcourt, Brace & Howe, 1920), pp. 77–78, and see also pp. 51–52, 67–72, 74, 79–81, 103–07. Second quote from ibid., p. 73. Costello, *Why Did We Go?* pp. 37–39, 46; Samuel Honaker, Memories of World War I, pp. 6–8, Samuel Honaker Papers, MHI; Elliot Macmorland, "Talk on North Russia," 7 Mar 77, p. 2, Elliot Macmorland Papers, MHI; Moore, *History of the American Expedition*, pp. 151–52, 155.

[38] Bruce Beals, "Coalition Warfare During the Allied Intervention in North Russia, 1918–19" (Master's thesis, Command and General Staff College, 1981), p. 24.

[39] Msg, Graves to Styer, 25 Dec 18, 000.2, World War I Organizational Records, AEF, Siberia, Records of U.S. Army Overseas Operations and Commands, RG 395, NARA; Memo, Maj R. E. Eichelberger for Adj Gen, HQ, AEFS, 16 Sep 18, General Correspondence, WWI Organizational Records, AEF, Siberia, RG 395, NARA; Goldhurst, *Midnight War*, pp. 123, 214; Carl Ackerman, *Trailing the Bolsheviki* (New York: Charles Scribner's Sons, 1919), pp. 186–89; Sylvian Kindall, *American Soldiers in Siberia* (New York: Richard Smith, 1945), pp. 85, 88; Memo, Adj Gen, HQ, AEFS, for All Commanding Officers, 7 Sep 18, sub: Factional Controversies Between Russians, General Correspondence, WWI Organizational Records, AEFS, RG 395, NARA; Betty Unterberger, *America's Siberian Expedition, 1918–20* (Durham, N.C.: Duke University Press, 1956), p. 76.

[40] Kindall, *American Soldiers in Siberia*, pp. 155–60, 189, 209–10; Telg 26, Col O. P. Robinson to Col Williams, 29 Jan 19, Historical file, AEFS, RG 395, NARA; Unterberger, *America's Siberian Expedition*, pp. 124–25; Graves, *Siberian Adventure*, pp. 193–94; Calhoun, "Wilsonian Way of War," p. 412. Quote from Ltr, Fred Bugbee to wife, 7 Sep 19, Joseph Longuevan Papers, MHI.

[41] Richard O'Connor, "Yanks in Siberia," *American Heritage* 25 (August 1974): 16; Intelligence Summary 118, Maj R. L. Eichelberger, 24 Mar 19, Historical file, AEFS War Diary, RG 395, NARA; Calhoun, "Wilsonian Way of War," pp. 419, 433; Unterberger, *America's Siberian Expedition*, p. 164; Kindall, *American Soldiers in Siberia*, pp. 101, 133.

[42] L. B. Packard, The American Expeditionary Forces in Siberia, 1918–19, Apr 19, pp. 84–86, Historical file, AEFS, RG 395, NARA; Telg, Consul Harris to State, 26 Sep 18, Historical file, AEFS War Diary, RG 395, NARA; George Kennan, *Soviet-American Relations, 1917–20*, vol. 2, *The Decision To Intervene* (Princeton, N.J.: Princeton University Press, 1958), pp. 399–400.

[43] Coffman, "Intervention in Russia," p. 69; Clarence Manning, *The Siberian Fiasco* (New York: Library Publishing, 1952), pp. 118–19.

44 Graves quote from Msg 200, Graves to Adjutant General, War Department (AGWAR), 5 Mar 19, Cablegrams to/from AGWAR, AEFS, RG 395, NARA. Goldhurst, *Midnight War*, p. 205; Unterberger, *America's Siberian Expedition*, p. 156. Wilson quote from Graves, *Siberian Adventure*, p. 355.

45 Rpt, Commanding Officer, Provisional Bn, 31st Inf, to Commanding Officer, U.S. Troops, Shkotovo, 23 May 19, sub: Report of Expedition to Maichi, Siberia, AEFS, RG 395, NARA.

46 L. L. Pendleton, "With the Siberian AEF," *Coast Artillery Journal* 62 (May 1925): 408–15; Rpt, Graves to Adj Gen, 25 Sep 19, sub: Operations to June 30, 1919, p. 20, Historical file, AEFS, RG 395, NARA.

47 Telg 84, Col Robinson to Col Williams, 27 Jun 19, General Correspondence, Organizational Records, AEFS, RG 395, NARA; Maj Gen William Graves, Report of Operations, July 1, 1919 to March 31, 1920, pp. 3–4, Historical file, AEFS, RG 395, NARA; Rpt, Sgt Herman Roush, 21 Jul 19, sub: Report of Intelligence Patrol no. 1, LeRoy Yarborough Papers, MHI; Rpt, Lt Col Eichelberger to Chief of Staff, AEFS, 10 Jul 19, sub: Conditions in the Suchan Mine District From June 27 Until July 7, Historical file, AEFS, RG 395, NARA; John White, *The Siberian Intervention* (Princeton, N.J.: Princeton University Press, 1950), pp. 276–83.

48 Schedule of Instruction Regimental Intelligence School, 31st Infantry, AEF Siberia; Digest of Instruction, Intelligence School, 31st Infantry, AEF, Siberia, April 21, 1919; Diary of Course—Military Intelligence—31st Infantry, April 22, 1919 to May 18, 1919. All in Yarborough Papers. Kindall, *American Soldiers in Siberia*, pp. 132, 139; Goldhurst, *Midnight War*, pp. 219–20; Rpt, Lt Col David P. Barrows to CG, 10 Jan 19, sub: Report in Detail of Operations of the Intelligence Section in Compliance With Memo No. 48, HQ AEF, Siberia, Series of 1918; Rpt, Lt Col R. L. Eichelberger to Chief of Staff, AEFS, 1 Jul 19, sub: Report of the Operations of the Intelligence Section, January 1–June 30, 1919; Memo, Chief of Staff, AEFS, for All Commanding Officers, 2 Sep 19, sub: Officers for Special Intelligence Work; Rpt, Capt Frank A. Paul to Commanding Officer, 31st Inf, 1 Jul 19. All in History file, AEFS, RG 395, NARA.

49 Memo for file, Col O. P. Robinson, Chief of Staff, AEFS, 21 Aug 19, 383.6, WWI Organizational Records, AEFS, RG 395, NARA; Kindall, *American Soldiers in Siberia*, p. 247.

50 Richard Luckett, *The White Generals: An Account of the White Movement and the Russian Civil War* (New York: Routledge and Kegan Paul, 1987), p. 62.

51 William McCain, *The United States and the Republic of Panama* (New York: Russell and Russell, 1965), p. 74.

52 Elbridge Colby, "Panamanian-American Relations in Chiriqui," *Current History* 12 (July 1920): 683.

53 Ibid., p. 683; Elbridge Colby, "American Powers in Panama," *Current History* 13 (March 1921): 450. Major Pace's efforts to stiffen the backbone of the local Panamanian police were reinforced by an American advisory mission to the Panamanian National Police. Sheldon Liss, *The Canal* (South Bend, Ind.: University of Notre Dame Press, 1967), p. 32.

54 Memo, Maj Gen C. W. Kennedy for Casper Y. Offutt, Charge d'Affaires, American Legation, Panama, 31 Jul 19, 370.6, 6083, Panama Canal Department, RG 395, NARA.

55 Ltr, Maj Gen C. W. Kennedy to Maj H. E. Pace, 6 Apr 20, 370.6, 6083, Panama Canal Department, RG 395, NARA.

[56] Msg 747, Maj Gen Kennedy to AGWAR, 4 Aug 20, 370.5, 6083, Panama Canal Department, RG 395, NARA.
[57] Coffman, "Intervention in Russia," p. 70.

7

THE INTERWAR YEARS 1920-1941

The two decades between the end of World War I and America's entry into World War II were relatively quiet ones for the U.S. Army. With few exceptions the government did not call upon the Army to undertake any foreign operations during this period. Such was not the case with the U.S. Marine Corps, which pulled constabulary duty in Santo Domingo (1916–1924), Haiti (1915–1934), and Nicaragua (1926–1933). The interwar years marked the zenith of the trend that had begun around the turn of the century of regarding the Marine Corps as the service of choice for the conduct of peacetime contingency operations. The American military establishment formally assigned intervention duty to the marines in 1927, when the Army and the Navy drew up the first joint document defining their roles and missions.

Under the agreement, the Marine Corps bore primary responsibility "for emergency service in time of peace for protection of the interests of the United States in foreign countries." Conversely, the Army was expected "to furnish land forces for occupation of foreign territory in protection of the interests of the United States" only "in exceptional cases." The 1927 agreement thus formalized what had already come to pass as the Marine Corps' preeminence in peacetime contingency operations.[1]

The Marine Corps' numerous experiences in overseas interventions during the first half of the twentieth century led it to publish the first American military manual devoted exclusively to the subject, the *Small Wars Manual* of 1935, revised and republished in 1940. Yet the marines were not alone in considering the problems associated with irregular conflict. Despite the 1927 agreement, these years also witnessed the development of small wars doctrine in the U.S. Army. Though the

Army's efforts in this regard were not as extensive as those of the Marine Corps, the principles that it codified during this period represented the culmination of a century of constabulary service at home and abroad.[2]

Overseas Duty in Panama, Germany, and China

The Army participated in only a few overseas operations of a constabulary nature during the interwar years. In Panama, U.S. military police deployed for two weeks in February 1921 to protect the residence of the country's president from angry mobs. Four years later, the Army sent troops twice more into Panama, first to supervise elections and then to quell rent riots in Panama City. Both operations were brief and had little impact other than to ensure that riot duty would remain a staple part of the Canal Zone garrison's training. The only other places where the Army saw external duty during the period were Germany and China. In Germany, the Army participated in the postwar occupation of the Rhineland. Although largely uneventful, the Army's five-year stay, 1918–1923, stimulated interest in military government matters, especially from an organizational and administrative standpoint. China, however, represented by far the Army's longest stint at overseas constabulary duty.[3]

The Army's presence in China stemmed from the Peking Relief Expedition of 1900. One consequence of the Boxer Rebellion was that the Western powers forced the Chinese government to permit them to station troops along the line of communications linking Peking to the sea whenever internal instability threatened either the lives or property of foreigners in China. In 1911 the foreign powers invoked that treaty when revolution swept the old Manchu dynasty from power. America's contribution to the international security detail consisted of the 15th U.S. Infantry, which arrived in China in January 1912 for what would ultimately turn out to be a 26-year stay.

For most of those years the 15th Infantry maintained a peaceful and leisurely lifestyle garrisoning the international quarter of Tientsin. During periods of civil war the regiment manned outposts along the Peking–Tientsin–Shanhaikwan railroad and contributed personnel for the "international trains" that patrolled the line. (*See Map 3.*) Each train carried a smorgasbord of American, British, French, Japanese, Italian, and, prior to World War I, German soldiers, as well as a contingent of Chinese chefs. The entire cavalcade had a comic opera flavor not unlike that which characterized similar duty along the Trans-Siberian Railroad, although the proceedings could turn deadly serious if a dis-

THE INTERWAR YEARS, 1920–1941

American (15th Infantry), French (Annamite), British, and Italian soldiers of the International Military Guard stand in front of their armored train on the Peking-Mukden Railroad in 1929.

gruntled warlord appeared astride the tracks. Fortunately, through a combination of luck, pluck, and a policy of permitting all sides use of the railroad, American soldiers were able to avoid becoming combatants in China's intermittent civil wars.[4]

Too small to be militarily effective, the 15th Infantry recognized that its primary function was symbolic, and it responded to the demands of China service accordingly. Although the regiment at times undertook field training to prepare for the possibility of another relief expedition to Peking, it focused most of its attention on spit and polish. Tailored uniforms and swagger sticks were the norm; one commander went so far as to replace all the pistols with wooden ones whose weight would not cause an unseemly crease in the men's uniforms. Though a bit extreme, the 15th's eccentricities were designed to help it fulfill its mission by inspiring awe and admiration on the part of the Chinese population. Bluff and swagger carried the 15th through more than one crisis during its long sojourn in China.[5]

Nevertheless, there was a limit to what the regiment could do, and as China's internal situation deteriorated the position of the U.S. troops

Spit and polish was the credo of the 15th Infantry in Tientsin.

became increasingly precarious. The Army repeatedly requested permission to withdraw the force, but to no avail, for the State Department feared that withdrawal would send the wrong signal, especially to imperialistic Japan. Even so, the Army's presence in Tientsin utterly failed to deter the Japanese from their aggressive designs. As the war between China and Japan escalated in the late 1930s, the State Department issued increasingly unsettling directives to the Tientsin garrison, including one that permitted the regiment to defend itself from assaults by disorganized soldiery but not from an attack made by organized units. Although the War Department protested bitterly, the 15th remained a hostage to the United States' China policy until 1938, when American diplomats finally decided to withdraw the soldiers lest they be caught in the advancing tide of the Sino-Japanese War.[6]

Sino-Japanese tensions also caused the one contingency deployment undertaken by the Army in China during the interwar years. When, in

THE INTERWAR YEARS, 1920–1941

Soldiers of the 31st Infantry defend the perimeter of Shanghai's foreign quarter in March 1932.

early 1932, fighting erupted between Chinese and Japanese troops in Shanghai, the United States sent the 31st U.S. Infantry from the Philippines to reinforce the U.S. marines and the European troops stationed in the city's international settlement. The regiment was poorly prepared for the mission. Fully one-quarter of the men had never fired their weapons, and the unit had rarely practiced civil disturbance duty. Shipped out with little information as to the situation in China, the regiment initiated a crash training program in riot and guard duty while en route, a program it continued once ashore at Shanghai. Upon debarkation the unit was placed under the control of the local U.S. Marine commander and given the task of guarding a segment of the international settlement's perimeter. The troops served as a neutral force, protecting foreign lives and property from both internal disorder and the fighting that swirled outside the boundaries of the Western enclave. Operating under strict rules of engagement, the infantrymen endeavored to achieve their objectives through tact, conciliation, and intimidation rather than by force. In this they were successful. During its four months in Shanghai, the 31st performed its duties without firing a shot or taking a casualty.

As the fighting outside the settlement died down, the Army requested permission to withdraw its men but—as in Mexico, Russia, and Panama—found that embarking upon an overseas expedition was easier than ending it. Uneasy about Japanese intentions, the State Department insisted that the 31st Infantry remain in China. The War Department countered that the regiment was not adequately trained for police work and was needed for Philippine defense. The Army might have found itself "shanghaied" by the diplomatic corps once again had not the Navy come to its aid. Disenchanted with the experience of having to work in close conjunction with its sister service and anxious to return Shanghai to its own exclusive preserve, the Navy generously offered to replace the soldiers with additional marines. The State Department accepted the offer and the 31st returned to the Philippines, never to see China again. In fact, when the Sino-Japanese conflict threatened to engulf Shanghai once more in 1937, the Navy insisted upon waiting for Marine reinforcements from California rather than accept more immediate assistance from Army forces in the Philippines.[7]

The Sources of U.S. Army Small Wars Doctrine

Given the Army's limited engagement in overseas constabulary operations during the 1920s and 1930s, one would not expect it to have devoted much attention to the subject during the interwar era. In fact, the Army's training, doctrine, and educational systems remained firmly oriented toward conventional warfare. And yet during the interwar years, the Army actually increased the amount of attention devoted to matters that lay at the core of the small wars experience, such as military government, overseas expeditions, and irregular warfare.

In part, the added emphasis was the natural consequence of the rising level of professional and educational standards throughout the Army during the early twentieth century. The complexities of modern warfare inculcated a dedication to continuous professional development. While this preparedness ethos was directed primarily at the Army's "core" responsibility of defending the nation in a major conflict, it spilled over into the "peripheral" areas of military science, like military government and guerrilla warfare—subjects that progressive military officers felt compelled to include as a part of a well-rounded professional education.

But the formulation of small wars doctrine was more than a mere academic exercise, for the military recognized that there were practical benefits to be derived from such study. The Army's five-year occupation of the Rhineland reemphasized the importance of military government as an integral part of the military art. Moreover, as Lt. Col. Ward Schrantz noted, "more than once in years gone by, American troops have been called upon to wage war against savage or semi-civilized foes and it is reasonable to suppose that the future may not be entirely devoid of such instances." World War I had shaken the industrialized West's domination of the less-developed world, thereby raising the specter of nationalistic uprisings. In the words of Capt. Charles A. Willoughby,

With the spread of democratic doctrine, half civilized people have promptly taken advantage of the magic formula of self-determination and flaunt it with great effect. Every colonial struggle becomes a struggle for 'freedom'; every unwashed savage becomes a potential hero of a war for independence.... From China to Mexico, the conception of government by the people, with the observance of certain outwardly republican forms, has repeatedly become a cloak for absolute anarchy, hopeless administrative mismanagement, or civil war.[8]

Although the United States was not a major colonial power, it did have significant interests in Asia and Latin America that, together with the interventionist policies espoused by the Roosevelt corollary to the Monroe Doctrine, dictated that the Army should be prepared to undertake occasional constabulary operations abroad, even if the Marine Corps had to carry most of the interventionist load. Nowhere was this truer than in Mexico, where any potential intervention was bound to involve significant numbers of Army troops. Indeed, it was the prospect of having to wage an extensive pacification campaign in Mexico that provided the greatest stimulus for the study of irregular warfare during the interwar period.

The Army drew upon a variety of sources in formulating its irregular warfare and pacification doctrines. Past Army policies and experiences, as recorded in textbooks and manuals, gave it a basis on which to build. Unfortunately, the relatively slight written record, coupled with the loss of constabulary veterans to death or retirement, meant that the Army was not able to tap the full richness of its own tradition. Nevertheless, the past contributed an essential ingredient to the Army's doctrinal efforts of the 1920s and 1930s, and fading memories were supplemented by historical research projects undertaken by officers at military schools.[9]

The Army also studied the experiences of others. During the 1920s and 1930s, several European nations confronted sporadic outbreaks of internal unrest and irregular warfare in their colonies and protectorates. The U.S. Army looked upon these irregular operations with some interest, because it believed that its own experiences in the Indian and

Philippine Wars were inadequate guides for the formulation of tactics and techniques utilizing modern weapons. Consequently, while students at Army schools occasionally studied small war operations of previous eras for wisdom on the conduct of irregular operations, they tended to focus their attention on more recent events. Of special interest were Thomas E. Lawrence's and Lettow von Vorbeck's guerrilla actions during World War I, and the postwar pacification campaigns waged by the French and Spanish in Morocco and by the British in Iraq and India.[10]

Professional military journals provided an excellent source of information about foreign experiences. During the 1920s and 1930s the Command and General Staff School regularly included a section on small wars and special warfare as part of its periodic review of articles published in American and foreign journals. Instructors and students sometimes even translated foreign works on irregular warfare. This material was then incorporated into the Army's small wars curriculum. The Army Air Corps, for example, based much of the content of the small wars instruction given at the Air Corps Tactical School upon the use of aircraft in Morocco and India, as well as the Royal Air Force's experiments with "air control" in the Middle East. Similarly, the Infantry School at Fort Benning, Georgia, studied Anglo-French uses of armored vehicles against tribal irregulars to learn what role modern weapons played in constabulary warfare. Such studies kept the Army abreast of contemporary European thinking.[11]

Given the Army's interest, it is somewhat curious that it did not expend an equal amount of attention on the activities of the U.S. Marine Corps. Part of the reason would seem to have been that the marines were not much further along than the Army in developing small wars doctrinal and curricular materials, at least during the 1920s.[12] There is also some evidence that the Army was not overly impressed with the performance of the marines in Central America. Capt. Matthew B. Ridgway's report on Marine operations in Nicaragua, which he compiled while serving on a commission created to supervise the Nicaraguan elections of 1928, contained some interesting observations but nothing that was startlingly new to the Army, and the report does not appear to have had any impact on the land service. Moreover, the head of the electoral commission, Army Brig. Gen. Frank R. McCoy, was extremely critical of the way the marines were conducting themselves in Nicaragua. A veteran of General Wood's campaigns in Moro Province, McCoy felt that the marines lacked aggressiveness and suffered from an inadequate intelligence service. He also believed that their efforts in the field were handicapped by an insufficient emphasis on civil programs, which he maintained should strive for "the development of communications, . . . the elimination of widespread corruption of the government, the improvement of health conditions and the extension and modernization of schools."[13]

McCoy's criticisms notwithstanding, there was some cross fertilization between the two services. Marine Corps officers drew upon a variety of Army writings in formulating their *Small Wars Manual*. Conversely, although the Army generally ignored Marine operations in detail, it benefited from those experiences to a modest degree by inviting Marine Corps officers to U.S. Army schools, either as students or lecturers. Marine officers in these capacities often presented papers on the corps' small wars experience, some of which, together with articles written by marines in professional journals, were used in formulating small wars instruction at Army service schools. Whether a greater exchange might have significantly altered either services' doctrine is somewhat problematical, as the emerging doctrines were virtually identical—not by virtue of coordination, but rather because the two had similar experiences and had independently derived similar lessons from the same basic sources.[14]

U.S. Army Small Wars Doctrine in the Interwar Period

During the 1920s and 1930s irregular warfare was incorporated into the course work of some of the Army's service schools, including the largest such institution, the Infantry School. Coverage of small wars at Fort Benning was generally confined to one or two conferences and several problems a year, just a fraction of the overall curriculum. Nevertheless, the courses conveyed the fundamental principles governing operations of an unconventional or counterguerrilla nature.

Initially, the basis for irregular warfare instruction in the Army was a brief three-page section on "minor warfare" in Training Regulation (TR) 15–70, *Field Service Regulations—Special Operations*, of 1922. Although similar in scope to earlier writings contained in the *Field Service Regulations* of 1905 and the *Infantry Drill Regulations* of 1911, TR 15–70 reflected a significant foreign influence, with many sections lifted almost verbatim from the British Army's *Field Service Regulations*. Similarly, much of the instructional material employed at the service schools was derived from another British source, Col. Charles E. Callwell's manual *Small Wars*, a classic distillation of European colonial warfare against the peoples of Africa and Asia.[15]

Following Callwell, the Army defined *small* or *minor wars* as

all campaigns other than those when both the opposing sides consist of regular troops. It comprises the expeditions against savages and semi-civilized races by disciplined soldiers; it comprises campaigns undertaken to suppress rebellions and guerrilla warfare in all parts of the world where organized armies are struggling against opponents who will not meet them in the open field. It thus obviously covers operations varying greatly in their scope and in their conditions.... The expression *minor war,* has in reality no particular connection with the scale on which any campaign may be carried out; it is simply used to denote, in default of a better term, operations of regular armies against irregular, or comparatively speaking irregular, forces.[16]

The Army included under this rubric campaigns of conquest or annexation, operations designed to suppress an insurrection or pacify an area, and punitive expeditions. Though Army writers believed that the principles of war were universally applicable to conventional and unconventional operations alike, they conceded that experience had shown small wars to be a distinct genre within the broader art of war. On the other hand, the Army also believed that the variety of small war campaigns made it impossible to draft any detailed instructions for their conduct. Consequently, it adhered to the approach laid down by Mahan a century earlier of explaining the nature of this type of warfare and outlining some of the principles governing its conduct without trying to formulate a completely autonomous small wars doctrine.[17]

Like Mahan before them, military instructors at the Infantry School taught their pupils that, to be successful at countering irregulars, they would have to adopt some of the enemy's tactics and discard aspects of conventional military science that were inappropriate to the situation. At the same time, they would have to capitalize on those features of modern military organization that could successfully be adapted to offset the enemy's advantages. Among the well-tried approaches endorsed by the Army were the development of march and camp procedures to foil ambushes and surprise attacks, the recruitment of friendly natives as scouts and auxiliaries, the establishment of a first-rate intelligence service to gather information on both the physical and political topography of the theater, and the formation of special units for reconnaissance and strike missions.[18]

Noting that undisciplined irregulars often neglected to take proper security precautions, Army texts endorsed the use of ambushes, night marches, and dawn raids to catch the guerrillas off guard. As in the past, the Army considered mobility to be of paramount importance in counterinsurgency operations, and it justified the continuation of horse cavalry in the force structure for that very reason. Use of artillery, on the other hand, was discouraged, in part because the advantages it conferred against a mobile and irregular foe were outweighed by its relative ponderousness. Moreover, artillery fire tended to disperse the enemy before the Army had a chance to come to grips with him. Unlike conventional warfare, the Army recognized that it benefited when its irregular foes were concentrated, for only then could Army regulars bring their superior firepower and training fully to bear. Consequently, unless it was needed to eject irregulars from mountain strongholds or entrenchments, heavy artillery was to be left at home in favor of light, pack-borne guns.[19]

Like its European counterparts, the U.S. Army believed that "in small wars the psychological factor is preeminent" because "all savage people respect power and are quick to detect weakness." Consequently, Army curricular materials echoed the long-established view that campaigns against semi-civilized peoples had to be prosecuted with vigor, both to wear down the guerrillas and to demoralize the population from whom the guerrillas drew their strength. Undertaking operations with insufficient forces, adopting a defensive posture, or otherwise yielding the initiative was deemed fatal, for the smallest guerrilla success would inflame popular passions and indefinitely prolong and complicate the struggle. The best course was to strike hard with a force adequate for the undertaking and to prosecute the war relentlessly to crush resistance before the enemy developed the will and the capability to engage in a prolonged, desultory guerrilla conflict.[20]

While the Army focused much of its attention upon the tactical and operational aspects of small wars, it recognized that combat was only part of the problem. In the words of one Command and General Staff School text, "Any officer can rapidly adapt himself to the [military] details of this type of warfare. What is more difficult is to understand the exact relation between the political and the military action, and the amount of each that should be used as the operation progresses."[21] Army texts urged small war commanders to obtain detailed knowledge of the political and cultural conditions under which they were operating. Aided by a well-organized intelligence service, the commander of a pacification campaign was expected to craft an operational plan that closely coordinated political and military factors for maximum advantage. Noting that "studiously prepared and well executed political plans . . . will often pave the way for military success," the Army urged its officers to presage any military operation with "a slow and methodical political preparation." By removing the causes of unrest, by reconciling the discontented population and inducing the irregular combatants to surrender, and by splitting the opposition into rival factions, "political action" was deemed essential to success.[22]

Nevertheless, Army texts followed the pattern established in the tactical realm by refraining from detailing precisely how "political action" programs were to be conducted. Variations in culture, custom, and circumstance made any fixed set of procedures for "political action" inappropriate. In fact, the Army believed that the delicate combination of political and military action necessary for the successful prosecution of a pacification campaign was only possible at the local level, and for that reason, interwar texts reiterated the Army's traditional insistence on decentralized command in operations of this type. The man on the spot was to be given the greatest possible leeway in tailoring his pacification and counterguerrilla programs to the exigencies of the moment.[23]

Traditionally, civil affairs lay within the domain of military law and government in the Army's doctrinal system.[24] This was no less true of the interwar era. The Army's experience in operating a military government in the Rhineland after World War I proved the catalyst for greater attention to civil affairs questions during the interwar years. Officers involved in the administration of occupied Germany complained that many soldiers were unprepared for their duties. This perception led Secretary of War Baker in late 1919 to direct the Army to publish an official military government manual. The Army balked, in part because it believed that the newly chartered League of Nations might radically alter the parameters of international law that governed the conduct of military occupations. More fundamentally, officers like Maj. Gen. James W. McAndrew, the commandant of the General Staff College, argued that the subject of administering foreign peoples was so varied that any attempt to codify procedures in a manual would be more misleading than helpful. Consequently, twenty years would pass before the Army finally published Field Manual (FM) 27–5, *Basic Field Manual, Military Government*, in 1940.[25]

The Army's procrastination did not mean that it ignored the subject of military government. Central to its approach to civil affairs during the interwar period was Col. Harry A. Smith's textbook *Military Government*, published in 1920. A veteran of the Philippine War, the occupation of Vera Cruz, the Mexican border crisis, and the occupation of Germany, Colonel Smith was well qualified to comment upon the subject of civil affairs. He took a historical approach, examining various applications of military government by the U.S. Army, as well as several military governments established by European powers. From these he derived principles that he hoped would guide officers charged with civil affairs responsibilities in the future. This method, traditional in the field of law where precedent is given great weight, ensured a high degree of continuity in the Army's approach to the administration of civil affairs. Consequently, the basic principles imparted by Smith and other experts of the interwar years (like Col. Irwin L. Hunt, Maj. Cassius Dowell, and Capt. Elbridge Colby) were virtually unchanged from those of Scott and Lieber nearly a century before.[26]

Colonel Smith and the rest of the Army's legal establishment based their analysis upon the prescription in GO 100 that occupiers "be strictly guided by the principles of justice, honor, and humanity." Morality and self-interest alike dictated this course, for as the 1940 field manual on military government explained,

A military occupation marked by harshness, injustice, or oppression leaves lasting resentment against the occupying power in the hearts of the people of the occupied territory and sows the seeds of future war by them against the occupying power when circumstances shall make that possible; whereas just, considerate, and mild treatment of the governed by the occupying army will convert enemies into friends.[27]

Following this line of argument, the Army elevated into formal doctrine those enlightened yet self-interested practices which it had always attempted to follow in the administration of occupied territory. Among these were the rapid restoration of normal social and economic life, the protection of personal and property rights, the inculcation among the troops of respect for social and religious customs, the perpetuation of indigenous law and administrative forms, and the retention of native officials in their posts. Of course, military necessity took precedence over all of these matters, but these precepts remained the ideals toward which an occupation government should aspire.[28]

Army doctrine held that a greater degree of social engineering was permissible during an intervention designed to correct the internal problems of a wayward state than might normally be tolerated during a more conventional occupation. Nevertheless, even under these conditions, Colonel Smith emphasized that nothing should be done that would significantly alter the subject society until close and careful examination had determined that the proposed measure was of such obvious benefit to the recipient as to override the prime directive of minimal interference. Smith warned his students of the perils of the ethnocentric tendency to make everything run as it did in the United States. "There should be no attempt to Anglo-Saxonize what cannot be Anglo-Saxonized," he wrote. "Do not try to make over the people, to change their habits or customs, nor to bend them to our way of thinking." This, of course, was easier said than done, for the process of changing or even assisting a culture, without alienating it, had always been the central dilemma of pacification and nation-building endeavors. Other than being aware of the problem, Smith, who was himself strongly paternalistic, had no pat solution to this difficult and perhaps insoluble aspect of overseas constabulary duty.[29]

Like his counterparts in the realm of irregular warfare, Smith recognized that psychological factors played a central part in the outcome of any military government operation. He therefore counseled that military governors make extensive efforts to acquaint themselves with the nature of their wards, not only to win their support, but to help the Army win acceptance of its actions from the American public at home and the international community abroad. Smith was well aware how the American public tended to react to stories of repressive measures against civilian populations, whether imposed by the Army in the West and the Philippines or, more recently, by the marines in the Caribbean. As another commentator noted, "what with political investigations, sobsters, and foreign ranters against our so-called imperialistic tendencies, [the Army officer] may find himself under surprising and peculiar cross fire."[30]

Based on historical experience, the interwar Army defined and disseminated guidelines regarding the mechanics of military government—guidance that eventually coalesced into doctrine with the publication of FM 27–5. Since the Spanish-American War, commanders charged with occupation responsibilities had established on an ad hoc basis special staff elements under such designations as the "Military Secretary for Civil Affairs," the "Office of Civil Affairs," or the "Officer in Charge of Civil Affairs," to help them perform these duties. Beginning in the 1920s, the Army directed that all war plans include a chapter devoted to military government and encouraged commanders to start planning for civil affairs early in a campaign. FM 27–5 went further, mandating that theater commanders establish civil affairs sections within their headquarters staffs whenever there was a prospect of occupation duty. Parallel offices were to be established at lower echelons of command. Whenever possible, officers (especially reserve officers) with prior military government experience or other civil expertise were to be assigned to civil affairs positions. These specialists were to bear the primary burden for planning and executing the Army's civil responsibilities within each echelon of command down to the tactical level. By creating staff positions dedicated to discharging such functions, the Army hoped to avoid two problems that had hampered past American military governments. First, the officers were to relieve overburdened tactical commanders of much (though not all) of the civil affairs burden. Second, by assigning military government staffs to geographical rather than tactical commands, the Army hoped to promote the continuity necessary for effective administration despite the constant relocation of tactical units. For the same reason, rotation of civil affairs personnel was to be kept to a minimum to maximize their expertise in a particular field or geographical area.[31]

To avoid the kind of civil-military disputes that had arisen during past pacification operations, Army officers attempted to make unity of command a sacrosanct tenet of military government doctrine. Civil and military functions were to be united in the commanding general, and while knowledgeable civilians might be consulted in the formulation of civil affairs plans, the execution of those plans was to remain exclusively in the hands of military personnel. Such a procedure would ensure close coordination of military and political action, preclude civil-military tensions, and ensure a "clean" government devoid of the type of unscrupulous civilian "carpetbaggers" who customarily sought to exploit occupation and pacification regimes for personal gain. Experience in the Caribbean and Siberia had demonstrated the necessity of close coordination of civil-military policy, however, and for that reason, some officers believed that the commander's staff should contain a representative from the State Department. But there was no doubt, at least insofar as the Army was concerned, that the State Department representative would be there purely to advise and coordinate, not dictate, policy.[32]

Once the machinery was in place, the Army planned to administer civil affairs according to the pattern established during the Progressive era. This was especially true in cases where the military government was established for the purpose of pacifying a disaffected area or intervening in the internal affairs of a "benighted" nation. Road-building and infrastructure programs would provide immediate "workfare" relief to the destitute, while laying the groundwork for future economic development. Sanitation and health care would be improved, prisons reformed, and antiquated governmental systems overhauled "in such manner as to constitute an object lesson in clean, economical and efficient government." A nonpoliticized civil service and a constabulary skilled in counterinsurgency work would be created to assist the occupation regime and carry its reforms forward once the Army had left. Finally, a revitalized system of primary and vocational education would be established because officers remained wedded to the notion that education was the ultimate fount of progress.[33]

Several studies undertaken at the Army War College during the 1930s concerning the internal stability of nations reinforced the traditional prescription for nation building. Based on analyses of upheavals like the French (1789), Russian (1917), and German (1918) Revolutions, War College committees charged with studying counterrevolutionary techniques advocated the concentration of power in the executive to smooth the coordination and execution of emergency measures, just as the Army favored centralizing all civil and military functions in the commanding general during a military government. Moreover, the War College concluded that to be successful a counterrevolutionary campaign had to be waged on a number of fronts simultaneously—educational, social, economic, political, and military. Socioeconomic reforms were considered particularly potent weapons if enacted in time, but often, the War College noted, governments implemented them too late. Ultimately, the Army recognized that political repression and military action, unsupported by at least a modicum of positive measures, were insufficient to stem the tide of revolution.[34]

Moderate policies and enlightened reforms were only half of the interwar Army's prescription for the suppression of insurrection and the administration of alien peoples. Instruction during the interwar years perpetuated the notion that the stick was still an important ingredient in the pacification of disaffected areas. Moreover, the Army continued to adhere to its traditional view that guerrilla warfare often violated the laws of war and was therefore punishable by extraordinary means. Army legal theoretician Elbridge Colby, for example, argued that warfare against guerrillas and semi-civilized peoples was qualitatively different from civilized warfare because of the difficulty of distinguishing combatant from noncombatant; consequently, stringent methods were entirely justified from both a practical and a legal viewpoint. Following Bell's dictum that "a short and severe war creates in the aggregate less loss and suffering than benevolent war indefinitely prolonged," Colby maintained that "excessive humanitarian ideas should not prevent harshness against those who use harsh methods, for in being overkind to one's enemies, a commander is simply being unkind to his own people."[35]

Based on such reasoning, the interwar Army continued to sanction many of the harsh methods traditionally associated with the repression of civilian and irregular resistance. Although the Army frowned upon executions and the employment of the "third degree," FM 27–10, *Rules of Land Warfare*, published in 1940, permitted methods such as communal retaliation, the confiscation or destruction of property, the taking of hostages, the levying of fines, the employment of military courts to bring guerrillas and their civilian allies to justice, the issuance of identity cards, and the imposition of restrictions on speech, press, assembly, and movement. Curricular materials, like those used at the Infantry School, also endorsed concentration as an effective population control and counterguerrilla measure, citing Bell's

Batangas campaign as the model counterinsurgency operation. Of course, even Colby admitted that humanity and morality (not to mention questions of internal discipline and political sensitivity) mandated restraint upon the Army's conduct, and the Infantry School warned its pupils that concentration required extensive planning so as to minimize human suffering. Nevertheless, despite the fact that stringent measures such as concentration or the destruction of the enemy's food supply "are perhaps not to our taste," the Army refused to proscribe such methods, insisting that "each case must be judged on its merits and that course chosen which promises the best results." The carrot and the stick remained inextricably intertwined in a somewhat uneasy, yet symbiotic, relationship.[36]

Army writers often turned to contemporary examples to illustrate how modern armies integrated political and military action in the prosecution of pacification campaigns. Of all the small war operations of the interwar years, those conducted by France and Spain against the Berber tribesmen of the Moroccan Rif attracted the most interest in U.S. military circles. Army officers saw in the Moroccan conflict, which involved a combination of regular and irregular warfare waged in an arid and mountainous region, conditions similar to those they believed the United States would face should it ever attempt to pacify Mexico. Consequently, the United States sent observers to Morocco on several occasions, while professional military journals covered the course of the campaign with some interest.[37]

U.S. military texts noted with approval how France tailored its conventional military forces to meet the unique circumstances of irregular warfare in Morocco. The French blended new weapons such as aircraft and tanks with more traditional techniques, including the extensive use of native auxiliaries, a general lightening of an otherwise heavy logistical system, the establishment of an efficient intelligence service, and a dedication to vigorous offensive action. In fact, French use of encirclement and cordon and sweep operations to clear areas of Rif rebels was probably the inspiration for the inclusion of similar tactics in the counterguerrilla sections of the U.S. *Field Service Regulations* of 1939 and 1941.[38]

American authors also noted with approval how Marshal Hubert Lyautey, France's proconsul in Morocco during the first quarter of the twentieth century and one of that nation's ablest counterinsurgency experts, skillfully interwove political programs with punitive measures, such as the destruction of villages, fields, and flocks, to produce a highly effective pacification campaign. Under Lyautey the French followed a course similar to that employed by the U.S. Army in Moro Province, building roads and markets and instituting improved forms of governmental administration, while carefully respecting certain fundamental social and religious customs indigenous to the region. Political and intelligence sections, staffed by experts in Moroccan culture, helped integrate the political and military aspects of the pacification effort into a cohesive whole. Indeed, American officers held France's use of "progressive military operations, closely seconded by liberal, economic policies" to be the very model of a modern pacification campaign.[39]

Theory Into Practice—Small War Exercises and Plans

In an era of relative inactivity, the only way in which officers could put doctrinal teachings into practice was through training problems and war plans. For the most part these exercises put participants into situations that Army leaders believed they might someday have to face, given foreseeable circumstances and the nature of U.S. policy. For example, one small wars problem used at the Infantry School during the 1920s and 1930s asked students how they would conduct a small, cross-border punitive expedition against bandits using a column of cavalry supplemented by armored cars, pack trains, and pack artillery. Another involved the suppression of an Indian revolt in the American Southwest using a similar force augmented by a detachment of Indian Scouts. Still other Infantry School problems, based on British experience policing the northwest frontier of India, tested officers' intellectual skills in convoy and march security operations against irregulars in an arid and mountainous environment, while a problem taken from Marine operations in Nicaragua examined similar questions under jungle conditions. Meanwhile, troops assigned to the Panama Canal Zone regularly trained in guerrilla and counterguerrilla tactics to be employed in the region's jungles. Included in these exercises were experiments in the employment of tanks in counterguerrilla operations—experiments that demonstrated the utility of armor both offensively and defensively in a tropical environment.[40]

While branch and garrison schools tested the tactical skills of their students, higher-level institutions, like the Command and General Staff School and the Army War College, focused on larger questions, such as the organization and transportation of the kind of small expeditionary force typically used in limited interventions and peacetime contingency operations. These exercises not only helped prepare students for the logistical aspects of expeditionary work, but introduced them to the notion that expeditionary forces had to be tailored to meet the circumstances under which they were to operate. In most cases, this amounted to eliminating heavy equipment and other impediments normally employed in conventional operations and using unconventional methods of transportation. Sometimes these studies and exercises also considered the civil and military policy questions likely to be encountered in such operations. Thus Leavenworth's offering on the subject of small expeditionary forces in 1921–1922 included a problem in "the organization of military government and the suppression of guerrilla warfare." Ten years later, Leavenworth students were working on similar problems, including one that postulated an American intervention in Cuba "to suppress the revolution, pacify the country and reestablish the constitutional government." Another problem, an intervention in a hypothetical country that looked suspiciously like Mexico, required students to organize a military government that would implement a progressive nation-building program.[41]

Officers transferred the lessons they had learned from classroom instruction and exercises into war plans. As was the case prior to World War I, most of the Army's interwar planning involved peacetime contingencies for the protection of U.S. interests abroad. As a rule, the studies were general in nature, providing little more than a foundation upon which more detailed plans could be based, should the necessity arise. Nevertheless, they offer concrete evidence of how the Army put classroom theory into practice.

War Plan Brown, for example, outlined how the Army would approach a counterinsurgency situation in the Philippines. It called for the use of both propaganda and genuine reform to retain the loyalty of the population at large and the native troops in particular. Propaganda was also to play a key role at home, as Plan Brown established a special office which, in cooperation with various patriotic societies, would conduct an "educational campaign for the purpose of crystallizing and holding public sentiment favorable to the policies of the government in relation to the suppression of the insurrection."[42]

In line with existing doctrine, Plan Brown envisioned a vigorous campaign in which native auxiliaries, infantry, and as many mounted troops as possible would relentlessly hunt down the insurgents. It also echoed doctrine in warning that with less civilized peoples like the Filipinos, "an act of generosity or plain justice is oftentimes regarded as a sign of weakness. They feign friendship but have little loyalty." An elaborate intelligence and counterespionage service was the proposed remedy to this situation. Finally, War Plan Brown required that troops bound for the Philippines be given an intensive course in "guerrilla warfare, bush and jungle fighting, sniping, scouting and patrolling, and leadership of small units." The plan placed special emphasis on fostering the type of individual initiative and self-reliance that was "so necessary in the type of warfare encountered in the Philippines."[43]

Although the Army prepared for contingencies in Asia, it focused most of its small war planning on Mexico and Central and South America, where the Monroe Doctrine and America's history of interventionist actions, at least up to the inauguration of the "Good Neighbor" policy in the mid-1930s, dictated that the Army be prepared to conduct similar operations in the future. Essentially, the Army envisioned three types of operations south of the border. The first consisted of a Vera Cruz–type landing and the seizure of a key port for the purpose of coercing the nation in question. Army planners were not overly confident, however, that such arm-twisting would have the desired effect, given the alleged mercurial nature of Latin society. Consequently, the Vera Cruz–style plan was reserved for interventions in Latin American countries where America's interests were unlikely to warrant resorting to a full-scale war and occupation.[44]

The second type of intervention was the "support" operation, in which the United States would launch a preemptive strike into a Caribbean Basin state for the purpose of thwarting a potential coup by pro-Axis "fifth columnists." The support plans anticipated that the host government would welcome the Army's arrival and that there would be little or no fighting as U.S. airborne and seaborne forces quickly secured airfields, ports, and critical government facilities. In accordance with the Army's small war teachings, the support plans recognized that commanders would have to be fully briefed on the historical, cultural, and political conditions of the nation in question and that "successful command in the area will therefore require not only military skill but also a high degree of political sagacity so that the commanders will be able to combine effectively diplomatic measures with the amount of force necessary." In fact, the Army deemed coordination of political and military affairs to be paramount and instructed intervention commanders to consult closely with foreign leaders and local American diplomatic representatives. The plans made equally clear, however, that the commander was not to be subordinated to the State Department, reiterating the Army's traditional insistence on autonomy and control during politico-military operations.[45]

The third and most traditional of the Army's small war plans involved the employment of military forces to enforce the Roosevelt corollary of the Monroe Doctrine. Based on prior Army and Marine experiences, the Army crafted a series of plans for the occupation, pacification, and administration of a number of Caribbean and Central American republics during the interwar period. Most of these plans assumed that these interventions would follow the pattern established in the past—that is, that the United States would effectively displace an existing foreign government for the purpose of restoring order and introducing political and administrative reforms. As in the Philippine plan, pacification entailed blending moderate policies and carefully considered reforms with an aggressive propaganda campaign and bold military action. While civil affairs personnel established a benign and paternal regime, U.S. military units would crush whatever guerrilla resistance materialized to the intervention by "taking to the bush in small patrols, ambushing the native troops in turn, learning how to live off the country, while holding all settlements and communications in sufficient force to make attack unprofitable."[46]

As was the case prior to World War I, the Army's most extensive intervention plan dealt with Mexico. Operationally, "Strategical Plan Green for the Occupation and Pacification of Mexico" called for the employment of massive numbers of American troops to overawe the population and secure the countryside from guerrillas and bandits. Infantry and especially cavalry, backed by pack trains and light trucks, were to bear the primary burdens of the counterguerrilla campaign, while heavy artillery, large vehicles, and other impediments were to be left behind. Forces earmarked for Mexican operations were to receive special training in security, as well as urban and irregular warfare. They would then sally forth to wage a relentless counterguerrilla campaign in the tradition of Crook, Bell, and Pershing, breaking down into small, mobile detachments for the conduct of night marches, ambushes, raids, and sweeps.[47]

War planners cautioned that Mexican irregulars would employ the "Amigo system," hiding their weapons and assuming the guise of peaceful inhabitants whenever it suited their purposes, just as Filipino insurgents had done at the turn of the century. To counter mufti-clad irregulars and their civilian allies, Plan Green called for the establishment of military tribunals, an elaborate intelligence system, and a 30,000-man native constabulary, whose familiarity with local terrain, customs, and language would greatly facilitate the pacification campaign. Officered by Americans experienced in constabulary work and trained according to the *Manual for the Philippine Constabulary*, the constabulary would not only play a central role in the pacification campaign, but would become the bulwark of the new government once sovereignty was restored. Consequently, its personnel were to be carefully picked and inculcated with a loyalty to the Mexican constitution rather than to any one person or political party.[48]

Following doctrine, Plan Green complemented the efforts of the troops in the field with a vigorous political campaign managed by a cadre of uniformed civil affairs experts. Proclamations and propaganda materials would be prepared, pledging minimal interference in Mexican customs and offering generous terms to those who laid down their arms. Civic action measures traditionally associated with U.S. pacification campaigns, such as cleaning the streets, improving government services, and feeding the destitute, would back these words with deeds. The plan further directed commanders to be "as mild and humane as the military necessities of the situation permit, in order not to prejudice the accomplishment of the primary object of the intervention," and expected "exemplary personal conduct . . . [by] all of the American forces." This combination of vigorous military action with "firm but just treatment" was, the planners hoped, "likely to have a great psychological effect, making the average Mexican realize quickly the hopelessness of resistance, and the advantages accruing from submission, and thus increasing the probability of a rapid and complete pacification."[49]

Although moderation was the predominant theme, a Plan Green document also counseled that "if Mexicans are treated with too much consideration, they think the cause for the good treatment is that they are feared and, once they think they are feared, they take every advantage. It is probably better to be firm and a little unjust than to be overindulgent." Proclamations drawn up in preparation for a possible intervention thus warned the Mexican populace that "acts of hostility or guerrilla warfare against us will lead to sharp reprisals, and we cannot be blamed for your consequent suffering." While the Army hoped that the intervention would be "as free from severity as possible," it continued to recognize the age-old truth that moderation alone was often insufficient to win a pacification campaign.[50]

Army Doctrine on the Eve of World War II

War Plan Green and similar exercises demonstrated that the U.S. Army had institutionalized many of the lessons learned from a century of constabulary service. By the eve of America's entry into World War II, it had developed doctrinal materials for the conduct of small war and civil affairs operations that synthesized European and American experience into a traditional carrot-and-stick doctrine—a doctrine that attempted to balance aggressive military action with nonmilitary programs designed to appease the civilian population and, if possible, to address some of its needs.[51] True, the study of small wars and civil affairs made up only a small part of the Army's overall training and doctrinal program, yet the material was there, ready to be tapped should the Army be called upon to perform such missions. If there were shortcomings in this doctrine, they stemmed from two sources. First, the doctrine was long on principles and concepts and short on details. Second, the doctrine tended to be scattered among a number of subject areas—small wars, military government, and expeditionary forces—rather than integrated into a single, cohesive body such as the marines achieved with the publication of their *Small Wars Manual*. Nevertheless, while not as sophisticated in terms of organization and packaging, in content the Army's small wars doctrine equaled that produced by the marines. Moreover, some of the doctrine's vagueness was by design, as the Army recognized that each pacification situation was unique and required its own carefully tailored solution. By explaining the basic features of small wars and military governments, Army doctrinal materials in the form of lectures, texts, and manuals preserved the core elements of its traditional approach to irregular warfare and provided the interwar officer corps with the tools to construct situation-specific programs should it be called to perform pacification duties.[52]

There were, however, two major storm clouds on the horizon that threatened to have an impact on the Army's approach to small wars. The first was America's entry into World War II. While the war would ultimately give the Army the opportunity both to test its military government doctrine and to experiment with partisan and special operations, the onset of the largest conventional military conflagration the world had ever known threatened to swamp the tiny boat of small wars doctrine and send it to oblivion.

The second challenge stemmed from the rise of communism. Guerrilla warfare had never figured prominently in the thinking of Marx, Engels, Lenin, or Trotsky. In fact, the one insurrectionary manual issued by the Soviet state during the interwar period contained only a single chapter on guerrilla warfare, written not by a Russian, but by an obscure Vietnamese Communist, Ho Chi Minh. Yet a new model of Communist warfare was being developed in Asia during the interwar period, a model that blended Communist principles of party organization and mass action with rising third-world nationalism and techniques of guerrilla warfare to produce what threatened to be a more virulent strain of revolutionary war. In 1941 a Marine officer warned his Army colleagues in an article carried by the *Cavalry Journal* that the Chinese Communist leader Mao Tse-tung was introducing a new sophistication to the art of revolutionary guerrilla warfare. Only time would tell whether the doctrines used to defeat tribal irregulars and Filipino guerrillas would work against this more sophisticated species of insurgency.[53]

Notes

[1] Although the two services had signed an agreement on Army-Navy responsibilities for coastal defense in 1920, the 1927 document was the first joint statement on the broader roles and missions of the U.S. armed forces. Quotes from Joint Board, *Joint Action of the Army and the Navy* (Washington, D.C.: Government Printing Office, 1927), pp. 2–3. Millett, *Semper Fidelis*, pp. 150, 174, 261; Challener, *Admirals, Generals, and American Foreign Policy*, p. 304.

[2] In addition to numerous articles in the *Marine Corps Gazette* during the 1920s and 1930s, see the following on the development of Marine Corps doctrine: U.S. Marine Corps, *Small Wars Manual* (Washington, D.C.: Government Printing Office, 1940); Ronald Schaffer, "The 1940 Small Wars Manual and the 'Lessons of History,'" *Military Affairs* 36 (April 1972): 46–51.

[3] McCain, *United States and Panama*, pp. 87–89; Liss, *The Canal*, p. 34; Memo, Maj Gen William Lassiter for Adj Gen, 4 Nov 25, sub: Intervention in Panama, Republic of Panama; Rpt, Maj Gen Charles Martin to CG, Panama Canal Department, 24 Oct 25, sub: Report of the Occupation of the City of Panama by the Panama Canal Division, October 12 to October 23, 1925. Both in 370.61, Panama Canal Department, RG 395, NARA.

[4] Jesse Cope, "American Troops in China—Their Mission," *Infantry Journal* 38 (1931): 178; Louis Morton, "Army and Marines on the China Station: A Study in Military and Political Rivalry," *Pacific Historical Review* 29 (February 1960): 52–53.

[5] Dennis Noble, *The Eagle and the Dragon: The United States Military in China, 1901–37* (New York: Greenwood Press, 1990), pp. 92, 103, 194–95; Charles Finney, *Old China Hands* (Garden City, N.Y.: Doubleday, 1961), p. 103.

[6] Morton, "Army and Marines on the China Station," pp. 68, 71.

[7] William Nolan, "America's Participation in the Military Defense of Shanghai, 1931–41" (Ph.D. diss., St. Louis University, 1978), pp. 88–90, 94, 104; W. H. Langdon, The Shanghai Operation, February–July 1932 [historical tactical study, Infantry School, Regular Course, 1936–37], pp. 9, 14; Howard Cahill, "The 31st Infantry in Shanghai," *Infantry Journal* 39 (1932): 165–75; Joseph Greene, The Occupation of the Shanghai Foreign Defenses, With Particular Reference to the 31st U.S. Infantry Expedition From Manila, January–July 1932 [Infantry School, Regular Course, 1936–37], p. 33.

[8] Ward Schrantz, "A Minor Operation in Morocco," *Infantry Journal* 33 (August 1928): 148; Charles A. Willoughby, "The French in Morocco," *Infantry Journal* 28 (January 1926): 7.

[9] For examples of research projects that endeavored to extract lessons from previous small war operations, see Benjamin Pope, "The Causes of the Boxer Uprising and the Battle of Tientsin," in *Monographs of the World War* (Fort Benning, Ga.: Infantry School, 1923), pp. 660–65; Langdon, Shanghai Operation; Greene, Occupation of Shanghai; C. T. Alden, The Engagement at Saahipa's Cota #1 on the Island of Jolo, P.I., in 1913, Advanced Course, 4th Section, Committee H, Infantry School, 1928–29; Fred Bugbee, "The AEF in Siberia," in *Monographs of the World War*; A Study of the Supply of the 31st Infantry, AEF, n.d., Longuevan Papers; Owen Rhoads, A Study of the Operations and Supply of the American Forces in the Suchan Mine Area, Siberia,

THE INTERWAR YEARS, 1920–1941

September 1918–January 1920, Individual Research Study (IRS) 90, CGS, 1932, Combined Arms Research Library (CARL), Fort Leavenworth, Kans.; I. C. Nicholas, A Critical Analysis of the AEF, Siberia, Including Relations With Other Allies, IRS 80, CGS, 1932, CARL.

[10] Maj Wallace, A Study of the Defeat of General Braddock on 9 July 1755, IRS 93, CGS, 1931; Capt Arthur, USMC, A Study of the War in German East Africa, 1914–18, IRS 33, CGS, 1930; G. G. Parks, A Critical Analysis of the Operations in German East Africa, 1914–18, IRS 94, CGS, 1934; G. L. McEntee, A Critical Analysis of the Campaign in the Soudan From a Supply Point of View, Army War College (AWC), G–4 Committee 1, 1922–23, AWC 253-1, MHI; George King, Outline of the Boer War in South Africa, 1899–1901, IRS 2, CGS, 1930; Hoffman Nickerson, "Irregular Warfare: The Role of Irregular Troops in Modern Conflict," *Army Ordnance* 22 (November–December 1941): 381–85; A. Stuart Daley, "Twentieth-Century Irregulars," *Infantry Journal* 48 (June 1941): 37–42; H. A. DeWeerd, "Was Lawrence a Great Soldier?" *Infantry Journal* 44 (May–June 1937): 197–204; Strategy of the South African and Russo-Japanese Wars, Rpt of Committee 6, AWC, 1926–27, AWC 338-6, MHI. That the study of old campaigns could still prove valuable was attested to by Maj. (future Lt. Gen.) Lucian K. Truscott, Jr., who wrote in 1937 that France's campaign against irregulars in Algeria during the 1830s and 1840s was "worthy of study because it illustrates and emphasizes many of the principles that are applicable to this special operation even in the modern age." L. K. Truscott, Jr., "Revue de Cavalerie," *Command and General Staff School Review of Military Literature* 17 (September 1937): 172.

[11] "British Operations Against Tribesmen on the Northwest Frontier of India," in *Infantry School Academic Department Instructional Matter*, 1934–35, 2d sec., vol. 5; "Tanks in Morocco," *Infantry Journal* 28 (May 1926): 560–61; Walter Muller, Historical Tactical Study. Light Tanks in Desert Operations—Morocco [student paper, Infantry School, Tank Course, 1936–37], p. 9; Richard Steinbach, Employment of Tanks and Armored Cars in India [student paper, Infantry School, Tank Course, 1938–39]; William Due, Plan and Conduct of Attack, A Special Operation—Mountain Warfare. Action of 1st Abbottabad Infantry Brigade (British) Near Damdil, India, 29th of March, 1937 [student paper, Infantry School, Regular Course, 1938–39]; Lecture, "Air Force in Minor Wars," in Air Force Course, 1929–30, Army Air Corps Tactical School, May 30, pp. 2, 14; Infantry School, *Infantry in Special Operations*, Special Text 13, Army Extension Courses (Fort Benning, Ga.: Infantry School, 1937); Command and General Staff School, *Mountain Warfare* (Fort Leavenworth, Kans.: Command and General Staff School Press, 1935); "Desert Warfare," *Infantry School Mailing List* 13 (January 1937): 65–99. For examples of foreign translations done at the Command and General Staff School, see W. O. Butler and H. M. Melasky, Some Lessons in Aviation Matters From the Riff Campaign (1925–26), IRS 14, CGS, 1935; Arthur Ehrhardt, *Guerrilla Warfare: Lessons of the Past and Possibilities of the Future* (Fort Leavenworth, Kans.: Command and General Staff School, 1936).

[12] The Marine Corps introduced small wars training into the curriculum of its Field Officers School at Quantico, Virginia, in 1926, four years after the Infantry School. Eventually, however, the marines surpassed the Army, culminating in the publication of the corps' *Small Wars Manual* in 1940.

[13] McCoy was instrumental in increasing the size and activity of the Marine contingent and in reorienting the Nicaraguan military away from being a conventional force and into a constabulary organization more appropriate for the task at hand. He also

added a public relations adviser to his personal staff to help defuse criticism of the war at home. Yet he was unable to get the home government to approve a more comprehensive civic action campaign, and in the end the United States withdrew the marines in 1933 with the rebel movement, led by a defiant Augusto Sandino, still intact. Matthew B. Ridgway, Notes on Military Operations of United States Naval Forces in Nicaragua, July 1927–October 1928, 30 Oct 28, box 2, Matthew B. Ridgway Papers, MHI; Msg, Brig Gen McCoy to Secy of State, 111, 5 Mar 28, pp. 4–6, 817.00/5450, Records of the State Department, RG 59, NARA. Quote from A. J. Bacevich, *Diplomat in Khaki: Major General Frank Ross McCoy and American Foreign Policy* (Manhattan: University of Kansas Press, 1989), pp. 129, 131.

[14] For evidence that the founders of Marine doctrine consulted Army sources, see Schaffer, "The 1940 Small Wars Manual," p. 46, and the bibliography of Harold Utley, Tactics and Techniques of Small Wars, Harold H. Utley Papers, USMC Historical Center, Washington, D.C. Many of the basic technical elements contained in the Marine Corps *Small Wars Manual*, such as small-unit infantry tactics, the use of pack transportation, etc., were essentially based on U.S. Army doctrines in those areas, leavened by the Marine Corps' own experience. For examples of papers given by marines attending Army schools, as well as articles written by marines that appeared in Army periodicals, see C. S. Baker, Supply and Evacuation in Minor Warfare, IRS 4, CGS, 1932; M. L. Curry, "Jungle Warfare Weapons," *Chemical Warfare* 20 (October 1934): 1444–48; AWC Rpt, Henry C. Davis, Military Government for a Latin-American Country in the Light of Our Santo Domingo Experience, 22 Jan 24, AWC 264–65, MHI; William Evans, Task Force and the Use of Aviation in Minor Wars, IRS 41, CGS, 1934; Roger Peard, "The Tactics of Bush Warfare," *Infantry Journal* 38 (1931): 409 (the same article also appeared in the *Cavalry Journal Mailing List* [15 March 1932]); G. C. Reid, Principles Deducible From Military Government of Haiti and Santo Domingo, Rpt of Committee 6, Sub-Committee 2, pt. 2, G–1 Course 16, AWC, 1924–25, AWC 287–6, MHI; Ross Rowell, Aircraft in Bush Warfare [student paper, Army Air Corps Tactical School, 1931]; H. Schmidt, Operations of the Intelligence Section of the 2d Brigade in Nicaragua, 1928–29, IRS 95, CGS, 1932; John Wood, Operations of the 9th Company, Guardia Nacional de Nicaragua, 11–17 April 1931 [student paper, Infantry School, Advanced Course, 1932–33]; Maurice Holmes, "With Horse Marines in Nicaragua," *Cavalry Journal* 39 (1930): 209–33. For examples of how Marine writings sometimes affected Army small wars instruction, see Infantry School, *Infantry in Special Operations*, p. 27; Lecture, "Air Force in Minor Wars," in Air Force Course, 1929–30, Army Air Corps Tactical School, May 30, p. 17; "A Skirmish in Nicaragua," *Infantry School Mailing List* 11 (January 1936): 231–49; General Service Schools, *Instructors' Summary of Military Articles for March 1922*, 10 April 1922, pp. 3–4. For examples of Army examinations of Marine operations, see Memos, Maj A. G. Campbell for Asst Commandant, AWC, 1 Apr 28, sub: U.S. Intervention in Haiti, and Col F. L. Bradman for Commandant, AWC, 31 Mar 28, sub: U.S. Intervention in Santo Domingo, both in AWC Course 1927–28, AWC 349–4, MHI.

[15] Compare the British *Field Service Regulations. I. Operations* (London: His Majesty's Stationary Office, 1909), pp. 196–97, with War Department, Training Regulation (TR) 15–70, *Field Service Regulations—Special Operations*, c. 1922, pp. 305–07, pars. 23b, 23c, 24b.

[16] Lecture, "Air Force in Minor Wars," in Air Force course, 1929–30, Army Air Corps Tactical School, May 30, p. 1.

THE INTERWAR YEARS, 1920–1941

[17] Infantry School, *Infantry in Special Operations*, pp. 24–25; Charles Callwell, *Small Wars: Their Principles and Practice* (London: Harrison & Sons, 1906), pp. 21, 25–27; Lecture, "Small Wars and Punitive Expeditions," in *Instructional Material, Infantry School*, 1925–26, vol. 2, *Tactics*; CGS, *Mountain Warfare*, p. 23; Parks, A Critical Analysis of the Operations in German East Africa, p. 27; War Department, FM 100–5, *Tentative Field Service Regulations, Operations*, Oct 39 (hereafter cited as FM 100–5, Oct 39), pp. 228–31; War Department, FM 100–5, *Field Service Regulations, Operations*, 22 May 41 (hereafter cited as FM 100–5, 22 May 41), pp. 238–40.

[18] TR 15–70, *Field Service Regulations—Special Operations*, c. 1922, p. 306; Lecture, "Minor Warfare," in *Instructional Material, Infantry School*, 1922–23, 1st sec., vol. 3; Lecture, "Minor Warfare," in *Instructional Material, Infantry School*, 1923–24, vol. 1, *Special Operations*; Lecture, "Small Wars and Punitive Expeditions," in *Instructional Material, Infantry School*, 1925–26, vol. 2, *Tactics*; Lecture, "Small Wars," in *Instructional Material, Infantry School*, 1930–31, vol. 3; CGS, *Mountain Warfare*, pp. 38–39.

[19] Lecture, "The Role of Cavalry," in *Instructional Material, Infantry School*, 1921–22, p. 5; Hamilton Hawkins, "The Role of Cavalry," *Cavalry Journal* 29 (1920): 264; Lecture, "Small Wars," in *Instructional Material, Infantry School*, 1930–31, vol. 3.

[20] Lecture, "Small Wars and Punitive Expeditions," in *Instructional Material, Infantry School*, 1925–26, vol. 2, *Tactics*. Quotes from Lecture, "Small Wars," in *Instructional Material, Infantry School*, 1930–31, vol. 3; CGS, *Mountain Warfare*, p. 24.

[21] CGS, *Mountain Warfare*, p. 40.

[22] Quotes from Infantry School, *Infantry in Special Operations*, p. 59. CGS, *Mountain Warfare*, p. 40.

[23] CGS, *Mountain Warfare*, p. 25; Infantry School, *Infantry in Special Operations*, p. 26.

[24] Although the Army drew a distinction between the terms *military government* and *civil affairs* during World War II, prior to that conflict military writers used the terms interchangeably to refer to the conduct of civil functions in areas under Army jurisdiction, regardless of the circumstances.

[25] Harry Coles, *Civil Affairs: Soldiers Become Governors* (Washington, D.C.: U.S. Army Center of Military History, Government Printing Office, 1964), p. 6; Memo, Maj Gen W. G. Haan, Dir, WPD, for Adj Gen, 4 Nov 19, sub: Manual of Military Government, WCD, 8334–5, RG 165, NARA.

[26] Harry Smith, *Military Government* (Fort Leavenworth, Kans.: Command and General Staff School, 1920); Harry Smith, "Four Interventions in Mexico. A Study in Military Government," *Infantry Journal* 17 (1920): 30–34, 125–31, 372–80. For other examples of how the Army employed historical analysis for the derivation of military government doctrine, see "Lecture Outline—Caribbean Policy of the United States," in CGS, 1st Year Course, 1930–31; Lecture, "Legal Principles," in CGS, 2d Year Course, 1931–32; Principles Deducible From Military Government of Porto Rico [sic] and Philippines, Rpt of Committee 6, Sub-Committee 1, pt. 2, G–1 Course 16, AWC, 1924–25, pp. 12–13, AWC 287–6, MHI; The Administration of Civil Affairs by Military Authority in Occupied Territory, Rpt of Committee 11, G–1 Course, AWC, 1927–28, AWC 341–11, MHI; "Military Government," *Mailing List of the General Service Schools* 2 (February–March 1923); Military Government, Supplement 1 to Rpt of Committee 5, G–1 Course, AWC, 1939–40, p. 9, AWC 1–1940.5A, MHI;

Administration of Civil Affairs in Occupied Territory, Rpt of Committee 9, G–1 Course 14, AWC, 1928–29, AWC 350–9, MHI.

²⁷ Smith, *Military Government*, p. 12. First quote from Col Irwin L. Hunt, Some Principles of Military Government, 28 Feb 33, G–1 Course 7, 1932–33, AWC, p. 5, AWC 391–A–7, MHI. "Military Government," *Mailing List of the General Service Schools* 2 (February–March 1923): 41–43. Second quote from War Department, FM 27–5, *Basic Field Manual, Military Government*, 30 Jul 40 (hereafter cited as FM 27–5, 30 Jul 40), p. 4.

²⁸ "Military Government," *Mailing List of the General Service Schools* 2 (February–March 1923): 41–43, 48; Smith, *Military Government*, p. 12; Lecture, Cassius Dowell, "Legal Principles," in General Staff School Course, 1922–23, p. 327.

²⁹ The Administration of Civil Affairs by Military Authority in Occupied Territory, Rpt of Committee 11, G–1 Course, AWC, 1927–28, pp. 4, 10. Quote from Smith, *Military Government*, pp. 9–11. Provost Marshal General's Plan. Military Government, Rpt of Committee 6, G–1 Course, AWC, 1934–35, app. to Committee Rpt, p. 43, AWC 1–1935–6, MHI.

³⁰ Smith, *Military Government*, pp. 7–8; "Military Government," *Mailing List of the General Service Schools* 2 (February–March 1923): 48. Quote from Burgo Gill, "Guerrilla Warfare," *Quartermaster Review* 13 (September–October 1933): 29.

³¹ The Army spent much time weighing the optimum organization for a civil affairs operation. It never fully resolved this question prior to World War II, in part because it recognized that each operation was unique and required tailored solutions. FM 27–5 attempted to provide a basic conceptual and organizational framework without overly constricting the local commander. "Military Government," *Mailing List of the General Service Schools* 2 (February–March 1923): 45–46; Smith, *Military Government*, p. 78; The Administration of Civil Affairs by Military Authority in Occupied Territory, Rpt of Committee 11, G–1 Course, AWC, 1927–28, pp. 11–12; Administration of Civil Affairs in Occupied Territory, Rpt of Committee 9, G–1 Course 14, AWC, 1928–29, pp. 1–3; Hunt, Some Principles of Military Government, 28 Feb 33, G–1 Course 7, 1932–33, AWC; Military Government, Supplement 1 to Rpt of Committee 5, G–1 Course, AWC, 1939–40, p. 89; Contributions by G–1 to the Various War Plans; Duties of G–1 at GHQ and on Higher Staffs; Problems of G–1 in War Games, Maneuvers, and on Reconnaissances; Staff Administration of Civil Affairs in Occupied Territory, Rpt of Committee 3, G–1 Course 5, AWC, 1925–26, AWC 311–3, MHI; FM 27–5, 30 Jul 40, pp. 3–12.

³² FM 27–5, 30 Jul 40, pp. 4–5; Principles Deducible From Military Government of Porto Rico [*sic*] and Philippines, Rpt of Committee 6, Sub-Committee 1, pt. 2, G–1 Course 16, AWC, 1924–25, pp. 12–13; Smith, *Military Government*, p. 80; Provost Marshal General's Plan. Military Government, Rpt of Committee 6, G–1 Course, AWC, 1933–34, AWC 401–6, MHI; Lecture, H. H. Slaughter, "The American Expeditionary Force in Siberia as a Part of Allied Intervention in 1918," in War Plans Course 21, 1933–34, pp. 23–24, AWC 405–A–21, MHI.

³³ Quote from Lecture, "Legal Principles," in CGS, 2d Year Course, 1931–32. Smith, *Military Government*, pp. 78–80, 85–86; Brown, "Social Attitudes of American Generals," pp. 78–79. The creation of a constabulary organized and equipped for internal security and counterinsurgency duty *a la* the Philippine Constabulary or the Cuban Rural Guard was given special importance, not only by the Army, but also by the State Department. In 1923 the department insisted that all Central American countries estab-

lish American-trained constabularies as part of the United States' general policy of bringing improved government and internal stability to the region. Richard Millett, *Guardians of the Dynasty* (Orbis Books, 1977), p. 43.

[34] Internal Stability of Nations, Rpt of Committee 8, Conduct of War Course, AWC, 1934–35, p. 2, AWC 6–1935–8, MHI; Internal Stability of Nations, Rpt of Committee 8, Conduct of War Course, AWC, 1935–36, pp. 3–4, AWC 6–1936–8, MHI.

[35] Military Government, Supplement 1 to Rpt of Committee 5, G–1 Course, AWC, 1939–40, p. 89. Colby quote from Elbridge Colby, "How To Fight Savages," *American Journal of International Law* (April 1927): 285, and see also p. 287. Bell quote from *Telegraphic Circulars*, p. 3.

[36] Quotes from Lecture, "Small Wars," in *Instructional Material, Infantry School*, 1930–31, vol. 3. War Department, FM 30–15, *Basic Field Manual—Military Intelligence*, 1940, pp. 4–5; Lecture, "Small Wars and Punitive Expeditions," in *Instructional Material, Infantry School*, 1925–26, vol. 2, *Tactics*; Military Government, Supplement 1 to Rpt of Committee 5, G–1 Course, AWC, 1939–40, p. 89; Cassius Dowell, *Military Aid to Civil Power* (Fort Leavenworth, Kans.: General Service Schools, 1925), pp. 44–45, 48, 52–53; Joseph Baker and Henry Crocker, *The Laws of Land Warfare Concerning the Rights and Duties of Belligerents* (Washington, D.C.: Government Printing Office, 1919), pp. 12–13, 18–19, 31, 131, 367–71; War Department, FM 27–10, *Rules of Land Warfare*, 1940, pp. 4–5, 7, 85–90; Lecture, "Minor Warfare," in *Instructional Material, Infantry School*, 1922–23, 1st sec., vol. 3; Gill, "Guerrilla Warfare," pp. 27–29; Burgo Gill, "This Guerrilla Warfare," *Military Engineer* 32 (November–December 1940): 442.

[37] McEntee, A Critical Analysis of the Campaign in the Soudan, AWC, G–4 Committee 1, 1922–23; Charles A. Willoughby, "Spanish Campaigns in Morocco," *Infantry Journal* 27 (August 1925): 126. For examples of Army interest in the Moroccan campaign, see C. B. Stone, "The Moroccan Campaign of 1925," *Infantry Journal* 28 (January 1926): 20–23; Maurice de la Rue-Barneville, "A Study of the Conditions of Warfare in Northeastern Morocco," *Journal of the Military Service Institution of the United States* 42 (March–April 1908): 211–18; Maurice de la Rue-Barneville, "Lessons From Moroccan Campaign," *Infantry Journal* 28 (April 1926): 472–75; "Tanks in Morocco," *Infantry Journal* 28 (May 1926): 560–61; Schrantz, "Operation in Morocco," pp. 148–54; Butler and Melasky, Some Lessons in Aviation Matters From the Riff Campaign.

[38] Infantry School, *Infantry in Special Operations*, pp. 40–43, 94; "Desert Warfare," *Infantry School Mailing List* 13 (January 1937): 84–98; CGS, *Mountain Warfare*, pp. 38; FM 100–5, Oct 39, pp. 228–31; FM 100–5, 22 May 41, pp. 238–40.

[39] Beckett, *Roots of Counter-Insurgency*, pp. 57–58; Douglas Porch, "Bugeaud, Gallieni, Lyautey: The Development of French Colonial Warfare," in *Makers of Modern Strategy*, ed. Peter Paret (Princeton, N.J.: Princeton University Press, 1986), pp. 391–94. Quote from Willoughby, "French in Morocco," p. 9. CGS, *Mountain Warfare*, pp. 25–26; Nelson Margetts, "Extracts From the Diary of an American Observer in Morocco," *Field Artillery Journal* 16 (March–April 1926): 130–31, 137, 147; Nelson Margetts, "Modern Warfare Versus the Riffians," *Army Ordnance* 6 (May–June 1926): 433–34. In contrast, Americans deplored Spain's lackluster counterinsurgency campaign in Morocco. Willoughby, "Spanish Campaigns," pp. 127–29.

[40] Training Orders 1, HQ, Panama Canal Division, 19 Feb 27; Training Memo 2, HQ, Panama Canal Department, 12 Mar 30; Program of Instruction, Panama Canal

Department; Field Training Period, January 1 to June 30, 1918, pp. 4, 7–8. All in 353, General Correspondence, Panama Department, RG 395, NARA. Lecture, "Small Wars—Desert Fighting," in *Instructional Material, Infantry School*, 1929–30, 1st sec., vol. 3; Lecture, "Mountain Warfare," in *Instructional Material, Infantry School*, 1929–30, 1st sec., vol. 2; Lecture, "Small Wars, Marked Problem No. 45—Advanced Course," in *Instructional Material, Infantry School*, 1929–30, 1st sec., vol. 3; Lecture, "Mountain Warfare," in *Instructional Material, Infantry School*, 1930–31, vol. 3; Lecture, "Small Wars—Desert Fighting," in *Instructional Material, Infantry School*, 1930–31, vol. 3; Lecture, "Tanks in Special Operations, Problem No. 14—Warfare Against Poorly Equipped Forces," in *Instructional Material, Infantry School*, 1933–34, vol. 2; Lecture, "Tanks in Security and Special Operations," in Illustrative Problem, sec. 13, Thirteenth Situation, *The Infantry School Academic Department Instructional Matter*, 1934–35, 1st sec., vol. 3; Lecture, "British Operations Against Tribesmen on the Northwest Frontier of India," *The Infantry School Academic Department Instructional Matter*, 1934–35, 2d sec., vol. 5; "A Skirmish in Nicaragua," *Infantry School Mailing List* 11 (January 1936): 231–49; Charles Howland, "The Infantry in the Canal Zone," *Infantry Journal* 26 (April 1925): 384; John Johnson, "Tanks in the Jungles," *Infantry Journal* 27 (September 1925): 268; Thomas White, "Jungle Fighting," *Infantry Journal* 29 (July 1926): 65–66; J. C. McArthur, "Jungle Warfare in Panama," *Infantry Journal* 10 (May–June 1914): 855–60; "Infantry in Jungle Combat," *Infantry School Mailing List* 12 (July 1936): 253–66; Lessons From the Experiences of the Fourteenth Infantry, 1937, Infantry School library; Infantry School, *Infantry in Special Operations*, pp. 77–86.

[41] *Annual Report, General Service Schools, 1921*, pp. 21, 23. First quote from *Annual Report of the Commandant of the General Service Schools, 1921–22, Program of Instruction*. *Annual Report of the Director of the General Service School, 1922–23*, p. 33; General Service Schools, "Expeditionary Force," *Command, Staff and Logistics, A Tentative Text* (Fort Leavenworth, Kans.: General Service Schools, 1929). Second quote from Lecture, "Legal Principles—Military Government Map Problem no. 2—Series 10, 8 Feb 1932," CGS, 1931–32. Lecture, General Service Schools, School of the Line, "Logistics," 1920–21, p. 585, CARL; A Study of the Supply of the 31st Infantry, AEF, n.d., Longuevan Papers; A Study of the Outstanding G–4 Features in War and Expeditions, With Conclusions as to Lessons That May Be Applicable to the Present Time: Mexican War, Mexican Punitive Expedition, Vera Cruz Expedition, Boxer Relief Expedition, Siberian Expedition, Russo-Japanese War, Tsingtao Expedition, World War, G–4 Course 15, AWC, 1927–28, Expeditions, AWC 344–6, MHI; Plans, Lessons, and Principles Deducible From British Campaigns the Iberian and Crimean Peninsulas, Sudan, South Africa, France, and Palestine, Rpt of Committee 6, G–4 Course 15, AWC, 1922–23, AWC 253–1, MHI; A Study of the Outstanding Features in the Following Wars and Expeditions, With Conclusions as to Lessons That May Be Applicable at the Present Time: The Mexican War, Civil War, China Expedition in 1900, Cuba and Philippines, 1898–1901, Mexican Punitive Expedition, 1916, World War, Siberia, 1918–19, Rpt of Committee 5, G–4 Course, AWC, 1926–27, pp. 4, 8, AWC 334–5, MHI; Memo, Lt Col D. A. Robinson for Asst Commandant, AWC, 29 Apr 33, sub: The Cavalry Division, p. 2, MHI; Smith, *Military Government*, pp. 75f.

[42] App. 2, Special Plan Brown, n.d., p. 3, Records of the Adjutant General's Office, Administrative Services Division, Operations Branch, Special Projects, War Plans—Color, 1920–48, 323, RG 407, NARA.

THE INTERWAR YEARS, 1920–1941

[43] First quote from Basic Plan—Brown, Philippine Department, 1923, 321. Philippine Department Plan Brown 1932, 313. Remaining quotes from Brown Plan, Hawaiian Department, Revision 1932, app. 3, Training, 31 Oct 32, 310. Brown Plan—Hawaiian Department, 1932, G–3 app., 312. All in RG 407, NARA.

[44] Army Strategical Plan Purple, 1928, 356; Memorandum for the Record (MFR), Lt Col Charles W. Furlong, c. 1930, sub: Comments on Strategical Plan Purple, 355. Both in RG 407, NARA.

[45] Quote from HQ, Caribbean Defense Command, Operation Plan of Caribbean Theater, 1 Dec 41, an. 1e, p. 7, RG 407, NARA. Caribbean Defense Command, Plan for Support of Costa Rica, Jul 41, 46, RG 407, NARA; John Child, "From 'Color' to 'Rainbow': U.S. Strategic Planning for Latin America, 1919–45," *Journal of InterAmerican Studies and World Affairs* 21 (May 1979): 255.

[46] Quote from Memo for Chairman, Subcommittee 2, A Succinct Account of the Economic, Political, Naval, and Military Situation in Central America With Particular Reference to the Causes That May Lead to Intervention on the Part of the US, in G–2 Course, AWC, 1929–30, p. 5, AWC 362–6, MHI. Plan for Intervention in Cuba, 9 Oct 20, 53, RG 407, NARA; Special Plan Tan (1924), app. WPD, pp. 10–11, 30–31, RG 407, NARA; Army Strategical Plan, Tan (1930 Revision), RG 407, NARA.

[47] Survey of the Vital Strategic Areas of the U.S. and Its Possessions. War Plans Division, War Plan Green, Committee 1, War Plans Division Course 6, AWC, 1921–22, p. 50, MHI; Strategical Plan Green for the Occupation and Pacification of Mexico (hereafter cited as Strategical Plan Green), Mar 26, pp. 3, 5, 259, RG 407, NARA; AEF Plan—Green, app. G–3, pt. 2, Organization, Training, Concentration, 1927, p. 3, 337, RG 407, NARA; App. WPD to Strategical Plan Green, Special Plan Green, 1926, p. 28, 269, RG 407, NARA; War Plan Green, War Plans Group 1, Preparation for War Course, AWC, 1935–36, p. 208, AWC 5–1936–18, MHI; War Department, MID, Situation Monograph, Special Plan Green, vol. 2, 31 Dec 28, AWC III–2.9B, MHI; Memo, Robinson for Asst Commandant, AWC, 29 Apr 33, sub: The Cavalry Division, p. 1; Memo, Army G–2 for WPD, 21 Jun 27, sub: Strategical Plan 2, Special Plan Green, Development file, Army Strategical Plan Green no. 2. Steps in the Development of the Plan, RG 407, NARA.

[48] War Department, MID, Special Plan Green, vol. 2, 1929, pars. 6180, 6700, AWC 111–2.9B, MHI; Memo, WPD for II and VIII Corps, 4 Sep 23, 1424, RG 165, NARA.

[49] First quote from Strategical Plan Green, Mar 26, pp. 20–21 and second quote from p. 4. War Department, MID, Situation Monograph, Special Plan Green, vol. 2, 31 Dec 28; Theater of Operations Plan—Green 2, an. 7, Plan for Military Government, Proclamations, Translations, etc., 1930, 265, RG 407, NARA.

[50] First quote from War Department, MID, Special Plan Green, vol. 2, 1929, par. 8000 (c)(2). Lecture, "War Plan Green," War Plans Group 1, Preparation for War Course, AWC, 1935–36, p. 146. Second quote from Theater of Operations Plan—Green 2, an. 7, Plan for Military Government, Proclamations, Translations, etc., 1930. Third quote from Strategical Plan Green, Mar 26, p. 21.

[51] The Army also experienced an awakening of interest in the utilization of partisan techniques during the late 1930s and early 1940s, as it observed one country after another turn to guerrilla or partisan tactics to resist Axis aggression. For insights into the Army's budding interest in partisan warfare, see Fred Wilkins, "The Guerrilla," *Cavalry Journal* (September–October 1941): 22–25; Cavalry School, *Cavalry Combat* (Cavalry School, 1937), pp. 13–15; "Partisan Warfare," *Cavalry Journal*

269

(September–October 1941): 31; Wilber Burton, "Guerrilla Warfare in China," *Coast Artillery Journal* 83 (March–April 1940): 120–24; "Soviet Guerrilla Warfare," *Cavalry Journal* (September–October 1941): 2–10; Bert Levy, "Guerrilla Warfare," in *The Infantry Journal Reader*, ed. Joseph Greene (Garden City, N.Y.: Doubleday, Doran & Company, 1943), pp. 5–6, 9–11; Nickerson, "Irregular Warfare," pp. 381–85; George Haig, "Guerrilla Warfare," *Field Artillery Journal* (February 1941): 110–14; George Haig, "Organization of a Guerrilla or Raider Unit," *Cavalry Journal* (September–October 1941): 26–29; Gill, "Guerrilla Warfare," pp. 27–29; Gill, "This Guerrilla Warfare," pp. 440–42; Daley, "Twentieth Century Irregulars," pp. 37–42; FM 100–5, Oct 39, pp. 228–31; FM 100–5, 22 May 41, pp. 238–40.

[52] The Administration of Civil Affairs by Military Authority in Occupied Territory, Rpt of Committee 11, G–1 Course, AWC, 1927–28, pp. 4, 10, 14–15, 17; Lecture, "Minor Warfare," in *Instructional Material, Infantry School*, 1922–23, 1st sec., vol. 3; Langley, *The Banana Wars*, pp. 222–23; Allan Millett, "'Cleansing the Augean Stables': The American Armed Forces in the Caribbean, 1898–1914," in *Essays in Some Dimensions of Military History* (Carlisle Barracks, Pa.: U.S. Army Military History Institute, n.d.), 4:123–41; Richard Millett, "Useful Lessons of the Caribbean Interventions," in *Essays in Some Dimensions of Military History*, 4:142–57.

[53] Beckett, *Roots of Counter-Insurgency*, p. 84; Walter Laqueur, *The Guerrilla Reader: A Historical Anthology* (New York: Meridan, 1977), pp. 151–52; Harold Nelson, *Leon Trotsky and the Art of Insurrection, 1905–17* (London: Frank Cass, 1988), pp. 14–15, 24–25, 31, 126; Lecture, "Capture and Occupation of Towns," in *Instructional Material, Infantry School*, 1922–23, 1st sec., vol. 4; Conrad Lanza, Communist Warfare, General Staff School, 1919–20; James Griffith, "Guerrilla Warfare in China," *Cavalry Journal* (September–October 1941): 12.

8

CONCLUSION: THE DEVELOPMENT OF SMALL WARS DOCTRINE IN RETROSPECT

Despite the fact that constabulary work was the U.S. Army's main source of employment prior to World War II, the Army never considered such duty to be of more than secondary importance when compared to major conventional operations. At first glance, the Army's preoccupation with one form of warfare while performing another seems incongruous, but there were several reasons why this was true.

Most of the Army's small war experiences occurred when the service was just beginning to evolve into a doctrinal-bound entity. The old Army believed that soldiers learned their trade best through experience, and prior to the twentieth century its publications rarely related more than the technicalities of drill, formation, and administration. Not until 1905 did the Army publish its first authoritative "doctrinal" manual in the modern sense, *Field Service Regulations*, and not until World War I did it establish a formal procedure for capturing "lessons learned." Consequently, when considering the state of small wars doctrine in the century between the Mexican War and World War II, it should be born in mind that the Army had little formal doctrine for any type of operation—conventional or unconventional—during about half that period.[1]

When the Army attended to doctrine, it focused primarily on conventional warfare because it considered major wars against modern, industrialized states to be more serious threats to national survival than desultory conflicts with irregular warriors. Although guerrilla warfare could prove nasty, most soldiers believed that regularly organized and disciplined troops would inevitably triumph over an irregular opponent. That the Army sometimes suffered from its "big war" fixation when engaging in irregular conflicts is indisputable. But without the impetus of a significant threat, counterinsurgency doctrine languished.[2]

The nature of the Army's small wars experience further discouraged officers from undertaking a coherent study of the subject. Unlike conventional warfare, where the enemy's military system roughly paralleled the Army's, America's small wars had occurred under an incredible variety of climatic, topographical, political, cultural, and tactical conditions. This diversity hindered a systematic approach to the study of small wars.[3] So too did the fact that counterguerrilla warfare consisted largely of small-unit actions, in which captains often played a more important role than generals. In the opinion of many officers, basic military skills were all that was required to combat guerrillas. Consequently, guerrilla warfare was not as attractive a field of inquiry to military theorists as the grandeur of Napoleonic-style campaigns.

Nor was it as rewarding. Counterinsurgency and occupation duty had generally proved to be an onerous and thankless undertaking. Whether on the Great Plains or in the jungles of Samar, the American public felt uneasy with some of the stringent measures the Army employed to pacify hostile populations. Such measures ran counter to American ideals and challenged the image of the United States as the personification of freedom and enlightenment. There has been internal opposition to most American wars, but the fact that small war and contingency operations typically occurred in peacetime, when the life of the nation was not directly threatened, heightened their divisiveness. The unpleasant nature of counterinsurgency operations and the criticisms they generated not only dampened the military's enthusiasm for this particular form of warfare, but contributed to a degree of amnesia within the military's corporate memory by discouraging frank and open examinations of the Army's experiences.

Ideology also contributed to the Army's uneasiness. Since the founding of the Republic, civilians and soldiers alike have shared a deep commitment to the principle of civil supremacy over military power. In practice, of course, the distinction between civil and military roles was dynamic and led to continuous friction between soldiers and statesmen over the control of military government and civil affairs functions. Nevertheless, the universal acceptance of the concept of civil supremacy created an intellectual bifurcation of state affairs that discouraged the institutionalization of the Army's experiences in sociopolitical matters into formal doctrine.

A final influence upon the position of small wars in Army thought was the officer corps' own self-image. American political philosophy was one factor that shaped this image. Another was the concept of officer professionalism that arose during the nineteenth century. Many officers believed that soldiers should devote themselves exclusively to purely military subjects to the exclusion of nonmilitary activities, especially politics. Such an attitude reinforced the Army's predisposition to relegate the highly political realm of small wars to the periphery of professional thought.[4]

The impact of professionalization, however, was mixed. Inherent in it was the idea that the professional must study all facets of his occupation, and, since the nation continued to require its soldiers to perform many nonmilitary roles, some officers applied the new professional methodology to the study of military government and irregular warfare. Moreover, there were officers, like Leonard Wood, who believed that the Army should play an active role in national affairs. Rather than seeing professionalism as a means of segregating the military from social and political life, Wood and his followers thought the Army's expertise in human leadership made it an ideal instrument for social engineering at home and abroad. These Armed Progressives had a major impact upon the way in which the Army conducted its overseas interventions and contributed to a gradual broadening of the concept of officership to include knowledge of political and social affairs. In fact, it was the many political requirements placed on officers as a consequence of their duties as pacifiers and administrators of America's overseas colonies and protectorates that stimulated the Army to expand gradually military curriculums to include subjects like history, government, language, and other liberal arts. The professionalization movement's effect on the Army's approach to the employment of military resources to political and social problems was therefore ambiguous, at once excluding and embracing it, depending upon the individual's conception of what "professionalism" meant. Yet the overall trend was toward a more encompassing definition.

The relative paucity of formal, written doctrine for counterinsurgency and military interventions notwithstanding, a striking continuity existed in the manner in which the Army performed operations of this type prior to World War II. Many factors contributed to this continuity. Perhaps the most important was the existence of broad, fundamental values, both in American society in general and in the military in particular. From the former, American soldiers drew upon a cultural heritage that included Judeo-Christian morality, the Protestant work ethic, and an espousal of the virtues of liberty, civic responsibility, representative government, social and economic opportunity, individualism, equality before the law, and the sanctity of private property. Less redeeming attributes, such as racism and ethnocentrism, also made up the cultural baggage of many American officers, as did the more positive impulses of American progressivism, a movement whose apogee (1900–1919) coincided with the Army's most intense period of overseas nation building. To these broad cultural and intellectual concepts, the Army as an institution added a generally conservative philosophy that cherished order, organization, efficiency, and a respect for authority. This is not to say that individual officers did not differ, at times profoundly, on the proper conduct of sociopolitical affairs. But ultimately American soldiers reflected the society and institutions from which they came, and they could not help but be influenced by the underlying currents of American civilization when called to administer foreign populations.[5]

Strong trends in the evolution of Western concepts of law and war also contributed to the continuity of Army actions. The official codification of these precepts by the U.S. Army through GO 100 (1863) and by the international community through the Hague Conferences of 1899 and 1907 provided the conceptual foundation upon which the Army based its treatment of guerrillas and occupied populations.

Another factor behind the continuity of Army actions was simply that similar situations tended to evoke similar responses. Although each operation was unique, sufficient similarities existed to encourage analogous actions. Whether in Mexico, Cuba, or the Philippines, the act of occupying a country and administering a foreign people generated many of the same types of issues. Order had to be imposed, the ravages of war and disease minimized, and the fabric of civil, political, and economic life restored. How the Army addressed these problems varied based on the exigencies of the moment, the policy aims of the U.S. government, the climate of public opinion at home and abroad, the personalities of the principal actors, and the internal dynamics of the occupied area, but many of the core questions were inherent in the nature of civil affairs and pacification. The same was true of counterguerrilla operations. Cheyenne warriors, Filipino guerrillas, and Bolshevik partisans may have operated within vastly different cultural, environmental, and military contexts, but all were governed by the same fundamental principles that have characterized guerrilla warfare for thousands of years. In all cases speed, stealth, surprise, intelligence, and civilian support were key to the irregular's survival, and in all cases the Army had to devise measures to counter these attributes—measures which, while they may have been situation-specific, reflected the essential truths of guerrilla warfare. Thus the nature of the events themselves contributed to the continuity of Army actions, at least at the broad, conceptual level, and it is no accident that this is

CONCLUSION: THE DEVELOPMENT OF SMALL WARS DOCTRINE IN RETROSPECT

exactly the level at which Army counterguerrilla and pacification doctrine was eventually written.[6]

Constabulary service played such a central part in military life during the late nineteenth and early twentieth centuries that the Army nearly always had on hand a significant cadre of veterans who were able to apply their knowledge to subsequent operations. Officers who first became acquainted with counterguerrilla and pacification techniques during antebellum Indian conflicts and the Mexican War later applied those same techniques during the Civil War, Reconstruction, and the post-1865 Indian wars. Long-service officers of the post–Civil War Army had multiple opportunities over the course of several decades to hone their frontier constabulary skills, and many of these men, together with a few veterans of the Civil War, went on to provide the Army's senior leadership during the Spanish-American and Philippine Wars. These conflicts, and subsequent operations in Cuba, China, and the Philippines, spawned an entirely new generation of constabulary veterans who collectively dominated the Army into the 1920s and 1930s. The career of General Pershing, who spent his first thirty years of service chasing Indian, Filipino, Moro, and Mexican irregulars, amply demonstrates the depth of experience available to the Army in the early twentieth century. The memories of such long-service constabulary veterans were invaluable assets and produced continuity in both operational thought and in the Army's approach to the management of semi-civilized peoples.[7] Moreover, although difficult to document and never formally institutionalized, it is reasonable to assume that older, experienced officers passed on to their less experienced colleagues the benefit of their experiences. The fact that personnel of different generations served side by side produced an overlap of experience and the opportunity for veterans to endow their younger contemporaries with some degree of accumulated wisdom, whether it be in the form of tactics and fieldcraft or more general lore about the nature of such operations. Although informal and irregular at best, such methods of transmission should not be discounted.

Finally, the Army did in fact institutionalize some of the fundamental tenets of small war and military government operations through a variety of mediums—articles, pamphlets, field notes, textbooks, classroom instruction, training problems, war plans, and manuals. Nowhere was this more evident than in the Army's approach to the administration of occupied populations and the treatment of irregulars, which was laid down in a chain of official publications beginning with GO 100 (1863) and continuing through the *Field Service Regulations* of 1905; the *Rules of Land Warfare* (1914, 1917); *The Laws of Land*

Warfare Concerning the Rights and Duties of Belligerents (1919); FM 27–10, *Rules of Land Warfare* (1940); and FM 27–5, *Basic Field Manual, Military Government* (1940).

One factor that is difficult to determine is the degree to which European precedents shaped American policies and programs. There were always individual officers who were cognizant of the way in which European powers conducted military operations. Most American manuals prior to the Civil War were adaptations of European manuals, while GO 100 creatively distilled and codified European concepts regarding the laws and customs of war. The writings of such men as Halleck and Marcy were influenced by European example, while the professional journals that emerged toward the end of the nineteenth century all carried reviews and reprints of foreign publications concerning irregular warfare. During the Philippine War, techniques like concentration and the water cure were clearly derived from Spanish and Filipino precedents, and several officers are known to have studied foreign treatises on the conduct of European colonial wars.[8]

It was not until after this war, however, that the Army began to study European example more closely, especially in regard to colonial affairs. Secretary Root amassed a library on European colonial administration to help guide him in the management of America's newfound insular empire. Similarly, while en route to assume the governorship of Moro Province, Leonard Wood stopped to discuss colonial administrative techniques with his counterparts in Egypt, Aden, India, Singapore, and the East Indies. Other Moro administrators likewise visited and studied neighboring British and Dutch colonies that had large Muslim populations. The War Department also compiled information on the way European armies organized their colonial military establishments, while military students occasionally studied European colonial campaigns, from Braddock's defeat and the Boer War to the Italian conquest of Ethiopia. For the most part, however, American soldiers derived their counterinsurgency and nation-building programs from experience, trial and error, and American tradition rather than any slavish adaptation of European procedure. In fact, American officers sometimes specifically rejected what they believed to be the European way of doing things. That certain parallels existed between American, British, and French counterguerrilla and colonial administrative policies had more to do with the common Western heritage shared by these nations and the similar problems such endeavors posed than any direct, causal relationship.[9]

Perhaps Europe's greatest influence on American doctrine, outside the realm of international law, occurred during the 1920s and 1930s,

Conclusion: The Development of Small Wars Doctrine in Retrospect

after most of the Army's imperial constabulary veterans had passed from the ranks. Both because the Army had failed to preserve fully its own rich heritage and because officers believed that technological advancements rendered past wars inadequate guides to the conduct of modern campaigns, Army writers after World War I relied heavily on Anglo-French experience in formulating doctrinal materials. Foremost among these were the writings of the British soldier Charles Callwell, from whom the U.S. Army derived the very term *small wars*, and the contemporary actions of the French in Morocco. While these provided valuable guides, there was little in them that American soldiers could not have derived from their own heritage, had they only bothered to preserve it in a more comprehensive form.

The doctrinal approach that emerged from the Army's counterinsurgency and intervention operations and its study of similar European experiences blended aggressive military action with nonmilitary incentives designed to control, pacify, and, if possible, "uplift" the population. This method can be best summarized as a carrot-and-stick approach.

Military action represented the "stick" side of Army small war campaigns. In counterguerrilla warfare, the Army's *modus operandi* was based upon continuous, aggressive small-unit action. Constant patrol work, offensive tactics, and night marches leading to dawn roundups characterized this method. Mobility, flexibility, logistical adaptation, and personal initiative were stressed. Passive measures, though sometimes necessary, were discouraged, not only because they gave the enemy the initiative, but also because of their adverse psychological effect on soldier and civilian alike. The Army recognized the importance of intelligence and the necessity of separating the population—both physically and mentally—from the influence of the militant elements, though it often had difficulty finding the right balance between the need to protect the population and the dangers of overdispersion. Specialist units, composed of either specially trained regulars, mounted scouts, or native auxiliaries, were also standard elements in the Army's counterguerrilla repertoire. Though few in number, specialist units provided the Army with vitally important reconnaissance, strike, and police capabilities. Both on the frontier and in the Philippines, native auxiliaries also played an integral part in the implementation of the ancient strategy of divide and conquer, as the Army successfully exploited ethnic, religious, or social fissures to undermine resistance. Such a strategy had to be handled with care, however, since the U.S. government's ultimate aim was peace and tranquility, not the promotion of permanent civil strife. Since experience had shown that native auxiliaries were prone to committing acts of atrocity and revenge that detracted from their usefulness as agents of pacification, most officers believed they should be employed with care.

The military recognized that small wars, like all human contests, were essentially struggles of will. However, it considered the question of will to be especially important in counterinsurgencies because they were peoples' wars in which the Army had to overcome not only an enemy army, but a hostile society as well. In wars of this kind, the conventional distinction between combatant and noncombatant was blurred. Once a popularly based insurgency had set in, many officers deemed it essential to strike not just at the enemy's military forces, but at the society that was sustaining them. Only in this way could the military bring the cost of war home to the people and discourage further resistance. This did not mean that the Army advocated improper behavior on the part of its soldiers toward civilians, but it did mean that it was willing to punish civilians for supporting insurgents. Punitive measures, such as the destruction of food and shelter, the imprisonment of guerrilla sympathizers, and the forced relocation of populations were employed not only for their military effect in denying these resources to the enemy, but for their moral effect. Genuine humanitarian concerns, as well as a recognition of the fickle nature of American public opinion, meant that the Army preferred not to employ stringent methods. Nevertheless, when faced with intractable guerrilla warfare, the Army repeatedly resorted to such measures to heighten the price of resistance so that people would lose heart and submit. Such an approach became an American tradition enshrined in the words and deeds of Washington, Mahan, Scott, Halleck, Grant, Sherman, Sheridan, Crook, Miles, Bigelow, Bell, Birkhimer, and Chaffee among others.

While the Army used combat operations and punitive measures as a "stick" to beat the heart out of the resistance, it also appealed to the minds of its enemies by offering them positive incentives to cease their resistance. The nature of the "carrots" proffered by the military varied under the circumstances. Invariably, the Army's first step was to soothe the inhabitants by promising peace, security, and a return to normal conditions of daily life. But that was only a start. In many cases officers looked beyond the immediate questions of law and order and sought to address what they regarded as the fundamental causes of unrest—ignorance, poverty, corruption, and injustice. They attempted to slay these dragons by establishing schools, modernizing economic infrastructures, imposing "clean" and efficient governments, and rewriting legal codes. These measures, firmly grounded on broad American values, Progressive impulses, and the tenets of

Conclusion: The Development of Small Wars Doctrine in Retrospect

GO 100, produced an American way of waging small wars and pacification operations.

Although the Army recognized the dual politico-military nature of small wars, it never quite settled upon the proper mixture of "carrot" and "stick" when dealing with an insurgency. The primary reason for this was that the Army realized that pacification was more alchemy than science, in which the policy of attraction and the policy of chastisement had to be blended in differing proportions to best meet the political, cultural, and military circumstances at hand. Nevertheless, most counterinsurgency veterans believed that experience had proved that sociopolitical measures could not beat an insurgency unless they were tied to strong military actions. Whether it was in Mexico, Georgia, Luzon, or the Sulu archipelago, Army officers had been forced to employ hard and sometimes unsavory measures after more benign methods had failed to achieve the desired results. Consequently, constabulary veterans believed that programs intended to win the favor of the populace could at best supplement, not supplant, military action.[10]

Unfortunately, this was one lesson that tended to become clouded with the passage of time. The Army's reluctance to record the degree to which hard measures had been responsible for its pacification successes, the gradual disappearance from the officer corps of experienced veterans, and the natural appeal of following a benevolent course, meant that Army texts during the interwar era tended to gloss over the harsh realities and to emphasize moderation above punitive action. While the adoption of moderate policies was both admirable and capable of producing positive results under the right circumstances, failing to give a full account of how firm, and occasionally hard, measures had proved to be equally necessary raised the danger that subsequent generations of soldiers might enter the small wars of the future with unrealistic expectations about the ability of benevolence alone to overcome an entrenched insurgency.

Another area that interwar doctrine failed to adequately address was that of civil-military coordination. Although they did not challenge the right of civilians to make policy, most officers questioned the wisdom of interjecting the restraints of civil and diplomatic life into the conduct of operations. They were especially disturbed when civil authorities provided unclear or vacillating instructions, as during the Mexican and Russian interventions, and when they violated the principle of unity of command by creating separate civil and military jurisdictions, as happened during the Civil, Indian, and Philippine Wars. Such actions placed commanders in untenable situations and produced power struggles between competing bureaucracies that hindered pacification operations. The Army, therefore, favored total unity of political and military effort, preferably under the command of a military officer. Civilian policy makers did not share this conclusion, however, and the problem of civil-military coordination was never resolved during the period covered by this study. Nor perhaps could it have been, for even if the bureaucratic relationships had been resolved, the very nature of politico-military operations mitigated against a set doctrinal solution to this problem. Soldiers can demand clear guidance, but the nature of politics is such that civilian leaders must be able to respond to the ever-changing political and diplomatic landscape. Clarifying bureaucratic lines of responsibility and making political leaders aware of the many pitfalls inherent in overseas contingency operations can help, but ultimately there is no organizational or doctrinal solution to the fact that the country will inevitably call upon soldiers to undertake politico-military tasks under difficult and ambiguous circumstances. The best preparation officers can have for such duty, baring personal experience, is to study previous historical situations to sensitize themselves to the kinds of dilemmas that counterguerrilla, civil affairs, and contingency operations typically pose.

The legacy of the Army's experience in small wars prior to World War II is thus somewhat ambiguous. On the one hand, the Army was generally successful in the military aspects of small wars. Naturally, every operation was not a success, nor was every commander equally gifted in conducting counterguerrilla campaigns. But by and large the Army proved flexible enough to adapt to the many challenges of the small wars environment, despite the relative paucity of formal, written doctrine for these operations. Although the Army undoubtedly would have been better served had it studied the problems associated with small wars and interventions more closely, the absence of formal doctrine had a positive side, in that commanders were free to adjust to local conditions and employ whatever methods worked best. Since guerrilla warfare is heavily influenced by local factors and since the irregulars America faced prior to World War II were not highly organized themselves, the absence of formal doctrine did not prove to be a major handicap. When the Army finally began putting small wars doctrine on a more formal basis in the 1920s and 1930s, it preserved the flexibility that had become characteristic of the Army's approach to these operations.[11]

The Army was less successful, however, in recasting the societies it came into contact with during the course of its pacification and intervention operations. Social engineering had proved to be a more difficult task than America's Armed Progressives had thought. Despite

CONCLUSION: THE DEVELOPMENT OF SMALL WARS DOCTRINE IN RETROSPECT

the military's many positive achievements in the area of civil affairs, often all it had really done was to superimpose American institutions on societies that were neither prepared nor entirely willing to accept them. Form proved easier to change than substance, for behind the facade of "modern" institutions there remained strong social and cultural forces that resisted change. Without the necessary value system to nurture them, American-based institutions either withered or became perverted.[12]

Changing values, however, was not an easy task. Values could not be changed by bayonets, as the nation learned during Reconstruction. Nor could they be imposed quickly, as dabblers in the Indian, Cuban, and Moro questions well knew. Most officers realized that U.S. policy was unrealistic in expecting the Army to apply "quick fixes" to deeply rooted social problems. Indeed, Army doctrine acknowledged the complexity of nation building and the perils of ethnocentrism by counseling officers to take a "go slow" approach that considered the cultural attributes of the indigenous population. Frequently, however, officers had difficulty following such instructions, in part because ethnocentrism is inherent in the very concept of nation building. No matter how sensitive soldiers may try to be to the needs of an indigenous culture—and such sensitivity is vital if soldiers are to successfully perform advisory and nation-building tasks—any effort to modernize, reform, or uplift a foreign society will inevitably lead to clashes of culture, values, and traditions that are not easily resolved. Internally generated changes in social, political, and economic institutions often produce great tension and stress. When such changes are imposed by an outside agent, the effect can be traumatic. Time after time, the United States found that indigenous body politics rejected transplanted American social and political institutions.

One way in which the Army tried to reduce the likelihood of rejection, as well as ease its administrative burdens, was by working through indigenous leaders and institutions. Unfortunately, the Army's limited and evolutionary approach to nation building, while perhaps pragmatic, also lessened its ability to transform what were often colonial, oligarchical, and exploitative systems into truly open, democratic societies. Although some, like the authors of the Plan Green pacification studies, may have believed that a radical redistribution of land or wealth might be necessary to break the grip of the traditional elites that dominated many "less developed" societies, most turn-of-the-century Americans were prepared neither philosophically nor politically to undertake such measures. Moreover, by rapidly restoring local self-government, the United States lacked the leverage to compel those elites to undertake anything that would fundamentally challenge their privileged position. The inability of the United States to compel the adoption of reforms that the indigenous elite viewed as inimical to its interests was a dilemma that the U.S. government faced in Mexico, Cuba, Russia, the Philippines, and in a different context, in the American South, and it would be a dilemma that the United States would face again in the post–World War II era.

The realization that militant progressivism had its limits left many turn-of-the-century officers ambivalent toward nation building as a whole. They were proud of the Army's accomplishments, yet unsure if their efforts would have any long-term effect. Nor did they ever find any alternative solutions to the perplexities of social engineering. Both government policy and national culture demanded that American soldiers continue to approach pacification with the same troika of moderate educational, economic, and governmental reforms that American society valued so highly. Similarly, while it may have made sense from a practical standpoint to refrain from thrusting American-style democratic institutions upon a society unaccustomed to these procedures, such restraint was difficult to effect, given the sentiments of the American public. Nor was there any likelihood that officers would be given the time they knew was needed to affect the cultural changes necessary to support modern democratic institutions. The result was that the military's basic approach to nation building remained unchanged, despite having proved only moderately successful in achieving long-term national policy aims. The difficulty of implementing a successful nation-building program was an important lesson that future policy makers, both inside the military and without, would ignore only at their peril.

Notes

¹ Nesmith, "Quiet Paradigm," pp. 1–3; Ney, *Evolution of the U.S. Army Field Manual*, pp. 47, 50–56; Crites, "Infantry Tactical Doctrine," pp. 12–14; Vetock, *Lessons Learned*, pp. 13, 16–17, 30, 37.

² Beckett, *Roots of Counter-Insurgency*, p. 109; "The Place of Doctrine in War," *Infantry Journal* 9 (July–August 1912): 136.

³ Gates, "Indians and Insurrectos," p. 59.

⁴ Samuel Huntington, *The Soldier and the State: The Theory and Politics of Civil-Military Relations* (Cambridge, Mass.: Harvard University Press, 1957), p. 255; Allan Millett, *Military Professionalism and Officership in America*, Mershon Center Briefing Paper 2 (Columbus: Ohio State University Press, 1977).

⁵ Morris Janowitz, *The Professional Soldier: A Social and Political Portrait* (New York: Free Press, 1960), pp. 233–55; Brown, "Social Attitudes of American Generals," pp. 30, 78–79, 212; Millett, *Politics of Intervention*, pp. 12–13; Lane, *Armed Progressive*, pp. 91–97; Gates, "Alleged Isolation," pp. 32–45; Gillette, "Occupation of Cuba," pp. 410–25; Bacevich, *Diplomat in Khaki*, pp. 15, 18.

⁶ Gates, "Indians and Insurrectos," p. 63.

⁷ Millett, *Politics of Intervention*, p. 7.

⁸ Miller, *Benevolent Assimilation*, p. 162; Efficiency Reports for James A. Ryan, 1891, 1900, 1901, 1902, 1903, 6509 ACP–1890, RG 94, NARA.

⁹ Bacevich, *Diplomat in Khaki*, p. 26; Gates, *Schoolbooks*, pp. 279–80.

¹⁰ Gates, "Indians and Insurrectos," p. 65.

¹¹ Linn, *Counterinsurgency in the Philippine War*, p. 169.

¹² Langley, *The Banana Wars*, pp. 222–23; Millett, "'Cleansing the Augean Stables,'" 4:123–41; Millett, "Useful Lessons of the Caribbean Interventions," 4:142–57.

SELECT BIBLIOGRAPHY

The extensive number of materials used makes a complete bibliography impossible. The following is a partial listing of the sources consulted.

Archival Sources

Carlisle Barracks, Pa. U.S. Army Military History Institute.
   Personal papers and manuscript collections of Bell, J. Franklin; Birkhimer, William E.; Brown, William C.; Bury, Frederick E.; Crook, George; Davis, George B.; Finley, John P.; Fiske, Harold; Gerhardt, Charles; Godfrey, Edward S., Sr.; Helmick, Eli; Henry, Guy V., Jr.; Hobbs, Horace P.; Honaker, Samuel; Kobbe, William A.; Longuevan, Joseph B.; Lyon, Samuel; McLaughlin, Clenard; McMaster, Richard H.; Macmorland, Elliot; Marmon, Joseph A.; Maus, Marion P.; Rhodes, Charles D.; Ridgway, Matthew B.; Sladen Family Papers; Steele, Matthew F.; and Yarborough, LeRoy.
   Spanish-American War Survey; Army War College curricular files, 1907–40.
Fort Benning, Ga. Infantry School. Student essays and Infantry School Academic Department instructional matter.
Fort Leavenworth, Kans. Command and General Staff College. Student papers and curricular materials.
Maxwell Air Force Base, Ala. U.S. Air Force Historical Research Center. Army Air Corps Tactical School curricular files.
Washington, D.C. Library of Congress.
   Personal papers and manuscript collections of Allen, Henry T.; Bliss, Tasker; Bullard, Robert L.; Corbin, Henry C.; Harbord, James G.; Merrill, John N.; Moseley, George Van Horn; Palmer, John McAuley; Pershing, John J.; Roosevelt, Theodore; Root, Elihu; Scott, Hugh L.; Wilson, James H.; and Wood, Leonard.
Washington, D.C. National Archives and Records Administration.
   Record Group (RG) 94, Records of the Adjutant General's Office.
   RG 120, Records of American Expeditionary Forces, 1917–21, including Records of the Punitive Expedition in Mexico and

Records of U.S. Forces in North Russia.
RG 140, Records of the Military Government of Cuba.
RG 141, Records of the Vera Cruz Military Government.
RG 153, Records of the Judge Advocate General's Office.
RG 165, Records of the War Department General Staff, including Records of the Military Intelligence Division, Records of the War College Division, Records of the War Plans Division, and Army War College monographs, reports, and studies.
RG 199, Records of the Provisional Government of Cuba.
RG 350, Records of the Bureau of Insular Affairs.
RG 393, Records of the U.S. Army Continental Commands. Part 5. Posts.
RG 395, Records of U.S. Army Overseas Operations and Commands, including Records of the Army of Cuban Pacification; Records of the China Relief Expedition; Records of the Division of the Philippines; Records of the Panama Canal Department; Records of the Punitive Expedition to Mexico; Records of U.S. Army Troops in China; Records of U.S. Expeditionary Forces, Vera Cruz; and World War I Organizational Records, AEF, Siberia.
RG 407, Records of the Adjutant General's Office. Administrative Services Division. Operations Branch. Special Projects, War Plans—Color, 1920–48.
Washington, D.C. U.S. Marine Corps Historical Center. Harold H. Utley Papers.
West Point, N.Y. U.S. Military Academy. George L. Welker Papers.

Dissertations

Beamer, Carl. "Gray Ghostbusters: Eastern Theater Union Counterguerrilla Operations in the Civil War, 1861–65." Ohio State University, 1988.

Brown, Richard. "Social Attitudes of American Generals, 1898–1940." University of Wisconsin, 1951.

Calhoun, Frederick. "The Wilsonian Way of War: American Armed Power From Veracruz to Vladivostok." University of Chicago, 1983.

Coats, George. "The Philippine Constabulary, 1901–17." Ohio State University, 1968.

Crouch, Thomas. "The Making of a Soldier: The Career of Frederick Funston, 1865–1902." University of Texas at Austin, 1969.

Dederer, John. "The Origins and Development of American Conceptions of War to 1775." University of Alabama, 1988.

DeMontravel, Peter. "The Career of Lieutenant General Nelson A. Miles From the Civil War Through the Indian Wars." St. Johns University, 1983.
Donnell, Guy. "U.S. Intervention in Mexico, 1914." University of Texas, 1951.
Fritz, David. "The Philippine Question: American Civil/Military Policy in the Philippines, 1898–1905." University of Texas at Austin, 1977.
Griess, Thomas. "Dennis Hart Mahan: West Point Professor and Advocate of Military Professionalism, 1830–1871." Duke University, 1968.
Grimsley, Christopher. "A Directed Severity: The Evolution of Federal Policy Toward Southern Civilians and Property." Ohio State University, 1992.
Hutton, Paul. "General Philip H. Sheridan and the Army in the West, 1867–88." Indiana University, 1981.
Jornacion, George. "The Time of the Eagles: U.S. Army Officers and the Pacification of the Philippine Moros, 1899–1913." University of Maine, 1973.
Linn, Brian. "The War in Luzon: U.S. Army Regional Counterinsurgency in the Philippine War, 1900–1902." Ohio State University, 1985.
Mangrum, Robert. "Edwin M. Stanton's Special Military Units and the Prosecution of the War, 1862–65." North Texas State University, 1978.
Mason, Joyce. "The Use of Indian Scouts in the Apache Wars, 1870–86." Indiana University Press, 1970.
Mulrooney, Virginia. "No Victor, No Vanquished: U.S. Military Government in the Philippine Islands, 1898–1901." University of California, Los Angeles, 1975.
Nolan, William. "America's Participation in the Military Defense of Shanghai, 1931–41." St. Louis University, 1978.
Parker, King Lawrence. "Anglo-American Wilderness Campaigning, 1754–64: Logistical and Tactical Developments." Columbia University, 1970.
Pfanz, Harry. "Soldiering in the South During the Reconstruction Period, 1865–77." Ohio State University, 1958.
Roberts, Larry. "The Artillery With the Regular Army in the West From 1866 to 1890." Oklahoma State University, 1981.
Smith, Sherry. "Civilization's Guardians: Army Officers' Reflections on Indians and the Indian Wars in the Trans–Mississippi West, 1848–1890." University of Washington, 1984.

Tan, Samuel. "The Muslim Armed Struggle in the Philippines, 1900–41." Syracuse University, 1973.
Thompson, Wayne. "Governors of the Moro Province: Wood, Bliss, and Pershing in the Southern Philippines, 1903–13." University of California, San Diego, 1975.
Ulrich, William. "The Northern Military Mind in Regard to Reconstruction, 1865–72: The Attitude of Ten Leading Union Generals." Ohio State University, 1959.
Waghelstein, John. "Preparing for the Wrong War: The United States Army and Low Intensity Conflict, 1755–1890." Temple University, 1990.
Welty, Raymond. "The Western Army Frontier, 1860–70." University of Iowa, 1924.
Woolard, James. "The Philippine Scouts: The Development of America's Colonial Army." Ohio State University, 1975.
Zuczek, Richard. "State of Rebellion: People's War in Reconstruction South Carolina, 1865–77." Ohio State University, 1993.

Books, Manuals, and Published Reports

Ackerman, Carl. *Trailing the Bolsheviki*. New York: Charles Scribner's Sons, 1919.
Albertson, Ralph. *Fighting Without a War*. New York: Harcourt, Brace & Howe, 1920.
Ambrose, Stephen. *Halleck: Lincoln's Chief of Staff*. Baton Rouge: Louisiana State Press, 1962.
—————. *Upton and the Army*. Baton Rouge: Louisiana State University Press, 1964.
Asprey, Robert. *War in the Shadows: The Guerrilla in History*. 2 vols. Garden City, N.Y.: Doubleday, 1975.
Bacevich, A. J. *Diplomat in Khaki: Major General Frank Ross McCoy and American Foreign Policy*. Manhattan: University of Kansas Press, 1989.
Bacon, Robert, and Scott, James, eds. *The Military and Colonial Policy of the United States: Addresses and Reports by Elihu Root*. Cambridge, Mass., 1916.
Baker, Joseph, and Crocker, Henry. *The Laws of Land Warfare Concerning the Rights and Duties of Belligerents*. Washington, D.C.: Government Printing Office, 1919.
Baldwin, Alice. *Memoirs of the Late Frank D. Baldwin, Major General, U.S. Army*. Los Angeles, 1929.
Ball, Harry. *Of Responsible Command: A History of the Army War*

College. Carlisle Barracks, Pa.: Alumni Association of the U.S. Army War College, 1983.
Bauer, K. Jack. *The Mexican War, 1846–48.* New York: Macmillan, 1974.
Beckett, Ian, ed. *The Roots of Counter-Insurgency: Armies and Guerrilla Warfare, 1900–45.* New York: Blandford Press, 1988.
Beede, Benjamin. *Intervention and Counterinsurgency: An Annotated Bibliography of the Small Wars of the United States, 1898–1984.* New York: Garland, 1985.
Beringer, Richard, et al. *Why the South Lost the Civil War.* Athens: University of Georgia Press, 1986.
Bigelow, John. *The Principles of Strategy, Illustrated Mainly From American Campaigns.* New York: Greenwood Press, 1968.
Birkhimer, William. *Military Government and Martial Law.* Washington, D.C.: James Chapman, 1892.
──────. *Military Government and Martial Law.* Kansas City, Mo.: Frank Hudson, 1904.
Bisbee, William. *Through Four American Wars.* Boston: Meador Publishing Company, 1931.
Blount, James. *The American Occupation of the Philippines, 1898–1912.* New York: G. P. Putnam's Sons, 1912.
Booth, Ewing. *My Observations and Experiences in the U.S. Army.* 1944.
Bourke, John. *On the Border With Crook.* Lincoln: University of Nebraska Press, 1971.
Brackett, Albert. *General Lane's Brigade in Central Mexico.* New York: J. C. Derby, 1854.
Braddy, Haldeen. *Pershing's Mission in Mexico.* El Paso: Texas Western Press, 1973.
Brownlee, Richard. *Gray Ghosts of the Confederacy: Guerrilla Warfare in the West, 1861–65.* Baton Rouge: Louisiana University Press, 1958.
Bruce, Robert. *The Fighting Norths and Pawnee Scouts.* New York, 1932.
Bugbee, Fred. "The AEF in Siberia." *Monographs of the World War.* Fort Benning, Ga.: Infantry School, 1923.
Callwell, Charles. *Small Wars: Their Principles and Practice.* London: Harrison & Sons, 1906.
Capers, Gerald. *Occupied City: New Orleans Under the Federals.* Manhattan: University of Kansas Press, 1965.
Carpenter, John. *Sword and Olive Branch: Oliver Otis Howard.* Pittsburgh, 1964.

Carte, Gene and Elaine. *Police Reform in the United States*. Berkeley: University of California Press, 1975.

Carter, William H. *The Life of Lieutenant General Chaffee*. Chicago, 1917.

Clark, W. P. *The Indian Sign Language*. Philadelphia: L. R. Hamesly, 1885.

Clendenen, Clarence. *Blood on the Border: The U.S. Army and the Mexican Irregulars*. London: Macmillan, 1969.

Cloman, Sydney. *Myself and a Few Moros*. Garden City, N.Y.: Doubleday, 1923.

Coffman, Edward. *The Hilt of the Sword*. Madison: University of Wisconsin Press, 1966.

_____. *The Old Army*. New York: Oxford University Press, 1986.

Cohen, Felix. *Handbook of Federal Indian Law*. Washington, D.C.: Department of the Interior, 1945.

Coles, Harry. *Civil Affairs: Soldiers Become Governors*. Washington, D.C.: U.S. Army Center of Military History, Government Printing Office, 1964.

Cooke, Philip St. George. *Cavalry Tactics*. 2 vols. Philadelphia: J. B. Lippincott, 1862.

Cornebise, Alfred. *Typhus and Doughboys: The American Polish Relief Expedition, 1919–21*. Newark: University of Delaware Press, 1982.

Costello, Harry. *Why Did We Go to Russia?* Detroit, Mich.: Harry J. Costello, 1920.

Crandall, Warren, and Newell, Isaac. *History of the Ram Fleet and the Mississippi Marine Brigade in the War for the Union on the Mississippi and Its Tributaries*. St. Louis, 1907.

Crane, Charles J. *The Experiences of a Colonel of Infantry*. New York: Knickerbocker Press, 1923.

Crook, George. *General George Crook: His Autobiography*. Norman: University of Oklahoma Press, 1960.

_____. *Resume of Operations Against Apache Indians, 1882 to 1886*. Washington, D.C.: War Department, 1886.

Cruz, Romeo. *America's Colonial Desk and the Philippines, 1898–1934*. Quezon City: University of the Philippines Press, 1974.

Daggett, Aaron. *America in the China Relief Expedition*. Kansas City: Hudson-Kimberly, 1903.

Daly, H. W. *Manual of Pack Transportation*. Washington, D.C.: Government Printing Office, 1910.

Davis, George. *The Elements of International Law*. New York: Harper & Brothers, 1903.

———. *Outlines of International Law*. London: Sampson, Low, Marston, Searle & Rivington, 1888.
Dawson, Joseph. *Army Generals and Reconstruction: Louisiana, 1862–77*. Baton Rouge: Louisiana State University, 1982.
Dilworth, Donald, ed. *The Blue and the Brass: American Policing, 1890–1910*. Gaithersburg, Md.: International Association of Chiefs of Police, 1976.
Dodge, Grenville. "The Army in the Philippines." *Military Order of the Loyal Legion of the United States, New York*. Series III, no. 18.
Dowell, Cassius. *Military Aid to Civil Power*. Fort Leavenworth, Kans.: General Service Schools, 1925.
Dunlay, Thomas. *Wolves for the Blue Soldiers*. Lincoln: University of Nebraska Press, 1982.
Ehrhardt, Arthur. *Guerrilla Warfare: Lessons of the Past and Possibilities of the Future*. Fort Leavenworth, Kans.: Command and General Staff School, 1936.
Elarth, Harold. *The Story of the Philippine Constabulary*. Los Angeles: Globe Printing, 1949.
Elliott, Charles. *The Philippines to the End of Commission Government*. Indianapolis: Bobbs-Merrill Company, 1917.
Ellis, Richard. *General Pope and U.S. Indian Policy*. Albuquerque: University of New Mexico Press, 1970.
Farrow, Edward. *Mountain Scouting*. New York, 1881.
Fellman, Michael. *Inside War: The Guerrilla Conflict in Missouri During the American Civil War*. New York: Oxford University Press, 1989.
Finney, Charles. *Old China Hands*. Garden City, N.Y.: Doubleday, 1961.
Flint, Roy. "The U.S. Army on the Pacific Frontier, 1899–1939." In *The American Military and the Far East*, Proceedings of the Ninth Military History Symposium, edited by Joe Dixon. U.S. Air Force Academy, 1980.
Forbes, W. Cameron. *The Philippine Islands*. 2 vols. New York: Houghton Mifflin, 1928.
Franklin, Charles. *History of the Philippine Scouts, 1899–1934*. Washington, D.C.: Historical Section, Army War College, 1935.
Funston, Frederick. *Memories of Two Wars*. New York: Charles Scribner's Sons, 1911.
Gates, John. "The Limits of Power: The U.S. Conquest of the Philippines." In *Great Powers and Little Wars: The Limits of Power*, edited by A. Hamish Ion and E. J. Errington. Westport, Conn.: Praeger, 1993.

_____. "The Pacification of the Philippines, 1898–1902." In *The American Military and the Far East*, Proceedings of the Ninth Military History Symposium, edited by Joe Dixon. U.S. Air Force Academy, 1980.

_____. *Schoolbooks and Krags*. Westport, Conn.: Greenwood Press, 1973.

Goldhurst, Richard. *The Midnight War: The American Intervention in Russia, 1918–20*. New York: McGraw-Hill, 1978.

Goodhart, Briscoe. *History of the Independent Loudoun Virginia Rangers*. Washington, D.C.: McGill & Wallace, 1896.

Gowing, Peter. *Mandate in Moroland*. Quezon City: Philippine Center for Advanced Studies, 1977.

Graber, Doris. *The Development of the Law of Belligerent Occupation, 1863–1914*. Columbia Studies in History, Economics, and Public Law 543. New York: Columbia University Press, 1949.

Graff, Henry. *American Imperialism and the Philippine Insurrection*. Boston: Little, Brown & Company, 1969.

Graves, William. *America's Siberian Adventure, 1918–20*. New York: Jonathan Cope and Harrison Smith, 1931.

Great Britain. *Field Service Regulations. I. Operations*. London: His Majesty's Stationary Office, 1909.

Grieb, Kenneth. *The United States and Huerta*. Lincoln: University of Nebraska Press, 1969.

Guthman, William. *March to Massacre*. New York: McGraw-Hill, 1975.

Hagedorn, Herman. *Leonard Wood*. New York: Harper & Brothers, 1931.

Haley, Edward. "Comparative Intervention: Mexico in 1914 and Dominica in 1965." In *Intervention or Abstention: The Dilemma of American Foreign Policy*, edited by Robin Higham. Lexington: University of Kentucky Press, 1975.

_____. *Revolution and Intervention: The Diplomacy of Taft and Wilson With Mexico, 1910–17*. Cambridge, Mass.: Massachusetts Institute of Technology (MIT) Press, 1970.

Halleck, Henry W. *Elements of the Military Art*. New York, 1846.

_____. *International Law; or, Rules Regulating the Intercourse of States in Peace and War*. New York: Van Nostrand, 1861.

Hartigan, Richard. *Lieber's Code and the Law of War*. Chicago: Precedent, 1983.

Hattaway, Herman, and Jones, Archer. *How the North Won*. Chicago: University of Illinois Press, 1983.

Healy, David. *The United States in Cuba, 1898–1902: Generals,*

Politicians, and the Search for Policy. Madison: University of Wisconsin Press, 1963.

Higham, Robin, and Brandt, Carol, eds. *The United States Army in Peacetime.* Manhattan, Kans.: Military Affairs/Aerospace Historian Publications, 1975.

Hinkle, Stacy. *Wings and Saddles: The Air and Cavalry Punitive Expedition of 1919.* El Paso: Texas Western Press, 1967.

Holley, I. B. *General John M. Palmer, Citizen Soldiers, and the Army of a Democracy.* Westport, Conn.: Greenwood Press, 1982.

Hopkins, Ernest. *Our Lawless Police.* New York: Viking, 1931.

Howard, Oliver. *My Life and Experiences Among Our Hostile Indians.* Hartford, Conn., 1907.

Huntington, Samuel. *The Soldier and the State: The Theory and Politics of Civil-Military Relations.* Cambridge, Mass.: Harvard University Press, 1957.

Hurley, Vic. *Jungle Patrol.* New York: E. P. Dutton, 1938.

Hutchins, James. "Mounted Riflemen: The Real Role of Cavalry in the Indian Wars." In *Probing the American West*, edited by K. Ross Toole. Santa Fe: Museum of New Mexico Press, 1962.

Hutton, Paul, ed. *Soldiers West: Biographies From the Military Frontier.* Lincoln: University of Nebraska Press, 1987.

Jamieson, Perry. *Crossing the Deadly Ground: U.S. Army Tactics, 1865–1899.* Tuscaloosa: University of Alabama Press, 1994.

Janowitz, Morris. *The Professional Soldier: A Social and Political Portrait.* New York: Free Press, 1960.

Jessup, Philip. *Elihu Root.* New York: Dodd, Mead & Company, 1938.

Jomini, Antoine Henri. *The Art of War.* Philadelphia: J. B. Lippincott, 1862.

Jones, Virgil. *Gray Ghosts and Rebel Raiders.* New York: Henry Holt, 1956.

Karnow, Stanley. *In Our Image: America's Empire in the Philippines.* New York: Ballantine Books, 1979.

Karsten, Peter. "Armed Progressives: The Military Reorganizes for the American Century." In *Building the Organizational Society*, edited by Jerry Israel. New York: Free Press, 1972.

Kennan, George. *Soviet-American Relations, 1917–20.* vol. 2. *The Decision To Intervene.* Princeton, N.J.: Princeton University Press, 1958.

Kent, James. *Commentaries on American Law.* 2 vols. New York: O. Halsted, 1826.

Kidd, Worth. *Police Interrogation.* New York: R. V. Basurio, 1940.

Kindall, Sylvian. *American Soldiers in Siberia.* New York: Richard

Smith, 1945.

Klare, Michael. "The Interventionist Impulse: U.S. Military Doctrine for Low-Intensity Warfare." In *Low-Intensity Warfare*, edited by Michael Klare and Peter Kornbluh. New York: Pantheon, 1988.

Lane, Jack. *Armed Progressive: General Leonard Wood*. San Rafael, Calif,: Presidio Press, 1978.

Langley, Lester. *The Banana Wars: United States Intervention in the Caribbean, 1898–1934*. Lexington: University of Kentucky Press, 1985.

Laqueur, Walter. *The Guerrilla Reader: A Historical Anthology*. New York: Meridan, 1977.

Leonard, Thomas. *Above the Battle: War Making in America From Appomattox to Versailles*. New York: Oxford University Press, 1978.

_____. "Red, White, and Army Blue. Empathy and Anger in the American West." In *The Military in America*, edited by Peter Karsten. New York: Free Press, 1980.

Levy, Bert. "Guerrilla Warfare." In *The Infantry Journal Reader*, edited by Joseph Greene. Garden City, N.Y.: Doubleday, Doran & Company, 1943.

Linn, Brian. *The U.S. Army and Counterinsurgency in the Philippine War, 1899–1902*. Chapel Hill: University of North Carolina Press, 1989.

Liss, Sheldon. *The Canal*. South Bend, Ind.: University of Notre Dame Press, 1967.

Lockmiller, David. *Magoon in Cuba: A History of the Second Intervention, 1906–09*. Chapel Hill: University of North Carolina Press, 1938.

Luckett, Richard. *The White Generals: An Account of the White Movement and the Russian Civil War*. New York: Routledge and Kegan Paul, 1987.

McCain, William. *The United States and the Republic of Panama*. New York: Russell and Russell, 1965.

McPherson, James. *Battle Cry of Freedom*. New York: Ballantine, 1988.

Magoon, Charles. *Reports on the Law of Civil Government in Territories Subject to Military Occupation by the Military Forces of the United States*. Washington, D.C., 1903.

Mahan, Dennis. *An Elementary Treatise on Advanced Guard, Out-Post, and Detachment Service of Troops With the Essential Principles of Strategy and Grand Tactics*. New York, 1847.

_____. *An Elementary Treatise on Advanced Guard, Out-Post,*

and Detachment Service of Troops With the Essential Principles of Strategy and Grand Tactics. New York: John Wiley, 1863.
Mahon, John. *History of the Second Seminole War*. Gainesville: University of Florida Press, 1967.
Manning, Clarence. *The Siberian Fiasco*. New York: Library Publishing, 1952.
Marcy, Randolph. *The Prairie Traveler, A Hand-book for Overland Expeditions*. Williamstown, Mass.: Corner House, 1978.
Maslowski, Peter. *Treason Must Be Made Odious*. Millwood, N.Y.: Kto Press, 1978.
Mason, Herbert. *The Great Pursuit*. New York: Random House, 1970.
May, Glenn. *Battle for Batangas*. New Haven, Conn.: Yale University Press, 1991.
_____. *Social Engineering in the Philippines*. Westport, Conn.: Greenwood Press, 1980.
Mercur, James. *Elements of the Art of War*. West Point, N.Y.: U.S. Military Academy Press, 1889.
Merritt, Wesley. *Merritt and the Indian Wars*. London, 1972.
Miles, Nelson. *Serving the Republic*. New York: Harper & Brothers, 1911.
Miller, Stuart. *'Benevolent Assimilation': The American Conquest of the Philippines, 1899–1903*. New Haven, Conn.: Yale University Press, 1982.
Millett, Allan. "'Cleansing the Augean Stables': The American Armed Forces in the Caribbean, 1898–1914." *Essays in Some Dimensions of Military History*. vol. 4. Carlisle Barracks, Pa.: U.S. Army Military History Institute, n.d.
_____. *The General, Robert L. Bullard and Officership in the U.S. Army, 1881–1925*. Westport, Conn.: Greenwood Press, 1975.
_____. *Military Professionalism and Officership in America*. Mershon Center Briefing Paper 2. Columbus: Ohio State University Press, 1977.
_____. *The Politics of Intervention: The Military Occupation of Cuba, 1906–1909*. Columbus: Ohio State University, 1968.
_____. *Semper Fidelis: The History of the United States Marine Corps*. New York: Macmillan, 1980.
_____, and Maslowski, Peter. *For the Common Defense*. New York: Free Press, 1984.
Millett, Richard. *Guardians of the Dynasty*. Orbis Books, 1977.
_____. "Useful Lessons of the Caribbean Interventions." *Essays in Some Dimensions of Military History*. vol. 4. Carlisle Barracks, Pa.: U.S. Army Military History Institute, n.d.

Mitchell, Frederick. "Fighting Guerrillas on the La Forche." In Military Order of the Loyal Legion of the United States, Commandery of the District of Columbia, *War Papers* 56. 1905.

Moore, Joel, et al., *The History of the American Expedition Fighting the Bolsheviki*. Detroit, Mich.: Polar Bear Publishing, 1920.

Morse, Charles. "The Relief of Chattanooga, October 1863, and Guerrilla Operations in Tennessee." In *Civil War and Miscellaneous Papers, Papers of the Military Historical Society of Massachusetts*. Boston: Military Historical Society of Massachusetts, 1918.

Mosby, John. *The Memoirs of Colonel John S. Mosby*. Boston: Little, Brown & Company, 1917.

Nash, Howard. *Stormy Petrel: The Life and Times of General Benjamin F. Butler, 1818–93*. Rutherford, N.J.: Fairleigh Dickinson University Press, 1969.

Nelson, Harold. *Leon Trotsky and the Art of Insurrection, 1905–17*. London: Frank Cass, 1988.

Nenninger, Timothy. *The Leavenworth Schools and the Old Army*. Westport, Conn.: Greenwood Press, 1978.

Ney, Virgil. *Evolution of the U.S. Army Field Manual, Valley Forge to Vietnam*. Combat Operations Research Group, CORG Memorandum 244, January 1966.

Noble, Dennis. *The Eagle and the Dragon: The United States Military in China, 1901–37*. New York: Greenwood Press, 1990.

Nohl, Lessing. "MacKenzie Against Dull Knife: Breaking the Northern Cheyennes in 1876." In *Probing the American West*, edited by K. Ross Toole. Santa Fe: Museum of New Mexico Press, 1962.

Noyes, Charles. "The Services of Graduates in China, 1900–01." *The Centennial of the United States Military Academy at West Point, New York*. vol. 1. Washington, D.C.: Government Printing Office, 1904.

Ochosa, Orlino. *The Tinio Brigade: Anti-American Resistance in the Ilocos Provinces, 1899–1901*. Quezon City, Philippines: New Day Publishers, 1989.

O'Connor, Richard. *The Spirit Soldiers*. New York: G. P. Putnam's Sons, 1973.

Otis, Elwell. "Filipino Characteristics as Manifested in Diplomacy and War." In *Civil War and Miscellaneous Papers of the Military Historical Society of Massachusetts*. vol. 14. Boston: Military Historical Society of Massachusetts, 1918.

———. *The Indian Question*. New York, 1878.

Owen, Norman, ed. *Compadre Colonialism: Studies on the Philippines*

Under American Rule. Ann Arbor: University of Michigan Press, 1971.
Palmer, Frederick. *Bliss, Peacemaker*. New York: Dodd, Mead & Company, 1934.
Parker, James. *The Old Army Memories*. Philadelphia: Dorrance & Company, 1929.
Parkhurst, Charles. "Incidents of Cavalry Service in Louisiana." In *Personal Narratives of the Battles of the Rebellion*. Rhode Island Soldiers and Sailors Historical Society 7. Providence, R.I.: Sidney S. Rider, 1879.
Parton, James. *General Butler in New Orleans*. Boston: Ticknor & Fields, 1866.
Perez, Louis. *Army Politics in Cuba, 1898–1956*. Pittsburgh: University of Pittsburgh Press, 1976.
Philippine Constabulary. *Manual for the Philippine Constabulary, 1907*. Manila: Bureau of Printing, 1906.
──────. *Manual for the Philippine Constabulary, 1907*. Manila: Bureau of Printing, 1922.
Pope, Benjamin. "The Causes of the Boxer Uprising and the Battle of Tientsin." In *Monographs of the World War*. Fort Benning, Ga.: Infantry School, 1923.
Porch, Douglas. "Bugeaud, Gallieni, Lyautey: The Development of French Colonial Warfare." In *Makers of Modern Strategy*, edited by Peter Paret. Princeton, N.J.: Princeton University Press, 1986.
Price, Barbara. *Police Professionalism*. Lexington, Mass.: D. C. Heath, 1977.
Prucha, Francis. *The Sword of the Republic*. Bloomington: Indiana University Press, 1969.
Purcell, Victor. *The Boxer Uprising*. London: Cambridge University Press, 1963.
Quirk, Robert. *An Affair of Honor: Woodrow Wilson and the Occupation of Veracruz*. Lexington: University of Kentucky Press, 1962.
Ramage, James. *Rebel Raider: The Life of General John Hunt Morgan*. Lexington: University of Kentucky Press, 1986.
Rattan, Donald. "Counterguerrilla Operations: A Case Study." In U.S. Army Office of Chief of Information. *Special Warfare, U.S. Army*. 1962.
Reedstrom, E. Lisle. *Apache Wars*. New York: Sterling Publishing, 1990.
Reston, James. *Sherman's March and Vietnam*. New York: Macmillan, 1984.

Rhodes, Benjamin. *The Anglo-American Winter War With Russia, 1918–19.* New York: Greenwood Press, 1988.

Rister, Carl. *Border Command: General Phil Sheridan in the West.* Norman: University of Oklahoma Press, 1944.

Romeyn, Henry. "Scouting in Tennessee." In Military Order of the Loyal Legion of the United States, Commandery of the District of Columbia, *War Papers* 59. 1905.

Ross, Charles. "Scouting for Bushwhackers in West Virginia in 1861." *War Papers Read Before the Commandery of Wisconsin, Military Order of the Loyal Legion of the United States.* Milwaukee: Burdick & Allen, 1903.

Ross, Steven, ed. *American War Plans, 1919–41.* New York: Garland, 1992.

Roth, Russell. *Muddy Glory: America's 'Indian Wars' in the Philippines, 1899–1935.* W. Hanover, Mass.: Christopher Publishing, 1981.

Saleeby, Najeeb. *The Moro Problem.* Manila, 1913.

Schofield, John. *Forty-Six Years in the Army.* New York: Century Company, 1897.

Schott, Joseph. *The Ordeal of Samar.* New York: Bobbs-Merrill, 1964.

Scott, Hugh. *Some Memories of a Soldier.* New York: Century, 1928.

Scott, William. *Ilocano Responses to American Aggression, 1900–1901.* Quezon City, Philippines: New Day Publications, 1986.

Sefton, James. *The U.S. Army and Reconstruction, 1865–77.* Baton Rouge: Louisiana University Press, 1967.

Sexton, Thaddeus. *Soldiers in the Sun.* Harrisburg, Pa.: Military Service Publishers, 1939.

Sheridan, Philip. *Personal Memoirs of P.H. Sheridan.* New York: Charles Webster, 1888.

Sherman, William. *Personal Memoirs of General W.T. Sherman.* New York, 1890.

Smith, Harry. *Military Government.* Fort Leavenworth, Kans.: Command and General Staff School, 1920.

Smith, James. *A Treatise on the Mode and Manner of Indian War.* Paris, Ky.: Joel R. Lyle, 1812.

Smith, Justin. *The War With Mexico.* 2 vols. New York: Macmillan, 1919.

Smythe, Donald. *Guerrilla Warrior: The Early Life of J.J. Pershing.* New York: Charles Scribner's Sons, 1973.

Stackpole, Edward. *Sheridan in the Shenandoah.* Harrisburg, Pa.: Stackpole Company, 1961.

Starr, Stephen. *The Union Cavalry in the Civil War*. 3 vols. Baton Rouge: Louisiana State University Press, 1979.

Stevenson, Roger. *Military Instructions for Officers Detached in the Field; Containing a Scheme for Forming a Corps of a Partisan, Illustrated With Plans of Manoeuvers Necessary in Carrying on Petite Guerre*. Philadelphia: Aitken, 1775.

Storey, Moorfield, and Lichauco, Marcial. *The Conquest of the Philippines by the United States, 1898–1925*. New York: G. P. Putnam's Sons, 1926.

Strakhovsky, Leonid. *Intervention at Archangel*. Princeton, N.J.: Princeton University Press, 1944.

Sweetman, Jack. *The Landing at Veracruz*. Annapolis, Md.: U.S. Naval Institute Press, 1968.

Swift, Eben. "Services of Graduates of West Point in Indian Wars." In *The Centennial of the United States Military Academy at West Point, New York*. vol. 1. Washington, D.C.: Government Printing Office, 1904.

Tan, Chester. *The Boxer Catastrophe*. New York: Columbia, 1955.

Taylor, John R. M. *The Philippine Insurrection Against the United States*. 5 vols. Pasay City, Philippines: Eugenio Lopez Foundation, 1971.

Telegraphic Circulars and General Orders, Regulating Campaign Against Insurgents and Proclamations and Circular Letters Relating to Reconstruction After the Close of War in the Provinces of Batangas, Laguna, and Mindoro, Philippine Islands, Issued by Brigadier General J. Franklin Bell, Batangas, Philippine Islands. HQ, 3d Separate Brigade, 1902.

Thomas, David. *A History of Military Government in Newly Acquired Territory of the United States*. New York: Columbia University Press, 1904.

Thompson, Gerald. *The Army and the Navajo: The Bosque Redondo Reservation Experiment, 1863–68*. Tucson: University of Arizona Press, 1976.

Thompson, Neil. *Crazy Horse Called Them Walk-a-Heaps*. St. Cloud, Minn.: North Star Press, 1979.

Tompkins, Frank. *Chasing Villa: The Story Behind the Story of Pershing's Expedition Into Mexico*. Harrisburg, Pa.: Military Service Publishing Company, 1934.

Toulmin, Harry. *With Pershing in Mexico*. Harrisburg, Pa.: Military Service Publishing Company, 1935.

Trotter, William. *Bushwhackers! The Civil War in North Carolina*. vol. 2. *The Mountains*. Greensboro, N.C.: Signal Research, 1988.

Twichell, Heath. *Allen: The Biography of an Army Officer, 1859–1930*. New Brunswick, N.J.: Rutgers University Press, 1974.

Unterberger, Betty. *America's Siberian Expedition, 1918–20*. Durham, N.C.: Duke University Press, 1956.

U.S. Army. Army Staff College. *Law Theses of the Staff Class*. vol. 2. *1910–11*. 1911.

———. *Military Government, Papers Prepared by the Class of 1908*. Fort Leavenworth, Kans., March 1908.

———. Cavalry School. *Cavalry Combat*. Cavalry School, 1937.

———. Command and General Service Schools. *Annual Report of Command and General Staff School, 1930–31*. 1931.

———. Command and General Staff School. *Mountain Warfare*. Fort Leavenworth, Kans.: Command and General Staff School Press, 1935.

———. *Problems, Second Year Course, 1931–32*. 1932.

———. *Special Operations*. 1937.

———. General Service Schools. *Annual Report, General Service Schools*. 1921, 1922.

———. "Expeditionary Force." *Command, Staff and Logistics, A Tentative Text*. Fort Leavenworth, Kans.: General Service Schools, 1929.

———. *Instructors Summary of Military Articles*. (eventually redesignated *Review of Current Military Writings*). 1922–41.

———. Infantry School. *Infantry in Special Operations*. Special Text 13. Army Extension Courses. Fort Benning, Ga.: Infantry School, 1937.

———. Service Schools. *Annual Report of the U.S. Infantry and Cavalry School for the Years 1882–91*. 1907.

U.S. Congress. House. *Instructions Issued to Military Officers in the Philippines*. 57th Cong., 1st sess., 1902, H. Doc. 596.

———. Senate. *Conditions in the Philippines*. 56th Cong., 2d sess., 1901, S. Doc. 167.

———. Philippine Committee. *Charges of Cruelty, etc., to the Natives of the Philippines*. 57th Cong., 1st sess., 1902, S. Doc. 205.

———. *Hearings Before the Committee on the Philippines*. 57th Cong., 1st sess., 1902, S. Doc. 331.

———. *Issuance of Certain Military Orders in the Philippines*. 57th Cong., 1st sess., 1902, S. Doc. 347.

———. *Trials or Courts-Martial in the Philippine Islands in Consequence of Certain Instructions*. 57th Cong., 2d sess., 3 March 1903, S. Doc. 213.

U.S. Joint Board, *Joint Action of the Army and the Navy*. Washington,

D.C.: Government Printing Office, 1927.
U.S. Marine Corps. *Small Wars Manual*. Washington, D.C.: Government Printing Office, 1940.
U.S. Military Academy. *Annual Report, U.S. Military Academy*. 1902–1920.
———. *The Centennial of the U.S. Military Academy at West Point, New York*. 2 vols. Washington, D.C.: Government Printing Office, 1904.
U.S. War Department. *Annual Reports of the War Department*. Washington, D.C.: Government Printing Office, 1899–1910.
———. "The Blockhouse System in South Africa." *Notes of Military Interest for 1901*. No. 36. Washington, D.C., 1902.
———. *Colonial Army Systems*. Washington, D.C., 1901.
———. *Correspondence Relating to the War With Spain*. 2 vols. Washington, D.C.: Government Printing Office, 1902.
———. "Extracts From the Report of Major General Adna R. Chaffee, Commanding U.S. Troops in China, on Military Operations in China." In *Reports on Military Operations in South Africa and China*. Washington, D.C.: Government Printing Office, 1901.
———. *Field Service Regulations, 1905*. Washington, D.C.: Government Printing Office, 1905.
———. Field Manual (FM) 27–5. *Basic Field Manual, Military Government*. 1940.
———. FM 27–10. *Rules of Land Warfare*. 1940.
———. FM 30–15. *Basic Field Manual—Military Intelligence*. 1940.
———. FM 100–5. *Field Service Regulations, Operations*. 1941.
———. FM 100–5. *Tentative Field Service Regulations, Operations*. 1939.
———. *General Orders and Circulars, Division of the Philippines*. 1901, 1902.
———. *Infantry Drill Regulations, 1911*. Washington, D.C.: Government Printing Office, 1917.
———. *Outline Description of U.S. Military Posts and Stations in the Year 1871*. Washington, D.C.: Government Printing Office, 1872.
———. *Philippine Commission Annual Reports*. 1903–14.
———. *Regulations for the Army of the United States, 1857*. New York: Harper & Brothers, 1857.
———. *Report of Major General E.S. Otis, USA, Commanding General of the Philippines, Military Governor*. Washington, D.C.: Government Printing Office, 1900.

———. *Reports on Military Operations in South Africa and China.* Washington, D.C.: Government Printing Office, 1901.

———. *Revised United States Army Regulations of 1861.* Washington, D.C.: Government Printing Office, 1863.

———. *Road Notes, Cuba, 1909.* 1909.

———. *Rules of Land Warfare.* Washington, D.C.: Government Printing Office, 1917.

———. Training Regulation (TR) 15–70. *Field Service Regulations—Special Operations*, c. 1922.

———. *The War of the Rebellion: A Compilation of the Official Records of the Union and Confederate Armies.* 53 vols. Washington, D.C.: Government Printing Office, 1880–1901.

———. Military Intelligence Division. *Military Notes on Cuba, 1909.* Washington, D.C., 1909.

———. Philippine Commission. Bureau of the Constabulary. *Philippine Constabulary Circulars, 1906–17.* n.d.

Utley, Robert. "The Contribution of the Frontier to the American Military Tradition." In *Harmon Memorial Lectures in Military History* 19. Boulder, Colo.: U.S. Air Force Academy, 1977.

———. *Frontier Regulars: The United States Army and the Indian, 1866–1890.* New York: Macmillan, 1973.

———. *Frontiersmen in Blue: The United States Army and the Indian, 1848–65.* New York: Macmillan, 1967.

———. *The Indian Frontier of the American West.* Albuquerque: University of New Mexico Press, 1984.

Vandiver, Frank. *Black Jack: The Life and Times of John J. Pershing.* 2 vols. College Station: Texas A&M University Press, 1977.

Vattel, Emmerich. *The Law of Nations.* Philadelphia: T. & J. W. Johnson, 1863.

Vetock, Dennis. *Lessons Learned: A History of United States Army Lesson Learning.* Carlisle Barracks, Pa.: U.S. Army Military History Institute, 1988.

Wagner, Arthur. *Organization and Tactics.* Kansas City: Franklin Hudson Publishing Company, 1906.

———. *The Service of Security and Information.* Kansas City: Hudson-Kimberly Publishing Company, 1893.

———. *The Service of Security and Information.* Kansas City: Hudson-Kimberly Publishing Company, 1903.

Waite, Carleton. *Some Elements of International Military Cooperation in the Suppression of the 1900 Antiforeign Rising in China With Special Reference to the Forces of the United States.* Los Angeles: University of Southern California Press, 1935.

Walker, Samuel. *A Critical History of Police Reform*. Lexington, Mass.: D. C. Heath, 1977.
Wallace, Ernest. *Ranald S. Mackenzie on the Texas Frontier*. College Station: Texas A&M University Press, 1993.
Washburn, Wilcomb E. *Red Man's Land—White Man's Law: A Study of the Past and Present Status of the American Indian*. New York: Charles Scribner's Sons, 1971.
Weigley, Russell. *The American Way of War*. Bloomington: Indiana University Press, 1973.
──────. *History of the United States Army*. Bloomington: Indiana University Press, 1984.
──────. "The Long Death of the Indian-Fighting Army." In *Soldiers and Civilians: The U.S. Army and the American People*, edited by Garry Ryan and Timothy Nenninger. Washington, D.C.: National Archives and Records Administration, 1987.
──────. *Towards an American Army*. New York: Columbia University Press, 1962.
Welch, Richard. *Response to Imperialism: The United States and the Philippine-American War, 1899–1902*. Chapel Hill: University of North Carolina Press, 1979.
Wert, Jeffrey. *Mosby's Rangers*. New York: Simon & Schuster, 1990.
Wharfield, Harold. *With Scouts and Cavalry at Fort Apache*. Tucson: Pioneer's Historical Society, 1965.
Wheaton, Henry. *Elements of International Law*. Philadelphia: Lea & Blanchard, 1846.
Wheeler, J. B. *A Course of Instruction in the Elements of the Art and Science of War for the Use of the Cadets of the United States Military Academy*. New York: Van Nostrand, 1879.
──────. *A Course of Instruction in the Elements of the Art and Science of War for the Use of the Cadets of the United States Military Academy*. New York: Van Nostrand, 1893.
White, Herbert. "The Pacification of Batangas." *The Centennial of the U.S. Military Academy at West Point, New York*. Washington, D.C.: Government Printing Office, 1904.
White, John. *Bullets and Bolos*. New York: Century Company, 1928.
White, John. *The Siberian Intervention*. Princeton, N.J.: Princeton University Press, 1950.
Williams, T. Harry. *The History of American Wars From Colonial Times to World War I*. New York: Alfred Knopf, 1981.
Williamson, James. *Mosby's Rangers*. New York: Sturgis & Walton, 1909.
Wilson, James. *China Travels and Investigations in the 'Middle*

Kingdom'—A Study of Its Civilization and Possibilities Together With an Account of the Boxer War. New York: D. Appleton, 1901.

──────────. *Under the Old Flag*. 2 vols. Westport, Conn.: Greenwood Press, 1971.

Wolff, Leon. *Little Brown Brother*. Garden City, N.Y.: Doubleday, 1961.

Woolsey, Theodore. *Introduction to the Study of International Law*. Boston: James Monroe, 1864.

Wooster, Robert. *The Military and United States Indian Policy*. New Haven, Conn.: Yale University Press, 1988.

Young, William. *Manoeuvers, or Practical Observations on the Art of War*. 1771.

Articles

In addition to the articles listed below, the following periodicals were consulted extensively: *Army and Navy Journal, Army Ordnance, Cavalry Journal, Chemical Warfare, Coast Artillery Journal, Field Artillery Journal, Journal of the Military Service Institution of the United States, Journal of the U.S. Artillery, Infantry Journal, Infantry School Mailing List, Marine Corps Gazette, Military Engineer, Military Review, Quartermaster Review*, and *United Service*.

Ambrose, Stephen. "Dennis Hart Mahan." *Civil War Times* 2 (November 1963): 30–35.

Berthoff, Rowland. "Taft and McArthur, 1900–01: A Study in Civil-Military Relations." *World Politics* 5 (October 1952–July 1953): 196–211.

Bonsal, Stephen. "The Philippines—After an Earthquake." *North American Review* 174 (March 1902): 409–21.

Boughton, D. H. "How Soldiers Have Ruled in the Philippines." *International Quarterly* 6 (September 1902–March 1903): 215–28.

Bourke, John. "Crook in Indian Country." *Century Magazine* 4 (March 1891): 643–60.

Bowen, Don. "Counterrevolutionary Guerrilla War: Missouri, 1861–65." *Conflict* 8 (1988): 69–78.

Brinsfield, John. "The Military Ethics of General William T. Sherman: A Reassessment." *Parameters* 12 (June 1982): 36–48.

Bronson, H. V. "Visayan Campaigns. The Insurrection of the Sugar Planters on Panay." *Military Historian and Economist* 2 (July 1917): 299–308.

Brownell, Atherton. "Turning Savages Into Citizens." *Outlook* 96

(September–December 1910): 921–31.

Bullard, Robert. "Among the Savage Moros." *Metropolitan Magazine* 24 (June 1906): 263–79.

———. "Preparing Our Moros for Government." *Atlantic Monthly* 97 (March 1906): 385–94.

———. "Road Building Among the Moros." *Atlantic Monthly* 92 (December 1903): 818–26.

Carpenter, Allen. "Military Government of Southern Territory, 1861–65." In American Historical Association, *Annual Report for the Year 1900* (Washington, D.C.: Government Printing Office, 1901): 465–98.

Castel, Albert. "The Guerrilla War, 1861–65." *Civil War Times Illustrated* 13 (October 1974): 3–50.

———. "Quantrill's Bushwhackers: A Case Study in Partisan Warfare." *Civil War History* 13 (1967): 40–50.

Cheatham, Gary. "'Desperate Characters': The Development and Impact of the Confederate Guerrillas in Kansas." *Kansas History* 14 (Autumn 1991): 144–61.

Child, John. "From 'Color' to 'Rainbow': U.S. Strategic Planning for Latin America, 1919–45." *Journal of InterAmerican Studies and World Affairs* 21 (May 1979): 233–59.

Colby, Elbridge. "American Control in the West Indies." *Current History* 12 (September 1920): 953–59.

———. "American Powers in Panama." *Current History* 13 (March 1921): 449–53.

———. "How To Fight Savages." *American Journal of International Law* (April 1927): 279–88.

———. "The Military Value of the Laws of War." *Georgetown Law Journal* 15 (November 1926): 24–34.

———. "Panamanian-American Relations in Chiriqui." *Current History* 12 (July 1920): 682–85.

Crozier, William. "Some Observations on the Peking Relief Expedition." *North American Review* 172 (January 1901): 225–40.

Cumberland, Charles. "Border Raids in the Lower Rio Grande Valley—1915." *Southwestern Historical Quarterly* 57 (January 1954): 285–311.

Curry, Richard, and Ham, F. Gerald. "The Bushwhacker's War: Insurgency and Counterinsurgency in West Virginia." *Civil War History* 10 (1964): 416–33.

Dunlay, Thomas. "General Crook and the White Man Problem." *Journal of the West* 18 (April 1979): 3–9.

Dyer, Brainerd. "Francis Lieber and the American Civil War."

Huntington Library Quarterly 2 (July 1939): 449–65.
Ellis, Richard. "The Humanitarian Generals." *Western Historical Quarterly* 3 (April 1972): 169–78.
Evans, Frank. "The French Campaign in Morocco." *U.S. Naval Institute Proceedings* (January 1934): 80–88.
_____. "A Model Moroccan Operation." *U.S. Naval Institute Proceedings* (February 1935): 173–76.
Finley, John. "The Mohammedan Problem in the Philippines." *Journal of Race Development* 5 (April 1915): 353–63.
_____. "Race Development by Industrial Means Among the Moros and Pagans of the Southern Philippines." *Journal of Race Development* 3 (January 1913): 343–68.
Freidel, Frank. "General Orders 100 and Military Government." *Mississippi Valley Historical Review* 32 (March 1946): 541–56.
Futrell, Robert. "Federal Military Government in the South, 1861–65." *Military Affairs* 15 (Winter 1951): 181–91.
Gabriel, Ralph. "American Experience With Military Government." *American Historical Review* 49 (July 1944): 630–43.
Gates, John. "The Alleged Isolation of U.S. Army Officers in the Late Nineteenth Century." *Parameters* 10 (September 1980): 32–45.
_____. "General George Crook's First Apache Campaign." *Journal of the West* 6 (April 1967): 310–20.
_____. "Indians and Insurrectos: The U.S. Army's Experience With Insurgency." *Parameters* 13 (March 1983): 59–68.
Gillette, Howard. "The Military Occupation of Cuba, 1899–1902: Workshop for American Progressivism." *American Quarterly* 25 (1973): 410–25.
Gowing, Peter. "Muslim-American Relations in the Philippines, 1899–1920." *Asian Studies* 6 (December 1968): 372–82.
Harris, Charles, and Sadler, Louis. "The Plan of San Diego and the Mexican-U.S. War Crisis of 1916: A Reexamination." *Hispanic-American Historical Review* 58 (1978): 381–408.
Hitt, Parker. "'Amphibious Infantry,' A Fleet on Lake Lanao." *U.S. Naval Institute Proceedings* 64 (February 1938): 234–50.
Howard, Oliver O. "Is Cruelty Inseparable From War?" *Independent* 54 (15 May 1902): 1161–62.
Hunt, Michael. "The Forgotten Occupation: Peking, 1900–01." *Pacific Historical Review* 48 (1979): 501–29.
Ileto, Reynaldo. "Toward a Local History of the Philippine-American War: The Case of Tiaong, Tayabas (Quezon) Province, 1901–02." *Journal of History* 27 (January–December 1982): 67–79.
Kennon, L. W. "The Katipunan of the Philippines." *North American*

Review 173 (August 1901): 208–20.

Kolb, Richard. "'Restoring Order' South of the Border." *U.S. Naval Institute Proceedings* 110 (July 1984): 56–61.

Leonard, Thomas. "The Reluctant Conquerors." *American Heritage* 27 (August 1976): 34–41.

McCormick, Medill. "The Army in Vera Cruz." *Outlook* 107 (30 May 1914): 233–34.

McCoy, Frank. "Patrolling the Rio Grande." *Military Historian and Economist* 2 (January 1917): 87–93.

McGinnis, Anthony. "Intertribal Conflict on the Northern Plains and Its Suppression, 1738–1889." *Journal of the West* 18 (April 1979): 49–60.

Mahon, John. "Anglo-American Methods of Indian Warfare, 1676–1794." *Mississippi Valley Historical Review* 45 (September 1958): 254–75.

Marvin, George. "Bandits and the Borderland." *World's Work* 32 (October 1916): 656–63.

May, Glenn. "Filipino Resistance to American Occupation: Batangas, 1899–1902." *Pacific Historical Review* 48 (1979): 531–56.

_____. "Resistance and Collaboration in the Philippine-American War: The Case of Batangas." *Journal of Southeast Asia Studies* 15 (March 1984): 69–90.

_____. "Why the United States Won the Philippine-American War, 1899–1902." *Pacific Historical Review* 52 (1983): 353–77.

"Messages From Mexico." *World's Work* 32 (August 1916): 430–36.

Miles, Nelson. "My First Fights on the Plains." *Cosmopolitan* 50 (May 1911): 792–802.

_____. "On the Trail of Geronimo." *Cosmopolitan* 51 (July 1911): 249–62.

"Military Government." *Mailing List of the General Service Schools* 2 (February–March 1923): 37–50.

Millett, Allan. "The General Staff and the Cuban Intervention of 1906." *Military Affairs* 31 (Fall 1967): 113–19.

_____. "The Rise and Fall of the Cuban Rural Guard, 1898–1912." *Americas* 29 (October 1972): 191–213.

Morton, Louis. "Army and Marines on the China Station: A Study in Military and Political Rivalry." *Pacific Historical Review* 29 (February 1960): 51–73.

Mosby, John. "Captain Blazer." *Harper's Weekly* 22 (May 1897): 519–20.

Nenninger, Timothy. "Tactical Disfunction in the AEF, 1917–18." *Military Affairs* 51 (October 1987): 177–81.

Nichols, William. "Fighting Guerrillas in West Virginia." *Civil War Times Illustrated* 6 (April 1967): 20–25.

Niepman, Ann. "General Orders No. 11 and Border Warfare During the Civil War." *Missouri Historical Review* 66 (January 1972): 185–210.

O'Connor, Richard. "Yanks in Siberia." *American Heritage* 25 (August 1974): 10–17, 80–83.

Offutt, Milton. "The Protection of Citizens Abroad by the Armed Forces of the United States." *Johns Hopkins University Studies in Historical and Political Science* 46 (1928): 409–579.

Olson, William. "The Concept of Small Wars." *Small Wars and Insurgencies* 1 (April 1990): 39–46.

Owen, Norman. "Winding Down the War in Albay." *Pacific Historical Review* 48 (1979): 557–89.

Palmer, Frederick. "Mexico." *Everybody's Magazine* 30 (June 1914): 806–20; 31 (July 1914): 65–74; 31 (August 1914): 198–205.

_____. "With the Little Brother of the Navy." *Everybody's Magazine* 30 (June 1914): 810.

Palmer, John. "Railroad Building as a Model of Warfare." *North American Review* 175 (December 1902): 844–52.

Paret, Peter. "Colonial Experience and European Military Reform at the End of the Eighteenth Century." *Bulletin of the Institute of Historical Research* 37 (May 1964): 47–59.

Parker, John. "The Last Phase of the Philippine Rebellion and the Problems Resulting Therefrom." *Review of Reviews* 21 (October 1901): 522–67.

Paschall, Rod. "Low-Intensity Conflict Doctrine: Who Needs It?" *Parameters* 15 (Autumn 1985): 33f.

Porter, Kenneth. "The Seminole Negro-Indian Scouts, 1870–1881." *Southwestern Historical Quarterly* 60 (January 1952): 358–77.

Prichard, James. "General Orders No. 59: Kentucky's Reign of Terror." *Civil War Quarterly* 10 (1987): 32–34.

Raines, Edgar. "Major General J. Franklin Bell, U.S.A.: The Education of a Soldier, 1856–1899." *Register of the Kentucky Historical Society* 83 (Autumn 1985): 315–46.

Remington, Frederick. "Indians as Irregular Cavalry." *Harper's Weekly* 31 (27 December 1890): 1004–06.

Richard, Carl. "'The Shadow of a Plan': The Rationale Behind Wilson's 1918 Siberian Intervention." *Historian* 49 (1986): 64–84.

Russ, William. "Administrative Activities of the Union Army During and After the Civil War." *Mississippi Law Journal* 17 (May 1945): 71–89.

Russell, Peter. "Redcoats in the Wilderness: British Officers and Irregular Warfare in Europe and America, 1740–1760." *William and Mary Quarterly* 35 (October 1978): 630–41.

Sageser, Adelbert. "Military Occupation of the Confederate States: Historical Lesson." *Current History* 9 (September 1945): 227–34.

Schaffer, Ronald. "The 1940 Small Wars Manual and the 'Lessons of History.'" *Military Affairs* 36 (April 1972): 46–51.

Seaman, Louis. "Native Troops for Our Colonial Possessions." *North American Review* 171 (1900): 847–60.

Smith, C. C. "An Expedition in Mindanao." *Army and Navy Courier* 4 (July 1928): 3–5; (August 1928): 7–9.

Smith, Justin. "American Rule in Mexico." *American Historical Review* 23 (January 1918): 287–302.

Smith, Wayne. "An Experiment in Counterinsurgency: The Assessment of Confederate Sympathizers in Missouri." *Journal of Southern History* 35 (August 1969): 361–80.

Smythe, Donald. "Pershing and the Disarmament of the Moros." *Pacific Historical Review* 31 (1962): 241–56.

Stegmaier, Robert. "Artillery Helped Win the West." *Kansas Quarterly* 10 (Summer 1978): 59–74.

Tan, Samuel. "Sulu Under American Military Rule, 1899–1913." *Philippine Social Sciences and Humanities Review* 32 (March 1967): 100–104.

Tate, Michael. "John P. Clum and the Origins of an Apache Constabulary, 1874–77." *American Indian Quarterly* 3 (Summer 1977): 99–120.

_____. "Soldiers of the Line, Apache Companies in the U.S. Army, 1891–97." *Arizona and the West* 16 (Winter 1974): 343–64.

Townsend, Henry. "Civil Government in the 'Moro Province.'" *Forum* 36 (July 1904): 138–49.

Trussell, John. "Seminoles in the Everglades." *Army* 12 (December 1961): 41–45.

Tyler, Ronnie. "The Little Punitive Expedition in the Big Bend." *Southwestern Historical Quarterly* 78 (1975): 271–91.

Utley, Robert. "Crook and Miles Fighting and Feuding on the Indian Frontier." *Military History Quarterly* 2 (Autumn 1989): 81–91.

Weinert, Richard. "The South Had Mosby; The Union, Major Henry Young." *Civil War Times Illustrated* 3 (April 1964): 38–42.

Welch, Richard. "American Atrocities in the Philippines: The Indictment and the Response." *Pacific Historical Review* 43 (1974): 233–53.

"What War With Mexico Means." *World's Work* 32 (August 1916):

424–30.

White, W. Bruce. "The American Indian as Soldier, 1890–1919." *Canadian Review of American Studies* 7 (Spring 1976): 15–25.

Worcester, Dean. "The Mexican Question in the Light of Philippine Experience." *Outlook* 107 (11 July 1914): 602–08.

INDEX

Aeroplanes, use in irregular operations, 207, 246, 255
Agua Prieta, 200–201
Aguinaldo, Emilio, 108–10, 113, 135
Allen, Brig. Gen. Henry T., 122, 127, 136, 154–56
Allied Supreme War Council, mission assignment to north Russia expedition, 210
American Expeditionary Force, Siberia (AEFS). *See* Siberia.
Amnesty programs, 26, 29, 40, 120, 260
Anderson, Maj. George S., 131
Anderson, Brig. Gen. Thomas M., 124
Apaches, 74–76, 82–85
Archangel, 208–09, 210
Armored vehicles, use in irregular operations, 207, 246, 255–56
Army
    challenges on the Western frontier, 58–59
    continuity in constabulary service, 275
    doctrine development, 230–31
    field code of conduct, 33
    institutionalization of small war tenets, 275–76
    involvement with Indian Bureau, 77–79
    irregular warfare instruction, 247, 273
    lessons from the Philippine War, 136–39
    modernization through frontier experience, 66
    Philippine Constabulary service versus Regular, 154, 176, 271
    public criticism against the, 68–69, 167, 252
    reforms and adaptation to modern warfare, 86–87
    study and influence of foreign counterinsurgency methods, 245–47, 255, 276–77
Army of Cuban Pacification, 169–71, 176
Army of Northern Virginia, 23
The Art of War, 14–15
Artillery, 248–49
Attraction, policy of
    failure and usefulness of, 135–36
    pacification of the Philippines and, 119, 157

Attraction, policy of—Continued
    versus policy of chastisement, 126–27, 279

Baker, Lafayette, National Detectives set up by, 46
Baker, Newton D., 201, 218, 228–29, 250
Baldwin, Capt. Frank D., 77
    Indian pacification and, 82–83
Bandholtz, Col. Harry H., 158
Basic Field Manual, Military Government, Field Manual (FM) 27–5, 250, 252, 276
Batangas, 132–35
Bell, Brig. Gen. J. Franklin, 133–34, 278. *See also* Colby, Capt. Elbridge.
    appointment to Army of Cuban Pacification, 170
    lyceum discussion on frontier experience, 88
    Philippine pacification and, 119, 125
    Telegraphic Circulars, 138–39
Bigelow, Capt. John, 278. *See also* Bullard, Col. Robert L.
    Army reform advocate, 86
    The Principles of Strategy, 89, 91, 164
    teachings from Indian warfare, 89–91
Birkhimer, Col. William E., 113, 130, 278
    Military Government and Martial Law, 101, 119, 126, 136–37
Blatchford, Brig. Gen. Richard M., commander of U.S. Canal Zone forces, 226–27
Blazer, Capt. Richard, 46. *See also* Forsyth, Maj. George.
Bliss, Brig. Gen. Tasker H., 193, 202
Bolshevik Revolution, 208
Bosque Redondo, 82–83
Bouquet, Henry, 11
Boxer Rebellion, 148, 240
Boyd, Capt. Charles T., 205
Brooke, Maj. Gen. John R., Governor of Cuba, 104–05
Brown, Col. William C., 203
Bryan, William Jennings, 112
Bullard, Col. Robert L., 135, 164, 200
    publication of *Military Pacification* by, 177–78

311

Butler, Maj. Gen. Benjamin F., 26, 28–29

Callwell, Col. Charles E., 4, 277
  Small Wars, 247
Carlton, Brig. Gen. James H., establishment of military-controlled reservation by, 82
Carpenter, Capt. J., 45
Carranza, Venustiano, 192, 198–99, 200, 204–05
Carrizal, 205
Cavalry. *See also* School of Application for Infantry and Cavalry.
  logistical adaptation, 70–71
  role in Mexican Punitive Expedition, 200, 203
  role in Philippine War, 115
  tactics. *See* Cooke, Brig. Gen. Philip St. George, *Cavalry Tactics.*
  use of horses versus Indian ponies, 72, 248
Cavalry regiments
  1st District of Columbia (D.C.), 45–46
  5th, 72
  6th, 72
  7th, 89–90
  13th, 204
Cavite Province, 130, 158
Chaffee, Maj. Gen. Adna R., 77, 132–33, 147, 148, 278. *See also* Boxer Rebellion.
  Indian pacification and, 82
  Peking Relief Expedition and, 150
  Philippine population concentration, 131
  policing of the Philippines, 153
Charity kitchens, 149
Chastisement, policy of, versus policy of attraction, 126–27, 279
Cheyenne, 67, 74
Chihuahua, 201, 203, 204, 205
China. *See also* Boxer Rebellion.
  interwar years Army operations in, 240
  U.S. expedition to, 147
Chiriqui Province, 226–29
Civil administration
  coordination with military jurisdictions, 279–80
  military government and, 26–27, 253
  military government and Philippine, 154
  Southern Reconstruction and, 56
  Vera Cruz, 196
Civil involvement, 5, 37. *See also* Pacification.
Civil War
  contribution to Army doctrine, 48
  counterguerrilla warfare, 40
  GO 100 and, 35

Civil War—Continued
  pacification policies, 24, 36
Civilians. *See also* Population.
  loyalty oath, 30–31
  prisoners and Lincoln, 29
  relationship with the army, 34, 278
  treatment of, 13, 16–17, 33, 101, 130, 157, 167, 178, 180, 200, 216, 220–21, 251–55, 259–60, 278
Clark, Capt. W. P., 87
  The Indian Sign Language, 65
Colby, Capt. Elbridge, 250–51, 254–55
Colon, 226
Columbus, New Mexico, raid, 200–202
Communists, 211, 214
  guerrilla warfare and, 261
Confederate Army, U.S. Army against, 41
Contingency operations
  definition of, 3–4
  factors of, 4
  political considerations in, 4
Cooke, Brig. Gen. Philip St. George, *Cavalry Tactics,* 66
Corbin, Brig. Gen. Henry C., 131
Counterguerrilla war. *See also* Army; Tactics and techniques, counterguerrilla.
  Army ruse in, 73
  creation of special units for, 45–47, 74–75, 116, 165
  moderation versus retaliation in, 40
  officer education and, 12, 60–63, 88–90, 136–38, 247–50, 256
  principles of, 247
  security concerns, 44
  strategic defense, 41
  strategies, 15, 37, 248
  tactics, 43–44, 277
  unconventional transportation in, 71
Counterinsurgency
  campaign example, 91
  definition of, 3
  factors of, 4
  foreign countries methods in, 152, 245–46, 255
  guide for commanders, 170
  political considerations in, 4
  reflection of American society values in, 273–74
  wills, a contest of, as an element in, 278
  A Course of Instruction in the Elements of Art and Science of War for the Use of the Cadets of the United States Military Academy, 61
Crook, General George, 30, 38, 46, 71, 278. *See also* Forsyth, Maj. George; Indian Bureau, Department of the Interior's.

INDEX

Crook, General George—Continued
  counterguerrilla war and, 42–43
  Indian pacification and, 83–84
  Indian scouts and, 69–70
  lessons from Indian warfare, 65
  Resume of Operations Against Apache Indians, 138
Crowder, Col. Enoch, 173
Cuba. *See also* Army of Cuban Pacification.
  American occupation of, 104, 169
  American progressivism in, 105–06, 172
  counterinsurgency plans for, 170–71
  demobilization of revolutionary army, 105, 169
  establishment of American military government in, 104–05
  nation-building problems, 106–08
  political system's reform, 169, 172, 174
  treaty of Paris and, 99
Curtis, Maj. Gen. Samuel R., 43
Czech Legion, 208–10, 219, 225–26

David, 226, 227–29
Davis, George B.
  The Elements of International Law, 136
  Outlines of International Law, 101, 136
Davis, Jefferson, 135
Destruction
  Chinese property, 150
  food supply, 67, 171
  Indian property, 60, 62
  policy of, 39, 129
  of property in the Philippines, 128, 129–30
  Southern property, 36–40
Doctrine, definition of, 5–6
Dougherty, Capt. Andrew J., 180
Dowell, Maj. Cassius, 250–51

Economic program
  Cuba and, 106, 172–73
  Indian pacification and, 85
  Moro pacification and, 162
  Philippines and, 154
  role in nation building, 102, 180–81, 254
Education programs, 253
  in Cuba, 106, 172
  establishment of school for Indians, 83, 85
  establishment of schools in China, 149
  in Mexico, 196
  in Moro Province, 163
  nation building and public, 102–03, 254
  in the Philippines, 121. *See also* Allen, Brig. Gen. Henry T.
  Reconstruction and, 55–56

An Elementary Treatise on Advanced-Guard, Out-Post, and Detachment Service of Troops, 15, 61
The Elements of International Law, George B. Davis, 136
Ewing, Brig. Gen. Thomas, Jr., 37

Farrow, 2d Lt. Edward, 71, 87
  Mountain Scouting, 65
Field service notes, 175
Field Service Regulations, 175, 247, 255, 271, 275
Field Service Regulations—Special Operations, Training Regulation (TR) 15–70, 247
Finley, Maj. John P., 162
Food control, 129–30
Forsyth, Maj. George, 74
Francis, David R., 211–12, 214
Freedmen's Bureau, 55–57
Fremont, Maj. Gen. John C., 28, 45
Frontier experience, 7
  lessons from, 11–13, 65–67
Funston, Maj. Gen. Frederick, 169
  response to bandits' insurgency in southern Texas, 200–201
  Vera Cruz operations' commander, 196–97
Furlong, Capt. John W., *Notes on Field Service in Cuba,* 170–71, 174

Gardener, Col. Cornelius, 122
General Orders (GO) 100, 34–35, 48, 136, 251, 274
  application to Philippine pacification, 126, 128, 131
  occupation policies and, 101
Geronimo, 75–76, 90
Gibbon, Brig. Gen. John, 66, 79–80
Gillem, Brig. Gen. Alvan, 45
Gillem's Cossacks, 45
Gilmore, Harry, 47
Glenn, Col. Edwin F., 179
  role in Philippine War, 118
Godfrey, Capt. Edward S., 61
Grant, Lt. Gen. Ulysses S., 36, 278
  contribution to Army doctrine, 48
Graves, Maj. Gen. William S. *See also* Kolchak, Admiral Alexander.
  commander of U.S. Siberia expedition, 209, 218–20
  dissension with allies in Siberia expedition, 220
  post–World War I U.S. policy implementation, 222–23
  Suchan Valley campaign, 223–25

313

Guam, treaty of Paris and, 99
Guerrilla
    population at large and, 40, 111, 129, 171
    techniques and counterguerrilla war, 42–44
    treatment of, 36. *See also* General Orders (GO) 100; Hague Conventions.
    versus partisan/war-rebel/bushwhacker, 33
Guerrilla Parties Considered With Reference to the Laws and Usages of War, 32
Guerrilla warfare. *See also* Counterguerrilla war; Counterinsurgency; Mexican-American War; Small wars; Vattel, Emmerich.
    challenge and strategies, 10–11, 27–28. *See also* Jomini, Baron Antoine Henri.
    laws of war versus, 254
    mapping program and, 170
    pacification policies and, 28
    Philippine, 110–11

Habeas corpus, 106
    Philippine pacification and, 123
Hague Conventions, 35, 274
Haiti, 191, 239
Halleck, Henry W., 17, 28–29, 32–33, 37, 276, 278
    International Law, 17, 101
Harrison, Brig. Gen. William Henry, 11
Hazen, William B., 77
Health and sanitation, 26, 253
    in China, 149–50
    in Cuba, 106, 172
    in Mexico, 196
    in the Philippines, 120, 161
Hitchcock, Maj. Gen. Ethan Allan, 33
Ho Chi Minh, 261
Howard, Maj. Gen. Oliver O., 56, 79. *See also* Indian Bureau, Department of the Interior's.
    Indian pacification and, 82
Huerta, Victoriano, 192, 198
Hunt, Col. Irwin L., 250–51
Hunter, Maj. Gen. David, 38

Ideology, civil/military roles, 272, 279–80
Indian Bureau, Department of the Interior's
    administration of the U.S. Indian policy by, 77–78
    nomadic tribes of the Great Plains and, 80
    trading posts and, 81–82
    transfer of responsibilities to War Department, 78–79
The Indian Question, 79

The Indian Sign Language, 65
Indian warfare, 7–9. *See also* Moro Province; *The Prairie Traveler.*
    Army fieldcraft in, 63
    Army's multiple column method against, 67, 69
    Army techniques for, 60
    Army winter campaign in, 67–68
    challenge and strategies, 10–11, 58–59, 69
    establishment of reservations and pacification, 82–83
    politico-military problem, 76–77
    teachings from, 88–89
    trading houses and pacification, 81–82
    U.S. Military Academy curriculum and, 12–13, 60–61
Indigenous auxiliary troop, 248, 277
    employment in Civil War, 44–45
    employment in Philippine War, 116, 131–32, 176
    Indian scouts as, 69–70, 83
    plans for, 180, 248, 257, 259
Industrial Trading Station, 162
Infantry. *See also* Infantry regiments.
    detail to China, 243
    mounted. *See also* School of Application for Infantry and Cavalry.
    role in counterguerrilla war, 44–45, 72
    role in Mexican Punitive Expedition, 200, 203
    role in Philippine War, 116
Infantry Drill Regulations, 175, 247
Infantry regiments
    3d U.S., 99
    9th U.S., 150–52
    13th Indiana Volunteer, 43–44
    14th Minnesota Volunteer, 99
    15th U.S., 240–42
    27th U.S., 225
    31st U.S., 225, 243
    33d U.S., 227
    36th Ohio Volunteer, 29–30, 43–44
Infantry School
    irregular warfare curriculum, 247–48, 254–55
    small wars exercises, 256–57
    study of foreign constabulary warfare experiences, 246
Intelligence, 179, 248, 277
    Mexican Punitive Expedition, 203–04
    in Panama, 227
    use in Cuba, 170
    use in Philippine War, 117–18, 132
    use in Siberia, 225
International internal disputes, United States arbitration of, 147

INDEX

International Law, 17
Irregular warfare doctrine, 245
Irregulars. *See also* Guerrilla.
  ambush of, 43
  Philippine *ladrone*, 157–58
  treatment of, 33

Japan
  in Siberia, 219–20
  war with China, 242
Jesse Scouts, 45
Johnston, 1st Lt. William T., role in Philippine War, 118
Jomini, Baron Antoine Henri, 14–15. *See also* Bullard, Col. Robert L.
Judicial issues
  Apache Indians and, 84
  in Cuba, 106
  Philippine Constabulary functions and, 156
  in the Philippines, 123
  at Vera Cruz, 196

Kanawha Valley, 38–39
Kennedy, Maj. Gen. Chase W., 227, 229
Kikuzo, Japanese General Otani, 219–20
Kirk, George, 45
Kobbe, Brig. Gen. William A., 130
Kolchak, Admiral Alexander, 220
  Bolshevik victory over, 225
  Wilson administration's support of, 222–23

The Law of Nations, 13–14
Lawrence, Thomas E., 246
Lawton, Capt. Henry W., 74–76
Lazelle, Col. Henry M., 43
Leavenworth. *See* School of Application for Infantry and Cavalry.
Leech Lake, Minnesota, uprising at, 58
Legion of Honor, 46
Lieber, Francis, 32, 48. *See also* General Orders (GO) 100.
  Lieber's code, 101
Lincoln, Abraham, 24–25
  military commissions and, 29
  pacification endeavors, 24–25
Little Big Horn, 67
Local units, role in counterguerrilla war, 44–45
Loudoun County, 39
Loudoun County Rangers, 45
Loudoun Valley, 133
Loyalty oath, 30–31
Lukban, General Vincente, 132
Lyautey, Marshal Hubert, 255–56

Macabebe scouts, 116–17
McAndrew, Maj. Gen. James W., 250
MacArthur, Maj. Gen. Arthur, role in Philippine pacification, 120–21, 128–29, 131
McClellan, Maj. Gen. George B., 25
  guerrillas and, 28
McCoy, Brig. Gen. Frank R., 166
  critique of the Marine Corps, 246–47
Mackenzie, Col. Ranald D., 77, 80, 82
McKinley, William, 112, 129, 130
  guidelines to Army's occupation, 100
  pacification of the Philippines and, 119
Magoon, Charles, 169, 172
Mahan, Dennis Hart, 12, 15–16, 278
  approach to Indian warfare, 60–61, 63
Malvar, General Miguel, 132, 133
Manual for the Philippine Constabulary, 156, 259
Manuals and military textbooks, 15, 61, 64–66, 89, 136–37, 155–56, 175, 247, 250–52, 254–55, 271, 275. *See also The Art of War; International Law; The Law of Nations.*
  integration of foreign countries methods in, 255
  international law, 101
Mao Tse-tung, 261
March, General Peyton C., 209, 214, 220–21, 226
Marcy, Capt. Randolph, 64–65, 71, 276. *See also The Prairie Traveler.*
Marinduque, 130
Marine Corps
  development of small wars doctrine, 246
  interwar years constabulary duty, 191–92, 239
Memorandum in Reference to the Methods To Be Employed in the Capture and Occupation of Latin American Cities, 197–98
Mexican-American War, 16–17
Mexican Punitive Expedition, 203–08
Mexico. *See also* Carranza, Venustiano; Huerta, Victoriano; Mexican-American War; "Strategical Plan Green for the Occupation and Pacification of Mexico"; Vera Cruz, American intervention in; Villa, General Francisco "Pancho."
  American war plans for, 179, 193–94. *See also A Study of the Pacification of Mexico and Establishment of Civil Government.*
  application of Philippine War lessons, 200

315

Miles, Lt. Gen. Nelson A., 58, 89, 138, 165, 171, 278. *See also* Geronimo; Indian Bureau, Department of the Interior's.
  counterguerrilla maneuvers, 87
  opening of military gymnasium by, 74
  raiders and pursuers exercise, 74, 171, 203
Military commissions
  in Civil War, 28–30
  in Philippines, 121, 128–29
Military government, 26–27. *See also Basic Field Manual, Military Government*, Field Manual (FM) 27–5; Birkhimer, Col. William E.; Smith, Col. Harry A., *Military Government*.
  civil administration and, 26–27, 250
  doctrine, 230–31, 244, 252–53
  principles of, 251
  psychological factor in, 252
  study of, 273
Mindanao, 128, 130, 159, 167
Miner, Col. Charles W., 176
Minor wars. *See* Small wars.
Mississippi Marine Brigade, 47
Mobility, 114
Monroe Doctrine, 147, 245, 258
Morgan, Col. John H., 28
Moro Exchange, 162
Moro Province, 160–65, 175–76, 177
  application of Indian warfare experience to, 159
  counterguerrilla tactics in, 164–65
  government organization in, 161
  population's makeup, 159
  U.S. district governors in, 163–64. *See also* Pershing, Brig. Gen. John J.; Wood, General Leonard.
  U.S. strategy in, 160–61
Mosby, Col. John S., 36, 39, 46, 133
Mountain Scouting, 65
Murmansk, 208–09
Murray, Col. Arthur, 132

Nation building
  agricultural transformation and, 161–62
  Army's approach to, 101, 162
  commerce and, 7, 81–82, 162, 255–56
  governmental reforms, 103, 122–23, 161, 180
  land redistribution as part of, 181
  problems experienced in, 281
  public works and, 105–06, 161, 173, 253
  social transformation and, 55–58, 102–03, 161, 180, 196–99, 251
  traditional prescription for, 253–54
Navajos, 82–83
Nicaragua, 181–82, 191, 239, 246–47, 256

No-quarter policies, 28–30, 36, 157, 200

Organization and Tactics, Arthur Wagner's, 89
Otis, Maj. Gen. Elwell S., 92, 159
  The Indian Question, 79
  pacification of the Philippines and, 119, 125
  Philippine War and, 110, 113

Pace, Maj. Herbert E., 227, 228–29
Pacification. *See also* Army of Cuban Pacification; Bullard, Col. Robert L.; General Orders (GO) 100; Jomini, Baron Antoine Henri; Military government; Nation building; *A Study of the Pacification of Mexico and Establishment of Civil Government;* Vattel, Emmerich.
  acculturation and Indian, 79–80
  Army's approach to, 26–27, 32–35, 176–78, 249–55
  conventional war versus, 48
  coordination of political and military factors in, 250
  definition of, 4–5
  doctrine, 245, 249–55
  influence of society's trends on, 91–92
  lessons from Philippine, 136
  Lincoln's endeavors, 24–26
  Philippine Constabulary and postwar Philippines, 156–57, 162
  political obstacles to, 27–28
  in the South, 55
Panama
  interwar years Army operations in, 240
  U.S. Chiriqui detachment in, 227–30
Panama City, 226, 240
Parral, 204
Partisan
  forces in Philippine war, 116
  forces in Siberia, 224
  treatment of, 33–34
  versus guerrilla/war-rebel/bushwhacker, 33
  warfare. *See* Guerrilla warfare.
  warfare strategies, 16
Partisan Rangers, 23, 33, 51. *See also* Mosby, Col. John S.
  creation of, 32
Patton, 1st Lt. George S., 207
Peking Relief Expedition, 148–53, 240
Penick, Col. W. R., 38
Pershing, Brig. Gen. John J., 74, 174. *See also* Indian Bureau, Department of the Interior's.
  Mexican Punitive Expedition and, 201–08
  Moro Governor, 162, 163

INDEX

Petite guerre. See Small wars.
Philippine Constabulary, 116–17, 154–58
Philippine Scouts, 116–18, 132, 156, 157–58
Philippine War. *See also* Taylor, Capt. John R. M.
  Army tactics in, 114
  Civil War precedents, 48, 133
  frontier service experience and, 113
  lessons from, 136–38
  Philippine Constabulary service during, 116–17
Philippines. *See also* Moro Province.
  civilian government and pacification, 122–23
  counterguerrilla principles applied in the, 85
  counterinsurgency campaign in the, 129, 134, 158
  guerrilla warfare in the, 110–12
  indigenous rebel forces in the, 108, 153
  pacification, 119–20, 147. *See also* Otis, Maj. Gen. Elwell S.
  post–Philippine War policing by United States of, 153–58
  treaty of Paris and the, 99
Plan Brown, 257–58
Plan of San Diego, 199, 205
Political considerations
  counterinsurgency/contingency operations, 4
  development of Philippine Federal Party, 123
Poole, Maj. Gen. Frederick C., commander of Allied forces in north Russia, 210
Pope, Brig. Gen. John, 31, 80, 82. *See also* Indian Bureau, Department of the Interior's.
Population. *See also* Civilians; Military government; Nation building; Pacification.
  concentration in the Philippines, 130–31, 158, 255
  control, 254
  demoralization of, 39
  establishment of reservations for Indian, 82
  Filipino organized brigands and, 153
  monitoring of Indian, 69
  occupation and respect of subject, 101
  Philippine guerrillas and, 125
  removal of, 37, 90
  support of guerrillas, 40, 111–12, 129, 171, 203, 277
  treatment of Indian tribes, 79–81
The Prairie Traveler, 64–65. *See also* Mountain Scouting.

Pratt, 1st Lt. Richard H., establishment of school for Indians by, 83
President, U.S. *See* Lincoln, Abraham; McKinley, William; Roosevelt, Theodore; Wilson, Woodrow.
The Principles of Strategy, Capt. John Bigelow, 89, 91, 164
Prisoners
  Communist, 225
  treatment of, 29, 33, 223
  treatment of Filipino, 131–32
  treatment of guerrilla, 36
  treatment of native, 62, 83
Proctor, Redfield, establishment of Indian soldier companies, 80–81
Progressive movement, 91–92
  pacification and, 280–82
  Spain's former colonies and, 102
Property
  confiscation, 31–32
  destruction of, 7, 36–38, 60, 128–29, 134, 150, 157, 164, 254
  Indian ownership of private, 82
  protection of military, 26
  respect of, 34
Provost marshal, 26–27
Puerto Rican Regiment, 227
Puerto Rico, 99

Racist attitudes, 124
Radical program, readmission of states to Union and, 56
Railroad
  protection, 41
  protection of the Peking–Tientsin–Shanhaikwan, 240–41
  protection of Trans-Siberian, 222–23
Reconstruction
  Army's approach to Southern, 55–56
  education programs and, 56
  land reform schemes and, 57
  military rule versus civilian governments, 56, 58
  Progressive movement and, 92
  radical/social programs and, 56
Ridgway, Capt. Matthew B., 246
Road building, 253
  in China, 149
  in Cuba, 173
  in Moro Province, 161
  in the Philippines, 120
Romanovka, 223–24
Roosevelt, Theodore, 147, 168–69, 226, 245
Root, Elihu, 103–04, 105, 135, 176, 276
Rosecrans, Maj. Gen. William S., loyalty oath and, 30

317

Rules of Land Warfare, Field Manual (FM) 27–10, 35, 179, 254, 275
Russia. *See also* Bolshevik Revolution; Siberia.
   allied intervention in, 210
   American contingent to northern, 210–11, 214
   attempt at non-Communist government in northern, 216, 218
   logistical problems of Allied expedition to north, 214
   pacification attempts in, 216–17, 221
Ryan, Maj. James, 203

Samar, 132–35
Schofield, Maj. Gen. John M., 32, 61, 82
   establishment of Indian soldier companies, 80–81
School of Application for Infantry and Cavalry, 175
   curriculum of, 88–89, 176
   establishment of, 86
   Spanish-language instruction at, 177
Schwan, Brig. Gen. Theodore, counterinsurgency in the Philippines and, 112
Scott, Maj. Gen. Hugh L., 77, 164, 201, 202, 278
   appointment to West Point, 177
Scott, Maj. Gen. Winfield, 7, 16
   military commissions against guerrillas, 28
Secretary of War, U.S. *See* Baker, Newton D.; Proctor, Redfield; Root, Elihu; Stanton, Edwin M.; Stimson, Henry; Taft, William Howard.
Seminole War, Second, 10, 11, 12–13, 67
The Service of Security and Information, Arthur Wagner's, 89, 138
Seymour, British Admiral Sir Edward, 148
Shanghai, 242–44
Shenandoah Valley, 38–39, 46, 74, 133
Sheridan, Lt. Gen. Philip H., 11, 36, 46, 65–66, 70, 74, 133, 278. *See also* Indian Bureau, Department of the Interior's.
   property devastation and, 38–39
Sherman, Maj. Gen. William T., 31, 36, 134, 278
   contribution to Army doctrine, 48
   Indian wars and, 58–59
   Reconstruction and views of, 57
Siberia. *See also* Russia.
   Allied expedition to, 218–22
   counterguerrilla war strategies in, 224–25
Sioux, 61, 67, 74, 89–90

Small wars. *See also* Counterguerrilla war; Counterinsurgency; Military government.
   concept of, 4
   conduct of, 5
   definition of, 15, 247–48
   doctrine, 244–45
   doctrine versus conventional warfare, 271–72
   experience under President Wilson, 230–31
   guerrilla warfare and, 47
   Infantry School exercises, 256–57
   lesson from, 175
   plans, 258–59
   psychological factor in, 249
Small Wars Manual, 239, 247. *See also* Marine Corps.
Smith, Col. Harry A., *Military Government,* 250–52
Smith, Brig. Gen. Jacob H., 133–34
Spanish-American War, 99–100, 108, 275
Special units, creation of counterguerrilla, 45–47, 74–75, 116, 165
Stanton, Edwin M., 45–46
State government, 56
Steele, Maj. Gen. Frederick, 38
Steele, Capt. Matthew F., 175
   Spanish-language instruction and, 177
Stewart, Col. George E., commander of U.S. north Russia expedition, 209–11, 214
Stimson, Henry, 181
"Strategical Plan Green for the Occupation and Pacification of Mexico," 259–60, 281
A Study of the Pacification of Mexico and Establishment of Civil Government, 180–81
Suchan Valley, 223–24, 225
Sullivan-Clinton campaign, 7
Sulu archipelago, 159
Sumner, Col. E. V., 88
Sumner, Brig. Gen. Samuel S., 125

Tactics and techniques, counterguerrilla
   in Civil War, 40–47
   against Indians, 12–13, 58, 67–76, 90
   interwar doctrine, 248–49
   in Philippines, 112–17, 128–30, 137, 157–58, 165
   urban, 197–98
Taft, William Howard, 122, 154, 169, 179, 181–82
   Philippine civilian government, 132
Taggart, Maj. E. F., 128
Tampico, 192

INDEX

Tayabas, 132
Taylor, Capt. John R. M.
  history of the Philippine War, 122
  The Philippine Insurrection Against the United States, 139
Telegraphic Circulars, General Bell's, 138–39
Tientsin, 150, 240–42
Torture, 131–32, 170–71, 203–04
Trading posts, 81–82. *See also* Industrial Trading Station.
Training. *See also* Field service notes.
  comprehensive program of troop, 86
  counterguerrilla warfare, 73–74, 171, 176, 206–07
Transportation, pack mules as, 71

Upton, Emory. *See also* Cooke, Brig. Gen. Philip St. George, *Cavalry Tactics.*
  A New System of Infantry Tactics for Double and Single Rank Adapted to American Topography and Improved Fire-Arms, 66
U.S. Military Academy
  curriculum, 7, 35, 177
  curriculum and Indian warfare, 12–13, 60–61
  international law curriculum and Indian warfare, 62
  role in preservation and transmission of frontier experience, 11, 61, 63
  Spanish instruction at, 177

Vattel, Emmerich, 13–14
Vera Cruz, American intervention in, 192–93, 196–99
Viatka, 210
Villa, General Francisco "Pancho," 199, 200, 205–08
  punitive expedition against, 201–04
Vladivostok, 208–09, 210, 218–19, 225–26
Vologda, 210
von Vorbeck, Lettow, 246

Wagner, Col. Arthur, 112, 175
  instructor at Leavenworth, 89, 176
  Organization and Tactics, 89
  The Service of Security and Information, 89, 138
War plans. *See also* Monroe Doctrine.

War plans—Continued
  coordination of political and military factors in small, 249–50
  inclusion of military government in, 252
  Mexico and, 179, 193–94. *See also* "Strategical Plan Green for the Occupation and Pacification of Mexico"; *A Study of the Pacification of Mexico and Establishment of Civil Government.*
  Philippines and. *See* Plan Brown.
  World War I allies, 209
War-rebel. *See* Irregulars.
War of the Rebellion, 48
Wayne, Maj. Gen. Anthony, 7, 11
West Point. *See* U.S. Military Academy.
Wheaton, Maj. Gen. Loyd, 135
Wheeler, Col. J. B., 61
Wild, Brig. Gen. Edward A., 38
Wilson, Brig. Gen. James H., 148
Wilson, Woodrow, 222
  Army's small wars experience under, 230–31
  contribution of U.S. troops to operations in Russia, 209–10, 218–19
  intervention at Vera Cruz, 192–93, 196–99
  order for expedition against General Villa, 200–204
  relationship with World War I allies, 209
  U.S. overseas interests under, 191–92
Wood, General Leonard, 75, 162, 164, 172, 174, 181, 193, 276
  Armed Progressives and, 273
  "colonial army" system, 176
  Moro Province governor, 161
  Progressivist governor of Cuba, 105–06
  strategy against the Moros, 165–68
Wool, Brig. Gen. John, 31
Woolsey, Theodore, *Introduction to the Study of International Law,* 101
World War I, 207–08
Wotherspoon, Brig. Gen. William W., 193
Wright, Col. George, 11

Yang-ts'un, 150
Young, Maj. Henry, 46. *See also* Forsyth, Maj. George.

Zamboanga, 162

☆ U.S. GOVERNMENT PRINTING OFFICE: 2004 312-177

www.ingramcontent.com/pod-product-compliance
Lightning Source LLC
Chambersburg PA
CBHW052051230426
43671CB00011B/1874